LEARNERS IN A CHANGING LEARNING LANDSCAPE

Lifelong Learning Book Series

VOLUME 12

Aims & Scope
"Lifelong Learning" has become a central theme in education and community development. Both international and national agencies, governments and educational institutions have adopted the idea of lifelong learning as their major theme for address and attention over the next ten years. They realize that it is only by getting people committed to the idea of education both life-wide and lifelong that the goals of economic advancement, social emancipation and personal growth will be attained.

The *Lifelong Learning Book Series* aims to keep scholars and professionals informed about and abreast of current developments and to advance research and scholarship in the domain of Lifelong Learning. It further aims to provide learning and teaching materials, serve as a forum for scholarly and professional debate and offer a rich fund of resources for researchers, policy-makers, scholars, professionals and practitioners in the field.

The volumes in this international Series are multi-disciplinary in orientation, polymathic in origin, range and reach, and variegated in range and complexity. They are written by researchers, professionals and practitioners working widely across the international arena in lifelong learning and are orientated towards policy improvement and educational betterment throughout the life cycle.

For other titles published in this series, go to
www.springer.com/series/6227

Jan Visser • Muriel Visser-Valfrey

Editors

Learners in a Changing Learning Landscape

Reflections from a Dialogue on New Roles and Expectations

 Springer

Dr. Jan Visser
Learning Development Institute
Jupiter, Florida, USA &
Eyragues, France
jvisser@learndev.org

Dr. Muriel Visser-Valfrey
Learning Development Institute
Jupiter, Florida, USA &
Eyragues, France
mvisser@learndev.org

ISBN 978-1-4020-8298-6   e-ISBN 978-1-4020-8299-3
DOI: 10.1007/978-1-4020-8299-3

Library of Congress Control Number: 2008925052

Editorial by Series Editors

This volume in the Lifelong Learning Book Series is a further flowering of the thinking and writing that first saw light in the *International Handbook of Lifelong Learning*, edited by David Aspin, Judith Chapman, Yukiko Sawano and Michael Hatton, published by Kluwer (now Springer) in 2001. In the *International Handbook* we laid down a set of agenda for future research and development, analysis and expansion, strategies and guidelines in the field of lifelong learning. It had become clear that the domain of lifelong learning was a rich and fertile ground for setting out and summarising, comparing and criticising the heterogeneous scope and remit of policies, proposals, and practices in its different constitutive parts across the international arena.

This volume is a further and more detailed enquiry into and development of some of the important issues that were raised in the *International Handbook* pertaining to an understanding of human learning and the essential features of being human, that contribute to making learning meaningful. The book was constructed by Jan Visser and his colleagues, through a process beginning with a dialogue around 32 questions, which were used as starting points for a process of group interactions "on line". This then led to a face-to-face workshop and panel discussion with a wider audience. This emphasis on evolving dialogue was central to the development of the book and is sustained in the manner in which the reader is invited into the dialogue and provided with concrete suggestions for ways of entering and participating in the conversation. Extremely helpful questions are formulated, resources identified for further exploration, and questions generated for comprehension, discussion and application.

Authors address critical questions and issues, such as: What is learning? Why do we learn? How do we learn on the Internet? What are the strengths and weaknesses of learning in formal and informal settings? How do we learn in a changing learning landscape? How do we respond to 'feral' learners, to those who are 'gifted' and those that are 'at risk'? What delivery strategies must be applied to facilitate learning in a context of distance and distributed modalities? What are the new online learning technologies and new online learner competences? What are the implications of emerging technologies of learning for influencing the learning landscape? What makes online instruction good and effective? And what are the basic principles of instruction arising from the new modalities and technologies of learning in the changed learning landscape? The enquiries, analyses and explorations with which Jan Visser and his colleagues address such issues, and the suggestions and recommendations that they derive from them and proffer here, have widespread implications and applicability to all those interested in and concerned about the topics, issues and problems of learning and learners in the 21st century.

This is a ground-breaking publication, which we believe helps carry forward the agenda of the Springer Series on Lifelong Learning. We thank the anonymous international reviewers and assessors who have considered the work and who have played such a significant part in the progress of this work to completion. We trust that its readers will find it as stimulating, thought-provoking and controversial as we who have overseen this project and its development have found it: we commend it with confidence to all those working in this field. We trust that this further volume in the Springer Series will provide the wide range of constituencies working in the domain of lifelong learning with a rich range of new material for their consideration and further investigation. We hope that it will encourage their continuing dialogue, critical thinking, research and development, academic and scholarly production, and individual, institutional and professional progress.

January 2008   David Aspin
                                                                   Judith Chapman

About the Authors

Michael F. Beaudoin is professor of education at the University of New England in Portland, Maine, where he was previously founding dean of a new college. He is recognized for designing and directing innovative projects, including several successful distance education programs. He has held senior administrative positions and faculty appointments at institutions in Maine, Massachusetts, Washington, DC and Germany, and has been a visiting scholar at institutions in Germany, China and Ghana. With over 75 publications and presentations, including two books, Dr. Beaudoin has written extensively in the field of distance education and related areas, frequently presents at conferences, and serves as an evaluator and consultant for distance education programs and courses.

John Bransford is an internationally renowned scholar in cognition and technology. He is the James W. Mifflin University Professor of Education at the University of Washington. Prior to 2003 he was Centennial Professor of Psychology and Education and co-director of the Learning Technology Center at Vanderbilt University. Dr. Bransford co-chaired several National Academy of Science and a National Academy of Education committees, resulting in the publication of multiple volumes on *How People Learn* and *Preparing Teachers for a Changing World*. He is director of the LIFE (Learning in Informal and Formal Environments) Center and serves on the International Board of Advisors for Microsoft's Technology and Learning program.

Ileana de la Teja is associate professor and researcher at the Télé-université in Montreal. She is also a consultant in competency-based learning in academic and corporate settings, and serves on the International Board of Standards for Training, Performance and Instruction. Her work has resulted in numerous publications and conferences on different aspects of online learning. She is co-author of *Instructor competencies: Standards for face-to-face, online, and blended settings* (2004), and *Evaluator competencies: Standards for the practice of evaluation in organizations* (2008). Ileana received her M.A. and Ph.D. degrees in educational technology from the Université de Montréal.

Mary Hall started her working life as an economist but re-engaged with education when her oldest child started Playcentre, a parent-run Early Childhood co-operative. Since then she has been involved in the sector in a wide range of roles from Early

Childhood teacher to school Trustee (Governor), university tutor, school administrator and policy advisor. She has been involved in the development of print-based and web-based learning materials as well as in the selection of educational personnel. Mary holds an honors degree in economics and is currently working towards her Masters in Education through the University of Southern Queensland's online program.

Deborah LaPointe is the assistant director of education development within the Learning Design Center at the Health Sciences Library and Informatics Center at the University of New Mexico. Her educational and professional background is in organizational learning and instructional technology with a specialization in distance learning. She is a recipient of the University Continuing Education Association's William Rainey Harper Research Award. Deb's research interests center on using synchronous and emerging technologies in the online environment to facilitate learning through peer interaction and group dynamics.

M. David Merrill, Ph.D. 1964 University of Illinois. He is an instructional effectiveness consultant, a visiting professor at both Florida State University and Brigham Young University Hawaii, and professor emeritus at Utah State University. He is internationally recognized as a major contributor to the field of instructional technology, has published many books and articles in the field and has lectured internationally. He received the 2001 AECT Life Time Achievement Award. Together he and his wife Kate have nine children and 37 + 4 (by marriage) grandchildren which he claims as his most important accomplishment.

Susan Mosborg is a research scientist at the LIFE (Learning in Informal and Formal Environments) Center at the University of Washington. Her current research investigates how people learn to collaborate to address complex challenges; in particular the role played by 'adaptive expert' and 'innovator designer' mindsets and by systems thinking and practice more generally. She received her Ph.D. in educational psychology from the University of Washington in 2004, where she studied historical sense-making. Earlier in her career she served as an educational policy analyst and as a high school social studies teacher.

Christina Rogoza joined the University of Manitoba in 2007 as an instructional designer in the Extended Education Department. Previously she served as the director for the Center for Learning, Teaching & Technology at the University of Texas Pan American. Her focus has been on faculty development in the appropriate pedagogical use of technology in curriculum design. She has taught in both traditional and online environments and is an instructor in the Worldwide Instructional Design System (WIDS) for performance based curriculum development. Her academic interests include research on technology enhanced learning and the relationship between epistemological beliefs and learning.

Mary Slowinski is director of curriculum design services at Bellevue Community College in Washington State where she works with faculty and administrators to integrate advances in the learning sciences and technology into campus-based and online courses. Prior to accepting this position, she received tenure as a faculty member and chaired the college's Digital Media Arts program. Mary is also a doctoral student in the learning sciences at the University of Washington, where she is investigating the use of technology to further shared inquiry and collaborative knowledge-building.

Timothy W. Spannaus, Ph.D. is program coordinator and senior lecturer in the instructional technology program at Wayne State University, Detroit, Michigan. He teaches courses in multimedia, message design, games and simulations and consults with business and industrial clients. Previously Tim was principal consultant with The Emdicium Group, Inc. He was president of ibstpi, the International Board of Standards for Training, Performance and Instruction, and ADCIS, the Association for Development of Computer-based Instructional Systems. Tim has contributed chapters to *The ID casebook* and was co-author of *Training manager competencies: The standards*. He is a frequent conference presenter, with papers on interactive technologies and faculty development.

J. Michael Spector is associate director of the Learning Systems Institute, professor of instructional systems, and principal investigator for the International Center for Learning, Education and Performance Systems at Florida State University. He earned a Ph.D. in philosophy from The University of Texas at Austin in 1978. His recent research is in the areas of intelligent performance support for instructional design, assessing learning in complex domains, and technology integration in education. Dr. Spector is editor of ETR&D—Development and edited the third edition of the Handbook of Research on Educational Communications and Technology.

Diana Stirling is a painter and educator who lives in the desert of the southwestern USA. Her particular interests include complexity theory and its potential application to the study of learning in the individual; ideas about how to create dynamic, individualized, computer mediated learning experiences; and ways to support self-directed learning through free access to information and the conscious exploration of human experience.

Slavi Stoyanov is a researcher at the Educational Technology Expertise Centre of the Open University of the Netherlands. He has a M.Sc. degree in psychology and educational sciences from Sofia University, Bulgaria, a M.Sc. in educational and training system design from Twente University (The Netherlands), and a Ph.D. in instructional technology from Twente University. His prior research interests are creative cognition, learning to solve ill-structured problems, cognitive mapping, individual differences in learning, and peopleware. Slavi Stoyanov is an advanced practitioner of Kirton's Adaptation/Innovation Inventory for measuring problem solving cognitive styles.

Jeroen J. G. van Merriënboer (1959) is professor of educational technology and scientific director of the Netherlands Laboratory for Lifelong Learning at the Open University of The Netherlands. He holds a Master's degree in psychophysiology from the Free University of Amsterdam and a Ph.D. in Instructional Technology from the

University of Twente. Main research themes are cognitive architecture and instruction, instructional design for complex learning, holistic approaches to design, and adaptive e-learning. He published over 100 journal articles and authored several books, including his prize-winning monograph *Training Complex Cognitive Skills* (1997) and his recent work *Ten Steps to Complex Learning* (2007).

Jan Visser is driven by the transdisciplinary quest to understand human cognition and learning in its broadest and deepest sense. He is a theoretical physicist (Delft University of Technology) and educational scientist (via Florida State's instructional design program), and studied philosophy at the Universities of Leiden and Amsterdam. Dr. Visser is founding president of the Learning Development Institute and directed previously UNESCO's Learning Without Frontiers. He has worked around the world to improve the conditions of learning; is a documentary filmmaker, a musician—who builds his own instruments, and has walked an average of ten miles a day since 1993.

Yusra Laila Visser is coordinator and trainer for the Digital Education Teacher's Academy, a collaborative program between Florida Atlantic University and the School Board of Broward County. In this capacity, she designs, develops, and implements targeted in-service teacher training courses focused on topics such as technology integration, project-based learning, and data-driven decision making. She also serves as researcher and secretary for the Learning Development Institute. In her consulting work she has served such clients as the World Bank, Verizon ESG, the Department of Homeland Security, Arthur Andersen, the United Nations, and Pearson PCS. Yusra holds a Ph.D. and Master's degree in instructional systems from Florida State University.

Muriel Visser-Valfrey is a communications researcher affiliated with the Learning Development Institute and works internationally as a consultant in health communication and education. Her work over recent years has focused on HIV and AIDS. Muriel has done extensive research on the role of teachers in HIV and AIDS prevention. Her other research interests include applying quantitative and qualitative research methods to examining issues such as the influence of attitude functions on alternate behaviors; the portrayal of HIV and AIDS in the media; the perceptions of rural communities about learning and health; and the impact of movies on adolescent smoking behavior.

Nancy Vye is a research scientist in the College of Education at the University of Washington. Previously, she was co-director of the Learning Technology Center at Vanderbilt University. Her research focuses on challenge-based learning, assessment, and uses of technology for designing curricula and assessment tools that enhance teaching and learning. Vye's work includes research on *The adventures of Jasper Woodbury*, a mathematics problem solving series, *Schools for thought*, a technology-based, educational reform initiative; *Betty's brain*, a pedagogical computer agent that teaches systems thinking and cause-effect reasoning, and most recently, *STAR.Legacy* software that supports problem-based learning.

Contents

Chapter 1
Let the Dialogue Begin: An Introduction

Jan Visser[1]

Abstract This brief introductory chapter highlights and describes the process that led to the creation of the present book. It argues that the process in question, which consisted of an elaborate form of evolving dialogue, was essential to the matter at hand, namely the deepening of understanding of human learning and of the essential features of being human that contribute to making learning meaningful. The chapter lists 32 questions that were formulated by 10 of the authors at the outset of the dialogue. These questions were the starting point for a process of group interactions that started online, then led to a face-to-face workshop and a panel discussion with a wider audience. Subsequently, the process proceeded again online as the chapters of this book evolved. The description of the above process will orient the reader to the context in which the author team worked. The chapter serves furthermore as an introduction to the organization of the book and its various components. It invites the reader into the dialogue and provides concrete suggestions for ways of entering the conversation from the outset.

1.1 The Elephant in the Dark

The book you hold in your hands is at once the result of dialogue, a manifestation of dialogue and a call for dialogue. The dialogue is about learning and, more specifically, the learners and the context in which they learn. Most people believe they know what learning is, but no one seems to know it fully. Hence the need to pull visions together, to make them interact, and to try and rise above the limitative truths contained in each person's separate vision.

Learning Development Institute

[1] In presenting this book to the reader, I like to highlight the spirit of teamwork that has created it. Authors take individual responsibility for their chapters and the editors do the same for the book as a whole as well as for structuring the dialogic process that generated it. However, this book would have been significantly different had authors and editors failed to discover the treasure of collective creativity that lies hidden in interaction, collaboration and dialogue.

J. Visser and M. Visser-Valfrey (eds.), *Learners in a Changing Learning Landscape*, © Springer Science+Business Media B.V. 2008

Understanding learning is like knowing the elephant in the ancient story of the blind men and the elephant. The story possibly originated in India and has been told differently in diverse cultures. Mowlana Jalaluddin Rumi (n.d.), in his poetic rendition of the tale, takes us to a dark house to which the elephant has been brought for exhibition by some Hindus. To see it, people enter into the darkness of the house, one by one. Their findings are reported in the following passage:

> *The palm of one fell on the trunk. 'This creature is like a water-spout,' he said.*
> *The hand of another lighted on the elephant's ear. To him the beat was evidently like a fan.*
> *Another rubbed against its leg. 'I found the elephant's shape is like a pillar,' he said.*
> *Another laid his hand on its back. 'Certainly this elephant was like a throne,' he said.*

The story illustrates the need for bringing different visions together to fully understand a complicated concept, whether it concerns an elephant in the dark or our as yet unenlightened perceptions of what it means to learn. This book purports to do exactly that. It brings together the observations, findings, analyses, conclusions, experiences, visions, and even speculative thought of 18 authors inspired by a challenge formulated in the following words:

> Today's learners find themselves in a learning landscape that is constantly and dramatically changing in terms of the modalities through which people learn; the purposes for which they learn; and the context, including temporal and spatial frames of reference, in which learning acquires its meaning. Learners are required to look at themselves as lifelong learners, putting greatly increased emphasis on learner self-efficacy, both individually and socially. It thus makes sense to ask ourselves deep questions about the learners, what to expect of them and how their roles and essential competencies should be defined. (Learning Development Institute, 2005)

What should learners be equipped with in order to flourish in this rapidly changing learning landscape? What does this imply for the conditions we put in place to foster learning? What does it mean in terms of preparing new generations of learners for the world in which they grow to learn and learn to grow?

1.2   Brief History and Future of the Dialogue

The idea to start facing the above challenge was prompted by an initiative of the International Board of Standards for Training, Performance and Instruction (ibstpi[2]) to conduct a study to identify the key competencies required of learners in today's world, taking into account particularly that significant processes of learning now take place on the Internet. The initiative was seen as important in its own right as

---

[2] Throughout this book, references to ibstpi—pronounced ibstípi, with the emphasis on the second syllable—are to ibstpi®, the registered trademark of the International Board of Standards for Training, Performance and Instruction.

most studies aimed at improving learning focus on the instructor and the parameters of the learning environment, rather than the learner. On the other hand it was felt that ibstpi's interest was too focused on the online learner and that broader questions needed to be asked, placing the learner in the context of a hugely complex learning landscape that is only partially determined by the formal education context and deliberate processes of learning.

Based on the above consideration, and while inspired by ibstpi's initiative, the Learning Development Institute proposed to run a dedicated workshop in conjunction with a Presidential Panel Session to be hosted by the Association for Educational Communications and Technology (AECT) at its annual convention in October 2005 in Orlando, Florida. This brought together ten individuals who initially started collaborating online. The majority of them then met face to face in Orlando at the workshop. They subsequently shared their ideas with the wider audience of attendees at the Presidential Panel Session that followed the next day. And they then took another two years to reflect further on the issues that had emerged, producing the chapters of this book.

In the context of the latter process, others joined in the effort, either invited by the original participants to become co-authors of chapters or sought out by the Learning Development Institute to write additional chapters. While doing so, authors stayed in touch and followed each other's efforts online as different draft versions of the chapters were posted to a Web site with restricted exclusive access for the authors. This led to yet further dialogue, which is reflected in the multiple cross-references that can be found dispersed throughout the book. When all core chapters of the book (Chapters 2–12) had reached a stage of development that appeared to be close to final, two additional authors—David Merrill and Muriel Visser-Valfrey—were invited to react to and reflect on the results and the process of the dialogue, respectively. Their 'meta-dialogic' considerations can be found in the final two chapters. The result now in the hands of the reader should not be seen as an end product. Rather, it is a crucial step in the process to move the debate beyond the relatively small circle of its proponents and thus involve the reader. Hence the title of this chapter, which is borrowed from the concluding sentences of another chapter in this book (Bransford, Slowinski, Vye, & Mosborg, p. 61).

In view of the aim to expand the dialogue to beyond the book, the authors have taken great care to list at the end of each chapter additional resources that readers can explore to deepen their insights. They have also formulated questions following the various chapters aimed at encouraging readers to expand their thinking beyond the content of the chapter in question. In some cases these questions bring issues together from a variety of chapters or they persuade the reader to look entirely outside what can be found in the book. Readers can take advantage of these 'questions for comprehension and application' individually or, better still, collaboratively. Indeed, the prospect that this work should be used as a textbook for advanced courses on different aspects of the sciences of learning and instruction, as well as in the wide array of areas of study that focus on human learning in informal settings, has been one of the leading thoughts in creating it. The questions provided typically do not have a simple or unique answer. Rather, they may lead to further questions. If so, they will have served their purpose of stimulating the dialogue beyond the book.

1.3 Questions Galore

There is virtually no end to the questions that can be raised about human learning and what constitutes the essence of those who engage in it, i.e., humans. To help the reader appreciate such abundance, and to serve as a guide towards understanding what motivated this dialogue from the start, I conclude with an overview of initial questions raised by the ten core proponents of the dialogue while they prepared themselves for the Orlando workshop. Those same questions can be found, together with their underlying rationale and initial reflective statements by most of the authors of this book, at the earlier mentioned Web site of the workshop (Learning Development Institute, 2005). In Table 1.1 these questions are listed in the chronological order in which they were posted by their authors.

The final chapter of this book explores what happened to these questions and the role they played in structuring and promoting the dialogue; in generating the ideas presented in this book; and in determining what remains unanswered. That same chapter may be read last to stimulate reflection about the book as a whole; it can equally be read first and serve as an advance organizer for what is to follow. The choice is left to the reader.

Table 1.1 Overview of initial questions raised by the authors to inspire the dialogue

Author	Question #	Question
Jan Visser	01	Is the online learner a distinct subspecies among the wider species of learners in general?
	02	What are the key changes that we notice in today's learning landscape and how can they be put into hierarchical order in terms of the importance of challenges posed to the learner?
	03	What does learning actually mean?
Diana Stirling	04	How does the design of the online software environment communicate expectations to learners? What gets communicated?

(continued)

Table 1.1 (continued)

Author	Question #	Question
	05	How does instructor use of online learning tools (e.g. software environment & its contents, email, etc.) communicate expectations to learners? What gets communicated?
	06	What do learners themselves expect in online environments? What role can/do those expectations play in the overall online learning experience?
Mike Spector	07	What makes a good/successful online course good/successful? Given an answer to that question, what role do the knowledge, skills and attitudes of online learners play in success? Which knowledge, skills, and attitudes are particularly critical to success of individual learners and the overall course?
	08	What might be different in answering what makes a good course good with regard to face-to-face and online courses?
	09	Many people have claimed that face-to-face classroom groups have identifiable "personalities" and further that these might affect which instructional strategies and activities are likely to be successful. Is this also true with regard to online courses?
Jeroen van Merriënboer	10	Shouldn't researchers in the field of instruction abandon the term online learning?
	11	Can online environments help to learn complex skills? If so, how?
	12	Do new requirements to online learners merely reflect the weaknesses of online learning environments?

(continued)

Table 1.1 (continued)

Author	Question #	Question
Deb LaPointe	13	Can assumptions about self, authority, and knowledge develop so that online learners come to see and know themselves as knowledge constructors? Do online learners learn to examine their underlying assumptions, reflect on alternative possibilities, and reframe their worldviews?
	14	Are we ready to facilitate learning for gamers, learners from diverse cultures, and learners recently returned from Iraq and Afghanistan? Can we quickly evolve and change to meet their learning needs? How do we do that?
	15	Are we preparing learners for creative global collaboration? Are we alerting learners to the fact that learners overseas are highly motivated and working in gifted communities? Do learners know that other countries are looking to them to create the next creative wave? Are we preparing learners to be creative collaborators?
Michael Beaudoin	16	Should the online instructor be lenient in assessing the invisible learner's minimal participation in online dialogue if other course requirements are satisfactorily met?
	17	Given that online course environments are generally enhanced by a community of scholars actively contributing to the course, especially via online discussions, can it be argued that the invisible learner's behavior is parasitic, in that s/he constantly takes from, but seldom contributes to, the course?

(continued)

Table 1.1 (continued)

Author	Question #	Question
	18	Is there evidence indicating that invisible learners, despite their minimal engagement in online interaction with instructor and peers, actually do learn and perform on graded assignments as well as or even better than the more visibly active students?
John Bransford	19	Whether taken online, face-to-face, or in a blended manner, we all probably agree that people need to become "lifelong learners". What are some aspects of lifelong learning that are especially important to make explicit?
	20	Can online learning environments (including blended environments) provide learning opportunities that are *more* interesting and productive for learners than traditional environments?
	21	Can online environments appeal to learners who are active problem posers, leaders and teachers, or must they be primarily "knowledge dispensing" environments.
	22	Can "online" learning open up new spaces for learning that are not currently being utilized?
Ileana de la Teja	23	What is the role of online learners in a multi-actor environment?
	24	What makes a successful online learner?
	25	Are online learners getting what they want/need?
Yusra Visser	26	What is the effect of anonymity (presence or lack thereof) on the learner, learning, and performance?

(continued)

Table 1.1 (continued)

Author	Question #	Question
	27	Some suggest that distance learning can be a superior method of instruction for supporting the achievement of certain outcomes. What is the basis of this claim, and how can the claim be validated?
	28	How do we measure opportunity costs (from the learner's vantage point) of different instructional modalities?
	29	What *really* is embodied learning, and how does it affect the effectiveness of instructional modalities?
Christina Rogoza	30	Does computer based collaborative learning rest on different epistemological assumptions and therefore require the development of new pedagogies?
	31	How is culture mediated in the design and delivery of online learning?
	32	Can the online learners be oriented to a disposition that opens up their personal learning space?

In determining the sequencing of the remaining chapters in this book, the editors have sought a compromise between recognizing some of the major lines of thought that run through this book and offering variety to the reader who reads them in sequence. However, absolutely no harm results from reading the following chapters in any order the reader chooses.

1.4   Resources for Further Exploration

Resources about the substance of the dialogue, those that relate to learning in its different guises, the actors involved in learning processes and the environment in which they operate are dispersed throughout the recommendations following all other chapters. I will refrain from repeating them here. However, few, if any, chapters list resources on the dialogic process itself. Following are a few that the interested reader may want to explore.

- Bohm, D. (1996). *On dialogue*. London, UK: Routledge. The physicist David Bohm devoted the last years of his life to studying dialogue and developing a kind of dialogic practice usually referred to as 'Bohmian.' Suspension of one's opinions and judgments is seen as crucial in the Bohmian dialogue to foster better listening and deepening insight through free association of thoughts in a small group context. The dialogue referred to in the present book is inspired by Bohm's ideas, but did not follow those ideas to the letter. Bohm's book *On dialogue* is composed of original material by David Bohm, selected and brought together by the book's editor, Lee Nichol.
- Bohm, D., Factor, D., & Garrett, P. (1991). *Dialogue – A proposal*. This influential paper carries a copyright notice giving "permission to copy this material and to distribute it to others for non-commercial purposes including discussion, inquiry, criticism and as an aid to setting up Dialogue groups...." Consequently, it is widely available on the Web. I recommend accessing it at http://www.infed. org/archives/e-texts/bohm_ dialogue.htm.
- Smith, M. K. (2001). Dialogue and conversation. In *The Encyclopaedia of Informal Education*. Available at http://www.infed.org/biblio/b-dialog. htm. This paper explores the ideas about dialogue of different authors, including David Bohm, Martin Buber, Paulo Freire, Hans-Georg Gadamer and Jürgen Habermas. It contains a rich overview of sources for further reading.
- Plato was of course a master of the use of dialogue as a way to understanding. An extensive list of links to Plato's work available on the Internet can be found at http://plato-dialogues.org/links.htm.

1.5   Questions for Comprehension and Application

1. This chapter lists 32 questions formulated by 10 authors at the start of their dialogue. Imagine that you had been invited as an eleventh member to this group and were asked to add some three questions to the ones already formulated. What would they be? As you start reading the book now, you may want to write those questions on, for instance, a 4' × 6' card that you keep with the book as your reading progresses. It will stimulate you to enter into a virtual dialogic relationship with the authors.
2. Our own experience is a forceful frame of reference for how we think about learning. Such experience may be the source of biases in how we interpret the world of learning. It may also positively contribute to providing anchor points for associating what you read with concrete instances of significant personal learning. Enhancing awareness of your personal learning history can thus be expected to make reading this book more meaningful to you. To help you

enhance such awareness, write a brief history of your most significant learning experiences throughout life, exploring why you judge certain experiences to have been of greater value and meaning to you than other ones while trying to identify the conditions that shaped such meaningful learning experiences. What appear to be key factors in making learning meaningful for you? Sample learning stories, on which you can model your own, were generated in the context of LDI's Meaning of Learning (MOL) research. They are available via http://www. learndev.org/MoL.html.

3. Consider this question in conjunction with the second 'question for comprehension and application' at the end of Chapter 14 (p. 289). If you were to carry the dialogue represented by this book forward, you would want to consider what different people have thought about the philosophical underpinnings and the practice of dialogue. The article by M. K. Smith (2001) in *The Encyclopaedia of Informal Education* mentioned above in Section 1.4 discusses and provides links to a variety of authors for further study. You should also do your own independent library and Internet research and read up on the issue of dialogue as a condition for learning and elucidation among members of a group. Make a selection of four authors whose ideas on dialogue you wish to study in greater depth. Compare their ideas and evaluate them against the backdrop of making informed choices concerning the future of this dialogue.

References

Bransford, J. D., Slowinski, M., Vye, N., & Mosborg, S. (in this volume). The learning sciences, technology and designs for educational systems: Some thoughts about change. In J. Visser & M. Visser-Valfrey (Eds.), *Learners in a changing learning landscape: Reflections from a dialogue on new roles and expectations* (pp. 37–67). Dordrecht, The Netherlands: Springer.

Learning Development Institute (2005). Web site of the Presidential Workshop and Panel Session at the International Convention of the Association for Educational Communications and Technology on *Learners in a changing learning landscape: New roles and expectations*, October 18–22, 2005, Orlando, FL. Retrieved October 5, 2007, from http://www.learndev.org/ibstpi-AECT2005.html.

Rumi, M. J. (n.d.). The elephant in the dark. In *Tales of Masnavi* (A. J. Arberry Trans.). Retrieved October 4, 2007, from http://www.khamush.com/tales_from_masnavi.htm.

Chapter 2
Constructive Interaction with Change: Implications for Learners and the Environment in Which They Learn

Jan Visser

Abstract Reflections regarding changes in the learning landscape and their implications for the (lifelong) learner are placed against the backdrop of an ecological perspective on learning. Learning—individually and as a feature of social behavior—is defined in relation to constructive interaction of complex adaptive systems with their wider environment. Human existence involves more and more that people interact online. Consequently, such interactions have increasingly become a crucial dimension of learning. Adapting to life—and thus also to learning—on the Net poses a certain challenge to those whose major life experience predates the digital era. However, more important than the changes brought about by technological innovation as such are the challenges posed by increased complexity of the world in which we live, the nature and scale of the problems it faces, and the changed nature of our productive and transformative presence in the world. The latter challenges require a fundamental rethinking of the purposes for which we learn, given the complex thinking educated individuals must be capable of. They also call for a strategic reorientation of the processes and environment that afford such learning. Tentative answers will be offered and questions will be raised regarding the implications of the referred challenges for today's learners and the learning ecology in which they operate.

2.1 Constructive Interaction with Change—The Reason Why We Learn

A good student is one who learns to think with his own head.
Italian-born French pianist Aldo Ciccolini in an interview
with Radio France on August 16, 2005

Humans distinguish themselves from other animals in their ability to go beyond merely adapting to their environment. They are actively and consciously involved in changing it. The change produced by some is the reason for others to react to such change, either by seeking to accommodate it in their lives or by producing

---

Learning Development Institute

J. Visser and M. Visser-Valfrey (eds.), *Learners in a Changing Learning Landscape*,
© Springer Science + Business Media B.V. 2008

further change. Thus, change has become a permanent feature of the human condition and so has the need to interact with it.

Our interaction with change can range anywhere on a continuum from destructive to constructive. In fact, not infrequently are our actions detrimental to ourselves or others. Nonetheless, it is natural for a species that is able to consciously contemplate the consequences of its actions to always seek behavior that, collectively, is considered constructive. For that to work it must be assumed that, as a species, we are able to entertain a dialogue among ourselves about what is right and wrong and that mutual understanding on ethical issues can be reached at levels that remain relatively uncorrupted by the forces of political and economic power. Considering the complexity and extent of challenges and problems faced by humankind at the current juncture in time, it makes sense for such a dialogue to extend across the planet. We may still be considerably removed from such an ideal state of affairs, however, it would be a mistake if we would not seek to define learning for the world we want, rather than for the world we have.

2.1.1 So, What is Learning?

For a book that explores what learners ought to be equipped with in order to flourish in today's changing learning landscape, I must first address the question 'What is learning?' My initial reflections on what it means to learn are based on personal experience. After all, attributing meaning is a personal matter.

As we transit through life, our perceptions about what it means to be a learning individual, what learning entails and how it impacts people will be marked by our personal experiences. Thanks to our ability to learn we change constantly and often profoundly throughout life. While this happens, the diversity of who we are as human beings and the different, constantly changing, circumstances in which we find ourselves cannot but produce a rich variety of ways in which we attribute meaning to the experience of learning. While any person's personal experience will be singular, it will easily be recognized that the examples that follow are far from extraordinary. Other people's learning life, while different from mine, will be both similar and similarly singular.

I spent a significant portion of my younger years preparing myself to become a physicist, going through formal university training. Having become what I wanted to be according to my boyhood dreams wasn't the end of my learning life, though. For instance, later in life I also learnt to make documentary films and did so entirely on my own through extensive reading and experimenting with 16 mm film equipment. In addition, I familiarized myself with and eventually became proficient in the Spanish language, starting my learning endeavor off by using a self-instructional book with accompanying audio recordings while later on using the real world as an opportunity for practicing my newly acquired skills. Interestingly, when I tried to do the same for Arabic I failed miserably on multiple attempts, whichever method I tried. I had meanwhile become an ardent advocate of self-directed learning, with part of my professional activities being dedicated to the development of distance education in different parts of the world. It wasn't easy, therefore, to admit my failure. It was even more difficult to accept my success when I finally learned Arabic effectively in a traditional face-to-face environment.

From the age of eight onward and throughout my adolescent years, as well as occasionally thereafter, I benefited from individual guidance by people much better than I when I learnt to play the piano and other keyboard instruments, such as the organ and harpsichord. I am still learning, often by trying things out for myself and by carefully listening to the performances by others.

In my late forties and fifties I familiarized myself with the instructional design field. Like in the case of physics, I did so in the formal context of a university environment, but this time only after serious negotiation about how I would use that setting. During that same period, I also learnt to construct complicated musical instruments, such as harpsichords, having acquired basic woodworking and cabinet making skills as a child by watching my father (the same way I learned such things as maintaining and repairing my bike). Other skills I still had to learn by following detailed written guidance or just by inventing them, based on what is perhaps best described as the use of common sense.

Besides the above more obvious instances of learning, I learnt numerous other things, such as overcoming shyness, accepting tragic and irreversible loss, and interacting gently with most of those I meet. None of these things were ever taught to me in any formal way or setting. I had to find out for myself, interacting with those whose advice I chose to accept and whose model I sought to emulate.

Looking back, and comparing my own learning experience as sketched above with the learning histories I got to know of other people, what strikes me most is the fabulous variedness of learning throughout people's lives. Such variedness reflects itself in many different dimensions, such as the purposes for which we learn, the specificity of our diverse motivations, the modality of the learning effort, its duration and the ways in which we seek to become different from who and what we were before the learning took place. While few would doubt that we can often dramatically change, thanks to our ability to learn, it frequently remains a mystery what suddenly seems to flip the switch between being an apprentice and the master of one's abilities.

Besides, it is not a mere matter of acquiring or having new abilities. Such abilities are quite futile if they are not integrated in an emotionally and intellectually meaningful overall perspective, i.e. one's life project or worldview. While I learnt many component skills, such as solving second-order partial differential equations; planing a piece of wood; editing a sequence of film shots; or presenting an argument in written form, those are not the things I feel added real value to my life. Without the more comprehensive perspectives of becoming a theoretical physicist, able to contribute to my field of interest; building musical instruments that I or other people would want to play; producing a documentary movie on an issue I felt passionate about; or being a contributing intellectual, none of the above skills, however competent I might have become at performing them, would have meant much to me.

Thus, my perspective on learning is one that is in the first place determined by awareness of the various comprehensive roles we wish to play in life. We want to be a good parent, a skillful carpenter, an effective teacher, a creative physicist, or a performing pianist who thinks with his own head rather than imitating someone else's performance.

2.1.2 A Matter of Definition

This book continues a process of collaborative reflection that started much earlier, first online and subsequently face-to-face during the 2005 annual convention of the Association for Educational Communications and Technology (Learning Development Institute, 2005). That reflection came in the wake of the initiative of the International Board of Standards for Training, Performance and Instruction (ibstpi, n.d.) to conduct a study of the competencies of successful online learners. In preparation for the above collaborative reflection 32 questions were formulated (Learning Development Institute, 2005). In this chapter I intend to address a small subset of those questions and will start off with one I originated myself, namely 'What does learning actually mean?' In fact, the previous section serves as a prelude to my exploration of that question. While initially formulating the above question and providing a rationale for it, I suggested that a response to it has something to do with one's perception of what it means to be human. So, I start from there.

My view of what it means to be human is a down-to-earth materialistic one. I see members of the human species as nothing more, but also nothing less, than pieces of organized matter-energy—just the same as rocks, plants, and other animals. What makes them special and somehow unique is the fact that, in the course of evolution, humans became endowed with sufficiently high levels of consciousness to allow them to reflect on their actions, to hold things in mind and contemplate them, carrying out thought experiments, and to foresee, to an extent, the consequences of what they intend to do. What exactly consciousness is; to what extent some form of it might be present in other species or be an exclusive feature of humans; what allowed it to emerge; and what the neuronal correlates are of consciousness are questions regarding which only recently some tentative insights have started to develop (e.g., Edelman & Tononi, 2000; Carter, 2002; Greenfield, 2002; Edelman, 2004; Koch, 2004, 2005; Steinberg, 2005).

While consciousness is not exclusive to humans, the particular level to which it evolved probably is. Edelman (2004), for instance, distinguishes between primary consciousness and higher-order consciousness, the latter having been made possible by neuronal development that eventually led to "the acquisition of semantic capability, and finally language, [which] gave rise to higher-order consciousness in certain higher primates, including our hominine ancestors (and arguably a number of other ape species)" (p. 58). It is this higher-order consciousness that confers, according to Edelman, "the ability to imagine the future, explicitly recall the past, and to be conscious of being conscious" (pp. 58–59).

Consciousness allows us to experience joy and sorrow as we transit through life. It is the cause of the eternal amazement with which we stand, generation after generation, in awe of who we are, where we came from, what we are here for, and where we are going. It is at the origin of our sense of belonging, of being part of a larger whole, an experience to which we give expression in religious beliefs; mythologies; evolving worldviews based on the methodical and disciplined pursuit of scientific insight; and great works of art. Within the above perspective, being human means having the unique faculty of participating consciously—for a brief moment—in the evolution of the universe. The latter affirmation, I hasten to add, is both an outrageous claim and a call to humility.

If one accepts the above vision of what it means to be human, then learning must be conceived of in a similarly broad perspective of purposeful interaction with a constantly changing environment to which we must adapt while being ourselves the conscious participants in creating the change. 'Constructive interaction with change' thus ought to feature prominently in a definition of human learning at this level, expressing what learning is ultimately all about. Besides, it should be recognized that not only individual human beings partake in such constructive conscious interaction with change, but that this same behavior equally applies to social entities at a variety of levels of complex organization of which humans are part.

Moreover, learning as conceived in this perspective is intimately interwoven with life itself. It is therefore not something one engages in merely from time to time, but rather a lifelong disposition, one that is characterized by openness towards dialogue. Hence, I define human learning as the "disposition of human beings, and of the social entities to which they pertain, to engage in continuous dialogue with the human, social, biological and physical environment, so as to generate intelligent behavior to interact constructively with change" (J. Visser, 2001, p. 453). When I first proposed this definition, I used the term 'undefinition' for it, referring to its intended purpose to remove the boundaries from around the existing, too narrowly conceived definitions of learning. I still think there is a great need to look at learning from a broader perspective than we habitually do and find others thinking likewise, such as the authors who contributed to the special issue of *Educational Technology* on broadening the definition of learning (Y. L. Visser, Rowland, & J. Visser, 2002) and the transdisciplinary group of researchers who participated in the two *Book of Problems* dialogues at the 2002 and 2003 annual conferences of the Association for Educational Communications and Technology (Learning Development Institute, 2004; J. Visser & M. Visser, 2003; J. Visser, M. Visser, & Burnett, 2004). However, I also recognize that in daily discourse the word 'learning' is used in a great many ways, each of which relates to only aspects of what is implied in the above definition. The next section therefore identifies different levels of human adaptive behavior, each of them having something to do with the reasons why we learn and the different kinds of learning we engage in.

2.1.3 Four Levels of Adaptive Behavior

Human adaptive behavior, and thus the learning associated with it, occurs at least at the following four levels of organizational complexity, some of which we share with other organisms (J. Visser, 2002, n.p.):

Level 1: Interaction with threats and opportunities in the environment through genetically transmitted preprogrammed responses, e.g., fight and flight responses.

Level 2: Acquisition of essential environment-specific abilities, such as mastery of the mother tongue, driven by an inherited predisposition to do so.

Level 3: Deliberate acquisition of specific skills, knowledge, habits and propensities, motivated by individual choices or societal expectations, usually by exposing oneself to a purposely designed instructional—or self-instructional—process.

Level 4: The development and maintenance of a lifelong disposition to dialogue with one's environment for the purpose of constructively interacting with change in that environment.

It can be argued (J. Visser, 2002,) that the above four levels of learning-related adaptive behavior in humans "represent a progression of increasingly higher levels of consciousness about one's role in life and in the world" (n.p.). Besides, "the four levels are not entirely distinct from each other" (n.p.). In fact, they often interact. Moreover, while the levels of adaptive behavior correspond to a hierarchy of increased consciousness about one's existence, the learning associated with these levels does not necessarily represent a similar hierarchy. Take the acquisition of skills such as 'to represent graphically the relationship between two variables' or 'to repair a punctured tire.' These are associated with Level 3 adaptive behavior. On the other hand, the procedures to acquire the skills in question are relatively simple and thus low level. A competent instructional designer will be able to explain the processes involved, sketching them out on the back of an envelope. In contrast, educational communication professionals, particularly those involved in helping humans to avoid, for example, health risks associated with their reproductive behavior (Level 1), are still searching for answers to the question how to intervene and promote effective learning in this vastly complex area, which involves attitudes and values, as well as related cognitive and motor skills and the ability to moderate emotion (e.g., Patel & Yoskowitz, 2005).

The comprehensive definition of learning provided in Section 2.1.2 above is of interest particularly if one wishes to contemplate learning from a perspective that includes the fourth level of adaptive behavior. It applies at the most comprehensive level of being human, the level at which we are most distinctively different from anything else that learns, such as non-human animals or machines. It goes beyond the narrower definitions that underlie most learning theories, starting with Hilgard's (1948) definition, which states that "learning is the process by which activity originates or is changed through training procedures…as distinguished from changes by factors not attributable to training" (p. 4), a definition that, according to De Vaney and Butler (1996), who cite it, has been particularly influential on the thinking of the behavioral school. More recent definitions no longer describe learning as the sole consequence of training or instruction. Driscoll (2000), analyzing different learning theories, concludes that current definitional assumptions about learning, in addition to referring to learning as "a persisting change in human performance or performance potential," specify as the cause of such persisting change "the learner's experience and interaction with the world" (p. 11).

Not everyone is happy with a comprehensive definition like the one referred to in the previous section. In the first place, such a broad definition is difficult to use in the operational context of intentionally designed instruction. Besides, it may be seen to stress the obvious. See for a brief polemic on the latter issue the exchange between Chadwick (2002) and J. Visser & Y. L. Visser (2003). Discomfort with more comprehensive definitions of learning probably arises from the fact that most common definitions of human learning contemplate adaptive behavior at Level 3, the level that most education professionals have been prepared to deal with to the exclusion of other levels. There is nothing wrong, at least not in principle, with focusing on a particular level and thus delineating learning more restrictively than is done in my earlier cited comprehensive definition as long as one is aware to be dealing with a particular segment or aspect of the rich reality of human learning. Jonassen (2002), for instance, uses a definition of learning referred to in connection with another question raised in this dialogue (De la Teja, Question 23, p. 7 in this volume), which focuses on learning as a "willful, intentional, active, conscious, constructive and socially mediated practice" (p. 45). While this definition stresses a number of undoubtedly important aspects of learning at Level 3, it excludes for instance the vast area of incidental learning associated with Level 4. However important a particular segment or aspect of learning may be at a practical level of intentional intervention in changing human performance capability to serve accepted societal goals—which in today's world is usually related to the interests of the prevailing economic model—by closing one's eyes to human functioning at a higher level of adaptive behavior one is at risk of developing human beings who increasingly lose the capacity to intervene in ever more complex situations at a time when the major problems the world faces are exactly situated at such higher levels of complexity.

In view of the above rationale, I thus argue that, at whatever level we interact with the development of human learning, we should always do so within the perspective of the highest level of complexity within which we expect people to be able to operate. Against the backdrop of that argument it is sad to observe how increasingly formal education, up to the highest level, is being dealt with as if it were a mere commodity (see for arguments defending this position Daniel, 2002, 2003, and for opposing arguments Jain et al., 2003).

2.2   A Changing Learning Landscape

Now that I have explained on the previous pages what I mean by learning, I shall attempt to clarify next what I see as the major characteristics of the current learning landscape, as contrasted with the challenges and opportunities learners of past generations were facing. I highlight two areas, namely (1) the changed nature of change and (2) the changed nature of the problems, challenges and opportunities we face. The latter area reflects the reality of a world which cannot be fully understood if we are unable or unwilling to engage in complex thinking processes.

2.2.1 Changed Change

Humans, as adaptive organisms, have of course changed extremely little over long periods of time, periods that cover many generations. Whatever changes there may have been, evolutionary processes are too slow for such changes to become noticeable within timeframes of the order of magnitude of a couple of generations. Conversely, the world in which humans live has undergone dramatic changes over the last one to two generations, changes that are much more dramatic than ever before. The process is ongoing and is expected to become even more spectacular (Spohrer, 2003). The major changes have to do with the phenomenon of change itself. Change has changed.

In the past, the rate of change was slow enough for each generation to prepare itself during the initial phase of its existence for the circumstances into which it was born. Those circumstances could be expected to prevail without much alteration throughout the lifespan. Thus, members of a particular generation were able to spend the rest of their lives living with what they had learned while they were young, being able to deal with most situations. Moreover, older generations still alive were perceived as storehouses of acquired wisdom that members of younger generations could access and validly apply in their own lives. That time has gone and it has gone forever.

By contrast, the world of the 21st century is characterized by change that is often perceived as turbulent and having a high level of unpredictability. The current and future generations will have to live with such unpredictability. This requires a high level of insight in and control over one's own capacity to learn, to an increased extent at Level 4 referred to earlier in this chapter, and to do so in a lifelong perspective. Learning to learn, in a conscious way, should therefore be a prime concern, starting from the time infants are being raised and continuing throughout life.

The wisdom of the elders is undoubtedly still to be treasured, but it will only remain a valid resource in the context of intergenerational dialogue as long as third and fourth age citizens retain the capacity to reframe, rethink and redefine their acquired insights in ever changing circumstances and younger people have the capacity and entertain the predisposition to incorporate such invaluable knowledge into their current reality. Furthermore, the possibility for such older citizens to share their wisdom and to make it interact with the learning of members of the younger generations may well be conditioned by their ability to use the technologies of the day and their associated symbol systems, which are a natural part of the world of the young, but with which older people often only become familiar with considerable difficulty, requiring them to learn as well.

2.2.2   Changed Problems, Challenges and Opportunities

Another way in which the learning landscape has become crucially different from what it looked like before has to do with a shift in emphasis regarding the purposes for which we learn. Put differently, it has to do with the nature of the problems, challenges and opportunities the world faces and the responsibilities we assume as actors in a problematized environment. Here I see the following key challenges:

- Complexity rather than linearity
- Uncertainty, chance and ambiguity rather than relative certainty
- Interconnectedness that challenges the ways in which we care for our creative diversity
- Science and technology challenging our perceptions of what it means to be human
- Power of potentially serious destructive intervention perpetrated increasingly at the level of individuals and relatively small groups

The above challenges are best appreciated against the backdrop of our evolutionary history. Most recent estimates put the age of the universe at 13.7 billion years (WMAP, 2005). Recent findings suggest that some form of life was present on earth at least 3.43 billion years ago (Allwood, Walter, Kamber, Marshall, & Burch, 2006; Awramik, 2006). Hominid development is supposed to have started between five and ten million years ago (Institute of Human Origin, 2001) whereas human development may have started somewhere between 100,000 to 200,000 years ago (Templeton, 2002).

For ease of comprehension, let us compress the timescale to seven days and let us pretend that the universe came into being at the start of the first day. Then early forms of life would have started to emerge on the sixth day. Hominid development would have started just about five minutes ago and human development a mere six seconds ago. Less than half a second ago on the chosen time scale (in reality 10,000 years) the so-called agricultural revolution took place, replacing the haphazard practice of hunting and food gathering by the sedentary practice of growing crops and raising livestock in an increasingly organized and planned manner, allowing food to be produced in excess of what was needed so that it could be preserved and stored for later use. This took away an important self-regulatory mechanism that had so far kept the world's human population at a more or less stable level—believed to have been eight million people—determined by the immediate availability of nature's resources in particular habitats. In fact, it replaced nature's control of humans by human control over nature and marked the start of a continual process of innovation building upon innovation, as each new innovation is usually at the origin of a new set of challenges and opportunities, calling for further intervention. It turned us into a species that actively and consciously uses its capacity to create knowledge for the purpose of changing the world in which it lives, riding on the waves of innovation by creating new innovations.

The consequences in that short time span of 10,000 years—less than half a second on our metaphorical seven-day time scale—have been stupendous. For instance, for millions of years the population size of our evolutionary ancestors had remained more or less stable at a level that nature could support. As the practice of agriculture abolished the self-regulatory constraint on population growth imposed by nature, we started to grow, little by little in the beginning, with ups and downs caused by the onslaught of and recovery from episodes of endemic diseases, but growth became increasingly more rapid the larger the population size and the better health, sanitary and nutritional conditions became. Thus, in 1960, after several million years of hominid development, the world population stood at three billion. It took no more than 40 years for it to double to six billion just before the end of the last century. Such startling expansion could not have taken place had it not been accompanied by ever more rapid technological development that could mitigate the problems created by too many people having to share only limited resources. The process led to fierce competition for available resources and thus the development of warfare and defense technology; it also led to the more beneficial processes of development of technologies through which additional or alternative resources could be accessed and already available ones could be used more efficiently.

Tremendous amounts of resources and effort continue to be expended until today on means to exert power over one another by force. This has escalated to such an extent that, according to Robert Nelson of the Union of Concerned Scientists in a discussion about the Reliable Replacement Warheads program (Science Friday, 2006), half a billion people can be killed in the first 30 minutes of a thermo-nuclear war using the currently existing nuclear capability of the US. The inability of the world, despite the tremendous efforts undertaken at the level of the United Nations system, to harmonize our scientific and technological capability with our political prowess to create a better and more just world is eloquently expressed in the title (and content) of a recent book, *Space-age science and stone-age politics* (Avery, 2005).

The above is but one of the many complex challenges facing today's world. There are many other challenges of a similarly complex nature. They are often intertwined with one another, further increasing the complexity of the problem space in which 21st century humans operate. They have to do with such questions as how to feed the nine billion people that are expected to populate the earth by the year 2050; how to care for and preserve our cultural and linguistic diversity in a world of all-encompassing open communication networks in which there is a risk of asphyxiation of weak cultures by dominant ones; how to use the resources available on the planet in a perspective of sustainable interaction with the environment; how to create a world in which living together in harmony is not under constant threat of the tensions caused by blatantly visible disparity in wealth and power; how to redefine what it means to be human in a world of scientific and technological development that increasingly allows humans to interfere with their very humanness; or how to ensure that humans around the globe behave so as to minimize the risk of pandemics, HIV and AIDS being a case in point.

In all the above cases there is an essential need to develop thinking that transcends the traditional disciplinary approaches. In other words, dealing with these issues requires a transdisciplinary mindset. Both the current structure of available educational offerings and related student attitudes are generally not conducive to developing the kind of deep and comprehensive insight that preconditions transdisciplinary thinking. There is little difference in this regard between the various levels at which the educational system operates, be they primary, secondary or tertiary. Marshall (2006) speaks in this connection of "an unbalanced learning environment [in which] the need for a deeper context of schooling is imperative" (p. 6). The school teaches separate content areas, or 'subjects,' often administered by different people, subject specialists, who are not seen to collaboratively serve a purpose greater than they themselves and their specific discipline. It leaves to the learner the task of bringing the parts together, creating meaning out of what is being taught, and to seek and discover the connections, building a whole that is more than the separate parts and that eventually encompasses the learners themselves, individually and socially. But the learner is already emotionally disengaged and rarely accomplishes what is assumed to happen. The reason is a simple and obvious one. Marshall asserts concisely the issue at stake when she explains that "learning occurs when meaning is constructed and…meaning is constructed when emotions are engaged and conceptual relationships and patterns are discerned and connected" (p. 7).

The underlying assumptions of how we learn and teach in school date back to the seventeenth century when Descartes introduced the principle of separation of what belonged to the mind (*res cogitans*) and what belonged to nature (*res extensa*), the assumption being that subjectivity is at odds with the serious pursuit of knowledge and that only the objectively verifiable counts. There is no doubt that the development of science as such has greatly benefited from applying Descartes' teachings, but it has at the same time detached those who know from what they know and led to sciences that are disconnected from the cultures to which they belong. Good scientists, of course, know better and they have always violated the principle as necessary, allowing science to move forward in a stepwise fashion. Bronowski (1978) calls it "a self-correcting activity" (p. 122) and explains:

> Science is an attempt to represent the known world as a closed system with a perfect formalism. Scientific discovery is a constant maverick process of breaking out at the ends of the system and opening it up again and then hastily closing it after you have done your particular piece of work. (p. 108)

Morin (2005) takes up the theme of complex thinking eloquently and comprehensively in a small compilation volume of his extensive work called, modestly, *Introduction à la pensée complexe* (Introduction to complex thinking). In his foreword he argues that the case for complex thinking cannot be made in a simplistic manner. The argument is in and of itself complex and must culminate in exercising thought capable of dealing with the real world, of entering into dialogue and negotiation with it. Such complex thought incorporates, according to Morin, as much as possible of the historically developed processes of reductive thought (pensée simplifiante), but refuses the mutilating consequences of a simplification "that sees itself as the representation of what real there is in reality" (p. 11—my translation).

Elsewhere, Morin (1999) draws specific lessons for what should be considered key issues for education for the future. True to his argument referred to in the previous paragraph, he calls these lessons 'complex lessons.' I include this 66-page document by Morin among the 'resources for further exploration' at the end of this chapter and encourage my readers to delve into these complex lessons, which are available online. Here I limit myself to a simple itemized listing of the main issues dealt with by Morin. Following is a paraphrased representation of the description that Morin outlines himself in the foreword to his complex lessons. Each of the bullet headings is a direct quote from Morin's referenced work. The rest is my own words and interpretation as well as commentary, except for the parts in quotation marks and referenced as such. I note that Morin's focus is on teaching; mine in this chapter is on learning and the role of the learner. My reformulation of Morin's ideas reflects my specific focus and vision.

- *Detecting error and illusion*

Under this heading, Morin alerts to the fact that the school focuses on knowledge but generally fails in letting the learner discover what knowledge is, denying the knower the privilege of knowing what it means to know; to be aware of the often fragile underpinnings of what we think we know; to be armed against misconception, error and illusion.

- *Principles of pertinent knowledge*

The question raised here relates to the habit of schools to confront learners with compartmentalized knowledge while failing to provide them with the opportunity to connect the parts among themselves and combine them into a whole that is more than the simple sum of the parts. Knowledge becomes pertinent by placing it in context. Doing so is the task of the learner—not that of the teacher, but it is the teacher's task to ensure that the opportunity exists as well as to help the learner prepare her or his mind to always seek the "mutual relations and reciprocal influences between parts and the whole in a complex world" (p. 2).

- *Teaching the human condition*

From our perspective as human beings (and what other perspective could we possibly have?), our humanness in all its multifaceted ways (biological, physical, social, cultural, etc.), seen as an integral component of the larger environment of which we are part, is the basis for our human presence and intervention in the world. Rediscovering what it means to be human, getting to see the "indissoluble connection between the unity and the diversity of all that is human" (p. 2), is the formidable challenge the learner faces when presented with the thoroughly disintegrated discipline-based knowledge that habitually characterizes what we still call education.

- *Earth identity*

This idea relates strongly to the points I made earlier in this section. Many of the problems, challenges and opportunities we face are of a planetary nature. It is no exaggeration to state that the future of our species is crucially dependent on how we relate to our earth identity. Thus, the way we learn and what we learn should take our planetary identity into account. Morin argues that therefore "the history of the planetary era should be taught from its beginnings in the 16th century, when communication was established between all five continents" (p. 2). I see no reason why this should be limited to the last five centuries. There has been significant cultural interaction among the peoples of the earth for much longer and major ideas that emerged thousands of years ago in one place continue to impact today's planetary population across the globe.

- *Confronting uncertainties*

Under this heading, Morin quotes the Greek poet Euripides as saying, 25 centuries ago: "The expected doesn't occur and [the gods] open the door for the unexpected" (p. 3 in Morin's text). He goes on to say that these lines are "more than ever relevant" (p. 3) today. Indeed, as I have argued above, change is no longer what it used to be and one of the key capabilities that citizens of the 21st century must possess is the ability to interact constructively with ambiguity, chance and unpredictability. Contrary to that conclusion, and as a consequence of how in the educational context knowledge tends to be presented as a series of separate areas of sure facts and procedures, learners continue to be faced with the challenge of figuring out how to "navigate on a sea of uncertainties, sailing in and around islands of certainty" (p. 3) and to discover how, in fact, the various disciplines they become familiar with are often far less focused on certainty than they appear or are presented to be.

- *Understanding each other*

It has long been known that it is generally better to first listen to each other, attempting to see the world as it is seen through other people's eyes, before taking action that might harm others and ourselves. The time at which I am writing these words, however, shows no shortage of serious violations of this principle. Such violations have become particularly dangerous as we live in times when the power to exercise significantly destructive action is not limited to states but is equally a weapon of coercion in the hands of individuals and small groups, such as terrorist cells. The problem is exacerbated by the pervasiveness of communication infrastructure that is able to show what happens in one part of the world almost instantaneously to everyone else on the globe. In a world of immense disparity and heightened levels of violence this cannot but create profound frustration and difficult to manage anxiety among individuals and governments. Thus, profound change of attitudes is of the essence. Or, as Morin argues, "Mutual understanding among human beings, whether near or far, is henceforth a vital necessity to carry human relations past the barbarian stage of misunderstanding" (p. 3). I have argued elsewhere (J. Visser, 2007) that "increased networking around the globe is an important condition for the formation of dynamic learning communities that are sufficiently global in outlook to become a basis for learning to live together (Delors et al., 1996) with the global concerns of our time" (p. 643). Not only is 'understanding each other' a key requirement for our time; it so happens that technological developments during the last two decades have made it easier for learners to find opportunities across cultural and geopolitical boundaries to practice the concept and give it personal meaning.

- *Ethics for the human genre*

Morin observes correctly that ethics is not the product of lessons taught. Ethics takes shape in the mind as one becomes more and more aware of one's identity, both individually and as a member of communities, the society, and the human species. Moreover, such elucidation of who one is and what meaning one wishes to attribute to one's life also leads to a sense of belonging, to finding one's place in the universe, a spiritual awareness that may find expression in religious experience, artistic creation and metaphysical perception. Thus, Morin asserts that "all truly human development must include joint development of individual autonomy, community participation, and awareness of belonging to the human species" (pp. 3, 4). Ethics is both personal and communal/societal. This has important implications for what ought to be done in preparing auspicious conditions for value clarification from an educational point of view. However, whether such conditions are in place or not, it remains a key challenge to the learner to always seek to participate in relevant contexts that allow for the development of a sense of individual, societal and species-related identity. A complicating factor in this regard continues to be the disintegrated way in which the world appears to learners in the perspective offered by most institution-based efforts at educating them. As long as schools do not attend to this problem, the burden is on learners to reconstitute the world from the pieces offered to them and to develop their sense of self, and of being good earth citizens, while interacting with other learning human beings who similarly engage in such efforts. The world of online learning is perhaps among the most propitious environments allowing important inroads to be made into this area of concern.

Having said the above, and while I recognize that the 'online learning space' is a relevant and important dimension of today's learning landscape, I shall argue below that I consider the notion 'online learner' an irrelevant and unhelpful concept—as do, for instance, Van Merriënboer and Stoyanov in their contribution to this volume (pp. 69–90). The online learning space is there in addition to the various other spaces in which people learn. The online learning space may at times be the dominant dimension of the environment in which one learns; at times it may be complementary or supplementary, or a merely rudimentary dimension of the learning space. The fact that it is there, and that the tools through which it exists represent a certain level of technological sophistication, requires of today's learners to be conversant with those tools and their various uses. Some of those uses may be culture sensitive, which adds a further challenge, considering that the online learning space is not restricted to a single culture.

2.3 Learning on the Net

Rumors about the superior usefulness of the Internet and its potential impact on learning are generally greatly exaggerated. Such exaggeration has led to a deformation of the perspective on the importance of technology for learning and the raising of expectations that are hardly ever met (e.g., Salomon, 2002). Those who make claims about the superior impact of technology often compare bad education via traditional means with the application of more enlightened principles of facilitating learning using technological means, tacitly assuming that the same level of enlightenment would not be possible in a technology-poor environment. I do not agree with such an assumption, which I view as uninformed and often based on limited imagination. Good thinking, good learning and good education can take place in almost any circumstance as long as the actors involved in the processes concerned are properly inclined and possess some basic competencies, the ability to listen being one of them. I contend that being passionate about what one teaches or learns is immensely more important than whatever technology. In fact, it remains an interesting question waiting to be researched to what extent technologization of the learning environment might adversely impact actors' disposition to develop passion about the matters at hand. The reportedly extraordinary abilities of Richard Feynman—a physicist whose passion for his subject is well documented—to teach to captivated audiences using no more than chalkboard and chalk (Sykes, 1994), lends support to my contention.

The problem of overemphasizing the importance of technology is furthermore exacerbated by the advertising practice of a commercial sector that does not miss an opportunity to induce into a naïve public the belief that there is a positive correlation between having the right gear and mundane measures of achievement practiced by the school system, such as making the grade. Defining technology *per se* as a factor of influence distorts visions of how pedagogy should be improved. Or, as Fishman (2006) argues: "Technology employed for 'business as usual' leads to the usual outcomes. You don't create improvements in teaching or learning by introducing technology; you create improvements in teaching and learning by improving teaching and learning!" (p. 2). Consequently, the challenges to learners and to those who help them learn generally have to do with issues that are unrelated to technology.

2.3.1 Is There Such a Thing as an Online Learner?

During the online dialogue and workshop that preceded the writing of this book, I raised the question "Is the online learner a distinct subspecies among the wider species of learners in general?" (J. Visser, Question 1, p. 4 in this volume) . The underlying thoughts that accompanied my question, particularly the reference to Dreyfus's (2001) claim that the online environment is incapable of accommodating "emotional, involved, embodied human beings" (p. 48) in ways that allow those who learn to reach proficiency and expertise, triggered off another question, namely "What really is embodied learning, and how does it affect the effectiveness of instructional modalities?" (Y. L. Visser, Question 29, p. 8 in this volume). Stirling (see pp. 4 and 5 in this volume) draws attention in Questions 4, 5 and 6 to the expectations created in learners due to their participation in online learning environments, features of which, and the ways in which those features are being used, affect the learners. In Question 8, Spector (p. 5 in this volume) also refers to learner expectations, suggesting that "many expect more in terms of improved learning from an online course than a face-to-face course." I doubt whether this is indeed the case, but agree with both Stirling and Spector that it is reasonable to assume that the environment in which one learns creates expectations—perhaps not only in the learners, but also in those who facilitate the learning—that are determined, at least in part, by the characteristics of that environment. Van Merriënboer suggests (Question 10, p. 5 in this volume) that the entire concept 'online' may just be too broad to usefully generate specific research questions. This suggestion, on the one hand, underlines that the environment is a likely factor (or set of factors) of influence, but, on the other hand, it also points to the need to become more specific in describing the various defining characteristics of learning environments. I would argue that, by extension of the same argument, such a differentiated approach in referring to the learning environment is similarly relevant in the case of online, face-to-face and hybrid learning settings.

Nonetheless, the online learning environment has its own specificities. For instance, it is able to facilitate kinds of learning, such as through global collaboration and online gaming (LaPointe's Questions 14 and 15, p. 6 in this volume) and allows kinds of learner behavior, such as 'invisible' and anonymous participation (Beaudoin's Questions 16–18 and Y. L. Visser's Question 26, pp. 6–7 and 7 in this volume, respectively) that are far less likely to occur in traditional settings. Besides, there are technical possibilities in the online environment that potentially allow new learning spaces to be opened up (see e.g. Bransford's Question 22, p. 7 in this volume) that may less easily come to mind to learners whose sole perspective is that of the face-to-face context. On the other hand, Rogoza's Question 30 (p. 8 in this volume) highlights the fact that, whatever the potentiality of the online environment, the reality often remains below what is potentially possible. Besides, as suggested by Question 26 (Y. L. Visser, p. 7 in this volume), this same environment may be responsible for generating in students a number of unintended and undesired behaviors that detract from reaching online learning's full potential.

When in the 15th century the printing press was invented and print materials came into wide use among the general public, the appearance of that particular technology did not result in the emergence of p-learning and p-learners. When Jan Amos Comenius published his Orbis Sensualium Pictus in 1658, calling attention, by doing so, to the importance of appealing to learners' senses by including illustrations in instructional text rather than capitalizing on learners' ability to process verbal information, it didn't result in isolating i-learning as a particular kind of learning, nor did the advent of instructional radio lead to r-learning or that of instructional use of TV to t-learning. Against the backdrop of a centuries old history of the use of media in education, there seems little logic in the current tendency to reserve a special place for such things as e-learning and m-learning for those instructional practices that involve the use of electronic communication via computer networking and handheld mobile devices, respectively.

The beauty of learners is that they are, well ... learners. They come to the world hardwired to explore their environment (Gopnik, Meltzoff, & Kuhl, 1999). They create their own path through life while moving along, together with their fellow learners. Faced with different opportunities in which particular modalities—such as face-to-face instruction or education at a distance via a variety of media—may be dominantly available, good learners—those who have not bought into the idea that there is only one way in which to learn—will find their way not just by exploring the initially chosen option but equally by accessing multiple additional opportunities beyond the given one. They escape from domestication and become feral (see also Hall's contribution to this book, pp. 109–133). Defining someone as an e-learner or distance learner, even within the framework of a particular instructional context, is tantamount to discouraging such a person from engaging in wider explorations and failing to recognize the enormous wealth there is in learning when left to determine its own path.

Thinking back of the learning experience I know best, my own, I'm pretty confident that I would never have learnt Arabic had I stuck to the idea that I should meet this challenge through self-instruction; I would not have become a competent musical instrument builder had I limited myself to merely following the guidelines of the harpsichord building manual that I had at my disposal and had I not sought further advice from other builders and craftsmen and experimented with several techniques of my own invention; I would not have deepened my understanding of physics had I not supplemented an already excellent university program with weekly discussions and work sessions with a fellow student and friend who had similar interests and had I not explored what was on offer at other universities in related fields; and, finally, my personality would have remained underdeveloped had I not been able to find my ways in the school of life and become increasingly better at feeling comfortable with who I am and at ease with the limitations of my being.

Obviously, one shouldn't generalize from the above (biased) sample-of-one. However, I would not have brought up my personal experience had it not been largely convergent with the findings of an analysis of the stories of the lifetime learning experience of hundreds of people from around the world (Y. L. Visser, & J. Visser, 2000; J. Visser, Y. L. Visser, Amirault, Genge, & Miller, 2002; M. Visser, & J. Visser, 2003), covering a spectrum ranging from academics in Europe and the USA of different ages to illiterate Aymara farmers in rural Bolivia. That research, which started accidentally at another annual convention of the Association for Educational Communications and Technology (J. Visser, Berg, Burnett, & Y. L. Visser, 2000), shows a similar propensity in those whose learning stories were collected to situate themselves as learners in environments that include a wide choice of learning spaces beyond those formally designed for specific instructional purposes. The learning human being wanders among those various spaces and should be encouraged to do so. Part of the work that schools could usefully undertake would be to make their students aware of and conversant with that wide range of learning spaces to which they potentially have access.

It will be clear from the above that my answer to the question whether online learners should be considered a subspecies among learners in general is a clear NO. 'Online learner' is at best an unhelpful concept. As said, its use could encourage learners to adopt too narrow a mindset in considering their options.

2.3.2   There are No Online Learners, but Learners Do Go Online and They Do So Increasingly Often

Some learners spend most of their learning time offline and will occasionally complement their learning effort through online explorations. Other learners may, in a particular context, primarily be driven by instructional events afforded to them online, but they will undertake additional offline explorations as well. Yet others will have opted initially for a hybrid learning environment, including both online and offline experiences, but they would still venture beyond what is given to them, offline as well as online. The crux is that intelligent learners, whatever their initial entry point into a particular learning effort, will continue to look around them, driven by their natural curiosity, to further enrich their learning experience both online and offline in any way they consider useful through all means at their disposal. I recognize that the above point of view clashes with some of the original core assumptions of the instructional design field. I am equally aware, though, that, over time, the field has become more open to alternative views that attribute greater importance to the autonomous role played by the learner. Such an alternative perspective is relevant and important considering that change in human behavior is not merely a goal in the context of predetermined social or economic processes—such as to serve corporate interests—but may often relate to human needs and desires in much more complex, non-linear ways, based on the long-term intricate interrelatedness of individual, communal and societal interests.

Dreyfus (2001) argues that learning by means of instruction develops according to the following seven stages: (1) novice; (2) advanced beginner; (3) competence; (4) proficiency; (5) expertise; (6) mastery; and (7) practical wisdom. He reasons that only the first three stages can adequately develop in the distance education mode. According to Dreyfus, reaching proficiency and expertise require "emotional, involved, embodied human beings" (p. 48), something that he fears the online environment is incapable of accommodating. Moreover, apprenticeship, which is necessary for the last two stages, calls for the physical presence of experts of flesh and blood.

I find Dreyfus's (2001) seven-stage analysis of the learning-through-instruction process relevant and useful. I also agree with him that emotional embodied involvement on the part of both learners and those who help them learn is crucial in the instructional context, particularly if the learning effort is directed at reaching more than mere competence. However, Dreyfus's conclusion that such emotional, involved and embodied presence is impossible in the distance education mode only holds if it is assumed that the various actors involved in what starts off as a distance education effort don't move beyond their starting point. If, however, as I argued earlier in this section, those same actors—who are all learners in the true sense of the word, whether their formal role in the educational process qualifies them as such or as instructors or facilitators—continue their explorations beyond the conditions of their starting point, Dreyfus would be wrong. Then competent learners (and other actors in the learning environment) will always find opportunities in their wider environment to create such embodied presence to the extent that they find useful to them. This requires a kind of 'learning intelligence' that involves entrepreneurship; creativity; the ability to communicate personal goals and negotiate conditions to reach them; and the autonomous capacity to monitor one's interactions with the world. In the wider context it requires 'mentorship' in the true sense of the word to be reinvented.

The term "mentor" derives from ancient Greek mythology. The story can be found in Homer's Odyssey. Mentor was the trusted friend of Odysseus and the tutor of his son Telemachus. We are told in the Odyssey[1] that the goddess Athena, the daughter of Zeus, on several occasions, appeared in the form of Mentor to give advice to Telemachus and Odysseus. The term "mentor" has since become synonymous of the kind of personal relationship that typically seeks to benefit the person who is being mentored. The beauty of Homer's account is, of course, that it tells us that you don't have to be Mentor himself to perform his functions. One can assume the shape of Mentor, as Athena did.

In essence, mentoring is a role that can be seen to represent one of the best sides of human nature, the disposition to dedicate oneself to the well-being of another person. I believe, based on personal experience, that the proliferation of online communication has created propitious and unique conditions for people around the globe to reconsider their options to serve as mentor for others and to benefit from mentoring.

2.4 Concluding Thoughts

I started this chapter off by arguing that there are good reasons to look at learning from the perspective of the various comprehensive roles we wish to play in life rather than that of the acquisition of neatly specified isolated competencies or well-separated areas into which the various known disciplines have organized—and disaggregated—knowledge. Subsequently, I discussed that learning can be associated with adaptive behavior and that in humans one can distinguish adaptive behavior at four different levels of organizational complexity. I then dwelt in some length on the importance of defining learning in ways concomitant with the levels of adaptive behavior in relation to which we learn, defending that those who create the conditions for learning should always have in mind that humans ought to be able to function at the highest level possible. This led to the conclusion that learning is best conceived of in a broad perspective of purposeful interaction with an environment to whose constant change we must adapt while being ourselves the conscious participants in creating such change. Consequently I restated, with reference to earlier work, a

---

[1] The full text is available at http://ibiblio.org/gutenberg/etext02/dyssy11b.txt.

definition of learning capable of representing such a broad perspective on learning and applicable to both individuals and social entities at different levels of complex organization.

In the next section I explored the fundamental changes that have taken place in the learning landscape, posing new challenges to the learner. Two areas were identified: (1) the changed nature of change and (2) the changed problems, challenges and opportunities humans face at the start of the 21st century. I also argued that technology is not among the determining features of the changing learning landscape. If indeed the changed nature of change and the changed problems, challenges and opportunities of our time lead to a fundamental reform of the kind of learning we engage in, then technological innovation will follow in its wake, rather than the other way around. What is needed in the first place is a profound rethinking of the key assumptions that underlie our vision of education. Based on Morin's (1999, 2005) work, I emphasized the need to focus on fostering complex thinking and cited seven key areas of concern defined by Morin to inspire much needed reform. I annotated these areas, focusing on their implications for the new roles expected of learners.

In the final section I discussed the online space as one of many spaces in which people learn and argued that defining learners as 'e-learners,' 'online learners,' or 'learners at a distance' does not do justice to the ingenuity of most learners in exploring multiple learning spaces rather than just one. I thus argued that the concept 'online learner' is an unhelpful concept and that it is better to do away with it while recognizing that learners—in de broad sense of the word and whatever their entry point into the complex learning landscape—do go online, occasionally or frequently. Recognizing that such is the case, the question can be asked in what areas learners should be competent to take full advantage of the multiple learning spaces to which they have or can create access in today's learning landscape. I leave the question with the reader (see also Section 2.7 of this chapter), but wish to offer the following bullet points as prompts for further thinking.

Today's learners should be competent in at least the following areas:

- Mastery of foreign languages
- Participation in or interaction with diverse cultural and social settings
- Negotiation of one's learning niche within the prevailing learning ecology
- Ability to listen
- Ability to question
- Ability to transcend the boundaries of disciplines, to look for linkages and to critically interact with change
- Aptitude to interact affectively with other actors in the learning landscape

Besides the learners, there are obvious implications as well associated with the above listing of learner competence areas for those who are responsible for creating a propitious learning environment, including teachers. However, the emphasis in my chapter is on the learner and not the teacher.

I finally wish to remark that the analysis provided in this chapter of the challenges that condition today's learning landscape contrasts sharply with how I perceive the current reality of academic life, both as regards students and faculty. The former are increasingly driven by pressure to obtain certificates, diplomas and degrees that give them access to jobs that may have little to do with what they actually learned in order to obtain those tokens; the latter live under the pressure of complying with the exigencies of an increasingly complex university bureaucracy, including the various formalities related to the ritual of tenurization. Within that context, education is more and more considered a commodity, a perspective that puts educators in the same category as other retailers, such as grocers. The fact that the commodity can now be traded online has exacerbated the situation. I believe this to be a dangerous development.

2.5   Resources for Further Exploration

- The best resource for further exploration of the ideas expressed in this chapter is you yourself. The next best resource is the people in your environment with whom you maintain close enough a relationship to share your more profound experiences with them. Writing down your personal learning history (as I have done, to an extent, in this chapter) and discussing it with friends can often provide deep insight into the multifaceted meaning of learning and the factors that foster it.
- One of the books I have found most enlightening on the subject of human learning, ever since it first came out in 1999, is *How people learn: Brain, mind, experience and school* (Bransford, Brown, & Cocking, 1999). The book is more than worth its money for having it on your shelf, but it can also be explored online at http://www.nap.edu/html/howpeople1/. The same year that *how people learn* came out another interesting book, *The scientist in the crib: Minds, brains, and how children learn* by Gopnik et al. (1999), also saw the light. It is an equally delightful read, one that reminds its readers of the tremendous opportunities in the life of the developing human organism to nurture its capacities to learn.
- Film director Majid Majidi's movie *Children of Heaven* (available on DVD) portrays eloquently how multiple learning spaces complement, compete and interact with each other in facilitating human growth. Watching the movie, particularly when done together, provides countless opportunities for reflection, individually and collaboratively, about the meaning of learning in different situations. While the setting and circumstances depicted in the movie may be far removed from those that readers of this chapter may be familiar with, readers will have no difficulty identifying with the experiences often movingly rendered by the actors and actresses, prompting recollection of one's own experiences and the desire to recount them to others.
- The idea that one needs a teacher in order to learn was part and parcel of the traditional conception of education. It no longer is. Enhanced learner autonomy and modes of education that reduce the role of the teacher or that put the teacher at a greater distance from the learner have contributed to dethroning the teacher in favor of focusing on the centrality of the learner. However, the ease with which the hypothesis of the essential role of the teacher is sometimes discarded may require more serious review. To fully appreciate the teacher-student relationship at its best one must watch the interactions between two of the great pianists of

our time, Daniel Barenboim and Lang Lang in a masterclass conducted by the former. At the time of writing, excerpts of it can be found on YouTube. The complete masterclass is included in a six-DVD set with the title *Barenboim on Beethoven: The complete piano sonatas.*

- Finally, anyone interested in finding out what learning really is can best explore the idea by simply practicing it in a conscious way. Readers currently enrolled in a course or program should take the opportunity to reflect on their own learning as it happens and the circumstances that surround it. Those not formally enrolled find no shortage of learning opportunities—for free or for pay—by exploring the Internet. Broadcasters such as TVO, CBC, BBC, and NPR offer podcasts or vodcasts of weekly, annual or occasional lectures or lecture series on diverse topics as well as general interest programs, such as Science Friday, online or on CD or DVD. Universities and some major journals, e.g. Nature, do likewise. Besides there are large repositories of resources that support educators and students at various levels of formal education, such as the National Repository of Online Courses and the European Gateway to Science Education, XPLORA. A Web search for any of the keywords in this paragraph will reveal countless learning opportunities. Branching out in other directions will reveal even more. You've never had it so good.

2.6 Questions for Comprehension and Application

1. The author argues in this chapter that the ability to master any or more of the traditional disciplines is as such insufficient for citizens of the 21st century to interact constructively with today's problems, challenges and opportunities. He offers various examples. Identify and discuss one or more issues, other than the ones mentioned in this chapter, that require thinking processes that cannot be limited to disciplinary approaches and that must thus benefit from a transdisciplinary perspective.

2. The author offers at the end of the chapter a short itemized list of areas in which today's learners should be competent to be effective learners. (i) Based on your reading of the chapter, what are some other areas of learner competence that you should like to add to this list? (ii) Discuss how the areas of learner competence identified by the author and those you wish to add yourself relate to the rationale presented in this chapter.

References

Allwood, A. C., Walter, M. R., Kamber, B. S., Marshall, C. P., & Burch, I. W. (2006). Stromatolite reef from the Early Archaean era of Australia. *Nature, 441*(7094), 714–718.
Avery, J. S. (2005). *Space-age science and stone-age politics.* Copenhagen: Danish Pugwash Group.
Awramik, S. M. (2006). Palaeontology: Respect for stromatolites. *Nature, 441*(7094), 700–701.

Bransford, J. D., Brown, A. L., & Cocking, R. R. (Eds.) (1999). *How people learn: Brain, mind, experience, and school.* Washington, DC: National Academy Press.

Bronowski, J. (1978). *The origins of knowledge and imagination.* New Haven, CT/London: Yale University Press.

Carter, R. (2002). *Exploring consciousness.* Berkeley, CA/Los Angeles: University of California Press.

Chadwick, C. (2002). What is learning? *Educational Technology, 42*(6), 64.

Daniel, J. (2002). Higher education for sale. *Education Today No. 3*, October–December 2002, p. 1.

Daniel, J. (2003). Debate McEFA. *Education Today No. 7*, October–December 2003, p. 9.

Delors, J., Al Mufti, I., Amagi, I., Carneiro, R., Chung, F., Geremek, B., Gorham, W., Kornhauser, A., Manley, M., Padrón Quero, M., Savané, M. -A., Singh, K., Stavenhagen, R., Suhr, M. W., & Zhou, N. (1996). *Learning: The treasure within.* Report to UNESCO of the International Commission on Education for the Twenty-first Century. Paris: UNESCO.

De Vaney, A., & Butler, R. P. (1996). Voices of the founders: Early discourses in educational technology. In D. H. Jonassen (Ed.), *Handbook of research for educational communications and technology* (pp. 3–45). New York: Simon & Schuster/Macmillan.

Dreyfus, H. L. (2001). *On the Internet.* London/New York: Routledge.

Driscoll, M. P. (2000). *Psychology of learning for instruction* (2nd ed.). Boston: Allyn & Bacon.

Edelman, G. M. (2004). *Wider than the sky: The phenomenal gift of consciousness.* New Haven, CT/London: Yale University Press.

Edelman, G. M. & Tononi, G. (2000). *A universe of consciousness: How matter becomes imagination.* New York: Basic Books.

Fishman, B. J. (2006). It's not about the technology. *Teachers College Record*, Date Published: July 06, 2006; ID Number: 12584. Retrieved July 13, 2006, from http://www.tcrecord.org.

Gopnik, A., Meltzoff, A. N., & Kuhl, P. K. (1999). *The scientist in the crib: Minds, brains, and how children learn.* New York: William Morrow and Company.

Greenfield, S. (2002). *The private life of the brain: Emotions, consciousness and the secret of the self.* New York: Wiley.

Hilgard, E. R. (1948). *Unconscious processes and man's rationality.* Urbana, IL (as quoted in De Vaney and Butler, 1996).

Ibstpi (n.d.). *International board of standards for training, performance and instruction: Current projects.* Retrieved May 28, 2006, from http://www.ibstpi.org/projects.htm.

Institute of Human Origin (2001). *Becoming human: Journey through the story of human evolution* (interactive web-based video). Retrieved June 19, 2006, from http://www. becominghuman.org/.

Jain, S. et al. (2003). *McEducation for all? Opening a dialogue around UNESCO's vision for commoditizing learning.* Retrieved June 2, 2006, from http://www.swaraj.org/shikshantar/mceducationforall.htm.

Jonassen, D. H. (2002). Learning as activity. *Educational Technology, 42*(2), 45–51.

Koch, C. (2004). *The quest for consciousness: A neurobiological approach.* Englewood, CO: Robert and Company.

Koch, C. (2005). The inchoate science of consciousness: New approaches could help quantify the mind-body gap. *The Scientist, 19*(17), 14–16.

Learning Development Institute (2004). *Book of problems: Presidential workshops and interactive discussion sessions at the International Conferences of the Association for Educational Communications and Technology, Dallas, Texas, November 12–16, 2002, and Anaheim, California, October 22–25, 2003.* Retrieved June 12, 2006, from http://www. learndev.org/BOP-AECT2002.html.

Learning Development Institute (2005). *Presidential workshop and panel session on learners in a changing learning landscape: Questions formulated by participating members.* Retrieved May 29, 2006, from http://www.learndev.org/ibstpi-AECT2005.html# anchor 1672398.

Marshall, S. P. (2006). *The power to transform: Leadership that brings learning and schooling to life.* San Francisco: Jossey-Bass.

Morin, E. (1999). *Seven complex lessons in education for the future*. Paris: UNESCO.

Morin, E. (2005). *Introduction à la pensée complexe* (Introduction to complex thinking). Paris: Éditions du Seuil.

Patel, V., & Yoskowitz, N. A. (2005, May). *The role of cognition in changing behavior: Understanding safe sex: Practices and HIV concepts*. Paper contributed to the special panel on 'The Scientific Mind and HIV/AIDS' at the Advanced International Colloquium on Building the Scientific Mind, The Hague, The Netherlands, May 17–20, 2005. Retrieved June 18, 2006, from http://www.learndev.org/dl/BtSM2005-Patel.pdf.

Salomon, G. (2002). Technology and pedagogy: Why don't we see the promised revolution? *Educational Technology, 42*(2), 71–75.

Science Friday (2006). Science Friday podcast on the *'Reliable Replacement Warhead' Program*. Retrieved July 13, 2006, from http://media.libsyn.com/media/sciencefriday/ scifri-2006070711.mp3.

Spohrer, J. (2003, October). *Nano-bio-cogno-socio-techno convergence for enhancing human performance: Perspectives on the great unsolved problems of learning*. Paper presented in the framework of the *Book of Problems workshop and panel discussion*, J. Visser, Chair, at the annual convention of the Association for Educational Communications and Technology held in Anaheim, CA, October 22–25, 2003. Retrieved July 29, 2006, from http://www.learndev.org/ppt/BOP-AECT2003-Spohrer.pdf.

Steinberg, D. (2005). Revelations from the unconscious. *The Scientist, 19*(17), 17–19.

Sykes, C. (1994). *No ordinary genius*. New York: W. W. Norton.

Templeton, A. R. (2002). Out of Africa again and again. *Nature, 416*(6876), 45–51.

Van Merriënboer, J. J. G., & Stoyanov, S. (In this volume). Learners in a changing learning landscape: Reflections from an instructional design perspective. In J. Visser & M. Visser-Valfrey (Eds.), *Learners in a changing learning landscape: Reflections from a dialogue on new roles and expectations* (pp. 69–90). Dordrecht, The Netherlands: Springer.

Visser, J. (2001). Integrity, completeness and comprehensiveness of the learning environment: Meeting the basic learning needs of all throughout life. In: D. N. Aspin, J. D. Chapman, M. J. Hatton, & Y. Sawano (Eds.), *International Handbook of Lifelong Learning* (pp. 447–472). Dordrecht, The Netherlands: Kluwer.

Visser, J. (2002, November). *Can we see the puzzle, rather than the pieces?* Paper presented in the framework of the *Book of Problems (or what we don't know about learning)* dialogue held at the International Conference of the Association for Educational Communications and Technology, Dallas, TX, November 12–16, 2002. Retrieved May 28, 2006, from http://www.learndev.org/BOP-AECT2002.html#anchor4078218.

Visser, J. (2007). Learning in a global society. In M.G. Moore (Ed.), *Handbook of distance education* (pp. 635–648). Mahwah, NJ/London: Lawrence Erlbaum.

Visser, J., & Visser, M. (2003). Talking about the unknown. *TechTrends, 47*(1), 5–8.

Visser, J., & Visser, Y. L. (2003). What's in a definition? A response to Clifton Chadwick. *Educational Technology Magazine, 43*(2), 58.

Visser, J., Berg, D., Burnett, R., & Visser, Y. L. (2002, February). *In search of the meaning of learning: A social process of raising questions and creating meanings*. Workshop held at the Annual Convention of the Association for Educational Communications and Technology, Long Beach, CA, February 16–19, 2000.

Visser, J., Visser, Y. L., Amirault, R. J., Genge, C. D., & Miller, V. (2002, April). *Second order learning stories*. Paper presented at the Annual Meeting of the American Educational Research Association (AERA), New Orleans, LA, April 1–5, 2002.

Visser, J., Visser, M., & Burnett, R. (2004). A cornucopia of problems: The importance of speculative thought and imagination. *TechTrends, 48*(2), 70–72.

Visser, M., & Visser, J. (2003, October). *"We closed our books and put them away." Learning stories from Mozambique - A critical reflection on communicating about the reality and future of learning*. Paper presented at the International Conference of the Association for Educational Communications and Technology (AECT), Anaheim, CA, October 22–25, 2003.

Visser, Y. L., & Visser, J. (2000, October). *The learning stories project*. Paper presented at the International Conference of the Association for Educational Communications and Technology, Denver, CO, October 25–28, 2000.

Visser, Y. L, Rowland, G., & Visser, J. (Eds.) (2002). Special issue of Educational Technology on 'Broadening the Definition of Learning.' *Educational Technology*, *42*(2) - entire issue.

WMAP (2005). Web site of the Wilkinson Microwave Anisotropy Probe. *How old is the universe?* Retrieved June 25, 2007, from http://map.gsfc.nasa.gov/m_uni/uni_101age.html.

Chapter 3
The Learning Sciences, Technology and Designs for Educational Systems[1]: Some Thoughts About Change

John Bransford, Mary Slowinski, Nancy Vye, and Susan Mosborg[2]

Abstract The idea that technology can be instrumental in connecting experts and novices who are separated by time or space inspired distance education pioneers over a century ago to take advantage of the innovations of their day—the printing press and postal system—to deliver the first correspondence courses. The technologies to facilitate learning at a distance have vastly evolved in the intervening years, becoming far more sophisticated and showing potential to break us free from old models of instruction. Yet instead of acting as transformative agents, the new technologies have often been assimilated to existing models, and it is not unusual to find ourselves strongly influenced by the methods found in the face-to-face classroom as we design instruction, monitor participant interaction, organize curricula, and conduct assessments in these new arenas. Still, the combination of a fast-changing, technologically-connected world and the expanding knowledge brought to our disciplines by advances in the learning sciences present an extraordinary opportunity for all of us to take part in the evolution and expansion of what we think of as 'teaching and learning.' Can technology help us reinvent how we prepare people for healthy and productive lives? This chapter asks that question and hopes to add at least a bit to the rich discussions in this book and sparked by it.

University of Washington—College of Education

[1] This chapter, and a number of studies reported in it, were supported by a grant from the National Science Foundation (NSF# 035445) to the LIFE Center (Learning in Informal and Formal Environments). We thank our LIFE Center colleagues and the NSF. However, the views expressed in this paper should be attributed to the authors and not to other LIFE members or to the NSF.

[2] Mary Slowinski's experience in developing and teaching with online learning environments that connect formal and informal learning, and her knowledge of work in this area, played an especially important role in this chapter. Nancy Vye, Susan Mosborg and John Bransford brought knowledge of the learning sciences to this chapter, including studies that we use to support our arguments. Overall, the paper represented a strong collaborative effort where everyone made unique contributions that enriched the chapter as a whole.

3.1 Introduction

Anyone who has been highly motivated to learn something new—especially something difficult—understands the advantages of finding experts who can help them. This is often not easy. Gaining access to instructional expertise has been a challenge throughout much of human history. Many secrets of success (e.g., how to make glass vessels, axe heads, or scalpels; how to read, write, or hula) were available only to a select few. In today's world, vast inequities still frustrate people's desires and opportunities to gain access to expert instruction (e.g., Banks et al., 2007; Darling-Hammond & Bransford, 2005; Ladson-Billings & King, 1990; National Research Council, 2000). Nevertheless, people throughout the world are beginning to act on the premise that increased access to learning opportunities is a moral imperative that can make far-reaching differences in peoples' lives.

A pioneering effort to increase access to learning opportunities is illustrated by the use of the correspondence course in the late 1800s (see Bergmann, 2001; Harris, 1967; Moran, 1993). The goal was to find ways to help learners who, for one reason or another, were unable to attend school in person. Technologies of the day, especially the printing press and the postal system, made the courses possible. Subsequent innovations added filmstrips and sometimes lantern slides—eventually progressing to radio broadcasts and audiocassettes, and to television and videotapes.

These, of course, were primarily one-way technologies. Initial presentations of information were followed by a lag while the student prepared a response. Opportunities for feedback and teacher-student dialogue were pretty much limited to asynchronous exchanges made in writing which, in turn, were further limited by the vagaries of the postal system.

Today's distance educators, by contrast, have a rapidly expanding array of Web-enabled technologies at their disposal, and more seamless opportunities for synchronous exchange. Even the venerable Open University, a forerunner in distance education, stopped televising lectures in late 2006, as its iconic late-night broadcasts 'succumbed' to the efficiencies of the Web (Jowit, 2006).

Digitally-based courses and their online delivery provide powerful examples of ways that new technologies can expand access to learning opportunities (Duffy & Kirkley, 2004; National Research Council, 2000). Internet technologies not only support a more rapid exchange between teacher and student—asynchronous as well as synchronous—they also provide new opportunities for interactivity among learners. While a great need to develop technology infrastructures still exists around the world, considerable strides are being made towards this end (e.g., Friedman, 2005; Smith & Casserly, 2006). Today, access to online learning is becoming much more common, and for people of means, rapidly expanding. Still, it is important to ask: Accessibility to what?

Some years ago, Weigel (2000) argued that most current attempts to create online learning environments suffered from a 'port the classroom to the Web' model. Based on our experiences, his point still rings true seven years later.

Look, for example, at the pioneering work taking place in Multi-User Virtual Environments (MUVEs) such as Second Life (http://secondlife.com/). You'll see some beautifully rendered virtual buildings and even campuses, quite like regular classrooms and universities. You'll see student-created avatars attending classes and learning from their teachers, asking questions and interacting—and they can do this from anywhere in the world. But essentially, these Second Life virtual classroom experiences are close imitations of the familiar 'first life' classroom experiences.

There are many reasons for these tightly parallel worlds. One reason becomes clear after reading postings to the Second Life educators' email list (see https://lists.secondlife.com/cgi-bin/mailman/listinfo/educators). Many of these educators, all of them pioneers, note that their students, academic administrators and funders *expect* education to look a certain way—namely, teachers presenting information to students. Therefore, despite the exciting new affordances of MUVE technologies to be explored, many educators working within these environments feel constrained to limit the degrees of innovation they can attempt at this point in time. Similarly, learner-participants themselves bring expectations of learning environments. For example, at the 2005 Association for Educational Communications and Technology conference where a number of the current authors presented (J. Visser, 2005), many presenters noted that students often described themselves as face-to-face learners who did not want to take 'less effective' courses online.

The 'porting the classroom' model and the students' desire for face-to-face learning environments would be fine if we knew that typical approaches to classroom-based teaching normally produce high-quality learning. Unfortunately, many approaches to K-12 and post-secondary instruction have often been found to leave a great deal to be desired (e.g., National Research Council, 2000, 2005; Weigel, 2000; see also Hall, in this volume).

Can modern-day technologies help change the educational landscape for the better in ways that serve our 'expanding educational access' goals while also yielding higher quality learning? It seems clear the answer is 'not without appropriate design considerations.' In the sections that follow we discuss some examples of possible ways to use models of effective teaching, learning, assessment and faculty collaboration to guide new uses of technology toward these ends.

We organize our discussion around Fig. 3.1, which was created by the LIFE Center (Learning in Informal and Formal Environments; see http://life-slc.org), to remind itself and others of the 'lifelong and lifewide' nature of human learning.[3]

Although only an approximation, the middle portion in Fig. 3.1 shows the percentage of time in a calendar year spent in formal educational settings such

---

[3] Our thanks to Reed Stevens, who designed this diagram with a visual artist following discussions with John Bransford and other members of LIFE Center's leadership. The diagram represents one of the shared working frameworks of the LIFE Center.

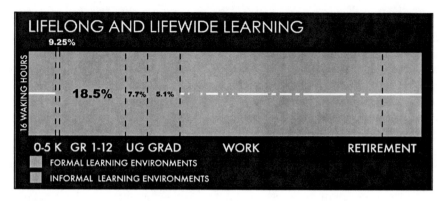

Fig. 3.1 The LIFE Center's representation of lifelong and lifewide learning

as schools, colleges and universities. The larger portion (assuming 16 waking hours) shows the approximate time spent in out-of-school settings. Clearly, much more time is spent in out-of-school settings than in-school settings. LIFE uses this diagram as a beginning point for exploring, among LIFE Center members and with others, issues such as informal learning in formal environments and vice versa, clearer definitions of their similarities and differences, the relative importance of different kinds of learning environments as people mature, and ways in which new technologies are affecting the boundaries between settings.

We discuss four ideas suggested by Fig. 3.1 that relate to this book's focus on changing learning landscapes. In particular, we consider:

1. The benefits and drawbacks of learning in informal versus formal environments, with an eye towards blending the strengths of each into more powerful designs for learning.
2. The kinds of post-graduation competencies required to adapt to fast-changing environments.
3. Implications of points (1) and (2) for new approaches to instruction (either online or face-to-face) and new assessment metrics.
4. The possible improvements upon present practices potentially afforded by new technologies, looking particularly at technology-enabled learning systems that (a) help us merge the unique strengths of learning opportunities that occur in both formal and informal settings, and (b) allow us to begin eliminating the 'silos' of instruction that often make it difficult for people to acquire the kinds of flexible skills and connected knowledge structures that can help them learn throughout life.

Each of these points is discussed below.

3.2   Strengths and Weaknesses of Learning in Informal vs. Formal Settings

Several years, ago one of the authors (JB) moved with his family to a small house on a river to enjoy the water. JB decided to study himself as he tried to learn bass fishing, first learning to fish on his own, then with various degrees of expert help. When growing up he had fished for pan fry like sunfish. But he'd never fished for bass.

For the first ten days JB tried 'discovery learning,' fishing every day with minnows, worms, and lures from his dock. He caught fish, but no bass.

As a next step in his experiment JB bought a book on bass fishing, to see what he'd been missing. One of the first statements in the book said, in short: *If you want to catch Bass, you have to fish where the bass are.* This hit him like a bolt of lightning. It was an SFO (sudden flash of the obvious)[4] but only in retrospect. In pictures and words, the book described the kinds of nooks and crannies where bass tended to live.

This was a revelation. The area surrounding JB's dock was nothing like the places suited for bass hangouts. So, JB ventured out in his kayak with bait and tackle, exploring other parts of the river close to home, searching for places matching the book's suggestions. Sure enough, JB soon began to catch bass—but only a few per trip.

Each trip on the river raised new questions and hunches, which led JB to new insights into particular nuances of the book's descriptions. These discoveries actually became more enlivening than catching the fish per se, and hence sustained him in his activities. Still, there were many questions that the original book, and several others he consulted, could not answer.

The next step in his experiment was to learn from people who knew the local river. This was not an entirely emotionally neutral decision. JB was an adult newcomer to an area where professors were often called 'overeducated fools.' Admitting to other adults that he needed help would simply confirm this belief. But he finally found the right people and summoned the courage to ask.

The bass book, of necessity, had provided generic information about bass and their habitats. The local people, in contrast, knew specifically where in the river bass tended to be found and also how the fish reacted during different seasons of the year—for example, that the bass swam at different depths depending on the water's temperature, and struck at different food and lure speeds depending on the time of the year.

Interestingly, however, many of the ideas held by the local fishing experts were not quite accurate. For example, one local fisherman explained that the bass started biting in the spring just a few weeks after pan fish started biting. He said he had always found lots of pan fish near a certain bush on the river, and noted they started

---

[4] We thank David McNeel for making us aware of this term.

biting right when the bush turned pink. He wasn't sure why—maybe the color attracted that species of fish.

Sometime later JB learned it was actually the ground temperature that triggered both the blooming of the bush and the feeding frenzy of the pan fish. He obtained this knowledge by reading another book on fish and their habits—a way of learning that went beyond the prevailing local expertise and placed it within a context of more broadly vetted knowledge.

Note that this deeper level of understanding was not necessary for the local fishermen *unless* they wanted to learn to fish in spots new to them. This point about procedural (local) knowledge versus more conceptual knowledge fits prevailing theory and research on transfer: Transfer effects are not as great nor as robust when one is simply learning surface connections and procedures versus 'learning with understanding' (e.g., Barron et al., 1998; Hatano & Inagaki, 1986; Hatano & Osuro, 2003; Judd, 1908; National Research Council, 2000; Wertheimer, 1949/1959).

Overall, the bass fishing example highlights a number of issues about learning in informal settings. First, trying to learn something by oneself (discovery learning) can be very difficult; hence access to expertise becomes highly valued. Second, learning general knowledge about one's intended activities (e.g., reading about bass fishing from a book) can be helpful, but making the connection between that general knowledge and the local situation can be difficult. Third, gaining access to local expertise can be much more helpful than a book that contains general knowledge, but local expertise is not always available nor easy to access, and it often lacks the level of understanding needed to go beyond surface contingencies and local explanations about their occurrences (e.g., the pan fish must like pink buds). Local expertise may be fine if one's activities remain local (although this is not always true [see Hatano & Inagaki, 1986]), but it must be checked against more broadly vetted information if one desires to function effectively in new environments.

We should also note that as JB attempted to learn bass fishing, he not surprisingly discovered a growing niche of high-tech, 'augmented reality' technologies on the market specially designed for fishing. He found out about (and coveted) special bass boats equipped with dual motors—a powerful gas motor to quickly reach fishing spots, paired with a quiet foot-controlled battery-driven motor for trolling. He learned about state-of-the-art water temperature gauges, and also about river depth gauges, digital fish finders, underwater video cameras, GPS devices for marking and re-finding successful fishing spots, special carbon rods that let one feel fish biting, and so forth. Each of these had the potential to bolster JB's fishing successes, but none of these technologies guaranteed success in and of themselves (except for the success of the people who made and sold the equipment).

Now, if we change our focus from informal learning to formal, we see different strengths and weaknesses at work. Typically, information provided in formal settings is more carefully vetted than many local stories about why things happen. However, what is missing from most formal educational environments is what was key in our bass fishing example: the opportunity to keep fishing—or at least to keep trying. Informal environments often offer opportunities for practice and for getting feedback about the degree to which new knowledge is helping to achieve one's goal. In many cases, formal education removes us from everyday opportunities for practice and instead places us into a 'unit' on fishing that provides only weak connections to our personal environments. When students are unable to make these connections and ask, 'Why is this relevant?' they often hear 'Trust me, you'll find this useful some day.'

Can technological advances help us merge the positive attributes of both informal and formal learning opportunities and reduce the negative ones? We return to this question later on.

3.3 Adaptivity to Rapidly Changing Environments

As noted earlier, Fig. 3.1 also raises questions about the competencies that people need after they graduate from formal education. Many argue that the world we face today and in the future will feature increasingly rapid change, which carries implications for what we will need to know and be able to do to succeed in life. This in turn has implications for what counts as effective curricula, instruction and assessment systems.

The bass fishing example discussed earlier is relevant to this point. The local area where JB fished changed with the seasons, but these changes 'according to season' were relatively constant and predictable. However many argue that with global environmental changes, even local changes may become more variable and intense.

J. Visser (in this volume) provides an excellent discussion of the roiling social transformations in the world and workplace, which also suggest the need to rethink our educational systems and practices. He observes, for example, that unlike the comparatively static work world of our forefathers and foremothers, "the world of the 21st century is characterized by change that is often perceived as turbulent and having a high level of unpredictability" (p. 30) which in turn requires "learning to learn" rather than mastering a discrete set of skills. Visser's argument fits well with the innovation literature (e.g., Augustine, 2005; Clough, 2005; Fullan, 2001; Nelson & Stolterman, 2002; Robinson & Stern, 1997; Rogers, 1962/2003; Von Hippel, 2005). From our reading of this literature, we think it fair to conclude that one of the major challenges we as educators face today is how to respond effectively to the quickened pace of change around us, our students, and our graduates. In a recent editorial in the *Journal of Engineering Education* one of us wrote:

> Not so many years ago, companies could come up with an innovative idea for a product or service and gradually refine it for 25 or more years. People could develop particular kinds of expertise and be successful for a lifetime. This made it possible for educational institutions (e.g., community colleges; four-year institutions) to teach job-specific skills and knowledge and know that most of this would still be useful in the workplace. Today, innovation cycles are often very short and educational systems are often insufficiently nimble. As educators, we may end up training students in specifics that are no longer useful once they reach the workplace. (Bransford, 2007, p. 1)

An additional example of today's accelerated change comes from the U.S. National Academy of Sciences' report *Rising Above the Gathering Storm* (Augustine, 2005).

There, Intel Corporation chairman Craig Barrett is quoted as saying: "If I take the revenue in January and look again in December of that year, 90% of my December revenue comes from products which were not there in January" (p. 17). This is extremely rapid change, of course. But even less frequent changes—in other sectors of the economy, culture, and physical environment—yield challenges we must meet. Rapid change is the backdrop against which educators' designs must live (National Center on Education and the Economy, 2007). In the following subsections we discuss three loci that affect adaptivity: adaptive people, adaptive organizations, and roles for technology in enabling their synergies.

3.3.1 Adaptive People: New Perspectives on Expertise

The fact and persistence of rapid change in our lives warrants a fresh look at expertise. Elsewhere, one of us summarized LIFE's view on this point as follows:

> It is often stated that experts are able to solve problems by applying previously learned (e.g., schematized) skills and knowledge in new settings. This is true, in part. If we encounter a problem that seems similar to previously solved problems, we are much more efficient at solving it (National Research Council, 2000). Nevertheless, people who function in rapidly changing environments must learn to navigate in situations where they are at the edges of their existing knowledge and skills. (Bransford, 2007, p. 1)

Learning at the edges of one's existing expertise is one way to describe *adaptive* expertise.

A number of researchers are beginning to build on the seminal work of Hatano and colleagues (Hatano & Inagaki, 1986; Hatano & Osuro, 2003) who first introduced the concept of 'adaptive expertise,' differentiating it from 'routine expertise.' Routine expertise involves developing a core set of competencies that can be applied throughout one's life with greater and greater efficiency. In contrast, adaptive expertise encompasses the willingness and ability to change core competencies and to continually expand the breadth and depth of one's expertise.

Often this involves the need to 'let go of old ways of doing things' (e.g., Schwartz, Bransford, & Sears, 2005). For example, a tennis player may take lessons and be told she is gripping the racket incorrectly. In order to reach a new level of performance, she will have to unlearn that behavior and take the time to learn a new one. In short, she'll have to get worse in order to get better in the long run, a process some psychologists refer to as "regression in the service of development" (Bever, 1982, p. 153). In the leadership literature, similar regressions that often accompany attempts to move away from old efficiencies and try something new have been referred to as "implementation dips" (Fullan, 2001, p. 40; Fullan, 2002, p. 17).

Ericsson's (2006) work on world-class experts in chess and in other domains illustrates how stellar performers—as they develop their expertise—resist premature automatization of skills and procedures to continually 'reinvent themselves' and push themselves to new heights. Ericsson does not explicitly refer to his world class-experts as adaptive experts, but we think it is a useful term for describing them.

It spotlights the process of intentionally seeking new challenges and insights during one's pursuits rather than resting on old laurels. Similarly, developing effective everyday (non world-class) expertise requires stepping out of one's existing comfort zones in order to increase one's abilities to think and perform (e.g., see Schwartz et al., 2005; Lin, Schwartz, & Bransford, 2006).

The idea that adaptive expertise often requires 'letting go' and 'unlearning' has implications for crafting effective teaching and learning experiences for others. For example, if we focus primarily on strong mastery of specific skills, we run the risk that the skills our students have learned will be out of date once they graduate. Data suggest that taking the extra time to learn skills 'with understanding' better prepares people to learn similar skills and adapt to new situations in the future (e.g., Hatano & Inagaki, 1986; Hatano & Osuro, 2003; Judd, 1908). For example, taking the time to understand the basic structure and function of software programs (compared to just learning to use them) can speed up people's abilities to learn and adapt to new programs when the software changes (Bransford & Schwartz, 1999).

Industry leaders also emphasize the need for team members who are flexible and can tolerate the momentary losses in efficiency that frequently accompany efforts to do things in a new way. Ideally, these losses in efficiency are short lived. For this, feedback opportunities are essential, and feedback that takes too long to inform the learner, or is carelessly targeted, can impede rapid learning and invention. As discussed below, this suggests that organizational structures play crucial roles in peoples' abilities to implement, evaluate, and enact mid-course corrections that allow them to change and improve.

3.3.2 Adaptive Organizations

Adaptive people need the support of adaptive organizations. A corollary of this point is that people need to understand how they are affected by different kinds of organizational structures so that they can better adapt to them and work to change them when necessary.

The economist Joseph Schumpeter (1942) coined the phrase 'creative destruction' to describe the process by which innovation creates new ideas and models that, in turn, 'destroy' old practices, methods, and industries—and consequently—jobs. A number of researchers and theorists are currently adding modern twists to this theory.

Martin and Austen (2002), for example, observe that "over the last two centuries, the rate of creative destruction has provided a sufficiently long cycle time … for new skills to be mastered and careers to take shape" (p. 6), whereas in our current situation "in many industries, the process of creative destruction has accelerated significantly. With more competitors, from more countries, and more diverse ideas in almost every industry, new concepts and models are being introduced ever faster" (p. 8).

Helping students learn to tolerate the ambiguity and frustration that often accompanies creative destruction—and to develop skills, knowledge, and habits of mind for innovation—appears to be an especially worthy goal for us educators to keep in mind. This includes the goal of helping students understand how organizational factors affect adaptivity, and how to become leaders when these factors get in the way (e.g., Nelson & Stolterman, 2002).

3.3.3 Adaptivity and Technology

An instructive example of the importance of technology for everyday learning and adaptivity surfaced during preparations for a panel session chaired by Jan Visser at the 2005 annual conference of Association for Educational Communications and Technology in Orlando, Florida (Visser, 2005). Our panelists, separated by miles and time zones, collaborated and corroborated online by contributing questions, thought papers and emails prior to meeting face-to-face. In fact, our dialogue was almost all carried out online until we came together in Florida. It required a leader, and Jan Visser played this role with humor, wisdom, insight and perseverance. Both leadership *and* technology were required for success.

As Jan helped our online dialogue flow, we all benefited from the shared curiosity, knowledge, and expertise of one another, and our own questions changed shape as a result. This online work did not eliminate the value of meeting face-to-face, but it seemed clear to us all that it greatly enhanced what was learned when we finally met. Had we been unable or unwilling to learn (informally) online, we would have missed a great deal.

However, as was also noted at the Orlando conference, some students may fail to participate in online learning because they believe they can only do their best in face-to-face environments. We may need to help students like these move beyond this self-limiting sense of their learning potentials and of what is needed for success in life, by providing learning experiences that merge the strengths of informal and formal learning and keep students from prematurely disengaging.

The value of technology-enhanced learning post-graduation can be seen in the evolution of the stock exchange industry. In *The new division of labor: How computers are creating the next job market*, authors Levy and Murnane (2004) examine the 1999 decision by the London International Financial Futures and Options Exchange (Liffe) to close down their traditional floor (or 'pit') trading and shift all trading to a digital trading network, which resulted in the loss of pit trader jobs.

The Chicago Mercantile Exchange (CME) took a slightly different tack in navigating the same marketplace shifts by providing existing and aspiring traders with opportunities to master this new, digital way of trading futures. They added an 'Education Center' (www.cme.com/edu/) to their website, provided a rich array of resources in a variety of media (printer-friendly written materials, slide shows, interactive media, trading simulators), and added formal online courses. Because the CME funds itself solely by charging fees per trade, it is in their best interest to not only introduce novices to futures and options trading, but also to assist all interested in this activity to succeed and thus, continue to trade.

This endeavor was met with enthusiastic and positive feedback by users, to which the CME responded by increasing its investment in trader education, partnering with a digital design firm to create an even more sophisticated online course, which culminates in the award of a certificate of completion. This newest course launched in January 2006; by July 2006 2,000 users from 17 different nations had registered to enter the course with over 600 working, chapter by chapter, towards the certificate. If this introduction to a new way of doing business required face-to-face learning, it is fair to say that many of those 2,000 users—at least the ones outside the Chicago area—would likely choose a different path.

Technology sites like these provide powerful examples for educators seeking to help students prepare for the future. However, moving in this direction requires that we view these kinds of online resources as 'prime' rather than as 'second choice' options for helping people learn. We also have an opportunity and obligation to help students learn to use the technological resources to support lifelong learning. Do we focus primarily on technology skills themselves by asking students to mimic our step-by-step instructions to learn how to use a piece of software, or do we help them learn to use technology as a means to purposeful ends? If we choose to do the latter, how do we accomplish this? One possibility is to ask students to assume a variety of more active roles within a group of learners, with each taking their turn at leading and following. Questions about instructional roles, and about assessments that surround efforts to use technology, are discussed next.

3.4   Approaches to Instruction and Assessment

3.4.1   The Importance of Leading and Following When Adaptivity is a Desired Outcome

We suggested earlier that an emphasis on being adaptive highlights the need to rethink how we define the roles of our students. Although some students may be reluctant to enroll in online courses in the belief they learn best face-to-face, today's youth are also by and large technological savants compared to many of their elders (e.g., Seely-Brown, 2006). As John Seely Brown (2006) points out, many of these 'digital natives' are already self-directed learners, having been strongly influenced by learning opportunities in their lives outside formal schooling. "This capacity for independent learning," he argues, "is essential to their future well-being, since they are likely to have multiple careers and will need to continually learn new skills they were not taught in college" (p. 18). He calls for educators to "re-conceptualize parts of our education system and at the same time find ways to reinforce learning outside of school" (p. 18).

3.4.2   Approaches to Instruction for Adaptivity

Cultivating 'self-directed learners' is an often-extolled goal—and also the group to which distance educators frequently appeal. But how do e-learning environments—predominantly modeled as they are on traditional, stand-and-deliver instruction—add value? Peter Vaill (1996), a management expert who has worked with hundreds of companies to help them manage change, uses the term "whitewater world" to describe many contemporary workplace environments and argues that success in these environments requires people to be self-directed learners. In an interview Vaill said:

> I would indict formal education. Formal education does not support self-directed learning. Formal education tends to support more the model of shut up and listen, we will tell you what you need to learn, we will tell you what book to read, we will tell you what the requirements for the term paper ought to be. We have kind of trained students over the decades to expect to be told what they are supposed to learn. (Vaill in Partners in Learning, 2007, n.p.)

Do we always—online or not—ask students to 'play student' and hence risk Vaill's indictment of formal education? Alternatively, should we follow Dewey's (1938/1997) advice that school—including, presumably, today's e-learning—should *be* life rather than solely a continual preparation for life?

In the context of Vaill's concerns, it is noteworthy that teaching often involves 'instruction first,' followed by practice (e.g., completing problems at the end of the textbook chapter). However, data from a number of studies suggest that first allowing students to generate their initial thoughts about a problem—inquiring, innovating, conceptualizing—helps prepare the students to better understand and appreciate the instruction they subsequently receive (e.g., Martin, Pierson, Rivale, Vye, Bransford & Diller, 2007; Schwartz & Bransford, 1998; Schwartz et al., 2005).

It is important to note that asking students to invent and adapt does not imply that we should always encourage 'discovery learning' above all else. The bass fishing example discussed earlier shows how 'discovery learning' helped set the stage for JB's new learning (e.g., by helping him use book knowledge to change his current practices). Nevertheless, JB would have undoubtedly made little progress had he simply remained in a 'discovery learning' mode.

Findings from a number of studies indicate that students' attempts to innovate and discover in response to an initially-presented challenge can create a 'time for telling' that sets the stage for deeper comprehension when expert knowledge is eventually presented (Schwartz & Bransford, 1998; Schwartz et al., 2005). In these studies, the expert knowledge was presented after students tried to do things on their own. The findings suggest that the old questions about who was right (e.g., Thorndike versus Dewey—or Piaget or other constructivists) are not useful ways to make progress in thinking about instruction and learning. Rather than 'either-or' it is the *balance* of attempts to inquire and innovate—coupled with opportunities to receive direct instruction and feedback—that needs emphasizing. In the bass fishing example, statements found in the bass book (e.g., *you need to fish where the bass are*) took on great significance because JB realized that his early attempts at discovery learning had totally missed this point. (For an experimental analog of this point see Martin et al., 2007.)

Another way to change students' traditional role as receiver of knowledge is to inject a higher ratio of leading to following; for example, by having students teach others (e.g., Biswas, Schwartz, Bransford, & TAG-V, 2001; Cognition and Technology Group at Vanderbilt, 2000). There are many phases to learning by teaching, and each can provide a foundation for new learning. For example, students are more motivated to learn, and they work harder, when they are preparing to teach others versus simply preparing to take a test (Biswas et al., 2001). People can also learn *while* teaching and during reflection periods *following* teaching (e.g., Darling-Hammond & Bransford, 2005) and by watching the actions of students whom they have taught (e.g., Okita & Schwartz, 2006). When orchestrated appropriately, these learning opportunities provide students with important practice in self-directed roles. Not only do learners make instructional choices by themselves, they can also quickly see the consequences of the instructional choices they have made.

Placing students in the role of collaborator and team member is another way in which the traditional role of students can be changed. However, simply having students work in groups does not necessarily develop the kinds of collaboration—or team functionality—that employers are seeking. Gregarious group members may take over the group process, and others simply follow along. Or a group may produce cacophony rather than symphony. Either pitfall robs everyone of the opportunity to learn and especially to learn what is hard about collaborating—namely, listening to others and learning from them, which often involves giving up cherished ideas that need to be changed (Schwartz et al., 2005). Further, in e-learning environments the physical co-presence that helps people interpret one another's actions and words, and to empathize, is absent; civility can be a challenge and perceived incivilities can gain a momentum of their own. For all these reasons, attention to building a positive social climate and setting the stage for students to learn as members of high-productivity teams—and to be able to quickly turn things around when faced with group dysfunction—is another crucial element in increasing our graduates' potential for success.

It can be especially difficult to help students experience 'workplace-like' collaborations that involve true 'distributed expertise.' The reason is that groups of students within a classroom often lack the kinds of deep distributed expertise characteristic of workplace environments. For example, imagine working on a multimedia project where one person is a video expert, one is a scriptwriter, one is a technology expert, and one is a content expert. Under these conditions, everyone has a role to play in producing a joint product, and the advantages of the collaboration are typically clear. However, this kind of distributed expertise is rare in any given classroom, face-to-face or at a distance.

Nevertheless, classes where members reflect a good mix of distributed expertise can be created, at least in part. One way is to use 'jigsaw teaching' methods that allow different subgroups of students to develop their expertise in particular areas and then create 'jigsaw groups' where people from the different expert subgroups work collaboratively on a common project. (e.g., Aronson, Blaney, Stephin, Sikes, & Snapp, 1978; Brown & Campione, 1994). Technology can be very useful in these settings; for example, it can be used to link students to the vetted knowledge that can help them develop their 'piece' of the expertise needed for problem solving, and it can facilitate the sharing of students' knowledge with one another as they work in both 'expert groups' and 'jigsaw groups.'

3.4.3 Approaches to Assessment When Adaptivity is a Goal

Measuring the effects of instructional practices is, of course, fundamental for gauging progress and for gaining feedback on the effectiveness of our teaching. A key question is: To what extent do our current assessments provide a clear indicator that we are helping our students develop the attitudes, skills and knowledge necessary for adapting to a 'whitewater world?'

Tests of student learning typically are 'one-shot' assessments that aim to measure a learner's ability to directly apply previously acquired skills and knowledge (e.g., Bransford & Schwartz, 1999; Schwartz et al., 2005). As such, these tests often provide an instrument that is much too blunt for assessing whether or not students are on a trajectory toward adaptive expertise. Further, during most tests of student learning, the students have no access to social, physical or technology resources to help them; in that sense, the assessments are purely instances of sequestered problem solving.

An alternative to these sequestered problem solving (SPS) assessments is to look at the degree to which particular types of learning experiences prepare students for accelerated future learning (e.g., Bransford & Schwartz, 1999). A number of these studies—involving comparison groups of students receiving different formats of instruction that are measured at more than one point in time subsequent to instruction—are discussed in Schwartz et al. (2005). The use of PFL (preparation for future learning) measures reveals the benefits of many approaches to instruction that remain invisible if only SPS assessments are used. The mechanisms of transfer that support future learning can include similarity-based transfer (e.g., Holyoak, 2005); dynamic transfer (e.g., Rebello et al., 2005; Dufrenes, Mestre, Thaden-Koch, Gerace, & Leonard, 2005; diSessa & Wagner, 2005; Hammer, Elby, Scherr, & Redish, 2005; Mestre, 1994) or a combination of the two (see Bransford, 2006; Pea, 2006; Schwartz, Varma, & Martin, 2006).

An emphasis on adaptivity from the perspective of preparation for future learning suggests new metrics for assessing not only student learning, but for assessing the success of courses themselves. For example, to what extent do students continue collaborating—leading and following—*after* a course is over? This question is not necessarily addressed by looking, at the end of the course, at the specific skills and content knowledge acquired only.

As one illustration of this point, consider a study by O'Mahony and his colleagues (2006) who studied the effects of two contrasting versions of a short course on new composite materials for airplane design being offered in a local aerospace work-place. Workshop participants were engineers drawn from different parts of the company, with different areas of expertise—and they tended not to know one another prior to the course.

One version of the workshop was a lecture by two experts in aviation and materials design. The second version of the workshop was based on the same basic information, but organized around a series of challenges, resources, and discussions about the challenges—and was designed by the same lecturers, in collaboration with the university learning scientists and the aerospace company's training personnel. In the challenge-based workshop condition, the engineers worked individually for a short time and then together in groups to solve each of four related challenges and to explore and consult the resources provided around these challenges. Although workshop participants were experienced engineers of various specialties, analysis of the videotapes revealed that, in the lecture condition, most of the questions were asked by the instructor, and workshop participants answered the instructor rather than discussed among themselves. In contrast, during the group discussions that were part of the challenge-based workshop, participants got to know one another's interests and strengths and often answered one another's questions.

While there is more work to be done to see how the social networks established in the workshops persist and grow in the workplace, initial data suggest that partici-pants in the challenge-based workshop not only learned new information about composite materials, but also learned about their fellow workers' areas of expertise and how to contact them to continue their mutual learning. Assessing the challenge-based condition for its effectiveness at potentially increasing the likelihood of future learning and collaboration by the participants provides a metric for measur-ing the effectiveness of courses that goes beyond the test scores students receive at the end of the course (in the aerospace study, both groups showed equal pre-to-post-test gains in learning key facts).

It is worth noting that there is an emerging body of data showing that back-ground knowledge about people with whom one works affects attitudes toward them (e.g., Bryk & Schneider, 2002; Lin & Bransford, 2005), memory and compre-hension of what they say and why (e.g., Davis, Lee, Vye, Bransford, & Schwartz, 2006), and reasoning and communication strategies (e.g., Bell et al., 2006). A simple illustration of effects of one's knowledge of others on communication strategies is illustrated in Box 3.1 (from a study by Bransford & Vye described in Bransford, Derry, Berliner, & Hammerness, 2005).

3.5 Technology, Learning, and Systems Integration

Our goal in this last section of the chapter is to explore the broader question of how new technologies—aligned with guidelines from the learning sciences—might enable us to (a) combine the unique strengths of learning in informal and formal settings to give us the best of both worlds, and (b) help break down the siloed walls of course-based teaching that can hinder learners' abilities to develop integrated

> **Box 3.1** Effects of personal knowledge on communication
>
> Imagine playing a game where you hear target concepts and try to get some-
> one you do not know to say them by providing clues but not giving direct
> answers. For example, in one study a participant received the target "red cor-
> vette" and said "A sports car made by Chevrolet that has the color of fire."
> Given the target "videodisc" she said "An interactive medium for video that
> came out before CD ROMs and was much bigger in size." For the target "brine
> shrimp" she said, "I'll pass on that one. It's too hard."
>
> Consider the same contestant when told that she was communicating with
> a person with whom she had worked for over a decade and knew very well.
> For "red corvette" she said, "What Carolyn drives—be sure to name the color."
> For "videodisc" she said, "What our Jasper program was published on when it
> first came out" (Jasper was an interactive videodisc program). For "brine
> shrimp" she said "The little orange things that are swimming around in the
> Ecosystem in my office." Knowing the person to whom she was talking pro-
> vided shortcuts to communication that otherwise were impossible to take.

knowledge structures that connect their entire program of study. This is a tall order, of course, and we have no illusions of being able to fill it. Our goal is simply to begin conversations that we hope will lead all of us as a field to create more adap-tive learning landscapes that increase opportunities for learning for all.

3.5.1 Merging the Advantages of Informal and Formal Learning Environments

Advantages of merging strong features of informal and formal learning environ-ments can be illustrated by considering once again the bass fishing example we presented earlier. JB's attempt to learn bass fishing illustrated the relative advan-tages (and disadvantages) of using 'local knowledge' versus more general 'vetted knowledge' to improve an everyday practice (bass fishing). Local knowledge (from local fishing experts) was directly relevant to JB's goals, but often incomplete or inaccurate (e.g., the idea that the pan fish were attracted to pink blossoms). Formal books offered more carefully vetted knowledge, but lacked connection to the local conditions and everyday experiences on the actual river JB wanted to fish, from which the local knowledge sprang.

It is worth noting that many times in formal settings, learners are not given the equivalent of *any* opportunities to fish. They therefore lack opportunities to generate questions from 'trips on the river' that they could otherwise bring back to the formal settings and use to enrich their learning. Indeed, much of formal education seems analogous to trying to teach landlocked people how to fish: no fishing waters are available for learners to truly explore on their own. Many students learn to do well in these kinds of 'landlocked' settings, but the depth of this learning can be hampered by the lack of opportunity to attempt to coordinate everyday experiences (e.g., trying to catch fish) with the more formal information presented in class.

A study headed by one of us (Mosborg, 2007)[5] shows how people's thinking and problem solving is affected by the degree to which they have had relevant everyday workplace experiences (analogous to JB's fishing experiences). The study involved a three-hour laboratory task originally designed by Cindy Atman and colleagues (Bursic & Atman, 1997; Atman, Chimka, Bursic, & Nachtmann, 1999) that asks engineering students and professional engineers to think aloud while designing a playground. The participants can also ask for any additional information they feel they need to accomplish their goals.

Previous studies had asked freshmen and senior engineering students to solve this task and analyzed their design processes (e.g., the students' use of time when moving through and among prototypical steps of the design process, and their information gathering behavior). Data indicated that seniors spent about the same amount of time on the task as the freshmen, but they asked for more information in more categories, and generally progressed more fluidly and iteratively through canonical phases of the design process (i.e., problem definition, information gathering, generating solution ideas, etc.).

Mosborg and colleagues compared the college students' approach to this design task with the approach taken by people who have been involved with design tasks 'in the real world.' The data have been collected and analysis has begun by focusing on a detailed transcription analysis of three contrastive case studies—one of a freshman engineering student (Amy); one of a professional engineering designer (John); and one of a professional industrial designer (Steve) highly experienced in playground design. The cases are analyzed against a backdrop of findings from a larger reference group (6 freshmen, 19 engineers, and 4 playground design experts).

Results are revealing the prominence of 'imagined social interactions' in the professionals' thinking as compared to that of the students. For example, the professionals know from experience that there will be a number of rounds of feedback cycles with the clients and stakeholders for whom they are building the playground (see Nelson & Stolterman, 2002). This helps explain another important finding; namely, that the professionals treated constraints as more malleable and negotiable than did the freshmen. Although the professionals devoted more effort to specifying initial conditions (including constraints) and to rendering them in greater detail, they also treated these specific conditions as subject to uncertainty and eventual negotiation. Two of the most common methods for re-negotiating these conditions were by anticipating a mid-course design review (which a majority of the professionals

---

[5] We thank researchers from the Center for Engineering Learning and Teaching (CELT) for their collaboration in making this study possible—especially Cindy Atman.

and none of the freshmen did) and by imagining ways of bringing greater financial and material resources to bear.

The findings point to the importance of giving more attention to the social aspects of design, which are often not apparent when students with little relevant workplace experience simply attempt to complete school tasks. More analyses of the data are being conducted, but the general results provide strong support for the idea that 'school tasks' and 'real world engineering and design tasks' are often separated by relatively large gaps of understanding, especially if people lack experience with the social contexts within which the work is operative and relevant.

Helping students connect formal learning to the everyday social interactions of the workplace is a major challenge. Although most of us as educators attempt to prepare our students for lives as professionals, we often run into the problem that 'wisdom can't be told' (e.g., Bransford, Franks, Vye, & Sherwood, 1989). Walker, Brophy, Hodge, and Bransford (2006) note the following:

> Preparing students for professional lives requires developing job skills that go beyond knowing how to apply engineering principles. Social competencies and ethical thinking are also critical to a successful engineering career. For example, professional engineers realize that failure to balance efficiency and quality can have significant consequences. They also know that persuading others requires a clear and concise message with well-represented data that supports their thesis. As well-intentioned educators, we often present students with advice about professionalism in the form of a list of important facts to remember (e.g., Accreditation Board for Engineering and Technology, 2004). However, *telling* the facts may not ensure that students understand why certain professional skills are important or learn to use them to solve problems in their everyday professional lives. (p. 49)

Walker et al. (2006) studied whether particular uses of video technologies could help students connect classroom instruction with real world practices. In their study, freshmen and senior bioengineering students received a web-based homework assignment where they were provided with a short set of principles about being professionals. For example:

> As a professional, you must learn to deal with competing demands. One involves conflicts between quality and efficiency—conflicts between taking the time to be very sure about the quality of an idea or product vs. delivering on a deadline. Knowing when to switch between quality and efficiency is an important key to success. (p. 51)

Additional principles highlighted three other areas of professionalism: interpersonal skills, safety, and lifelong learning.

After logging on, students read the 'professional advice' passage and responded to several questions presented in web form—including their perception of its perceived benefit and importance. Students used a four-point scale to rate the benefit of the advice (1 = 'not at all' to 4 = 'very beneficial') and how much the advice changed their thinking about life after graduation (1 = 'not at all', 4 = 'a lot'). Students were also asked to identify the advice they found most and least important and explain why, and to describe a situation they had experienced or heard about that exemplified the advice.

During the initial trial, all students tended to rate the advice as 'obvious' and 'self-evident.' This was not surprising given the literature on 'wisdom can't be told' (e.g., Bransford, Franks, Vye, & Sherwood, 1989). Following the initial trial, freshmen and seniors were randomly assigned to two different groups for Trial 2. The control group simply rated the advice a second time and also generated examples of how it applied to their experiences. The experimental group *eventually* rated the advice a second time, but they were *first* asked to think about the principles they had read during Trial 1 while watching a seven-minute video segment reenacting the NASA engineers' and managers' discussion of whether or not to launch the Challenger Space Shuttle (Englund, 1990). Students were asked to pay special attention to the O-Ring expert. He did not want to launch the next day but for a number of reasons—including poor efforts to communicate verbally and visually (e.g., to show data)—his advice was challenged and he eventually gave in to the larger group who wanted to launch.

For the freshmen, watching the video with the professional principles in mind had large effects on their subsequent ratings; they now rated the advice as more influential and relevant. Further, as mentioned, on the first trial the freshmen students in both the experimental and control groups initially described the advice as 'obvious' and 'self-evident.' Such comments on the post-test were notably absent from the remarks of the students who had seen the video. Students' self-generated statements also showed changes for the video condition. For example, one said: "It should all be very obvious and yet I see none of it is mundane but very important, especially at a time such as that" (Walker et al., 2006, p. 54). Freshmen in the video condition were also able to generate many more examples of the professional principles on Trial 2 than were those in the control group.

For seniors the results were different. They still tended to rate the advice as obvious, but on both Trial 1 and Trial 2—irrespective of the video condition—they were able to map many of the principles into their everyday experiences. Examples included: "I've worked in several academic research labs, and … I've noticed that people notice my work more when I present it better;" "I have worked on many teams, and I realize how important unity is;" and so forth. Most of the senior bioengineers in this study had had 'real world' experiences and hence did not need the video to help them interpret the particular advice used in the study. For freshman, however, the opportunity to think of the professional principles in the context of the video had very noticeable effects on their ability to understand and appreciate its relevance.

There are also more immersive ways to integrate internships and other fieldwork directly into the heart of students' course of study. Consider engineering education, for example. Even during the freshman year of a degree program, many opportunities exist to assign students field projects in which they can work—often collaboratively—to develop innovations that are truly useful (see, for example, Olin college, available at http://www.olin.edu/on.asp). Such opportunities do not have to yield patentable innovations, of course; they merely need to be new for the students involved in the classes. A noteworthy point about many of the courses at Olin is that student projects involve a set of clients with whom the students work to solve problems. When done appropriately, this can allow the students to develop early on the kinds of 'client centered' socially-grounded mental models that were important in the Mosborg study (2007) noted above.

Technology offers unprecedented possibilities to connect students working at different workplace sites with opportunities for peer feedback and co-learning, and with instructor feedback and learning about workplace needs. Imagine, as an analogy, technology that could have allowed JB on his fishing trips to connect online with other learners who were fishing elsewhere, plus connect to broader sets of knowledge just when it was needed (e.g., to find out what kind of lure was working best in his area at that very moment or to connect with experts who could look at digital shots of JB's surroundings and give him advice.) Similarly, imagine technology that could provide the students working on Olin projects to get just-in-time ideas from professors and other students in their class.

A good example of the beginnings of this kind of technology-enhanced scenario is the 'capstone internship' that students take as a required course in the Digital Media Arts program of Bellevue Community College in Washington State. Prior to enrollment in the class, students seek and secure a position in an environment that is closely aligned with their area of study. They work under the supervision of a digital media content professional for a contracted number of hours in the studio, on the set, or in the workplace. While students are given some assistance in finding an appropriate internship, the process is intended to be self-directed, much like a job search.

Once the internship is secured and the student enrolled, course instruction occurs entirely online. With feedback from the instructor, students craft and refine their learning objectives for the internship, submit detailed weekly logs to the instructor outlining their activities and general observations about their position and duties, post responses to reflection questions on the course site discussion boards, and have access to each other's blogs. In culmination, they write a final report documenting and reflecting on their experience, including their preparation for future professional development.

The online environment allows for asynchronous exchange not only with the instructor, but among learners who are on different time schedules and at different points in their internships. What is more, the opportunity to participate in the internship course without having to travel to attend weekly classes face-to-face makes the sizable time commitment to an on-site internship possible.

The feedback from the students, and from graduates of the program, suggests that this kind of carefully tailored internship experience helps students feel very prepared for the workplace. Students' comments indicate that spending time at the studio working alongside professionals—while also being prompted to think about what they were doing, seeing, and feeling—created a synergistic set of experiences that not only deepened their media production (i.e., discipline-specific) skills but also increased their self-awareness of themselves in the context of their new careers and in relationship with their peers. If these students can stay connected to their cohorts through technology (something they are encouraged to do), this should help their preparation for future learning even more.

Ideally, of course, programs such as the one described above would be moved from 'capstones' to 'stepping stones' where students start to make formal and informal links early in their educational career. There are many reasons for believing that this could have an important effect on learning. For example, an increasing number of researchers are studying K-12 students' informal learning competencies and finding that they are often highly sophisticated yet invisible to teachers in formal settings (e.g., Barron et al., 1998; Banks et al., 2007; Bell et al., 2006; Heath, 2004; Moll, Amanti, Neff, & Gonzalez, 1992; Pea, Bell, Barron, & Stevens, 2005; Stevens, O'Connor, & Garrison, 2005). If we could use these 'funds of knowledge' (Moll et al., 1992) as meaningful stepping-stones and design them into meaningful paths, we can begin to capture some of the positive aspects of informal learning (e.g., locally relevant knowledge) and link these to formal educational instruction.

Technology can be used to bridge informal and formal learning opportunities. For example, Bell and colleagues (2006) are equipping students with media cameras and asking them to capture key aspects of their everyday experiences that they can then bring back to their classrooms. If JB, our would-be bass fisherman, were in this study, he would bring back fishing scenes that could then be related to a number of topics, including biology and ecology.

It seems worth noting that attempts to help students connect everyday and workplace experiences with formal education might benefit from exposure to two or three different kinds of experiences rather than only one. This conjecture is based on the cognitive literature, which suggests that a single concrete experience (e.g., an example) can lock students into that context, whereas two or three allow them to abstract the similarities and differences. The studies we know that support this point are all based on laboratory studies (e.g., Gick & Holyoak, 1980, 1983; Gentner & Markman, 2005). Still, the application of these ideas to optimal arrangements of everyday work and life experiences seems like a useful one to explore. In addition, helping students frame particular experiences as instances of more general principles can also facilitate transfer to other tasks (e.g., Judd, 1908).

3.5.2 Can Technology Help to Bridge the 'Silos of Expertise' That Can Hinder Learners' Knowledge Integration?

We end this section by discussing one additional issue that is relevant to this book's theme of reshaping the landscapes of learning. It is a *systems* issue that involves the challenge of helping students develop across-course skills, attitudes and knowledge structures that support expert judgment and problem solving in our fast changing global environment (e.g., Chi, 2006; Ericsson, 2006; National Research Council, 2000). If we continue to teach in course-based or discipline-based 'silos,' it can be very difficult to achieve the kind of transdisciplinarity that Jan Visser discusses in his opening chapter for this book.

Our concern about silos is related to a major principle from the study of learning; namely, the importance of helping students develop knowledge structures that are organized around 'big ideas' that are integrative and generative. The importance of this point is discussed in Wiggins and McTighe's (2005) book on the use of 'working backwards' strategies for creating high quality learning experiences (see also National Research Council, 2005). Wiggins and McTighe suggest (1) beginning with a careful analysis of what we want students to know and be able to do; (2) exploring how to assess students progress in achieving these goals; and (3) using the results of 1 and 2 to choose and continue to improve instructional strategies. It is important to note that point (1) goes beyond creating a list of 'mile wide and inch deep' factual and behavioral objectives. Bruner (1960) provides a clear articulation of this issue:

> The curriculum of a subject should be determined by the most fundamental understanding that can be achieved of the underlying principles that give structure to a subject. Teaching specific topics or skills without making clear their context in the broader fundamental structure of a field of knowledge is uneconomical .... An understanding of fundamental principles and ideas appears to be the main road to adequate transfer of training. To understand something as a specific instance of a more general case—which is what understanding a more fundamental structure means—is to have learned not only a specific thing but also a model for understanding other things like it that one may encounter. (pp. 31 and 25, respectively)

Bruner's quote refers to the curriculum of a subject, but we suspect he would agree that it is also relevant for designing entire *programs* of study and asking how they fit the needs of students once they graduate. Working at the level of programs is very difficult to accomplish, of course. A major reason is that people who teach within programs of study rarely get opportunities to talk with colleagues who teach the next (or preceding) course sequence in order to clarify how to provide a better learning corridor for the students in a program, much less colleagues in other discipline areas. These kinds of coordination activities take a great deal of time, and time is a highly precious commodity (see especially Y. L. Visser, in this volume).

One approach to this issue, an approach that is still in a fledgling phase of development yet has shown promise is to use video and audio technologies to capture and share the expertise of different faculty members, workplace employers, students and others. A key to making this work is to have groups develop a set of common 'anchoring' challenges or cases, and then ask experts from different disciplines to comment on the challenges. This can be accomplished by posting challenges on the web and conducting short interviews via telephone and recording them via audio. The audio clips are then edited, sent to the experts for their 'ok' and used as resources that can help teachers and their students see how common cases can be viewed from multiple points of view.

The present authors' work in this area involved several 'anchored collaboration' projects that began a number of years ago when members of the Cognition and Technology Group at Vanderbilt (CTGV) used the first 12 minutes of the movie 'Raiders of the Lost Ark' as an anchor for joint learning from multiple perspectives. In this portion of the film, the main character (Indiana Jones) finds the Golden Idol, barely escapes a number of harrowing events and makes his getaway in a seaplane. We asked people with backgrounds in science, mathematics, ethics, geography and other areas to point out things that were relevant to their disciplines. The result was that the experts all learned from one another and the students also experienced changes in their own thinking that were prompted by the anchored comments (see Cognition and Technology Group at Vanderbilt, 1997).

A short while later, Michael, Klee, Bransford, and Warren (1993) extended this idea to a college course in speech therapy. This study investigated whether or not differences existed in what learners noticed in speech therapy sessions after receiving two different kinds of instruction about three approaches to speech therapy that were based on different theoretical frameworks: behavioral, sociolinguistic, and Vygotskian).

Students in instructional group #1 learned in ways that had been used in many previous classes designed to teach speech therapy. They read and discussed textbook descriptions to learn about different theories and approaches to speech therapy—but never saw them applied to the same case.

Students in instructional group #2 watched video clips of a therapist doing speech therapy and were asked to discuss what they noticed. They then saw additional videos of experts from each of the theoretical backgrounds noted above.

At the end of the class, the two groups performed equally on tests of factual memory. However, on tests of transfer, the 'common anchor with multiple perspectives' group (group # 2) did a much better job of analyzing and explaining new speech therapy sessions. It is also noteworthy that each of the three experts who contributed to the study by commenting on the anchoring case (they had each done this individually) were extremely motivated to see the videos of their colleagues.

Work by Dan Schwartz (September 21, 2000, personal communication) also demonstrated the value for faculty of 'anchored collaborations.' He used a seven-minute video of a six-month old infant who had, for the first time, been introduced to a voice-activated mobile (it moved and played music when the child made a sound). Colleagues of Schwartz, in the Peabody Psychology department, were each asked, separately, to view the video and make comments on what they noticed and how their ideas related to broader literatures. There was an amazingly broad range of responses, and all were highly engaged. As faculty watched the responses of their colleagues, they gained a much deeper appreciation of the areas of expertise of their colleagues that previously had been invisible to them.

Over time, members of the CTGV developed a set of STAR Legacy software shells that helped systematize this 'challenge cycle' process of beginning by asking participants to write down their initial thoughts about a given challenge, providing them with opportunities to explore expert resources and multiple perspectives around the challenge, and then iteratively revisit their initial thinking, writing down new insights, and working in groups to discuss insights and burning questions about the initial challenge (e.g., CTGV, 2000; Schwartz, Lin, Brophy, & Bransford, 1999). This general format has been used in a variety of settings, including teacher preparation (PT[3] Group at Vanderbilt, 2003) via an online resource center that helps teachers work more effectively with students with special needs (iris.peabody.vanderbilt.edu); leadership development (Partners in Learning, 2005, 2007); Bioengineering (Bransford, Vye, Bateman, Brophy, & Roselli, 2004); and business training (e.g., O'Mahony et al., 2006; Vye, Martich, & McBrian, 2003).

Within the framework of our current discussion, the most important point is the development process used to build STAR Legacy modules. The process involves the use of simple technologies that make collaboration possible even though people are busy or physically distant from one another. As noted earlier, a key phase of development is to build challenges and then collect the resources for the challenges by using phone interviews, asking experts to audiotape or videotape themselves, and so forth. Overall, technology can aid in collecting the expertise of a wide variety of people on any given topic.

With the help of a development team, faculty and their students can also add to the set of resources (or to the list of challenges), which provides another method by which students can try out new roles in the classroom. Over time, individual teachers and their students can thus become 'conductors' of resources, introducing the perspectives of a broad array of experts during the course of in-class challenges. As conductors, the teachers or students do not have to personally 'play every instrument;' instead they can know when to bring in particular areas of expertise that fit their momentary needs. This process can also be used to help students build team and collaboration skills, which, as mentioned earlier, have been identified as being crucial to their future success.

Another possibility for breaking down existing teaching silos is to use MUVEs (multi-user virtual environments) to create interactive educational journeys or challenges that require learners to acquire information from multiple disciplines in order to successfully navigate and solve the presented challenge. As an example a research group or a class of 'pioneering teachers and students' might build a virtual, three-dimensional moon landscape where learners have to collaborate to survive in conditions of extreme temperatures, no atmosphere, lots of dust, no water, and so forth. The right set of interactive experiences—complete with opportunities to fail and try again—could help students learn about topics not only in physics and biology, but in engineering, architecture, psychology, sociology, politics and other areas. Teachers could learn along with the students, and thus could receive the kind of continuous and rapid updating of their knowledge needed for our fast changing world.

It is noteworthy that there is already a very dedicated and creative group of educators working in multi-user virtual environments such as Second Life, a widely used MUVE, and that these educators are highly collaborative. The authors are newcomers to Second Life, but have already witnessed the impressive collaboration, innovation, sense of community and cumulative creation with which this 'world' is being built (e.g., Bransford & Gawel, 2006).

Of course, quality control is an issue for all educational environments—including MUVEs. To ensure environments are of merit, one possibility might be to create a space for commentary coupled with a peer review system. As an example, the adequacy of the designs could be reviewed (e.g., for the accuracy of moon-based physics in the example earlier); the instructional strategies and learning-taking place could be measured; and suggestions for improving the environments and learning experiences could be collected. If this type of peer-review came to be considered equal in quality and stature to peer-reviewed journal publications, the world might witness a new kind of journal structure—one that is more explicit and interactive than text and still pictures, accessible from anywhere in the world via the internet, filled with tools, objects and environments that could be interoperable and, ideally, sharable across disciplines and institutions.

As we noted earlier in this chapter, doing this requires both technology and outstanding leadership. It is unlikely to happen simply because the technology exists.

3.6 Summary and Conclusions

We began this chapter by noting that learning something new—especially something difficult—often highlights the advantages of finding experts who can help, and that gaining access to instructional expertise has been a challenge throughout much of human history. New technologies are helping us solve the access problem, but we also need to ask 'access to what?'

We organized our discussion around a visual representation created by the LIFE Center (Fig. 3.1) that serves as a reminder of the lifewide and lifelong learning spaces within which people find themselves. The LIFE Center is joining with many other researchers around the world to develop a more differentiated view of learning as it occurs in a variety of settings. The goal is to help the field create new, transformative theories of learning that are both empirically grounded and useful for helping people learn.

Our discussion focused on four ideas suggested by Fig. 3.1 that relate to this book's focus on changing learning landscapes. In particular:

1. We used the bass fishing example to explore some of the benefits and drawbacks of learning in informal and formal environments, with an eye towards blending the strengths of each into more powerful designs for learning.
2. We looked at the kinds of post-graduation competencies needed for the current century and argued for the need to cultivate adaptivity to fast-changing environments in response to our 'whitewater world.'
3. We discussed how a combination of points 1 and 2 above suggested some possible new approaches to instruction (either online or face-to-face) and new assessment metrics.
4. We explored whether and how new technologies might allow us to improve upon present practice by looking at technology-enabled learning systems that allow us to (a) help us merge the unique strengths of learning that occur in both formal and informal settings, and (b) begin breaking through the 'siloed walls' of instruction that often make it difficult for people to acquire the kinds of transdisciplinary skills, attitudes and knowledge structures that can help them learn throughout life (see J. Visser, in this volume).

It is our hope that the ideas we have collected and presented here, as well as those presented throughout this volume, will motivate educators and researchers to continue and deepen the conversations that brought these pages to print. The combination of a fast-changing, technologically-connected world, and the expanding knowledge brought to our disciplines by advances in the learning sciences, present an exceptional opportunity for all of us to take part in the evolution and expansion of what we think of as 'teaching and learning.' Let the dialogue begin—or continue—and deepen our collective effectiveness in assisting our learners and graduates—as well as ourselves—to flourish and succeed.

3.7 Resources for Further Exploration

We recommend the following Web based resources for further exploration in connection with the issues discussed in this chapter.

- LIFE (Learning in Informal and Formal Environments) Center. Available at http://life-slc.org
- The Chicago Mercantile Exchange Education Center. Available at http://www.cme.com/edu/
- Olin College. Available at http://www.olin.edu/on.asp
- Second Life, 'a 3D online digital world imagined, created and owned by its residents.' Available at http://secondlife.com/
- Second Life Educators Mailing List. Available at http://tinyurl.com/qfw4
- VaNTH, CAPE and Adaptive Learning Technologies. Available at http://www.isis.vanderbilt.edu/Projects/VaNTH/
- Partnership for 21st Century Skills. Available at http://www 21stcenturyskills.org/index.php
- The Sloan Consortium ('A Consortium of Institutions and Organizations Committed to Quality Online Education'). Available at http://www. sloan-c.org/index.asp

3.8 Questions for Comprehension and Application

1. Informal learning can occur anywhere and at any time. Identify something that you have learned informally during the past two weeks, and note who you learned this from and where. Did the setting of your learning experience influence your understanding or retention? How was your experience different from what it might have been if you had learned it in a more formal setting such as a classroom? Can you explain?
2. Identify a face-to-face course that you feel would benefit from being delivered online or as a blended course (partially face-to-face, partially online, and possibly partially in informal or workplace settings). Why did you choose this particular course? What aspects did you feel would translate well to online delivery? What aspects of the class would you reserve for face-to-face learning? Why?
3. As Spector (Ch. 12 in this volume) points out, good assessment of student learning in formal instruction is often considered hard to achieve. What are two or three of the most pressing challenges surrounding assessment in a fast-changing, technologically connected world? Are there new alternatives for assessment that are emerging? What advantages do they have and what challenges do they face?

References

Accreditation Board for Engineering and Technology (2004). *Sustaining the change*. Baltimore: ABET. Retrieved September 21, 2007, from http://www.abet.org/ papers.shtml.

Aronson, E., Blaney, N., Stephin, C., Sikes, J., & Snapp, M. (1978). *The jigsaw classroom*. Beverly Hills, CA: Sage.

Atman, C. J., Chimka, J. R., Bursic, K. M., & Nachtmann, H. L. (1999). A comparison of freshman and senior engineering design processes. *Design Studies, 20,* 131–152.

Augustine, N. (2005). *Rising above the gathering storm: Energizing and employing America for a brighter economic future*. Washington, DC: National Academies Press. Retrieved September 21, 2007, from http://www.nap.edu/catalog.php?record_id=11463.

Banks, J. A., Au, K. H., Ball, A., Bell, P., Gordon, E., Gutierrez, K., Heath, S. B., Lee, C., Lee, Y., Mahiri, J., Nasir, N., Valdes, G., & Zhou, M. (2007). *Learning in and out of school in diverse environments: Life-long, life-wide, life-deep*. Seattle, WA: The LIFE Center (The Learning in Informal and Formal Environments Center) and the Center for Multicultural Education, University of Washington. Retrieved September 21, 2007, from http://life-slc.org/wp-content/up/2007/05/Banks-et-al-LIFE-Diversity-Report.pdf.

Barron, B. J. S., Schwartz, D. L., Vye, N. J., Moore, A., Petrosino, A., Zech, L., Bransford, J. D., & The Cognition and Technology Group at Vanderbilt (1998). Doing with understanding: Lessons from research on problem- and project-based learning. *Journal of the Learning Sciences, 7,* 271–311.

Bell, P., Bricker, L., McGaughey, M., Lee, T., Reeve, S., Zimmerman, H., & Tzou, C. (2006, April). *How children in a multicultural, low-SES community learn science across social settings*. Paper presented at the annual meeting of the American Educational Research Association, San Francisco.

Bergmann, H. F. (2001). "The silent university": The society to encourage studies at home, 1873–1897. *New England Quarterly, 74*(3), 447–477.

Bever, T. G. (1982). Regression in the service of development. In T. G. Bever (Ed.), *Regression in mental development: Basic phenomena and theories* (pp. 153–188). Hillsdale, NJ: Lawrence Erlbaum.

Biswas, G., Schwartz, D., Bransford, J. D., & the Teachable Agent Group at Vanderbilt (TAG-V) (2001). Technology support for complex problem solving: From SAD environments to AI. In K. D. Forbus & P. J. Feltovich (Eds.), *Smart machines in education: The coming revolution in educational technology*. Menlo Park, CA: AAAI/MIT Press.

Bransford, J., & Gawel, D. (2006). Forward: Thoughts on Second Life and learning. In D. Livingstone, & J. Kemp, J. (Eds.), *Proceedings of the Second Life Education Workshop, part of the Second Life Community Convention*. Second Life Community Convention, San Francisco, August 18–20, 2006. Paisley, Scotland: University of Paisley Press.

Bransford, J., Vye, N., Bateman, H., Brophy, S., & Roselli, B. (2004). Vanderbilt's Amigo3 project: Knowledge of how people learn enters cyberspace. In T. Duffy & J. Kirkley (Eds.), *Learner-centered theory and practice in distance education: Cases from higher education* (pp. 209–234). Mahwah, NJ: Lawrence Erlbaum.

Bransford, J., Derry, S., Berliner, D., & Hammerness, K. (2005). Theories of learning and their roles in teaching. In L. Darling-Hammond & J. Bransford (Eds.), *Preparing teachers for a changing world: What teachers should learn and be able to do* (pp. 40–87). San Francisco: Jossey-Bass.

Bransford, J. D. (2006, November). *Transfer, adaptivity and innovation*. Paper presented at the National Science Foundation's workshop on Multidisciplinary Perspectives on Transfer, Expertise, and Innovation, Washington, DC.

Bransford, J. D. (2007). Preparing people for rapidly changing environments. *Journal of Engineering Education, 96,* 1–3.

Bransford, J. D., & Schwartz, D. L. (1999). Rethinking transfer: A simple proposal with multiple implications. *Review of Research in Education, 24,* 61–100.

Bransford, J. D., Franks, J. J., Vye, N. J., & Sherwood, R. D. (1989). New approaches to instruction: Because wisdom can't be told. In S. Vosniadou & A. Ortony (Eds.), *Similarity and analogical reasoning* (pp. 470–497). New York: Cambridge University Press.

Brown, A. L., & Campione, J. C. (1994). Guided discovery in a community of learners. In K. McGilly (Ed.), *Classroom lessons: Integrating cognitive theory and classroom practice* (pp. 229–272). Cambridge, MA: MIT Press.

Bruner, J. (1960). *The process of education.* Cambridge, MA: Harvard University Press.

Bryk, A., & Schneider, B. (2002). *Trust in schools.* New York: Russell Sage Foundation.

Bursic, K. M., & Atman, C. J. (1997). Information gathering: A critical step for quality in the design process. *Quality Management Journal, 4*(4), 60–75.

Chi, M. T. H. (2006). Two approaches to the study of experts' characteristics. In K. A. Ericsson, N. Charness, P. J. Feltovich, & R. R. Hoffman (Eds.), *The Cambridge handbook of expertise and expert performance* (pp. 21–30). New York: Cambridge University Press.

Clough, G. (2005). *Educating the engineer of 2020: Adapting engineering education to the new century.* Washington, DC: National Academy of Engineering, National Academies Press. Retrieved September 21, 2007, from http://books.nap.edu/catalog.php?record_id= 11338.

Cognition and Technology Group at Vanderbilt (1997). *The Jasper Project: Lessons in curriculum, instruction, assessment, and professional development.* Mahwah, NJ: Lawrence Erlbaum.

Cognition and Technology Group at Vanderbilt (2000). Adventures in anchored instruction: Lessons from beyond the ivory tower. In R. Glaser (Ed.), *Advances in instructional psychology: Educational design and cognitive science* (Vol. 5, pp. 35–100). Mahwah, NJ: Lawrence Erlbaum.

Darling-Hammond, L., & Bransford, J. (Eds.) (2005). *Preparing teachers for a changing world: What teachers should learn and be able to do.* San Francisco: Jossey-Bass.

Davis, J., Lee, T., Vye, N., Bransford, J., & Schwartz, D. (2006, June). *The role of people knowledge in learning narrative and domain content.* Paper presented at the 7th International Conference of the Learning Sciences, Bloomington, IN.

Dewey, J. (1938/1997). *Experience and education.* New York: Simon & Schuster.

diSessa, A. A., & Wagner, J. R. (2005). What coordination has to say about transfer. In J. P. Mestre (Ed.), *Transfer of learning from a modern multidisciplinary perspective* (pp. 121–154). Greenwich, CT: Information Age Publishing.

Duffy, T. M., & Kirkley, J. R. (2004). *Learner-centered theory and practice in distance education: Cases from higher education.* Mahwah, NJ: Lawrence Erlbaum.

Dufrenes, R., Mestre, J., Thaden-Koch, T., Gerace, W., & Leonard, W. (2005). Knowledge representation and coordination in the transfer process. In J. P. Mestre (Ed.), *Transfer of learning from a modern multidisciplinary perspective* (pp. 155–216). Greenwich, CT: Information Age Publishing.

Englund, G. (1990). *Challenger.* [Television Film]. King Phoenix Entertainment.

Ericsson, K. A. (2006). An introduction to the Cambridge handbook of expertise and expert performance: Its development, organization, and content. In K. A. Ericsson, N. Charness, P. J. Feltovich, & R. R. Hoffman (Eds.), *The Cambridge handbook of expertise and expert performance* (pp. 21–30). New York: Cambridge University Press.

Friedman, T. L. (2005). *The world is flat: A brief history of the twenty-first century.* New York: Farrar, Straus & Giroux.

Fullan, M. (2001). *Leading in a culture of change.* San Francisco: Jossey-Bass.

Fullan, M. (2002). The change leader. *Educational Leadership, 59*(8), 16–20.

Gentner, D., & Markman, A. B. (2005). Defining structural similarity. *Journal of Cognitive Science, 6,* 1–20.

Gick, M. L., & Holyoak, K. J. (1980). Analogical problem solving. *Cognitive Psychology, 12,* 306–365.

Gick, M. L., & Holyoak, K. J. (1983). Schema induction and analogical transfer. *Cognitive Psychology, 15,* 1–38.

Hall, M. (in this volume). Getting to know the feral learner. In J. Visser & M. Visser-Valfrey (Eds.), *Learners in a changing learning landscape: Reflections from a dialogue on new roles and expectations* (pp. 109–133). Dordrecht, The Netherlands: Springer.

Hammer, D., Elby, A., Scherr, R. E., & Redish, E. F. (2005). Resources, framing, and transfer. In J. P. Mestre (Ed.), *Transfer of learning from a modern multidisciplinary perspective* (pp. 89–120). Greenwich, CT: Information Age Publishing.

Harris, W. J. A. (1967). Education by post. *Adult Education, 39*(5), 269–273.

Hatano, G., & Inagaki, K. (1986). Two courses of expertise. In H. Stevenson, J. Azuma, & K. Hakuta (Eds.), *Child Development and Education in Japan* (pp. 262–272). New York: W. H. Freeman.

Hatano, G., & Osuro, Y. (2003). Commentary: Reconceptualizing school learning using insight from expertise research. *Educational Researcher, 32*(8), 26–29.

Heath, S. B. (2004). Ethnography in communities: Learning the everyday life of America's subordinated youth. In J. A. Banks & C. A. M. Banks (Eds.), *Handbook of research on multicultural education* (2nd ed., pp. 146–162). San Francisco: Jossey-Bass.

Holyoak, K. J. (2005). Analogy. In K. J. Holyoak & R. G. Morrison (Eds.), *The Cambridge handbook of thinking and reasoning* (pp. 117–142). New York: Cambridge University Press.

Jowit, J. (2006, December 10). *No more late-night particle physics as OU broadcasts last programme*. The Guardian. Retrieved September 21, 2007, from http://education. guardian.co.uk/higher/news/story/0,,1968741,00.html.

Judd, C. H. (1908). The relation of special training to general intelligence. *Educational Review, 36*, 28–42.

Ladson-Billings, G., & King, J. (1990). Cultural identity of African-Americans: Implications for achievement. Aurora, CO: Midcontinental Regional Education Laboratory.

Levy, F., & Murnane, R. J. (2004). *The new division of labor: How computers are creating the next job market*. Princeton, NJ: Princeton University Press.

Lin, X. D., & Bransford, J. D. (2005, April). *People knowledge: A useful ingredient for bridging cultural differences between teachers and students*. Paper presented at the annual meeting of the American Educational Research Association, Montreal, Canada.

Lin, X., Schwartz, D. L., & Bransford, J. (2006). Intercultural adaptive expertise: Explicit and implicit lessons from Dr. Hatano. *Human Development, 50*, 65–72.

Martin, R., & Austen, H. (2002). Innovation vs. implementation: Mastering the tensions. *Rotman Management*, Spring/Summer, 6–11.

Martin, T., Pierson, J., Rivale, S. R., Vye, N. J., Bransford, J. D., & Diller, K. (2007). The function of generating ideas in the Legacy Cycle. In W. Aung (Ed.), *Innovations 2007: World innovations in engineering education and research*. Arlington, VA: International Network for Engineering Education and Research (iNEER).

Mestre J. (1994, February). Cognitive aspects of learning and teaching science. In S. F. Fitzsimmons & L. Kerpelman (Eds.), *Teacher enhancement for elementary and secondary science and mathematics: Status, issues, and problems* (section 3, pp. 1–53). Washington, DC: National Science Foundation (NSF 94–80).

Michael, A. L., Klee, T., Bransford, J. D., & Warren, S. F. (1993). The transition from theory to therapy: Test of two instructional methods. *Applied Cognitive Psychology, 7*, 139–154.

Moll, L., Amanti, C., Neff, D., & Gonzalez, N. (1992). Funds of knowledge for teaching: Using a qualitative approach to connect homes and classrooms. *Theory into Practice, 31*(2), 132–142.

Moran, L. (1993). Genesis of the open learning institute of British Columbia. *Journal of Distance Education, 8*(1), 43–70.

Mosborg, S. (2007, April). *Beyond the problem given: Contrasting approaches to problem structuring among professional and student designers*. Poster presented at the annual meeting of the American Educational Research Association, Chicago.

National Center on Education and the Economy (2007). *Tough choices or tough times: The report of the New Commission on the Skills of the American Workforce*. San Francisco: Jossey-Bass.

National Research Council (2000). *How people learn: Brain, mind, experience, and school* (expanded edition). Washington, DC: National Academies Press.

National Research Council (2005). *How students learn: History, mathematics, science in the classroom*. Washington DC: National Academies Press.

Nelson, H. G., & Stolterman, E. (2002). *The design way: Intentional change in an unpredictable world: Foundations and fundamentals of design competence*. Englewood Cliffs, NJ: Educational Technology Publications.

Okita, S., & Schwartz, D. (2006, June). *When observation beats doing: Learning by teaching.* Paper presented at the 7th International Conference of the Learning Sciences, Bloomington, IN.

O'Mahony, K., Bransford, J., Lin, K., Richey, M., Vye, N., Clark, H., & Swanson, K. (2006, April). *From metal to composites manufacturing: Preparing Boeing engineers for future learning.* Paper presented at the annual meeting of the American Educational Research Association, San Francisco.

Partners in Learning. (2005). *School leader development: Building 21st century schools.* [Compact Disc]. Redmond, WA: Microsoft Corporation.

Partners in Learning (2007). *School leader development: Assessing 21st century learning.* [Compact Disc]. Redmond, WA: Microsoft Corporation.

Pea, R. (2006, November). *Transfer and expertise in informal settings.* Paper presented at the National Science Foundation's workshop on Multidisciplinary Perspectives on Transfer, Expertise, and Innovation, Washington, DC.

Pea, R., Bell, P., Barron, B., & Stevens, R. (2005, April). *Informal learning in everyday settings.* Paper presented at the annual meeting of the American Educational Research Association, Montreal, Canada.

PT³ Group at Vanderbilt (2003). Three AMIGOs: Using "anchored modular inquiry" to help prepare future teachers. *Educational Technology Research and Development, 51*(1), 105–123.

Rebello, N. S., Zollman, D. A., Allbaugh, A. R., Englehardt, P. V., Gray, K. E., Hrepic, Z., & Itza-Ortiz, S. F. (2005). Dynamic transfer: A perspective from physics education research. In J. P. Mestre (Ed.), *Transfer of learning from a modern multidisciplinary perspective* (pp. 217–250). Greenwich, CT: Information Age Publishing.

Robinson, A. G., & Stern, S. (1997). *Corporate creativity: How innovation and improvement actually happen.* San Francisco: Berrett-Koehler.

Rogers, E. M. (1962/2003). *Diffusion of innovations* (5th ed.). New York: Free Press.

Schumpeter, J. A. (1942). *Capitalism, socialism and democracy.* New York: Harper & Row.

Schwartz, D., Varma, S., & Martin, L. (2006, November). *Dynamic transfer and innovation.* Paper presented at the National Science Foundation's workshop on Multidisciplinary Perspectives on Transfer, Expertise, and Innovation, Washington, DC.

Schwartz, D. L., & Bransford, J. D. (1998). A time for telling. *Cognition and Instruction, 16,* 475–522.

Schwartz, D.L., Lin, X., Brophy, S., & Bransford, J. D. (1999). Toward the development of flexibly adaptive instructional designs. In C. M. Reigeluth (Ed.), *Instructional-design theories and models: A new paradigm of instructional theory* (Vol. 2, pp. 183–213). Mahwah, NJ: Lawrence Erlbaum.

Schwartz, D. L., Bransford, J. D., & Sears, D. L. (2005). Efficiency and innovation in transfer. In J. P. Mestre (Ed.), *Transfer of learning: Research and perspectives* (pp. 1–51). Greenwich, CT: Information Age Publishing.

Seely-Brown, J. (2006). New learning environments for the 21st century: Exploring the edge. *Change, 38,* 18–25.

Smith, M., & Casserly, C. (2006). The promise of open educational resources. *Change, 38,* 8–17.

Spector, J. M. (in this volume). What makes good online instruction good: New opportunities and old barriers. In J. Visser & M. Visser-Valfrey (Eds.), *Learners in a changing learning landscape: Reflections from a dialogue on new roles and expectations* (pp. 251–266). Dordrecht, The Netherlands: Springer.

Stevens, R., O'Connor, K., & Garrison, L. (2005). Engineering student identities in the navigation of the undergraduate curriculum. *Proceedings of the American Society for Engineering Education.* Retrieved September 21, 2007, from http://www.asee.org/ acPapers/2005-1989_Final.pdf.

Vaill, P. B. (1996). *Learning as a way of being: Strategies for survival in a world of permanent whitewater.* San Francisco: Jossey-Bass.

Visser, J. (Chair) (2005, October). *Learners in a changing learning landscape: New roles and expectations—A dialogue motivated by an ibstpi research project.* Panel session at the annual meeting of the Association for Educational Communications and Technology, Orlando, FL.

Visser, J. (in this volume). Constructive interaction with change: Implications for learners and the environment in which they learn. In J. Visser & M. Visser-Valfrey (Eds.), *Learners in a changing learning landscape: Reflections from a dialogue on new roles and expectations* (pp. 11–35). Dordrecht, The Netherlands: Springer.

Visser, Y. L. (in this volume). Postsecondary education in the changing learning & living landscapes. In J. Visser & M. Visser-Valfrey (Eds.), *Learners in a changing learning landscape: Reflections from a dialogue on new roles and expectations* (pp. 135–163). Dordrecht, The Netherlands: Springer.

Von Hippel, E. (2005). *Democratizing innovation.* Cambridge, MA: MIT Press.

Vye, N. J., Martich, D., & McBrian, L. (2003). A case-based e-learning program for healthcare professionals: Design considerations and outcomes. In A. Rossett (Ed.), *Proceedings of E-Learning 2003: World Conference on E-Learning in Corporate, Government, Healthcare, & Higher Education.* Norfolk, VA: Association for the Advancement of Computing in Education.

Walker, J. M. T., Brophy, S. P., Hodge, L. L., & Bransford, J. D. (2006). Establishing experiences to develop a wisdom of professional practice. *New Directions for Teaching and Learning, 108,* 49–53.

Weigel, V. (2000). E-learning and the tradeoff between richness and reach in higher education. *Change, 32*(5), 10–15.

Wertime, R. (1979). Students, problems and "courage spans." In J. Lockhead & J. Clements (Eds.), *Cognitive process instruction: Research on teaching thinking skills.* Philadelphia: The Franklin Institute Press.

Wertheimer, M. (1945/1959). *Productive thinking.* New York: Harper & Brothers.

Wiggins, G., & McTighe, J. (2005). *Understanding by design* (2nd ed.). Upper Saddle River, NJ: Prentice-Hall.

Chapter 4
Learners in a Changing Learning Landscape: Reflections from an Instructional Design Perspective

Jeroen J.G. van Merriënboer and Slavi Stoyanov

Abstract Both learners and teachers find themselves in a learning landscape that is rapidly changing, along with fast societal and technological developments. This paper discusses the new learning landscape from an instructional design perspective. First, with regard to what is learned, people more than ever need flexible problem-solving and reasoning skills allowing them to deal with new, unfamiliar problem situations in their professional and everyday life. Second, with regard to the context in which learning takes place, learning in technology-rich, informal and professional 24/7 settings is becoming general practice. And third, with regard to the learners themselves, they can more often be characterized as lifelong learners who are mature, bring relevant prior knowledge, and have very heterogeneous expectations and perceptions of learning. High-quality instructional design research should focus on the question which instructional methods and media-method combinations are effective, efficient and appealing in this new learning landscape. Some innovative instructional methods that meet this requirement are discussed.

Both learners and teachers find themselves in a learning landscape that is constantly and dramatically changing in terms of the modalities through which people learn, the purposes for which they learn, and the context in which learning acquires its meaning. This chapter reflects on this phenomenon from an instructional design perspective. Instructional designers, on the basis of studying learning as a natural human drive, try to construct or select instructional methods in the attempt to make learning effective, efficient, and appealing under specified circumstances. They typically do so on the basis of an analysis of, among other aspects, what ought to be learned, in which context or under which conditions it is learned, and by whom it is learned. Researchers in the field of instructional design carefully investigate the conditions under which particular methods yield desired effects and organize those methods in instructional design models or theories. In this chapter, we will first sketch the new learning landscape in terms of changes in contents, changes in contexts, and changes in learners. Then, we will briefly

Educational Technology Expertise Center, Open University of The Netherlands

J. Visser and M. Visser-Valfrey (eds.), *Learners in a Changing Learning Landscape*,   69
© Springer Science+Business Media B.V. 2008

discuss the implications for selecting instructional methods, that is, the implications for the field of instructional design.

4.1 Changing What is Learned

In order to deal with rapid societal and technological changes, people more than ever need problem-solving and reasoning skills that allow them to deal with new, unfamiliar situations in their professional and everyday life. This focus on complex skills or professional competencies implies the integration of knowledge, skills, and attitudes in such a way that transfer of learning is enhanced. Thus, learning is no longer primarily about reaching specific learning objectives, but about the ability to flexibly apply what has been learned in new problem situations.

These changes determine a shift away from the traditional instructional design paradigm, which can be defined along the following five dimensions: (a) from well-structured towards ill-structured problems; (b) from domain-specific towards domain-general competencies; (c) from cognitive towards metacognitive processes; (d) from 'expert-novice' towards 'expert-expert' performance mappings, and (e) from specific learning objectives towards authentic reference situations. Instructional design typically begins with defining learning outcomes, then identifies the cognitive processes and structures involved in achieving these outcomes, determines the relevant methods and techniques to activate these cognitive and personality dispositions, and finally measures the effects of the instructional arrangements according to particular criteria. Defining learning outcomes is related to analyzing possible reference situations for a particular educational program, which contains a set of ill-structured problems. This means confronting learners with authentic real-life situations and constructing a set of ill-structured learning tasks representing these situations. The question, however, is not only to involve learners in solving ill-structured problems but also to provide them with necessary and sufficient operational support, which is matched to the individual needs and preferences of learners. Learning to cope with ill-structured learning tasks requires not only domain-specific knowledge and skills but also domain-general competencies. Domain-general competencies are based on metacognitive strategies that operate on the cognitive structure and processes, which themselves are bound up with domain-specific knowledge and skills. Observing and comparing the performances of high profile professionals provides valuable information for the ways these experts behave in ill-structured problem situations, which can be used for modeling instruction in the most effective way.

The direction in the five dimensions is an attempt of the instructional design paradigm to react adequately to the scale, rate and dynamicity of the changes that the society is experiencing nowadays (see J. Visser's argumentation on the nature of change, in this volume, pp. 17–19). With regard to the five dimensions, it should be clear that the changes along the dimensions imply an extension rather than a replacement, the poles are inclusive rather than exclusive. Thus, whereas ill-structured problems become increasingly important, this does *not* imply that well-structured problems are of no interest to the field of instructional design anymore. Ill-structured situations contain some routine or recurrent procedures as well. They are important pre-conditions for handling complex, non-routine skills. The same argumentation, emphasizing inclusiveness rather than exclusiveness, applies to the other four dimensions. Furthermore, the 'novel' poles of the dimension are not new in the sense that they have never been studied before. What is new is that they now have the highest priority in order to address current societal and technological developments. The following sections briefly explore each of the five change dimensions in the instructional design paradigm.

4.1.1 From Well-Structured to Ill-Structured Problems

The capability of solving problems is widely recognized as the most important competence that students should acquire to behave adequately in various professional contexts (Ge & Land, 2004; Jonassen, 2004; Merrill, 2002). Current theories of problem solving mostly reflect the results of research conducted on well-structured problems, while "...ill-structured problems are ill understood" (Pretz, Naples, & Sternberg, 2003, p. 9). The focus on ill-structured problems is determined by the new challenges, which the society faces nowadays (see J. Visser's argumentation for the new societal and technological problems, challenges and opportunities, in this volume, pp. 19–21). Ill-structured problems are characterized by the availability of incomplete data or insufficient access to information; the existence of alternative and often conflicting approaches; the lack of a clear-cut problem-solving procedure; no agreement on what can be accepted as an appropriate solution, and a solution that may not always be recognizable as such (Jonassen, 2004; Schön, 1996). Another distinguishing feature of ill-structured problem solving is the combination of multi-contextual influences and dynamics of uncertainty (Mirel, 2004). Often, the problem solver has to take different perspectives on a problem before finding one that gives insights into viable solution paths (Pretz et al., 2003).

Recent research points out that different intellectual skills are needed for solving well-structured problems, which rely on *applicative* or recurrent skills that are highly domain-specific, and ill-structured problems, which rely not only on applicative but also on *interpretive* or non-recurrent skills that are less domain-specific (Cho & Jonassen, 2002; Hong, Jonassen, & McGee, 2003; Van Merriënboer, 1997). In this respect, the meaning of domain-specific and domain-general competencies is also changing because the combination of both is needed to solve ill-structured problems.

4.1.2 From Domain-Specific to Domain-General Competencies

Domain-specific knowledge, skills, and attitudes are a substantial part of professional competence. But sometimes they are not sufficient for adequately responding to the challenges posed by ill-structured problem situations. Then, another type of competencies is required to manage the problem-solving process, in particular, the analysis of the problem situation, the generation of alternative solutions, the selection of the most appropriate solution for the given situation, and its implementation into practice. Pretz et al. (2003) describe these domain-general competencies as 'metacognitive' components of professional competence. This is indicated by the fact that these components emphasize the regulation, monitoring, and control of problem-solving activities to make the best use of technical, domain-specific knowledge and skills (Chambres, Izaute, & Marescaux, 2002; Metcalfe & Shimamura, 1996; Zimmerman & Campillo, 2003).

Domain-general competencies may prevent the negative effects of *functional fixedness* (Davidson, 2003; De Bono, 1990; Gick & Holyoak, 1983; Holyoak & Thagard, 1995; Keane, 1997; Weisberg & Alba, 1981) and *analysis-paralysis* (Von Wodtke, 1993), which are often present in ill-structured problem solving. Functional fixedness reflects the hindering effect of past experiences on problem solving, emphasizing the negative role of a problem-solving strategy that works well for certain tasks, but not for other tasks. When functionally fixed, people tend to look for existing solutions and easily jump to conclusions, completely ignoring the opportunity to identify better solutions. Analysis-paralysis is the tendency to spend unlimited time on analyzing the problem situation and generating ideas, with an inability to select among alternative solutions, draw conclusions, and plan the next steps in the problem-solving process. In an experimental study, conducted recently, we found that domain-general problem solving support generated a significant difference in the problem-solving production of people confronted with an ill-structured situation. The data also provided evidence that domain-general support, which applied brainstorming with only a remote and postponed reference to the problem, was more effective than brainstorming with a direct reference to the problem. Domain-general support produced qualitatively better solutions that were more original.

No significant difference between the two types of problem solving domain-general support was found in relation to the number of ideas (fluency), although mean figures of the brainstorming with a direct reference to the problem were higher (Stoyanov & Kirschner, 2007).

The results of this study can be explained by different cognitive processes that underlie domain-specific and domain-general problem solving competencies. The next section focuses on these structures and processes while paying special attention to 'the paradox of knowledge structure.'

4.1.3   From Cognitive to Metacognitive Processes

Most research on problem solving refers to the limited capacity of working memory as the most important cognitive factor to deal with (Hambrick & Engle, 2003; Kirschner, 2002; Paas, Renkl, & Sweller, 2004; Van Merriënboer & Sweller, 2005). However, several cognitive theories emphasize the crucial role of long-term memory as well (Lubart & Mouchiroud, 2003; Robertson, 2001; Wenke & Frensch, 2003).

Whereas long-term memory may be unlimited in terms of storing information elements, the retrieval of relevant information elements may cause problems in ill-structured problem-solving situations. Then, the information might actually be available but not be accessible, which affects problem-solving performance of both novices and experts. Most of the issues related to the role of long-term memory in ill-structured problem situations and the negative problem solving effects such as functional fixedness, dominant thinking patterns, routine expertise, and negative transfer, can be explained by the 'paradox of knowledge structure.' A recent study provided empirical evidence for the existence of this phenomenon (Stoyanov & Kirschner, 2007). The 'paradox of knowledge structure' states that the structure of knowledge both enables and restricts ill-structured problem solving. Knowledge organizes itself in knowledge structures (patterns, schemas), which are absolutely necessary for successful problem solving. They are easily recognizable, repeatable, give rise to expectancy, provide useful short-cuts to the solutions, and offer a platform for interpreting incoming information and communicating new solutions.

Knowledge structures, however, may have a detrimental effect that hinder problem solving, especially in ill-structured situations. A knowledge structure can establish a dominance, which forces the problem solver to see and follow only one path and not be aware of other possibilities (Anderson, 1983; De Bono, 1990; Quillian, 1988). People tend to quickly pick and apply a dominant problem-solving schema without investigating the problem situation for possible alternative solutions. Because of that, individuals are prone to select an inappropriate schema. Once a knowledge structure presents itself, the tendency is for it to get larger and more firmly established. This makes it very difficult to break off and jump into an alternative line. A person with insufficient knowledge structures might be unable to look at the information in a meaningful way, but a person with strong knowledge structures might not be able to look at the information in a new way.

Recent research on experts' problem solving performance in ill-structured situations emphasizes the crucial role of meta-cognitive knowledge and strategies for regulation, monitoring and control of problem solving activities, which could prevent the negative effects of the 'paradox of knowledge structure' (Jonassen, 2004; Pretz et al., 2003; Zimmerman & Campillo, 2003). Metacognitive processes operate on the internal representations of the problem solver, such as cognitive schemas, mental models, and plans. Metacognition emphasizes two essential functions: self-management and self-appraisal (Paris & Winograd, 1990). Self-management refers to 'metacognition in action,' that is, operational support of problem solving in terms of analysis of the problem situation, idea generation, idea selection, and solution implementation. Self-appraisal refers to self-reflections on cognitive and affective processes in a problem-solving situation. Awareness about the existence of the 'paradox of knowledge structure' is metacognitive knowledge. The next step is successfully managing this phenomenon, i.e. promoting the enabling part and suppressing the restricting part.

Studies on expertise provide evidence that the 'paradox of knowledge structure' should be attributed to not only novices but to the high profile professionals as well (Ericsson & Kintsch, 1995; Ericsson, 2003; Holyoak, 1991). High levels of domain knowledge can sometimes be an impediment to problem solving limiting the search space to readily available ideas.

4.1.4 From Expert-Novice to Expert-Expert Mappings

Research on expert-novice differences has been very fruitful to determine cognitive factors that play a role in the acquisition of expertise (Chase & Simon, 1973; Chi, Feltovich, & Glaser, 1981; De Groot & Gobet, 1996; Frensch & Sternberg, 1989). Comparing the performances of experts in different professional domains has equally proven valuable (see Ericsson, 2003; Ericsson & Charness, 1994). Holyoak (1991) identified issues in expert performance that cannot easily be explained by findings from classical novice-expert research: Experts do not always easily accomplish what novices accomplish with difficulties; expert search strategies are extremely varied and often opportunistic; expert performance does not show continuous improvement with practice; knowledge can sometimes be transferred across domains; the teaching of expert rules often does not lead to expertise; expertise depends on induction, retrieval, and instantiation of schematic knowledge structures rather than the acquisition and use of highly specific production rules, and skilled performance depends on the parallel integration of multiple sources of information rather than serial information processing.

It has become clear that not only novices but also experts need specific support to improve their performance (Stoyanov & Kirschner, 2004). Investigating what makes one expert better than another expert in ill-structured problem situations is a valuable research target in the field of learning and instruction. Such research may identify specific skills and underlying cognitive and metacognitive processes, such as factors related to 'deliberate practice' (Ericsson, 2003), which may have important consequences for instructional design.

4.1.5 From Learning Objectives to Authentic Reference Situations

The formulation of learning objectives has always been a critical part of the instructional design process. Traditional design models analyze a learning domain in terms of distinct objectives, after which instructional methods are selected for reaching each of the separate objectives. This often yields instruction that is fragmented and piecemeal (Van Merriënboer, Clark, & de Croock, 2002). Holistic design models (e.g., Van Merriënboer & Kirschner, 2007) stress the importance of highly integrated sets of objectives, and reference situations are used to ask the learner to demonstrate that such an integrated set of objectives has been reached. The real-life reference situation puts learning objectives in a broader context and makes them meaningful. Integrated sets of objectives should thus be formulated as a reference to real-life contexts, in which learners have to apply their acquired knowledge, skills, and attitudes to perform authentic tasks, thus promoting far transfer.

To conclude this section, it is important to stress that developments in 'what is learned' must have clear implications for instruction. Nowadays, there is an increasing emphasis on whole, meaningful learning tasks as the driving force for learning (Merrill, 2002; Van Merriënboer & Sweller, 2005). Instructional methods primarily pertain to experiential learning in real or simulated task environments, and include the design of learning tasks or learning experiences, the sequencing of those experiences, and ways to scaffold the learning process (see Van Merriënboer, Kirschner, & Kester, 2003). As a rule, the learning tasks are ill-structured and allow for several acceptable solutions. They make a strong appeal to domain-general skills that sustain problem solving and reasoning. Problem sequencing and scaffolding help learners to develop expert approaches, which also ask for "metacognitive" skills that allow for independent learning, such as information problem solving, self-assessment and self-regulation skills, and learning-to-learn. And finally, assessment of complex task performance is not based on distinct learning objectives but on the learner's ability to integrate knowledge, skills, and attitudes in such a way that real-life problems are effectively dealt with in a specified set of reference situations.

4.2   Changing Contexts

In addition to changes in what is learned, there are also major changes in the contexts in which learning nowadays occurs. Time- and place-independent learning in technology-rich, informal and professional settings is becoming general practice. Maybe even more important, modern society and education are developing from a production economy to a service economy, where educational services are available on-demand and customized for the individual learner ('mass individualization'). These changes in context have important implications for our thinking about the delicate relationship between instruction and technology, or, methods and media.

4.2.1   Time- and Place-Independent Learning

Changing contexts result, among other factors, from new technologies that allow for time- and place-independent learning. In modern societies, people have 24-hour opportunities to connect to other people and to vast information resources through mobile phones, MP3 players, Personal Digital Assistants, laptop computers, and devices for ubiquitous computing, ambient intelligence, and augmented intelligence. These technologies have built-in affordances that allow for the realization of many instructional methods that sustain a wide range of different types of learning. The conspicuous consequences are that people learn more and more in out-of-school contexts, at all stages in their life ('lifelong learning'), and in ever-changing, highly heterogeneous groups of learners.

With regard to learning outside school, there is a remarkable increase of learning activities in informal and in professional settings. There are at least three causes for this phenomenon. First, as already discussed above, the combination of professional and domain-general competencies is becoming increasingly important in our society. Real-life settings are indispensable for learning those competencies (Merrill, 2002). Second, due to fast technological and societal changes, domain-specific knowledge and skills are quickly becoming obsolete. Thus, there is an obvious need to regularly update those knowledge and skills and learn outside school. Third, learning outside school is facilitated by the availability of new technologies, which enable learners to study materials, consult others, and discuss with peers anywhere, anytime.

A strongly related issue is the upsurge of lifelong learning, reflecting the idea that it is never too soon or too late for learning. Lifelong learning, often in non-formal settings, is becoming a necessity to survive in a society in which jobs and technologies quickly change. The idea of informal lifelong learning is very close conceptually to the definition of learning as a natural drive and a human disposition towards adapting to the constantly changing environment (see definition of learning and four level of adaptive behavior by J. Visser, in this volume, pp. 15–16). Learning is becoming a constant attribute of personal human life, not only for adapting but also for pleasure, satisfying curiosity, and, in terms of Maslow (1970), self-actualization and self-fulfillment. Instructional design focuses more on creating conditions in formal educational settings for enhancing lifelong learning, as informal activity, to accomplish personal aspirations and social goals in the most effective and efficient way. This raises new questions for the field of education and instructional design (European Commission, 2000). Some research questions are directly related to changes in what is learned and changes in contexts, for instance, which new competencies are needed for lifelong learning (new basic skills) and how can new technologies help to realize time- and place-independent lifelong learning (ICT tools)? Other questions are related to necessary changes in instructional methods, such as which new instructional methods are suitable to sustain lifelong learning (learning innovations) and how should lifelong learners be given proper help and advice (guidance)? Finally, new research questions pertain to societal and organizational changes, such as how can it be ensured that people have time and means for lifelong learning (human resource development) and how can lifelong learning be valued and reinforced by organizations and the society at large (valuing learning)?

With regard to groups in which learning takes place, there are also major changes. Rather than participating in one-and-the-same year group for a relatively long period of time, learners increasingly participate in more than one learning network, and the composition of those networks continuously changes. The typical composition of such learning networks is heterogeneous, including learners with different cultural and professional backgrounds, prior knowledge, and learning goals. In addition, rather than one teacher there may be several people in the network taking on roles related to teaching, such as a tutor-role, an expert-role, a coaching-role, and so forth. Probably the most conspicuous development is that learning networks are often virtual. For instance, they may take the form of Web-based learning communities. Wenger (1998) discusses learning communities as one kind of "community of practice", which is a social construct that places learning in the "...context of our lived experience of participation in the world" (p. 3). Web-based learning communities and communities of practice are sometimes seen as a new paradigm for learning in the 21st century. Interestingly enough, this development into the direction of communities goes hand in hand with a further development of individualized and personalized instruction.

4.2.2   On-Demand Education

In the last decades, new technologies 'technically' enabled the individualization of instruction. Nevertheless, up until now individualization in education has not been very successful because highly individualized learning trajectories can only be realized if the number of *possible* trajectories is very large. Thus, there is the need to develop a large amount of learning tasks and instructional materials beforehand in order to make individualization possible—and this threatens its cost-effectiveness. Only since the upsurge of Web technologies it has become possible to develop instruction for very large target groups. And thanks to the combination of technologies and large groups individualization is now not only technically feasible, but also becoming cost-effective. This process is known as 'mass individualization' or 'mass customization', and may be expected to yield an enormous increase in the flexibility of education (Schellekens, Paas, & Van Merriënboer, 2003). Traditional mass media (books, television and radio) are more and more intertwined and replaced with personalized media that provide adaptive online learning, that is, information and support that is tailored to the particular needs and preferences of individual users and learners.

Salden, Paas, and Van Merriënboer (2006; see also Van Merriënboer & Luursema, 1996) discuss adaptive online learning with a focus on the dynamic selection of learning tasks. They describe adaptive learning as a straightforward two-step cycle: (1) assessment of learner characteristics, and (2) the selection of learning tasks of a particular difficulty and a particular level of provided support. Three types of models can be distinguished.

- In system-controlled models, some educational agent (teacher, online learning application) selects the optimal learning task for a particular learner from all available tasks.
- In shared responsibility models, some educational agent selects a suitable subset of learning tasks for a particular learner from all available tasks, after which the learner makes, on-demand, a final selection from this subset. Thus, there is partial system control (i.e., selecting the subset) and partial learner control (i.e., selecting the final task).

- In on-demand advisory models, an educational agent may or may not select a suitable subset of tasks, but the learner is advised on his or her selection of the next task to work on.

With regard to system-controlled models, Kalyuga and Sweller (2005) conducted a study in the domain of algebra in which both the level of difficulty and the given support for the next task were adapted to the mental efficiency of the learner. In the adaptive group, learners were presented with algebra tasks at three different difficulty levels. If their cognitive efficiency was negative for tasks at the lowest level, they continued with the study of worked examples; if their cognitive efficiency was positive for tasks at the lowest level but negative for tasks at the second level, they continued with simple completion tasks (i.e., they had to complete a partially given solution); if their cognitive efficiency was positive for tasks at the lowest and second level but negative for tasks at the third level, they continued with difficult completion tasks, and, finally, if their cognitive efficiency was positive for tasks at all three levels, they continued with conventional problems. Each learner in the adaptive condition was paired to a learner in the control condition, who served as a yoked control. As expected, higher gains in algebraic skills from pre-test to post-test and higher gains in cognitive efficiency were found for the adaptive group than for the control group.

A drawback of system-controlled models is that (1) learners have no opportunity to learn how to select their own learning tasks and plan their own learning, and (2) the lack of any freedom of choice over tasks may negatively affect learners' motivation. With regard to the first point, a gradual transfer of responsibility over task selection from the system to the learner, as his or her self-regulation skills further develop, may be desirable. A first pilot study has been conducted to compare a system-controlled model with a shared-responsibility model on motivation/interest and learning outcomes (Corbalan, Kester, & Van Merriënboer, 2006). Results show that learners in the shared-responsibility group report, as expected, a higher interest in the training and also tend to outperform learners in the system-controlled group. With regard to the second point, research indicates that *some* freedom of choice indeed has positive effects on motivation, but *too much* freedom may lead to stress, high mental effort, and demotivation (Iyengar & Lepper, 2000; Schwartz, 2004). Thus, a shared-responsibility model in which the system makes a pre-selection of suitable tasks, and the learner makes the final selection, is expected to be superior to a completely free on-demand model in which the learner has to select one task from a very large set of available tasks.

Finally, advisory on-demand models may or may not make a pre-selection of tasks but give learners advice on the task-selection process. They explicitly help learners to apply cognitive strategies for assessing their own performance and keeping the scores in a so-called *development portfolio*, for interpreting evaluation results of their performances, for matching evaluation results with the qualities of available learning tasks, for making an informed selection from those tasks, for planning their own work on those learning tasks, and so forth. First, an effective model provides heuristic 'rules-of-thumb' rather than algorithmic rules. This forces learners to reflect on their performance and may facilitate transfer to other learning domains and educational settings. Second, an effective model takes explicated strategies rather than feedback principles as a basis. This may help learners to develop cognitive strategies for regulating their own learning (Kicken, Brand-Gruwel, & Van Merriënboer, 2005).

4.2.3   Technology Versus Instruction

New technologies set high expectations. But in the field of education they typically failed to live up to the expectations. For instance, radio, television and even microcomputers did not greatly affect teaching practices in schools (Clark, 1994; Kozma, 1994; Russell, 2001; WCET, 2006). Internet research agency Gartner group (2002) identified a Hype Cycle representing the maturity, adoption and application of specific technologies, including learning technologies. The Hype Cycle consists of five phases: (1) technology trigger, (2) peak of inflated expectations, (3) disillusionment, (4) slope of enlightenment, and (5) plateau of productivity. Most if not all of the technologies applied for educational purposes go through these stages. But the sad reality is that up until now, most of the learning technologies never reached the final two stages. Some authors argue that this is due to the fact that hardware and software issues have overshadowed more important people issues (Constantine, 2001; Kuniavsky, 2003; Holtzblatt, Wendell, & Wood, 2005). Nowadays, a shift toward people issues can be observed in the use-case movement, contextual design, and scenario building—but probably the most remarkable achievement is the concept of peopleware (Constantine, 2001; De Marco & Lister, 1999), which includes the whole range of people issues from gathering user experiences to managing teams of designers.

"Good software does not come from use-case tools, visual programming, rapid prototyping, or object technology. Good software comes from people. So does bad software" (Constantine, 2001, p. xvii). The main difficulty in designing software applications for educational and training purposes is conceptual and not technological in nature. The potential added value is not in the new technology or medium itself, but in their combination with appropriate instructional methods. New technologies and media are neither the problem nor the solution for instructional design. The promise that new technologies and media are a panacea for problems in the field of learning and instruction merely generates a feeling of 'deja vu all over again.' Online learning is neither good nor bad. As indicated by Spector in this volume, combined with the wrong methods "...online teaching [is] as an alien ritual performed by people wearing masks whispering in the dark" (p. 262). Only combined with appropriate instructional methods it may add value to learning.

Related to the Hype Cycle is the ongoing debate on the so-called non-significant effect of technology on learning (Clark, 1994; Kozma, 1994; Russell, 2001; WCET, 2006). Have new technologies a positive impact on learning or not? Too often, researchers have tried to answer this question without taking instructional methods into account (e.g., is learning from the computer screen better than learning from a book?). A better approach might be to study the conditions under which particular media-method combinations have an effect on learning, including not only a broad range of learning outcomes (recall, application, transfer) but also invested time, mental effort, and satisfaction. Then, it will probably show that 'high tech' in learning does not necessarily lead to positive effects. In contrast, it is the 'high touch' that makes the difference: The amount of personal attention, involvement and interaction are key and technology, whether high tech or low tech, must be placed in their service (Spitzer, 2002).

To conclude this section, contextual changes clearly affect the use of instructional methods. On the one hand, online learning makes experiential learning in simulated task environments only possible to a certain degree. That is, it should be perfectly clear that online learning alone would never be sufficient to educate medical doctors, who need to practice with patients of flesh and blood; lawyers, who need to practice in real courts of justice; or carpenters, who need to practice with real wood and tools. But, on the other hand, more and more instructional methods can be realized in online tools and mobile devices, and new media-method combinations emerge with their own specific affordances. For instance, methods that stimulate learners to construct knowledge may use the interactive possibilities of hypermedia; methods that help learners to learn from each other may take form in Web-based learning communities, and methods that aim at the just-in-time provision of information during professional task performance may take advantage of mobile technologies (e.g., presenting operating instructions on-demand on a mobile phone, PDA, or augmented reality glasses). Furthermore, the selection of instructional methods will no longer be based on the general characteristics of a whole 'target group' but on the specific characteristics of an individual learner.

4.3   Changing Learners

This brings us to the topic of the changing learner. At an abstract level, it is tempting to assert the emergence of the 'online learner,' a new species that is directing its own learning, that is focusing on the development of flexible problem-solving skills, that is having a rich mix of (online) media at its disposition, and that is expecting instruction that is fully tailored to its personal needs. But at the individual level, differences *between* individual learners may have far greater implications for the selection of instructional methods than the emergence of the so-called online learner. The following sections explore the implications for instruction of changes in learners' age, prior knowledge and experience, and learning styles.

4.3.1   The Older Learner

Lifelong learning will evidently mean that more and more elderly people become involved in both formal and informal learning. A substantial body of research has demonstrated that cognitive aging is accompanied by a reduction of working-memory capacity, a general slowing of mental processes, and a decline of the ability to process irrelevant information (for a review, see Reuben-Lorenz, 2002). Van Gerven, Paas, Van Merriënboer, and Schmidt (2000) relate these phenomena to cognitive load theory (Sweller, Van Merriënboer, & Paas, 1998; Van Merriënboer & Sweller, 2005), the core idea of which is that working-memory capacity is limited and should therefore be managed with great care. The theory claims that this can be achieved by minimizing the level of so-called extraneous cognitive load, which is the portion of load that does not directly contribute to learning (e.g., because it is allocated to integrating information sources, searching for information, weak-method problem solving, etc.), and maximizing the level of germane cognitive load, which directly contributes to learning (e.g., constructing cognitive schemas, automation). Since instructions based on cognitive load theory deal with cognitive limitations in that they lead to an efficient use of the available resources, it can be hypothesized that they are especially effective when elderly people are involved.

A first set of studies tested this hypothesis by comparing learning by studying worked examples with learning by solving conventional problems (Van Gerven, Paas, Van Merriënboer, & Schmidt, 2002). According to cognitive load theory, novices in a domain learn more from studying worked examples than from solving the equivalent problems because the latter impose a high extraneous cognitive load. Due to the cognitive limitations of older learners, it is expected that the advantage of worked examples above conventional problems is even larger for them than for young learners. As predicted, the results of Van Gerven et al. show that especially for older learners (above 60 years), who are novice in a domain, the efficiency of studying worked examples is higher than the efficiency of solving conventional problems, in that less training time and cognitive load leads to a comparable level of performance.

Another set of studies was specifically concerned with online learning (Van Gerven, Paas, Van Merriënboer, Hendriks, & Schmidt, 2003). Often online learning involves multimedia where learners study an animation or picture that is explained by a text. Such presentations can be either unimodal, when both animation/picture and the (written) text are presented visually, or multimodal, when the animation/picture is presented visually but the (spoken) text is presented in auditory mode. Multimodal instruction is expected to be superior to unimodal instruction, because it uses both the visual and auditory subsystems of working memory and so increases the effectively available working-memory capacity. Furthermore, older learners are expected to profit more from multimodal instruction than younger learners. The results of Van Gerven et al. indeed show an interaction of modality and age on cognitive load, indicating that older learners have a disproportional large advantage from the multimodal instruction. Summarizing, there is growing evidence that effective instructional methods for older online learners are different from effective methods for younger online learners, due to a significant decrease in working-memory capacity of the elderly.

4.3.2   The Expert Learner

Lifelong learning also implies that more and more learners are not novices in a particular learning domain, but are at various stages of expertise development. Recent research indicates that this level of expertise is a major factor to be taken into account when selecting instructional methods. Kalyuga, Ayres, Chandler, and Sweller (2003) provide a review of research results on the 'expertise reversal effect,' which indicates that instructional methods that are effective for low-expertise learners are often ineffective for high-expertise learners, and vice versa. For example, Kalyuga, Chandler, and Sweller (1998), using novices, demonstrated the so-called split-attention effect: Students who were presented diagrams and text in a format that separated the two sources of information learned less than students given materials that integrated the texts into the diagrams. Physical integration reduced the need for mental integration and reduced extraneous cognitive load. As levels of expertise increased, the difference between the separate and integrated conditions first disappeared and eventually reversed with the separate condition superior to the integrated condition. Indeed, rather than integrating the diagrams and text, totally eliminating the text was superior. The text had become redundant for these more expert learners.

Initially, using complete novices, both the diagrams and text were essential for learning. Under such conditions, extraneous cognitive load could be reduced by physically integrating the two sources of information in order to reduce the need for learners to mentally integrate them. Reducing the need for mental integration reduces extraneous cognitive load. As expertise increased, the textual explanations became less and less important. Eventually they were unnecessary, but if presented to learners with more experience in the area in an integrated format, they were hard to ignore. Processing such redundant information imposed an extraneous cognitive load for these more expert learners, thus reducing their learning. The redundancy effect had replaced the split-attention effect as expertise increased, providing an example of the expertise reversal effect.

Similar results were obtained by Yeung, Jin, and Sweller (1998) using purely textual materials. McNamara, Kintsch, Songer, and Kintsch (1996) found that low-knowledge learners benefited from additional explanatory text intended to increase coherence whereas high-knowledge individuals benefited most from the sparser text. Kalyuga, Chandler, and Sweller (2000) found that among novices, dual mode, auditory/visual presentations were superior to visual only presentations, demonstrating the modality effect. With more experience, the auditory component became redundant and was best eliminated. Using novices Tuovinen and Sweller (1999), and Kalyuga, Chandler, Tuovinen, and Sweller (2001) demonstrated the worked example effect in which worked examples were superior to solving the equivalent problems. With increasing knowledge, the effect first disappeared and then reversed. Worked examples become redundant for more knowledgeable learners and so impose an extraneous cognitive load. All these examples of the expertise reversal effect have strong implications for the design of instruction and indicate that instructional methods for learners with relevant prior knowledge are different from methods for learners without relevant expertise.

4.3.3   The 'Gaming Generation'

A common claim is that young learners learn in new ways and have new conceptions and styles of learning. They would be better able to learn by trial-and-error, to seek helpful resources, to try out solutions, and so forth. This may be true for a subgroup of young learners, but research also points out that there are surprisingly large differences in students' perceptions of instructional methods and learning environments. For instance, Könings, Brand-Gruwel, and Van Merriënboer (2005) studied the perceptions of young Dutch students (13–16 years of age) who were confronted with an educational innovation, characterized by the use of meaningful learning tasks, more independent learning, and individualization. Whereas some students perceived this innovation as desirable and an impetus for their learning, others perceived it as undesirable and not helpful at all for promoting their learning.

The differences in the perceptions of students can, among other things, be a function of either their level of achievement (low vs. high) or their cognitive style. It is important to make a clear distinction between *level* (how much?) and *style* (in what way?) constructs. Level-type constructs are, for instance, abilities, knowledge, skills, and competencies. Style-type constructs are, for instance, learning styles and cognitive styles. Styles should also be distinguished from process constructs (e.g., learning or problem solving strategies). Actually, different levels and styles can be identified during different stages of a process. Style and behavior are not necessarily in agreement with each other. People are capable of behaving differently from their preferred style—but this is always at the expense of more invested effort, energy and time. In an experimental study on the effects of type of problem solving support and cognitive styles (innovator vs. adaptor) on ill-structured problem solving, we did not find a significant difference of the cognitive style for problem solving on the originality of ideas (Stoyanov & Kirschner, 2007). The results confirmed the hypothesis that styles are about preferences, not about level. Both cognitive styles were capable to generate original ideas, none of them was better than the other, but learners with different cognitive styles solved problems in different manners. It was the type of problem solving support that explained the substantial part of the variations in problem solving production. The same study supported the hypothesis related to coping behavior. The participants in the experiment performed equally well in both preferential and compensation conditions. Effective, efficient and flexible learning requires not only the application of learning strategies consonant with the preferred style, but also the ability to shift to less congenial learning styles when these are more effective in a particular situation.

Elaborating on these results, we recently started a project aimed at developing and testing an integrated instructional approach that combines two theoretical perspectives on adaptation: adapting instructional strategies to style (style-strategy interaction) and adapting them to achievement (achievement-strategy interaction). In the theoretical model of the study, learning style is defined according to the theoretical tradition that makes an extensive empirical validation to distinguish style, level, and process constructs (De Ciantis & Kirton, 1996; Honey & Mumford, 1992; Kirton, 2003). The integrated style-by-strategy/achievement-by-strategy approach will be tested against preferential adaptive approaches (i.e., chosen strategy is the preferred one for a student's style) as well as compensatory adaptive approaches (i.e., chosen strategy compensates for the weaknesses of the student's style). The integrated instructional approach supports students to build a learning strategy that is oriented towards learning to solve ill-structured problems. The learning resources are designed to accommodate the strong features of a particular learning style, to compensate for the weak characteristics of this style, and to continuously take the learner's level of performance into account.

To summarize, adapting instruction to learner's differences in achievement or differences in style have been considered as two confronting positions for a long time. But recent investigations show that it is possible and desirable to adapt instruction to the needs of individual learners by taking both their style and their achievement into account: Style-by-strategy and achievement-by-strategy interactions complement each other and should not be considered separately. This flexible approach allows instructional designers to develop adaptive instruction that is effective and appealing for many groups of learners, including the 'gaming generation'.

4.4 Discussion and Implications

The learning landscape is drastically changing in terms of what is learned, the contexts in which learning takes place, and who is learning. The field of instructional design has to reflect these changes in its research agenda and propose adequate solutions. First of all, instructional designers must become *aware* of the major changes in the learning landscape. This is not a trivial issue. In the practical field, it is not uncommon for designers and teachers to apply instructional design models that were developed in the 1970s and 1980s—models that do no longer meet today's requirements. Second, instructional designers must develop a research agenda that enables the development of instructional design models and guidelines that fit the new learning landscape.

Traditional instructional design models focus on one particular domain of learning such as procedural, declarative or attitudinal learning (compartmentalization); they typically divide this learning domain in small parts (fragmentation), and they focus on the realization of specific learning objectives rather than transfer of learning (transfer paradox). These models cannot deal with current changes in what is learned, that is, the movement towards ill-structured problem solving, domain-general competencies, expert learning, metacognitive skills, and broad reference situations. New models are needed, which use real-life learning tasks as the driving force for learning. These learning tasks are somewhere on the continuum from ill-structured to well-structured problems, and different types of learning tasks might be identified that involve different cognitive and metacognitive processes. These different types of tasks would require different instructional arrangements in terms of sequencing, scaffolding, and information support.

With regard to the context in which learning takes place, time- and place-independent learning, outside school, lifelong, in heterogeneous groups is becoming general practice. On the one hand, this enables the development of communities of practice such as web-based learning communities. On the other hand, individualization and personalization of instruction becomes cost-effective due to the fact that a very large—potential—target group is dealt with. The main message for instructional design is not to be obsessed by new technologies and media. E-learning, for instance, refers to a motley collection of methods (presenting text on the screen, asking ready-made questions, showing video clips and animations, evoking discussions in asynchronous and synchronous discussion groups, engaging learners in highly interactive games and simulations, etc.) that invoke very different types of learning. This is not helpful to generate valuable research questions. Instead, the field of instructional design must focus on particular media-method combinations and carefully investigate the conditions under which those combinations yield desired outcomes.

With regard to the learners in the new learning landscape, notions such as "the online learner" are also too general to be helpful for doing research in instructional design. It suggests a homogeneity that simply does not exist. Effective instructional methods for different subgroups of online learners (e.g., young vs. old, high- vs. low-expertise, and positive vs. negative perceptions) seem to be much more diverse than the difference between methods for so-called online learners and 'traditional' learners. Moreover, what we need to develop for the future are not instructional methods for an intangible group of online learners, but methods that are tailored to the personal needs of individual learners. Only then will we be serious in putting the learner at the center of the learning environment, whether it is online or not.

To summarize, the new learning landscape is characterized by more emphasis on complex skills and higher-order skills; by new technologies that allow for flexible time- and place-independent learning as in Web-based learning communities, and by better opportunities to adapt instructional methods to individual learner characteristics such as age, level of expertise, learning styles, and perceptions. High-quality instructional design research is badly needed and should focus on the question which instructional methods or media-method combinations are effective, efficient and appealing for teaching complex and higher-order skills, in a highly flexible fashion, and by taking learners' individual needs and preferences into account.

4.5   Resources for Further Exploration

- Claxton, G. (1999). *Wise up: The challenge of lifelong learning.* New York: Bloomsbury. British psychologist and educator Guy Claxton advocates direct immersion, soft thinking, and imagination as useful tools for lifelong learning. A refreshing view on education in the 21st century.
- Jonassen, D. H. (2004). *Learning to solve problems: An Instructional design guide.* San Francisco: Pfeiffer. This book by David Jonassen stresses that problem solving is the most important skill students can learn in any setting. The main

thesis is that different types of problems require different instructional design solutions.

- Spector, J. M., Ohrazda, C., van Schaack, A., & Wiley, D. A. (2005). *Innovations in instructional technology: Essays in honor of M. David Merrill*. Mahwah, NJ: Lawrence Erlbaum. This thought provoking set of essays on learning, instructional design and learning technologies deals with innovations and future directions in instructional technology. With an epilogue by David Merrill himself.
- http://www.nosignificantdifference.org/. This website is a repository of studies that found no significant difference in student outcomes between alternate modes of education delivery. Based on the work by Thomas L. Russell.

4.6   Questions for Comprehension and Application

1. This chapter discussed major changes in what people learn in our modern society, with an increasing focus on problem solving, domain-general competencies and metacognition. What are in your view the main causes for these changes and the main implications for the design of instruction?
2. The 'paradox of prior knowledge' states that past experiences both enable and restrict the quality of problem solving in new problem situations. Under which conditions dominate, in your opinion, either the enabling effects or the restricting effects of prior knowledge? Explain your answer.
3. This chapter discussed the technology hype cycle. Discuss at least three learning technologies and their development according to the hype cycle. Is there a particular learning technology you expect to reach the last phase of the cycle in the near future? Why do you think so?
4. Suppose you have to design a workshop on presentation skills for both an experienced group of older bank employees and a group of high school students from the 'gaming generation.' On which aspects would the workshops for the two groups differ from each other?

References

Anderson, J. (1983). *The architecture of cognition*. Harvard, MA: Harvard University Press.

Chambres, P., Izaute, M., & Marescaux, J. P. (Eds.) (2002). *Metacognition: Process, function and use*. London: Kluwer.

Chase, W., & Simon, H. (1973). Perception in chess. *Cognitive Psychology, 4*, 55–81.

Chi, M., Feltovich, P., & Glaser, R. (1981). Categorization and representation of physics problems by experts and novices. *Cognitive Science, 5*, 121–151.

Cho, K., & Jonassen, D. (2002). The effects of argumentation scaffolds on argumentation and problem solving. *Educational Technology, Research and Development, 50*(3), 5–22.

Clark, R. (1994). Media will never influence learning. *Educational Technology, Research and Development, 42*(2), 21–29.

Constantine, L. (2001). *The peopleware papers. Notes on the human side of software.* Upper Saddle River, NJ: Prentice-Hall.

Corbalan, G., Kester, L., & Van Merriënboer, J. J. G. (2006). Towards a personalized task selection model with shared instructional control. *Instructional Science, 34*(5), 399–422.

Davidson, J. (2003). Insights about insightful problem solving. In J. Davidson & R. Sternberg (Eds.), *The psychology of problem solving* (pp. 149–175). New York: Cambridge University Press.

De Bono, E. (1990). *Lateral thinking for management.* London: Penguin Books.

De Ciantis, S., & Kirton, M. (1996). A psychometric reexamination of Kolb's experiential learning cycle construct: A separation of level, style, and process. *Educational and Psychological Measurement, 56*, 809–820.

De Groot, A., & Gobet, F. (1996). *Perception and memory in chess: Heuristics of the professional eye.* Assen: Van Gorcum.

De Marco, T., & Lister, T. (1999). *Peopleware: Productive projects and teams* (2nd ed.). New York: Dorset House Publishing.

Ericsson, K. (2003). The acquisition of expert performance as problem solving: Construction and modification of mediating mechanisms through deliberate practice. In J. Davidson & R. Sternberg (Eds.), *The psychology of problem solving* (pp. 31–83). New York: Cambridge University Press.

Ericsson, K. A., & Charness, N. (1994). Expert performance. *American Psychologist, 49*(8), 725–748.

Ericsson, K. A., & Kintsch, W. (1995). Long-Term Working Memory. *Psychological Review, 102*, 211–245.

European Commission (2000). *A memorandum on lifelong learning.* Brussels: European Commission.

Frensch, P., & Sternberg, R. (1989). Expertise and intelligent thinking: When it is worse to know better? In R. Sternberg (Ed.), *Advances in the psychology of human intelligence* (Vol. 5, pp. 157–188). Hillsdale, NJ: Lawrence Erlbaum.

Gartner group (2002). *Predicts 2003. Knowledge & content management, collaboration & e-learning.* Retrieved December, 4, 2002, from www3.gartner.com/1_researchanalysis/.

Ge, X., & Land, S. (2004). A Conceptual framework for scaffolding ill-structured problem-solving process using question prompts and peer interaction. *Educational Technology, Research and Development, 52*(2), 5–22.

Gick, M., & Holyoak, K. (1983). Schema induction in analogical transfer. *Cognitive Psychology, 15*, 1–38.

Hambrick, D., & Engle, R. (2003). The role of working memory in problem solving. In J. Davidson & R. Sternberg (Eds.), *The psychology of problem solving* (pp. 207–229). New York: Cambridge University Press.

Holtzblatt, K., Wendell, J., & Wood, S. (2005). *Rapid contextual design.* San Francisco: Morgan Kaufmann.

Holyoak, K. (1991). Symbolic connectionism: Toward third-generation theories of expertise. In A. Ericsson & J. Smith (Eds.), *Toward a general theory of expertise* (pp. 301–335). Cambridge, MA: Cambridge University Press.

Holyoak, K., & Thagard, P. (1995). *Mental leaps.* Cambridge, MA: MIT Press.

Honey, P., &. Mumford, A. (1992). *The manual of learning styles.* Maidenhead, Berkshire: Peter Honey.

Hong, N., Jonassen, D., & McGee, S. (2003). Predictors of well-structured and ill-structured problem solving in an astronomy simulation. *Journal of Research in Science Teaching, 40*(1), 6–33.

Iyengar, S. S., & Lepper, M. R. (2000). When choice is demotivating: Can one desire too much of a good thing? *Journal of Personality & Social Psychology, 79*, 995–1006.

Jonassen, D. H. (2004). *Learning to solve problems. An Instructional design guide.* San Francisco: Pffeifer.

Kalyuga, S., & Sweller, J. (2005). Rapid dynamic assessment of expertise to optimize the efficiency of e-learning. *Educational Technology, Research and Development, 53*(3).

Kalyuga, S., Ayres, P., Chandler, P., & Sweller, J. (2003) The expertise reversal effect. *Educational Psychologist, 38*(1), 23–31.

Kalyuga, S., Chandler, P., & Sweller, J. (1998). Levels of expertise and instructional design. *Human Factors, 40*, 1–17.

Kalyuga, S., Chandler, P., & Sweller, J. (2000). Incorporating learner experience into the design of multimedia instruction. *Journal of Educational Psychology, 92*, 126–136.

Kalyuga, S., Chandler, P., Tuovinen, J., & Sweller, J. (2001). When problem solving is superior to studying worked examples. *Journal of Educational Psychology, 93*, 579–588.

Keane, M. (1997). What makes an analogy difficult? The effect of order and causal structure in analogical mapping. *Journal of Experimental Psychology: Language, Memory & Cognition, 23*, 946–967.

Kicken, W., Brand-Gruwel, S., & Van Merriënboer, J. J. G. (2005, May–June). *Advisering bij het kiezen van leertaken: Veilig op weg naar vraaggestuurd onderwijs [Advice on the selection of learning tasks: A safe approach to on-demand education]*. Paper presented at the OnderwijsResearchDagen (ORD), May 30–June 1, Gent, Belgium.

Kirschner, P. A. (2002). Cognitive load theory: Implications of cognitive load theory for the design of learning. *Learning and Instruction, 4*, 251–262.

Kirton, M. (2003). *Adaption – Innovation in the context of diversity and change*. London: Routledge.

Könings, K. D., Brand-Gruwel, S., & Van Merriënboer, J. J. G. (2005). Towards more powerful learning environments through combining the perspectives of designers, teachers and students. *British Journal of Educational Psychology, 75*, 645–660.

Kozma, R. (1994). Will media influence learning? Reframing the debate. *Educational Technology, Research and Development, 42*(2), 7–19.

Kuniavsky, M. (2003). *Observing the user experience. A practitioner's guide to user research*. San Francisco: Morgan Kaufmann.

Lubart, T., & Mouchiroud, C. (2003). Creativity: A source of difficulty in problem solving. In J. Davidson & R. Sternberg (Eds.), *The psychology of problem solving* (pp. 127–148). New York: Cambridge University Press.

Maslow, A. H. (1970). *Motivation and personality* (2nd ed.). New York: Harper & Row.

McNamara, D., Kintsch, E., Songer, N. B., & Kintsch, W. (1996). Are good texts always better? Interactions of text coherence, background knowledge, and levels of understanding in learning from text. *Cognition and Instruction, 14*, 1–43.

Merrill, M. D. (2002). First principles of instruction. *Educational Technology, Research and Development, 50*(3), 43–59.

Metcalfe, J., & Shimamura, A. (Eds.) (1996). *Metacognition: Knowing about knowing*. Boston: MIT Press.

Mirel, B. (2004). *Interaction design for complex problem solving: Developing useful and usable software*. San Francisco: Morgan Kaufmann.

Paas, F., Renkl, A., & Sweller, J. (2004). Cognitive load theory: Instructional implications of the interaction between information structures and cognitive architecture. *Instructional Science, 32*, 1–8.

Paris, S., & Winograd, P. (1990). How metacognition can promote academic learning and instruction. In B. Jones & L. Idol (Eds.), *Dimensions of thinking and cognitive instruction* (pp. 15–51). Hillsdale, NJ: Lawrence Erlbaum.

Pretz, E., Naples, A., & Sternberg, R. (2003). Recognizing, defining, and representing problems. In J. Davidson & R. Sternberg (Eds.), *The psychology of problem solving* (pp. 3–30). New York: Cambridge University Press.

Quillian, M. (1988). Semantic memory. In A. Collins & E. Smith (Eds.), *Readings in cognitive science: A Perspective from psychology and artificial intelligence* (pp. 80–101). San Mateo, CA: Morgan Kaufman.

Reuben-Lorenz, P. (2002). New visions of the aging mind and brain. *Trends in Cognitive Science, 6*(9), 394–400.

Robertson, S. (2001). *Problem solving*. Sussex: Psychology Press.

Russell, T. (2001). *The no significant difference phenomenon: A comparative research annotated bibliography on technology for distance education* (5th ed.). Montgomery, AL: IDECC.

Salden, R. J. C. M., Paas, F., & Van Merriënboer, J. J. G. (2006). A comparison of approaches to learning task selection in the training of complex cognitive skills. *Computers in Human Behavior*, *22*, 321–333.

Schellekens, A., Paas, F., & Van Merriënboer, J. J. G. (2003). Flexibility in higher professional education: A survey in business administration programmes in the Netherlands. *Higher Education*, *45*(3), 281–305.

Schön, D. (1996). *The reflective practitioner: How professionals think in action*. London: Arena.

Schwartz, B. (2004). *The paradox of choice: Why more is less*. New York: HarperCollins.

Spector, J. M. (in this volume). What makes good online instruction good? New opportunities and old barriers. In J. Visser & M. Visser-Valfrey (Eds.), *Learners in a changing learning landscape: Reflections from a dialogue on new roles and expectations* (pp. 251–266). Dordrecht, The Netherlands: Springer.

Spitzer, D. (2002). Don't forget the high-touch with the high-tech in distance learning. In A. Rossett (Ed.), *The ASTD e-learning handbook. Best practices, strategies, and case studies for an emerging field* (pp. 165–174). New York: McGraw-Hill.

Stoyanov, S., & Kirschner, P. A. (2004). Expert concept mapping method for defining the characteristics of adaptive e-learning: ALFANET project case. *Educational Technology, Research and Development*, *52*(2), 41–56.

Stoyanov, S., & Kirschner, P. A. (2007). Effect of problem solving support and cognitive styles on idea generation: Implications for technology-enhanced learning. *Journal of Research on Technology in Education*, *40*(1), 77–85.

Sweller, J., Van Merriënboer, J. J. G., & Paas, F. (1998). Cognitive architecture and instructional design. *Educational Psychology Review*, *10*, 251–296.

Tuovinen, J., & Sweller, J. (1999). A comparison of cognitive load associated with discovery learning and worked examples. *Journal of Educational Psychology*, *91*, 334–341.

Van Gerven, P. W. M., Paas, F., Van Merriënboer, J. J. G., Hendriks, M., & Schmidt, H. G. (2003). The efficiency of multimedia learning into old age. *British Journal of Educational Psychology*, *73*, 489–505.

Van Gerven, P. W. M., Paas, F., Van Merriënboer, J. J. G., & Schmidt, H. G. (2000). Cognitive load theory and the acquisition of complex cognitive skills in the elderly: Towards an integrative framework. *Educational Gerontology*, *26*, 503–521.

Van Gerven, P. W. M., Paas, F., Van Merriënboer, J. J. G., & Schmidt, H. G. (2002). Cognitive load theory and aging: Effects of worked examples on training efficiency. *Learning and Instruction*, *12*, 87–105.

Van Merriënboer, J. J. G. (1997). *Training complex cognitive skills*. Englewood Cliffs, NJ: Educational Technology Publications.

Van Merriënboer, J. J. G., & Kirschner, P. A. (2007). *Ten steps to complex learning*. Mahwah, NJ: Lawrence Erlbaum.

Van Merriënboer, J. J. G., & Luursema, J. J. (1996). Implementing instructional models in computer-based learning environments: A case study in problem selection. In T. T. Liao (Ed.), *Advanced educational technology: Research issues and future potential* (pp. 184–206). Berlin: Springer.

Van Merriënboer, J. J. G., & Sweller, J. (2005). Cognitive load theory and complex learning: Recent developments and future directions. *Educational Psychology Review*, *17*, 147–177.

Van Merriënboer, J. J. G., Clark, R. E., & de Croock, M. B. M. (2002). Blueprints for complex learning: The 4C/ID-model. *Educational Technology, Research and Development*, *50*(2), 39–64.

Van Merriënboer, J. J. G., Kirschner, P. A., & Kester, L. (2003). Taking the load of a learners' mind: Instructional design for complex learning. *Educational Psychologist*, *38*(1), 5–13.

Visser, J. (in this volume). Constructive interaction with change: Implications for learners and the environment in which they learn. In J. Visser & M. Visser-Valfrey (Eds.), *Learners in a changing learning landscape: Reflections from a dialogue on new roles and expectations* (pp. 11–35). Dordrecht, The Netherlands: Springer.

Von Wodtke, M. (1993). *Mind over media.* New York: McGraw-Hill.

WCET (2006). *Non significant difference phenomenon.* Retrieved February 20, 2006 from www. nosignificantdifference.org/.

Weisberg, R., & Alba, J. (1981). An examination of the alleged role of "fixation" in the solution of "insight" problems. *Journal of Experimental Psychology: General, 110,* 169–192.

Wenger, E. (1998). *Communities of practice.* Cambridge: Cambridge University Press.

Wenke, D., & Frensch, P. (2003). Is success or failure at solving complex problems related to intellectual ability? In J. Davidson & R. Sternberg (Eds.), *The psychology of problem solving* (pp. 87–126). New York: Cambridge University Press.

Yeung, A., Jin, P., & Sweller, J. (1998). Cognitive load and learner expertise: Split-attention and redundancy effects in reading with explanatory notes. *Contemporary Educational Psychology, 23,* 1–21.

Zimmerman, B., & Campillo, M. (2003). Motivating self-regulated problem solvers. In J. Davidson & R. Sternberg (Eds.), *The psychology of problem solving* (pp. 233–262). New York: Cambridge University Press.

Chapter 5
The Influence of Epistemological Beliefs on Learners' Perceptions of Online Learning: Perspectives on Three Levels

Christina Rogoza

Abstract This chapter will discuss the influence of epistemological beliefs on learners' perceptions of alternate learning environments such as online learning. Epistemological assumptions will be examined on three levels addressing institutional, faculty, and individual learner perspectives. Questions to be explored include: What are the dominant beliefs about knowledge and knowing in our educational system today? What are our students' beliefs about knowledge and knowing? How do we account for them and how do they align with a new paradigm of learning and a non-localized learning environment?

5.1 Introduction

We come to know by intentionally guiding a generative dance of knowing and knowledge, using the interactions and relationships between knowledge and knowing as the source of generative power, and prior knowledge as a tool.

Rowland, Shall We Dance (2004)

Research has shown that personal epistemological beliefs impact on learning and the development of higher order thinking skills (Schommer, 1990). Although there have been numerous studies that have investigated student epistemological beliefs there has been little agreement about what dimensions they encompass (Hofer & Pintrich, 1997). Most studies have addressed the concept within linear developmental frameworks and little attention has been given to the interplay between the learner, the instructor, and the context or learning space. This discussion will explore these relationships and examine assumptions about epistemology and its impact on learners' ability to adapt to new environments such as online learning. Three epistemological perspectives will be explored from the institutional, faculty, and learner levels.

Most current models of teaching and learning derive from the positivist paradigm of scientific and industrial thinking (Rowland, 2004). This is reflected

Nova Southeastern University

across many college campuses with traditional instructional practices that focus on transmission of knowledge from instructor to learner with the measurement of learner success being the ability to reproduce that knowledge. However, the broader societal context in which we learn is changing. Change is turbulent and unpredictable in an ever increasing complex environment. As technology continues to drive the development of the knowledge era, the need for continuous, lifelong learning is becoming a necessity. Learners need to develop problem solving and critical thinking skills and go beyond being passive recipients of knowledge to being active participants in identifying their learning needs and collaboratively constructing knowledge.

The emergence of flexible, technology infused curricula allows learners to go beyond the limits of static location and time specific learning. As such, learners need to build capacity to adapt to new technologies and build learning networks. Essentially they need to open and expand their learning space.

Learners enter higher education with personal epistemologies, i.e. with beliefs about what knowledge is and how it is accessed. Their assumptions about knowledge have been shaped by their experiences in education over the years and this enculturation into learning will influence their learning expectations (Schoenfeld, 1983). For example, students who have come from a learning environment that focuses on rote learning of facts will most likely be oriented to a preference for a traditional approach and they may not be receptive to new ways of learning.

However, there is evidence that learner epistemologies do change over their college career (Perry, 1970). As students move from simple to more complex epistemologies they will be able to improve their problem solving skills to handle complexities (Hofer, 2001). This epistemological development can be embedded in the design of curricula but it is largely dependent on the instructor's ability to be receptive to its role in developing competent learners.

Spector and De la Teja (2001) argue that instructors come inadequately prepared to address new learning environments and the lifelong learning needs of their students. Instructors need to be made aware that their epistemological assumptions influence their teaching practice and this in turn shapes learner epistemological beliefs and the learning space.

Teaching practices are shaped by current instructional design models that were developed in the 1970s and 1980s. Curriculum continues to be designed from a linear perspective with a focus on specific learning objectives. Unfortunately this approach does not work well when dealing with complex problem solving with real world applications. Instructional design approaches need to focus on flexible learning environments that facilitate higher order thinking skills (Van Merriënboer & Stoyanov, in this volume).

Learning is a dynamic process and is influenced by the interaction between the learner, the instructor, and the learning space. The learning landscape today exists as multiple contexts and dimensions and comprises individual and collective experiences (Visser, 2001). It is essential that the education system respond to this and move learners to a new level. This discussion proposes that enabling learners to navigate within a continuously changing dynamic can be facilitated with an enhanced focus on epistemological development of learners, instructors, and the institutional context.

5.2   What is Epistemology?

The term epistemology comes from the Greek episteme (knowledge) and logos (theory), hence the theory of knowledge. Epistemology is concerned with the nature of knowledge and knowing, including the source and evaluation of knowledge (Hofer, 2004). Personal epistemology refers essentially to the beliefs that individuals hold about knowledge. Such beliefs influence how learners engage in the learning process (Schommer, 1990).

Personal epistemological beliefs are usually tacit and learners may in most cases not be aware of them nor how they influence how they learn. Making them explicit is the first step in examining how they shape the learning process. How do you know what you know? What is that thing that we call knowledge? Where do you get it? What is its relationship to learning? I asked Erin (not his real name) a second year biology student, to articulate his thoughts on his personal epistemological beliefs.

Q. What is your understanding of knowledge?

A. To me knowledge is accumulated information that you learn through your experiences in life. You have experiences, you learn from those experiences and once you learn from them that becomes knowledge.

Q. What is the connection between learning in the classroom and knowledge?

A. Um...learning in the classroom...you don't learn what you need to survive, you know. Like general knowledge you learn...I guess how to live. School is just book smarts, facts, stuff like that. You know knowledge is like doing...knowing what you have to know... mmm...I don't know...it's a big grey area right there for me.

Q. What is your preferred learning environment? Online or face-to-face?

A. I would much rather learn face-to-face. There has to be some sort of human interaction between the professor and the student in order for me personally to learn, 'cause staring at a computer screen doesn't help—doesn't do anything for me. I need a specially designated time that I am going to be in class to learn.

Erin has drawn a distinction between the formal learning found in the classroom and informal learning outside of the classroom. When asked about the connection between learning and his concept of knowledge, he is able to explain his understanding of knowledge in the school environment, i.e., he sees knowledge as being represented as facts. He is definitive about how he gains knowledge describing it as something that happens in a specific location at a specific time.

However, he has difficulty articulating his understanding of how informally acquired knowledge is represented and says that this is a 'grey' area for him. In addition, he has indicated that he values the informal learning that occurs outside of the classroom. He says that 'book smarts' don't help you how to survive in the world. Hence, Erin goes to school to gather bits of knowledge with the understanding that it may or may not be helpful to him in his life.

This student like most students at the college level, enter the adult learning landscape, be it institutional, online, or otherwise, with some general framework of their concept of knowledge and learning. They have a personal epistemology that they have formulated over the years and it is this that mediates their learning experiences (Perry, 1970; Belenky, Clinchy, Goldberger, & Tarule, 1986). The learning environment to which the learner has been exposed influences epistemological development. Therefore, attention needs to be directed to the learning environment and the implicit epistemological assumptions that it brings to the learning table.

5.2.1 How Does the Education System Reflect Epistemological Assumptions?

What is the nature of the learning environment for today's learners and how does this align with their personal expectations and understanding of learning? Learning occurs in the world and is a contextualized activity. Our world today is technology driven and the growth in the amount of information available is doubling every five to seven years (Hirumi, 2002). This rapid rate of technological change is impacting on education in ways not seen since the industrial age. Students today need to be competent in problem solving, critical thinking, and in analyzing and synthesizing this deluge of information. In addition, learners need to be adaptable and flexible in their learning strategies as they respond to new situations. These are competencies that are required for being successful in today's world. Therefore, students' abilities need to be developed to become independent, self-directed, and lifelong learners.

Constructivist theory may be responsive to these demands. Constructivism asserts that knowledge does not exist independently of the learner and that learning becomes a personal interpretation of the world (Von Glasersfeld, 1989). Hence, constructivism takes an approach to teaching and learning that emphasizes the facilitation of the construction of knowledge and its application in various contexts. Learners today are faced with increasingly complex problems. Instructors thus need to help them recognize that knowledge is fluid and that they will always be working with incomplete information (LaPointe, 2005). This requires different approaches to instructional practices with the aim of assisting learners to actively engage in roles as problem solvers.

Despite the growing acceptance and application of constructivist theory in educational arenas, Bransford (2005) argues that learning environments (face-to-face, online, and blended) continue to be knowledge dispensing milieus. Although constructivist rhetoric fills the halls of universities and colleges there appears to be meager evidence of its application in university classrooms.

Traditional approaches to education are mired in the mechanistic paradigm of the Industrial Age. The concept of knowledge is derived from positivism where it is considered as something objective that can be transferred from expert to novice, in this case the expert being the teacher and the novice being the student. Students essentially are "empty vessels" ready to be filled with the facts of knowledge.

The most efficient way of accomplishing this is to structure classrooms and curriculum delivery in a way that allows for the smooth transfer of this repository of knowledge. Hence institutions of learning are structured around a division of labor model where students are 'produced' as units of learning similar to widgets in a factory. Knowledge is the resource that is the input into the production cycle. The architecture of education reflects this paradigm of positivism and continues to bear its mark on education today. Organizational hierarchies, rote learning, mechanistic tests, unions, and the ivory tower syndrome are all artifacts of this industrial thinking (Morrison & Osborne, 2005).

5.2.2 The Learning Space Newly Defined

The influence of the epistemological assumptions of the architecture of education can be significant and has implications for how the learning space is conceptualized. The term learning space brings many things to mind. For some it may be a visual of a physical location, i.e., a learning space may be a typical classroom with rows of desks. For others, it may bring to mind the types of relationships they had with other learners and teachers. The idea of a learning space is multifaceted. An approach taken by J. Visser (2000) in addressing this concept is to first examine what is meant by learning. He advocates for an ecological perspective of learning where human learning occurs in multiple contexts, multiple dimensions, and is an individual and collective experience. He argues that learning occurs within the context of change and hence builds human capacity to adapt.

> Human learning is the disposition of human beings, and of the social entities to which they pertain, to engage in continuous dialogue with the human, social, biological and physical environment, so as to generate intelligent behavior to interact constructively with change. (Visser, 2001, p. 453)

This ecological perspective moves beyond the subjective/objective perspective of positivism and presents the integrated nature of learning, the learner, and the learning space. In this view, the learner does not objectively engage in a learning process within a static learning space. All three entities are facets of a dimension rather like a wave and the ocean. As the wave cannot be separated from the ocean, so too the learner and learning cannot be separated from the learning space.

What would Erin's understanding be of this ecological approach? As Erin stated, he would agree that learning of any value takes place in the world and occurs as an experience in an interaction with one's environment. However, he noted that 'book learning' is a separate matter and occurs in a rigidly contextualized, structured environment—an environment that Erin accepts as appropriate for this kind of learning. Hence, Erin holds two simultaneous distinct perspectives of learning and the learning space. On the one hand, he assumes an objectivist view of knowledge and applies that in his formal learning space. On the other hand, his approach to informal learning that occurs outside of the classroom rests on a subjective perspective of knowledge where he seems comfortable with the experiential nature of knowledge. However,

Erin has exhibited difficulty in justifying this inconsistency in his understanding of knowledge. This epistemological dissonance will become more of a problem as the learning landscape becomes transformed through technology. Technology will see the blurring of boundaries between formal and informal learning environments as formal learning becomes non-localized in a virtual environment.

5.2.3   A Changing Learning Landscape

The pervasiveness of technology is reshaping the learning landscape in our world today (Burnett, 2005). Technology has become an aspect of the human condition and as such is dissipating the subjective/objective aspects of experiences. We are at a pinnacle in the redefining of our relationship with machines as we become more interdependent with technology. The use of the Internet is an example of how our learning space is expanding. Burnett (2005) defines this human-machine interaction as digital ecology and notes that technology has become a part of learning systems and the learning space.

This symbiotic relationship between humans and technology, although pervasive, is invisible and is extending the human mind and body in ways that may not be explicitly known by the subject. For example, the use of cell phones has released persons from having to be in a specific location to communicate and share information with others. Therefore, people are physically more mobile and able to extend their mental reach. However, the human capability that this technology has allowed remains as an underlying tacit awareness. Erin, for example, may communicate by cell phone with another class member about some subject matter problem. The solution to the problem may be negotiated while Erin is sitting in a restaurant. However, Erin may still maintain that learning did not really take place outside of the classroom.

The emphasis on the integration of technology into the curriculum of higher education is seen as supporting the generic learning outcome of information literacy. Unfortunately this can translate into a focus for learning in which it becomes simply a process of adding new sets of skills and knowledge to the learner's existing palette. The danger in this approach is that the process of updating skills becomes associated with learning. True learning involves much more than just 'adding to.' It equally involves the need to unlearn and 'let go' of assumptions and procedures (Bransford, 2005). Issues arise as to how learning environments support this and how willing the learners are to opening up their learning space and following these new pathways.

5.2.4   The Online Learner

There is no doubt the learning landscape is continuously changing, as is reflected, among other things, in the increase of online delivery of curriculum. In higher education, Chief Academic Officers identifying online education as a critical long-term strategy grew from 49% in 2003 to 58.4% in 2006. Overall online enrollment increased from 1.98 million in 2003 to 3.3 million in 2006 (Sloan Consortium, 2006).

This trend in online learning will continue to increase but how does the online learning environment align with student expectations and understanding of learning? Research has shown that online learners need to be more self-directed than traditional learners in a face-to-face environment. To be successful the online learner needs to have additional competencies that include self-discipline, initiative, commitment, time management skills, and organization skills to work independently (Simonson, Smaldino, Albright, & Zvacek, 2003). Hongmei (2002) suggests that self-motivated and self-disciplined students are most likely to succeed in online learning. However, studies by Belenky et al. (1986) on practicing nurses who were taking online courses, suggest that students felt a need to be told what to do and when to do it. They demonstrated dependent behaviors and reliance on their instructor.

These findings are antithetical to the tendency to stereotype today's students as independent learners and able to easily adapt to any environment including online opportunities. After all, are not today's students natural online learners? Van Merriënboer (2005) suggests that this perception of young learners or the 'gaming generation' is a broad generalization that only applies to a subgroup of learners. Research has found that young students (13–14 years of age) can be resistant to educational innovation that emphasizes independent learning and do not necessarily perceive it as being helpful to their learning.

We have seen how Erin feels about learning online. Erin has definite preconceived ideas about when, where, and how he likes to learn which happens to be in a traditional face-to-face environment. However, the reality of today's world suggests that learners need to think beyond these limiting paradigms.

Technology has facilitated the development of a knowledge-based society which has created different learning needs and learners must build capacity to adapt to new learning environments. The role of education is to help students develop the 'habits of mind' to develop adaptive expertise that will prepare them for the realities of today's world (Bransford, 2005). The role of educators is to create the conditions of learning that push students beyond current comfort zones to accept new understandings of knowledge and innovative ways of learning.

5.2.5   Learners' Epistemology

It is important to understand how students make epistemological sense of their learning environment. Learners enter college with an epistemological framework and preconceived ideas about their needs as learners (Schoenfeld, 1983). These beliefs may inhibit or enhance their ability to adapt to new learning environments.

There is no single theoretical framework for conceptualizing epistemological beliefs. Instead a number of different frameworks have been put forward (Hofer &

Pintrich, 1997). Research on epistemological beliefs and their impact on learning began with Perry (1970) who posited a model that suggested the sequential development of epistemological beliefs. His findings concluded that students go through stages in the development of their epistemological beliefs moving from simple to more complex. For example, he found that undergraduate students enter college with a perspective that knowledge is certain and rests solely with authority figures such as the instructor. However, senior students exhibited a move to a more constructivist understanding of the uncertainty and subjectivity of knowledge.

Other research places personal epistemology within a multi-dimensional model. Schommer-Aikins & Hutter (2002) explored epistemology as a system of beliefs that reside in dimensions that exist independently and are represented on continuums. Hofer's (2004) model was factored to four dimensions of epistemological beliefs (Fig. 5.1). They are applied to the learner as follows:

Certainty of knowledge. At one end of this continuum, the learner views knowledge as representing absolute truth and certainty. These learners do not tolerate ambiguity and do not tend to engage in evaluative thinking. The development along this continuum occurs as a movement from a fixed to a more fluid view where at the other end, the learner accepts that there is no absolute knowledge and that it is continuously evolving.

Simplicity of knowledge. At one end of this continuum the learner views knowledge as concrete, discrete, and consisting of knowable facts that can be transmitted from expert to novice. This belief is characteristic of the 'surface learner' who is comfortable with rote learning. At the other end, the learner views knowledge as contingent, contextual, and relative. This learner would see learning from a systems perspective and see the interconnectedness of knowledge.

Source of knowledge. This dimension refers to where the locus of knowledge resides. At one end of the continuum the learner would see knowledge as existing external to the self—such as when it is seen as invested in some kind of authority. For example, authority may be represented in textbooks, professors, parents, and church leaders. At the other end, learners would view knowledge as subjective and see themselves as active participants in the construction of knowledge.

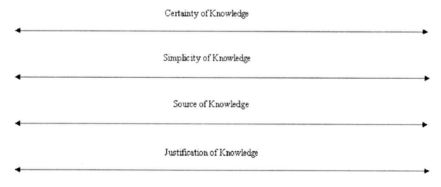

Fig. 5.1 Epistemological dimensions

Justification for knowing. This dimension addresses how the learners justify and evaluate their beliefs. At one end of the continuum they might justify their beliefs using external sources of authority or simply go by what they feel is right. At the other end they would engage in evaluation of the evidence, the expertise of the authority, and their personal integration of knowledge with this evidence.

Kuhn, Cheney, and Weinstock (2000) also proposed a developmental perspective of epistemological beliefs but within a subjective/objective framework. Beginning at the objective level, the learner views knowledge as an external reality and knowable with certainty. As development occurs, the learner would begin to see knowledge as being subjectively understood and therefore their source of knowledge relocates to the self. This transition begins the development of personal epistemological beliefs to a constructivist understanding, where knowledge is understood to be subjectively interpretive. Eventually, they suggest there is reconciliation between the two constructs.

This framework further defines epistemological beliefs as being domain specific. For example, students may have beliefs about knowledge in the area of mathematics, i.e., that knowledge is certain and falls within the objectivist realm. This may differ from their beliefs about knowledge in the discipline of art for example, i.e., that knowledge is subjective and relative.

In Erin's case his epistemological beliefs in the subjective and objective domains are not subject specific but rather are defined with respect to the learning space. For example, he views the institutional learning environment as concerned with objective knowledge and any learning that occurs outside of that as constituting subjective knowledge.

Erin's assumptions can affect the way he engages in learning both within and outside of the institutional environment. For example, his beliefs about school learning as being mainly about facts will focus his learning strategies on fact gathering and memorization with little attention to evaluation of that knowledge. This epistemological orientation might constrict his openness to inquiry.

There is evidence that there are interventions that will effect epistemological belief change in learners moving them from simple to more complex reasoning (Hofer, 2004). Sandoval and Reiser (2004) argued that although the facilitation of epistemological inquiry may be imbedded in the curriculum of some disciplines, it should be made more explicit to support this development.

5.2.6   Opening the Learning Space

Although traditional paradigms of teaching and learning may be dominant in colleges, the force of constructivism is weaving its way into higher education. Instructional practices based on constructivist theory are evidenced in such things as the use of authentic assessments and increased focus on interaction. However, it cannot be assumed that all learners welcome constructivism and this raises the issue of how learners' personal epistemologies integrate with the epistemological

Table 5.1 Constructivism and epistemological dimensions

Epistemological dimension	Constructivism
Certainty of knowledge	Knowledge is contextual and relative
Simplicity of knowledge	Knowledge is complex
Source of knowledge	Knowledge is subjectively constructed
Justification of knowing	Knowledge is evaluated

principles of constructivism. In terms of Hofer's (2004) four knowledge dimensions, constructivist epistemology can be mapped onto the dimensions as illustrated in Table 5.1.

Development along some of these domains may be particularly problematic for students as it can involve a great deal of epistemological stretch. In Erin's case he sits at one end of the continuum in the simplicity and certainty of knowledge domains and his source of knowledge is externally located in traditional resources such as the professor and the textbook. If pedagogical practices in the classroom took a constructivist approach Erin might be very uncomfortable. He would not necessarily be receptive to the view that knowledge is subjectively constructed. In constructivist classrooms students are encouraged to learn from others and to actively participate in discussion groups. Erin might find this disconcerting when after all he came to hear the expert on the subject.

Erin's epistemological beliefs may also impact on his openness to alternative learning environments. Tsai & Chuang (2005), in a study of 324 high school students in Taiwan, found that students holding more constructivism orientated epistemological beliefs tended to prefer Internet-based learning environments.

Erin has stated that he prefers a face-to-face environment and feels that he could not learn outside of the classroom. Remember that Erin had categorized his school learning as involving objective knowledge, i.e. facts. He had also categorized the informal learning that occurs outside of the classroom as involving more experiential learning and subjective kinds of knowledge. What would happen if Erin were to change his view on the type of knowledge that he learns in the classroom? For example, if he moved to an epistemological position of understanding knowledge as contextual, would he become more self-directed in his learning as he assumes the responsibility for evaluating the kinds of knowledge presented to him? Perhaps this epistemological development would make him more receptive to the possibilities of online learning. Also, if he was to move on the source of knowledge continuum toward accepting that there are viable and expert resources in the online environment, would that predispose him to accepting the online environment as an acceptable alternative to classroom based learning?

Erin has demonstrated that he is aware of his epistemological inconsistency. However, that seems to have been a tacit awareness made explicit through direct questioning about his understanding of knowledge and its connection to learning. This paper proposes that it is this epistemological dissonance (Fig. 5.2) that provides the portal for epistemological development. Inconsistencies in epistemological beliefs may provide transition points to move learners to more complex epistemo-

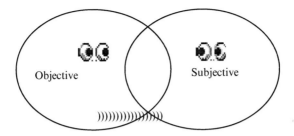

Fig. 5.2 Reconciling epistemological dissonance

logical beliefs. These change points allow for learners' reflection on their conflicting beliefs and incentive to seek reconciliation through alternative ways of viewing knowledge. Hence, the issue for course development and design would be to create a learning environment where instructors would attend to explicating learners' tacit awareness of their personal epistemological beliefs and facilitate epistemological development.

5.2.7 Instructors' Epistemology

Much of this discussion has focused on the relationship between student epistemological beliefs and how these can enhance or restrict the students' ability to adapt to a changing learning landscape. However, an essential consideration that factors into the learning space is the presence of the instructor. Instructors bring their own epistemological beliefs into their teaching practice and these in turn influence their instructional strategies just as a learner's epistemological beliefs influence their learning strategies. For example, an instructor teaching an introductory psychology course might teach it from a 'just the facts' objectivist perspective that would entail lecture style transmission of knowledge and multiple choice testing for evaluation of that knowledge. The instructor may feel that this is appropriate based on his epistemological beliefs about the nature of knowledge in that discipline.

In addition, the traditional architecture of the educational system imposes constraints on the instructor. The factory model of education is based on economies of scale resulting in large classes that inevitably dictate the design and delivery of course curricula.

Additionally, if instructors have been fortunate to receive any training at all in instructional design for curriculum development, it most likely would have been from an objectivist paradigm. This is even more likely as rigorous standards for accountability are seeing the increasing use of mechanized and standardized testing procedures and curriculum development based on principles of scientific management drawn from business and industry (Vrasidas, 2000).

Instructional design for online and classroom settings needs to take a constructivist approach to facilitate the development of higher order thinking skills. However, instructors are inadequately prepared in applying constructivist epistemology in their teaching practice whether in traditional classrooms or online (Spector & De la Teja, 2001). For example, those objectivist educators who do teach online tend to transfer traditional pedagogical strategies used in the classroom to the online environment, i.e. the transmission of knowledge through lecturing. Essentially, text on a blackboard becomes text on a computer screen or the talking head in the classroom becomes the talking head in a multimedia mode. Again the instruction is designed to transfer objective knowledge into the learner's head. Hence, the online environment is not a newly transformed learning space but more of the same.

Besides, those instructors who have adopted constructivist approaches in their teaching practice may continue to hold tacit assumptions that the learning experience in an online environment is inferior to that of a traditional classroom space. They may blame the lack of interaction between instructor and student as one of the factors that diminish the learning experience. There is merit in the argument given that distance education did hail from a correspondence model where students often learned in isolation from each other and the instructor. However technology can now enable both synchronous and asynchronous interaction between learners and between the learner and the instructor. The problem lies in their understanding of the interaction of the technology and new approaches to teaching and learning.

The transformation of the distance learning environment into a dynamic experience may occur with the development of epistemological understanding of the instructor. As instructors move to a more constructivist approach this may facilitate the opening of the learning space to new ways of teaching and learning. This process may happen concurrently as learners' epistemologies are transformed.

5.2.8   Instructional Design and the Online Environment

Education has been cited as a contributor to the development of the learner along the epistemological dimensions from simple to more complex (Hofer, 2001). Constructivist theory also aligns with this aim. However, constructivism does not have a history of being embedded in the design and delivery of curriculum based on traditional instructional design models.

Instructional design derives from a behaviorist tradition with an emphasis on quantifiable behavioral objectives. Language like terminal behavior, measurable tasks, and taxonomies of behavior continue to be heard in instructional design departments in colleges today. Cognitive science later began to have an influence on instructional design but both cognitivism and behaviorism are grounded in positivism where the goal of instruction is the transfer of objective knowledge (Ragan & Smith, 1994). This is a particular problem not only for face-to-face traditional classroom delivery but online delivery as well. Internet-based course delivery and course management systems (CMS) have been adopted by thousands of institutions of higher education but the adoption of these technologies brings with it a set of epistemological assumptions that are embedded in the systems' architecture (McDonald, Yanchar, & Osguthorpe, 2005). The structural design of CMS platforms promotes the instructor as the source and expert of a knowledge repository. Emphasis is placed on the organization and sequencing of learning objectives and the measurement of outcomes. The system is structured in such a way that it forces course development in a linear fashion and essentially is a continuation of the objectivist paradigm. The design of the system was not meant to support the facilitation of meaning making and epistemological beliefs (Wineburg, 1991).

Stirling (2005) argues that software for the online environment does not have to necessarily be designed or used from an objectivist paradigm. She advocates for creative ways of using the learning platforms, i.e. collaborative web based art projects. Indeed if the assumption is that constructivist pedagogy facilitates the development of necessary skills for today's learners, the fault does not lie in the technology but with the instructional design for the online environment.

Learning systems must respond to today's learning needs. Effective and responsive learning systems need to be designed from a constructivist perspective to include holistic approaches, customization, collaboration, diverse teams, networking, and complexity (Van Merriënboer, 2005; Reigeluth, 2005).

Technology and the online environment are providing promising alternatives to monitor epistemological activities and move learners into more complex epistemological thinking (Tsai & Chuang, 2005). Sandoval and Reiser (2004) developed Explanation Constructor, an online prompting program that makes explicit students' inquiry practices in the science curriculum. Key to the design of the program is the scaffolds that it provides in guiding students to formulate and evaluate their explanations in reference to their approach to scientific investigation. Their findings indicate that technological tools can function to articulate students' epistemological beliefs in relation to their discipline.

Bell and Linn (2000) developed SenseMaker, a software tool to facilitate explanation construction and make thinking visible. Windschitl (2000) integrated technology into science curricula to support student inquiry practices and subsequent epistemological development. These and other epistemological tools are being developed to help students articulate their thinking across disciplines (Bell & Linn, 2000; Hirumi, 2002). However, the use of these tools is dependent on the skills of the professors and more importantly their willingness to incorporate these into their curriculum design.

5.3 Summary and Conclusion

Change in the world is happening at a rate never before experienced and the development of the lifelong learner is a critical issue in education. Learners need to understand the importance of adapting to online learning opportunities and that learning does not begin and end within a set limited timeframe. They will continue to learn throughout their lives and this will not always occur in traditional educational settings. Today's learners need to be receptive to alternative ways of learning and go beyond their comfort zones as they learn to adapt to a changing learning landscape.

The beliefs that learners hold about knowledge may constrict or open up their learning space. For example, learners who view knowledge as discrete, concrete facts might expect traditional instructional practices that involve a transmission of knowledge approach. These learners might find comfort in the lecture style of instruction in a typical classroom environment. Their learning space would be predictable and knowable. On the other hand those learners who view knowledge as relative and contextual, might be more inclined to venture into other learning environments such as online learning and virtual worlds.

Learner epistemologies can be shaped through pedagogy and instructional design (Baxter-Magolda, 1992; Hofer, 2004). If the epistemology in the learning environment is grounded in objectivism, the curriculum design and delivery will be content driven and the instructor will assume the role of transmitter of this content. If learners have been immersed in this paradigm for most of their years in formal education, it would be reasonable to assume that they might not be comfortable in a process driven constructivist environment.

Instruction should support the development of higher order thinking skills grounded in sophisticated epistemological beliefs. Abd-El-Khalick and Lederman (2000) emphasized the importance of actually making epistemological development an instructional goal in the curriculum. Providing instruction to students about epistemological beliefs and how those beliefs affect classroom learning needs to be made explicit, a practice that is not the norm in most disciplines (Sandoval & Reiser, 2004).

Instructors are key to facilitating this development. They need to understand that their epistemological assumptions shape those of their students as well. In addition, their tacit epistemological assumptions will influence their receptivity to learning new skills to engage in non-traditional learning environments. Not only is there a need to attend to student adaptation to new learning environments but that of the instructors as well.

Research has provided evidence that epistemological development is important for higher level learning. In addition, this paper proposed that it may have impact on student perception of the learning space. It may influence their receptiveness to alternate learning environments such as online learning. More research needs to be done on the measurement and understanding of the relationship between epistemological beliefs and student receptivity to online learning. In addition, as technology continues to be infused into the higher education system, developing instructional interventions that facilitate the development of students' personal epistemological beliefs is a salient area for continued research.

However, a holistic approach needs to be taken in examining epistemological beliefs. Student epistemological beliefs are not static and are influenced by the epistemological assumptions of their instructors and the education system itself. It is a constant interplay between the learner, instructor, and the learning space.

This reality can be somewhat of a moving target and will require new approaches for continuous study. Cross-disciplinary dialogue is essential in addressing strategies for epistemological development in curriculum. However, institutions need to first recognize that this is an area that requires focus. Administrators and faculty need exposure to the connection between epistemological development and how it can prepare students for learning in the digital age. This will require careful facilitation to throw out old assumptions based on the industrial model of education.

5.4 Resources for Further Exploration

- Hameroff, S. R., Kaszneiak, A. W., & Scott. A. C. (1994). *Toward a science of consciousness. The first Tucson discussions and debates.* Cambridge, MA: MIT Press. This book is a compilation of 56 articles on consciousness from various disciplines including but not restricted to philosophy, cognitive science, neuroscience, and quantum theory. It provides a comprehensive foundation of various epistemological perspectives couched in each disciplinary context.
- Hofer, B., & Pintrich, P. (2002). *Personal epistemology: The psychology of beliefs about knowledge and knowing.* Mahwah, NJ: Lawrence Erlbaum. This book provides an overview of the theoretical and methodological approaches to the study of personal epistemology from a psychological and educational perspective.
- Ferrari, M., & Sternberg, R. (1998). *Self-awareness: Its nature and development.* New York: Guilford Press. This book examines the philosophy of mind and cognitive science and its relevance to education. It provides an introduction to the field of research on the development of the self. Contributions are included from leaders in the fields of philosophy, comparative psychology, and developmental psychology creating an inviting dialogue on human nature itself.
- Huemer, M. (2002). *Epistemology: Contemporary readings (Routledge Contemporary Readings in Philosophy).* New York: Routledge. This book introduces both contemporary and historical work in epistemology. It provides an overview of the nature of knowledge with works drawn from those philosophers that have made significant contributions to the field.
- Website: http://www.learndev.org. This website provides a rich resource of international scholarly papers, dialogue, reports, and events hosted by the Learning Development Institute (LDI). LDI is a transdisciplinary learning network with the aim to "establish the conditions of growth for comprehensive learning environments that can, in an open and flexible way, respond to diverse and changing learning needs of people and communities."

5.5 Questions for Comprehension and Application

1. At the beginning of the chapter, Erin is asked a couple of questions about his beliefs regarding what it means to learn and become knowledgeable. His answers are subsequently analyzed by the author throughout the chapter. Do you think the author's analysis is fair? If so, why? If not, or if not entirely, why not

and how else might his answers have been interpreted? If at all opportune, for instance if you study this book as part of a collaborative effort with fellow students or professional colleagues, discuss and compare your observations with those of others. What makes you agree or disagree?

2. Suppose you were asked the same questions that prompted Erin's responses, what would *your* answers have been and what would they have been 10, 20 or 30 years ago? Have your beliefs about learning changed over time? If so, how and why? Are you now better able to articulate such beliefs than you were in the past? How has your thinking improved? Do you feel compelled to think this through more deeply? Discuss your thoughts and observations with others.

3. Consider a discipline (say physics, history, mathematics, literary creation, etc.) or transdisciplinary area of concern (e.g. related to problems such as sustainable living, climate change or poverty alleviation). Choose the area you feel most profoundly attached to intellectually and emotionally. How do the professionals working in that area agree on what it means to know? How do they build consensus? How do they deal with disagreement? What does this imply for how the field in question develops and how it should be taught? Consider your own teaching and/or learning in that area. How does it conform to the epistemological underpinnings of the field? If there is discrepancy between existing practice of teaching and learning and those epistemological underpinnings, how should the practice of teaching and learning in the area of concern be rethought? Discuss your views with colleagues.

References

Abd-El-Khalick, F., & Lederman, N. G. (2000). Improving science teachers' conceptions of the nature of science: A critical review of the literature. *International Journal of Science Education, 22*(7), 665–701.

Baxter-Magolda, M. B. (1992). Students' epistemologies and academic experiences: Implications for pedagogy. *Review of Higher Education, 15*(3), 265–287.

Belenky, M. F., Clinchy, B. A., Goldberger, N. R., & Tarule, J. M. (1986). *Women's ways of knowing*. New York: Basic Books.

Bell, P., & Linn, M. (2000). Scientific arguments as learning artifacts: Designing for learning from the web. *International Journal of Science Education, 22*(8), 797–817. Retrieved September 23, 2007, from http://www.designbasedresearch.org/reppubs/bell-Linn.pdf.

Bransford, J. (2005, October). Five thoughts on online learning and preparation for the twenty first century. In J. Visser (Chair), *Presidential Workshop and Panel Session on Learners in a changing learning landscape: New roles and expectations—A dialogue motivated by an ibstpi research project*. International annual conference of the Association for Educational Communications and Technology (AECT), Orlando, FL, October 15–18, 2005. Retrieved September 23, 2007, from http://www.learndev.org/ibstpi-AECT2005.html#anchor 186580.

Burnett, R. (2005). *How images think*. Cambridge, MA: MIT Press.

Hirumi, T. (2002). Student-centered, technology-rich learning environments (SCenTRLE): Operationalizing constructivist approaches to teaching and learning. *Journal of Technology and Teacher Education, 10*(4), 497–537.

Hofer, B. K. (2001). Personal epistemology research: Implications for learning and teaching. *Educational Psychology Review, 13*(4), 353–383.

Hofer, B. K. (2004). Exploring the dimensions of personal epistemology in differing classroom contexts: Student interpretations during the first year of college. *Contemporary Educational Psychology, 29*, 129–163.

Hofer, B., & Pintrich, P. R. (1997). The development of epistemological theories: Beliefs about knowledge and knowing and their relation to learning. *Review of Educational Research, 67*(1), 88–140.

Hongmei, L. (2002). *Distance education: Pros, cons, and the future*. Paper presented at the Annual Meeting of the Western States Communication Association (WSCA), Long Beach, CA, March 2–5, 2002.

Kuhn, D., Cheney, R., & Weinstock, M. (2000). The development of epistemological understanding. *Cognitive Development, 15*, 309–328.

LaPointe, D. (2005, October). Reflections on three questions I am trying to answer. In J. Visser (Chair), *Presidential Workshop and Panel Session on Learners in a changing learning landscape: New roles and expectations—A dialogue motivated by an ibstpi research project*. International annual conference of the Association for Educational Communications and Technology (AECT), Orlando, FL, October 15–18, 2005. Retrieved September 23, 2007, from http://www.learndev.org/ibstpi-AECT2005.html#anchor 180718.

McDonald, J. K., Yanchar, S. C., & Osguthorpe, R. T. (2005). Learning from programmed instruction: Examining implications for modern instructional technology. *Educational Technology Research and Development, 52*(2), 84–98.

Morrison, J., & Osborn, H. (2005). Implementing organic education: An interview with Hugh Osborn. *Innovate* 2(2). Retrieved September 23, 2007, from http://www.innovateonline. info/index.php?view=article&id=236.

Perry, W. G., Jr. (1970). *Forms of intellectual and ethical development in the college years: A scheme*. New York: Holt, Rinehart & Winston.

Ragan, T. J., & Smith, P. L. (1994). Opening the black box: Instructional strategies examined. In M. R. Simonson, N. Maushak, & K. Abu-Omar (Eds.), *Proceedings of selected research and development presentations at the 1994 national convention of the Association for Educational Communications and Technology* (pp. 665–681). (ERIC Document Reproduction Service No. ED 373 749). Retrieved September 23, 2007, from http://eric.ed.gov/ERICDocs/data/ericdocs2sql/content_storage_01/0000019b/80/13/4e/3f.pdf.

Reigeluth, C. M. (2005). New instructional theories and strategies for a knowledge-based society. In J. M. Spector, C. Ohrazda, A. V. Schaack, & D. A. Wiley (Eds.), *Innovations in instructional technology* (pp. 207–217). Mahwah, NJ: Lawrence Erlbaum.

Rowland, G. (2004). Shall we dance? A design epistemology for organizational learning and performance. *Educational Technology Research and Development, 52*(1), 33–48.

Sandoval, W. A., & Reiser, B. J. (2004). Explanation-driven inquiry: Integrating conceptual and epistemic scaffolds for scientific inquiry. *Science Education, 88*, 345–372. Retrieved September 23, 2007 from http://www3.interscience.wiley.com/cgi-bin/home.

Schoenfeld, A. H. (1983). Beyond the purely cognitive: Belief systems, social cognitions, and metacognitions as driving forces in intellectual performance. *Cognitive Science, 7*, 329–363.

Schommer, M. (1990). Effects of beliefs about the nature of knowledge on comprehension. *Journal of Educational Psychology, 82*, 498–504.

Schommer-Aikins, M., & Hutter, R. (2002). Epistemological beliefs and thinking about everyday controversial issues. *The Journal of Psychology, 136*(1), 5–20.

Simonson, M., Smaldino, S., Albright, M., & Zvacek, S. (2003). *Teaching and learning at a distance* (2nd ed.). Columbus, OH: Merrill/Prentice-Hall.

Sloan Consortium (2006). *Making the grade: Online education in the United States*. Retrieved September 23, 2007, from http://www.sloan-c.org/publications/survey/ survey06.asp.

Spector, M. J., & De la Teja, I. (2001). *Competencies for online teaching. Eric Digest*. Syracuse, NY: ERIC Clearinghouse on Information and Technology.

Stirling, D. (2005, October). Learners in a changing learning landscape: New roles and expectations. One learner's reflections. In J. Visser (Chair), *Presidential Workshop and Panel Session on Learners in a changing learning landscape: New roles and expectations—A dialogue motivated by an ibstpi research project.* International annual conference of the Association for Educational Communications and Technology (AECT), Orlando, FL, October 15–18, 2005. Retrieved September 23, 2007, from http://www. learndev.org/ibstpi-AECT2005.html# anchor182249.

Tsai, C. & Chuang, S. (2005). The correlation between epistemological beliefs and preferences toward Internet-based learning environments. *British Journal of Educational Technology, 36*(1), 97–100.

Van Merriënboer, J. G. (2005, October). Learners in a changing learning landscape: Reflections from an instructional design perspective. In J. Visser (chair), Presidential Workshop and Panel Session on *Learners in a changing learning landscape: New roles and expectations—A dialogue motivated by an ibstpi research project.* International annual conference of the Association for Educational Communications and Technology (AECT), Orlando, FL, October 15–18, 2005. Retrieved September 23, 2007, from http://www. learndev.org/ibstpi-AECT2005. html#anchor185098.

Van Merriënboer, J. J. G., & Stoyanov, S. (in this volume). Learners in a changing learning landscape: Reflections from an instructional design perspective. In J. Visser & M. Visser-Valfrey (Eds.), *Learners in a changing learning landscape: Reflections from a dialogue on new roles and expectations* (pp. 69–90). Dordrecht, The Netherlands: Springer.

Visser, J. (2000, November). *Learning in the perspective of complexity.* Presentation at Santa Fe Institute (SFI) Seminar on Learning in the Perspective of Complexity, Santa Fe, NM, November 10, 2000. Retrieved September 23, 2007, from http://www.learndev.org/ppt/ SFI2000/sld001.htm.

Visser, J. (2001). Integrity, completeness and comprehensiveness of the learning environment: Meeting the basic learning needs of all throughout life. In: D. N. Aspin, J. D. Chapman, M. J. Hatton, & Y. Sawano (Eds.), *International handbook of lifelong learning* (pp. 447–472). Dordrecht, The Netherlands: Kluwer.

Von Glasersfeld, E. (1989). Cognition, construction of knowledge, and teaching. *SYNTHESE, 80*(1), 121–140. Retrieved September 23, 2007, from http://srri.nsm.umass.edu/ vonGlasersfeld/onlinePapers/html/117.html.

Vrasidas, C. (2000). Constructivism versus objectivism: Implications for interaction, course design, and evaluation in distance education. *International Journal of Educational Telecommunications, 6*(4), 339–362.

Windschitl, M. (2000). Supporting the development of science inquiry skills with special classes of software. *Educational Technology, Research and Development, 48*(2), 81–96.

Wineburg, S. S. (1991). On the reading of historical texts: Notes on the breach between school and academy. *American Educational Research Journal, 28*(3), 495–519.

Chapter 6
Getting to Know the Feral Learner

Mary Hall

Abstract Feral learning offers a positive language and a conceptual framework that transcends the distinctions between formal and informal education, allowing educators and policy makers to deconstruct the implicit limitations of what we have become used to thinking of as teaching-and-learning. This in turn opens up a broader field of possibilities for effectively nurturing learners and cultures of learning. The theoretical basis of feral learning grows out of constructivist theory, with particular reference to the work of Rogers (1967) and Mezirow (1990, 1991). It returns to first principles by positioning learning as an instinctual and intrinsic part of growth and development. This chapter considers the nature of learning, explores the characteristics of feral learning and environments conducive to it and goes on to consider the roots of these ideas in the literature about constructivist theory, transformative learning theory, and flexible delivery. It concludes with a discussion of some of the issues facing formal education in our ability to nurture the feral learner.

6.1 Introduction and Context

Context is important. Each person who reads these words will paint them with the colors of their own experience and will create a unique and individual interpretation. The scope of my own experience and understanding informs, and also limits, the views I present here. You may have different experiences and interpretations. I invite you to explore those as you engage with what you read.

The main focus of this chapter is on personal (individual) learning in environments where access to C21st information and communication technologies is relatively easy. However, the arguments and insights developed in this context may be extrapolated to 'low-tech' educational settings, to learning organizations (Senge, 1990) and learning societies (Faure et al., 1972) as well as the learning each of us does purely for ourselves as we pursue our daily lives. "Interactivity. Many-to-many

---

Independent innovator, analyst and writer

communications. Pervasive networking. These are cumbersome new terms for elements in our lives so fundamental that, before we lost them, we didn't even know to have names for them." (Adams, 1999, n.p.). I have provided some indicative connections to these other areas; however those discussions generally are beyond the scope of this chapter.

6.1.1 The Traditional Classroom

Throughout this chapter, I refer to *the traditional classroom*—what Bransford, Slowinski, Vye, & Mosborg (this volume, Chapter 2) call "the gold standard for teaching and learning". Let me acknowledge from the outset that *the traditional classroom* is a stereotype that does not do justice to the innovative and effective practices of some of today's teachers.

But, while classroom practice in many educational institutions today is vastly different from what I and my peers experienced in the 1960s and 1970s, *the traditional classroom* remains a useful label for a particular set of practices and experiences of formal education that educators and society at large still tend to regard as the natural default. If you are one of those whose classroom practice or experience transcends that stereotype, I apologize and ask you to bear with me.

6.2 What is Feral Learning?

The feral learner is unconstrained by the boundaries of curriculum, school hours, academic discipline, or assessment criteria. Feral learners learn, primarily, for learning's sake. Feral learning is to academic study what pure research is to product development. It is about discovering what might be 'out there' rather than reaching pre-defined targets. Understanding the feral learner starts with acknowledging that *learning* (as compared to *being taught*) is a natural, instinctual human activity.

The typical dictionary definition for the adjective 'feral' relates the word to the Latin 'fera' (wild animal) and 'ferus' (wild). More specifically, it refers to the existence of an animal in a wild or untamed state, or to it having returned to such a state from domestication. Lundin (1997, p. 16) uses the word in connection with learning and tells us that "A university lecturer... marking her students' papers, found references to writings by key people in the field...she had not yet read .... from ...the Internet! She dubbed this 'feral learning.'"

There is no question that any learner, feral or otherwise, can benefit from appropriate instruction or exposure to other people's expertise (see also Bransford et al. in this volume, pp. 37–67). The question is, what constitutes 'appropriate?' The next section of this chapter identifies a set of core characteristics that may help us to answer that question.

6.2.1 What Feral Learning Looks Like

Feral learning is by nature respectful, transparent, complex, holistic, seamless, student-led and a-curricular. In this section, we explore each of these attributes. As you will see from the following discussion they are not mutually exclusive, but rather different angles from which we can glimpse what lies at the wild heart of learning—the quest for survival, and wisdom.

6.2.1.1 Respectful

There is nothing new or unique about the notion that effective learning environments should be respectful. It is enshrined in international law, in the principle of *responsive and reciprocal interactions* practiced by early childhood educators, as *unconditional positive regard* in person-centered counseling, and in the religious doctrine of *love your neighbor as yourself*. The Declaration of the Rights of the Child, proclaimed by the UN General Assembly in 1959, specifies in its Principle 2: "The child…shall be given opportunities and facilities…to enable him to develop physically, mentally, morally, spiritually and socially in a healthy and normal manner and in conditions of freedom and dignity" (United Nations Office of the High Commissioner for Human Rights, 1959).

When *learning* is understood not simply as imprinting curriculum content, but as the lifelong process of creating and refining a holistic relationship with the world (see also Section 6.3.2 on *transformative learning* in this chapter), the need for educators to be respectful—unconditionally accepting of the learner's right to be as they are—becomes paramount. Rogers (1967) who coined the phrase *unconditional positive regard*, described this as "a basic trust…a prizing of the learner as an imperfect human being with many feelings, many potentialities. The facilitator's prizing or acceptance of the learner is an…expression of…trust in the capacity of the human organism" (p. 60).

The philosophy of reciprocal and responsive relationships in a respectful, student-led learning environment underpins many schools and early childhood education (ECE) settings already in existence, such as Montessori schools, Rudolf Steiner (Waldorf) schools, Sudbury model (democratic) schools, the deschooling movement, and New Zealand's Playcentre movement. Perversely, these environments are generally regarded as 'alternative' education. The respectful learning environment however does not always survive the transition from theory into practice, particularly where there is a significant difference in age and status between the teacher and those taught. The volume of literature on deficit modeling, hidden curriculum, alternative education, and the need to actively promote self-esteem and resilience in schools provides ample evidence of this.

In *Sarah Laughed*, Ochs (2005), retells the stories of famous Biblical women. In the first chapter, she attributes this powerful insight to Eve: "Eve was struck by the way the fellows [Adam, Abel, and Cain] failed to distinguish between knowledge as a possession that made you feel powerful, and knowledge as a stance in the world, an inquisitive approach to becoming a deep and complex human being" (p. 7). To be respectful, inclusive, open-minded, is to acknowledge the potential for learning from the unfamiliar, regardless of social status or power structures. This is an essential part of that "inquisitive approach to becoming a deep and complex human being" that generates new experiences and the opportunity to learn from them. To be disrespectful, exclusive, or narrow-minded, to behave as if knowledge is a possession or a source of power over others, is to deny that potential and thus to reject the opportunity for learning.

6.2.1.2 Transparent

For a feral learner, whatever is learned, whether by design or by accident, is by definition part of the learning experience. There is no room for a *hidden curriculum*. The crucial question is not *whether* our students are learning, but *what* they are learning. Rather than prescribe limits to 'valid' learning, one of the key roles for the instructor of feral learners is to unbundle their experience so as to guide them through parts of the learning landscape that both parties perceive, and to help them recognize the significance of aspects that are unique to their own experience.

For this reason, the instruction process, where there is one, should be made transparent in the sense that the mechanism of instruction is not a 'black box'. It remains visible; there are no dark, hidden areas where the light of genuine enquiry may not shine. Limits to the scope of relevant learning may be negotiated, but in a way that contributes to the co-construction of knowledge between instructor and instructed. Even in idyllic Eden, Ochs's (2005) Eve does not cope well with God's unilateral decision to create a structured learning environment by imposing limits that Eve is not party to:

> God, acting with compassion, knowing that with knowledge comes pain, was not keen to share…as if imagining Eve could be protected and kept innocent. But…Eve…found neither joy nor safety in her bewilderment…. Even if God meant well in wishing to preserve her ignorance, Eve would become a learner just the same. (p. 8)

Transparency requires that in formal education settings, a context and purpose are made explicit. The 'rules of the game' can then be understood and negotiated effectively. For example, if we make candles, are they for lighting, to decorate with, or an aromatherapy tool? If we need a light source, then using high grade lavender oil is probably not a priority. For aromatherapy, it may be the most important consideration. For decoration the quality of light or aroma may matter less than texture, shape and color.

This may be particularly important in developing adaptive expertise where, as Bransford et al, (this volume) observe, the "process of intentionally seeking new challenges and insights during one's pursuits" (p. 45) is of key importance and learners must thus be prepared to leave their "existing comfort zones in order to increase…[their] abilities to think and perform" (p. 45). Too often, those of us with expertise attempt to hide this part of our own experience from those of us who are seeking to develop it. We present simply the end result, thus removing the opportunity to model persistence, evolution of ideas, lateral thinking, and reflective practice.

The shared understanding that develops from negotiating the learning process creates a clear contract between learner and teacher. It provides a scaffold for learners to create their own personal interpretation of the experience, and the possibility that learners and teachers together may create a solution that is actually better than the original model.

However well-intentioned, creating barriers between feral learners and the open spaces of their natural learning environment tends to make them feel not safe, but trapped. In a feral learning environment, teachers (if there are any), peers and learners establish a relationship of trust and mutual respect through transparency in the instruction process. Each acknowledges the validity and value of the others' essential humanity and life experience (prior learning), both the success and failure.

6.2.1.3 Complex

Feral learners do reduce and analyze information in manageably small quantities. However they may then also add value and complexity to their understanding of the world by recognizing many permutations of existing knowledge. So where a standard curriculum might focus on four or five key connections between five items in a linear, pentagonal or spiral pattern, feral learners may find themselves pursuing any or all of the possible connections between them.

Feral learning is not necessarily chaotic or undisciplined. It is however dictated by the complexity of the learner's whole understanding, not simply the part of it that is claimed by one academic discipline or another. As a feral learner, the things that I learn from watching my son's pet rat give birth to 13 baby rats; a block course on The Art of Managing Difficult People; and parent interviews with my son's teachers, are not necessarily arranged in a rigid matrix within my understanding as "Parenting/1987", "Pet care/2005", etc. Each is fluid—infinitely flexible in its connections to other items in my life experience.

Techniques for working with feral learners must therefore focus less on reducing the scope of knowledge to a discrete series of lessons, disciplines or curriculum areas and more on the overall connectedness of things, and on acknowledging learning as and when it occurs. Silverman (2004) describes this approach as fluid, by contrast with the more rigid crystalline nature of traditional curricula.

Britain and Liber (1999) and Britain (2004) describe two ways of managing the complexity of a natural knowledge environment in education. The traditional one is to reduce, or *attenuate* the complex information that exists in the environment to a more simple level by applying a variety of filters. The reciprocal process, on the other hand, is to *amplify* the knowledge of the individual or organization into the knowledge environment where it connects with other bits and pieces of knowledge to become part of that larger, more complex system. We do this for example by publishing a paper or making a presentation.

Traditional pedagogies break down complex knowledge environments into manageable 'chunks' (attenuation), in essence defining what is worth knowing by what the instructor knows or the curriculum prescribes. This approach may be appropriate for replicating knowledge of relatively stable mechanical processes, but it is much less effective for dealing with environments or concepts that are complex and/or rapidly evolving. Significantly, this means it does not cater well to a genuinely innovative approach.

6.2.1.4   Holistic

A holistic approach is needed in order to deal with complexity. We must recognise that new learning not only affects the immediate context but may lead to modifications in the learner's whole knowledge system as it accommodates the new combinations and permutations that become possible as a result.

To nurture the feral learner, we need to review our underlying approach to designing both curriculum and learning environments. Whether the ultimate objective is to help learners survive or achieve wisdom, the educator's goal should be to help them assimilate experience. This is the process of making meaning, in which the meaning schemes and perspectives that frame the learner's internal landscape are constantly evolving to coexist with the external landscapes of their world.

Senge, Scharmer, Jaworski, & Flowers (2004) speak of transformational change (learning) as an holistic mechanism whereby living entities move from repetition of the known present into new and unknown futures (evolution). In their view "the whole exists through continually manifesting in the parts, and the parts exist as embodiments of the whole." (p. 6). They reject the mechanistic perception that the whole is simply the sum of its component parts, asserting that "This is a very logical way of thinking about machines. But living systems are different" (p. 5). This perception is "stolen from us when we accept the machine worldview of wholes assembled from replaceable parts" (p. 7).

Marks (1985) considers self-organization to be an important feature of evolving systems. In his words: "Constructive rationalism gives rise to designed or made orders, like cars, or silicon chips, buildings or…armies….All of these have been designed for…definite purposes" (n.p.). However, "it is not possible…to know all the relevant facts needed to design complex social institutions" (n.p.). Marks thus goes on to say: "We need to recognise the importance of…self-generating or spontaneous orders to which the ideas of purpose and design do not apply. Organisms, languages, market economies, societies are orders which were not designed: they evolved" (n.p.).

6.2.1.5   Seamless

The way I learn is continuous and consistent over time. In other words, learning is seamless—but institutions aren't. Moving from one to another can create the illusion of discontinuities throughout the lifetime that do not really exist.

Looking through the array of educational theories and models related to specific life stages it is easy to form the impression that as a child I must have learned in a way that was quite different from the way I do now. In some ways this may be true, in that like everything else these processes may evolve. However, the things that make each of us who we are, such as genetic coding, cognitive style, personality and the way we each make meaning from our experience, remain if not static, at least consistent.

To work effectively with feral learners we must recognize that while their learning processes do evolve, an individual does not learn differently because they are old enough to attend a tertiary institution instead of secondary, or because they are in the workplace not the classroom. It is not so much their learning process that changes, but the context in which that learning is viewed.

6.2.1.6 Student-Led, A-Curricular

A feral learner does not always need to be taught, although there will always be circumstances where the guidance of a more experienced or skilled practitioner is invaluable (see also Bransford et al., in this volume). Traditional classroom teaching, though, is curriculum-driven, while feral learning is student-led, determined by the readiness of the learner to assimilate new experiences and information. Teaching feral learners is not so much like training dogs as training cats—a much more difficult activity.

Feral learning is continuous through time (is seamless—see above), disciplines and the limits of prescribed curriculum. If a learner perceives a connection between apparently unrelated topics such as the life of Napoleon, how to make waffles and quadratic equations, then curriculum and pedagogical approach need to be flexible and open enough to accommodate them in this. Siemens (2007) speaks in this connection about "permeable learning spaces so that we can reach out to the broader world, to have experts, communities, and networks of teachers" (n.p.). To accommodate the feral learner we need to develop not only permeable learning spaces, but permeable curricula as well.

Some educators of course are very familiar with this kind of approach. The Sudbury School model, and some forms of home schooling provide useful examples of how this open approach to curriculum can work. The New Zealand Early Childhood Curriculum, Te Whāriki, for example, describes *curriculum* as "… the sum total of the experiences, activities, and events, whether direct or indirect, which occur within an environment designed to foster children's learning and development." This not only permits but requires a rigorously child centered approach from educators. And for good reason: infants and very young children are the ultimate feral learners and will engage with whatever holds their interest, but only so long as it genuinely continues to do so.

6.2.2 *Where Do We Look for Feral Learners?*

Feral learners are not a breed apart. Feral learning is by its nature something we all do. Some of us however are more easily 'domesticated' than others. Some groups may be identified as more intrinsically feral than others. Aside from infants and the very young, whom we have already touched upon, some of these groups are identified below.

6.2.2.1 ...Gifted and Able Students

Visual-spatial learners may be among the most naturally feral learners—the ones who daydream or draw pictures through the teacher's careful explanation and then ask apparently unrelated questions, who seem almost willfully obtuse when lessons are broken down into easy steps, who find disciplined, consistent effort hard to sustain. For these learners, the boundaries and disciplines of the curriculum-led classroom or course of instruction may constitute active barriers to deep learning. Silverman and Freed (2006) associate giftedness with a visual-spatial learning style and speak of fluidity and gestalt learning moments as characteristic of these learners. They assert that "spatial learners are systems thinkers—they need to see the whole picture first before they can understand the parts (p. 4) and warn that "Rote memorization and drill...are actually damaging for visual-spatial learners, since they emphasize the student's weaknesses instead of their strengths" (p. 4). They furthermore characterize visual-spatial learners as learners who are "gestalt, "aha" learners...[who] can be taught out of order" (p. 4); who are "usually disorganized and miss details" (p. 5); who are "highly aware of space but ...[pay]... little attention to time" (p. 5); who "can't show their work because they arrive at conclusions intuitively" (p. 5); and who are at risk of being under stress as "they have no systems to fall back on: no trial-and-error processes, no sequential cues" (p. 7).

6.2.2.2 ...The at Risk

It is worth noting that the characteristics Silverman and Freed (2006) attribute to visual-spatial learners may also be associated with so-called "learning disabilities" such as dyslexia and ADD. Both Silverman and Freed (2006) and Gilbertson (2003) point out that this group includes some of the most creative and influential figures of recent times. Silverman (2004) refers in this connection to a study

> conducted in the Arapahoe County juvenile court system [which] revealed that 15 percent of incarcerated youth tested in the top 3 percentile on standardized intelligence scales (Harvey & Seeley, 1984; Seeley, 1984, 2003). ... Fifteen percent is five times the number... [that] would be predicted by chance. The majority exhibited a "fluid" or "spatial" learning style, in which the right hemisphere is favored over the left hemisphere. Such children are often unrecognized ... as sequential methods of instruction fail to reach them. (p. 1)

6.2.2.3 ...Nerds and Geeks

According to Prensky (2004, personal communication), feral learning is exactly what gamers expect and thrive on in a gaming environment. These virtual environments provide situated problem solving, incremental acquisition of new skills, strategic thinking, goal orientation, and the opportunity to follow a path simply to see where it leads. LaPointe's chapter (in this volume) contains a fuller discussion of virtual gaming environments.

Within this landscape, feral learners may come to value their journey and their destination in a way that satisfies both their thirst for knowledge and their hunger for success. They may, therefore, be less inclined to accept the tradition that *being taught* is a satisfactory alternative to self-directed and personally meaningful *learning*. For these learners, reusable learning objects, digital game based learning, just-in-time training and total immersion via cultural exchanges and the like may provide more effective learning than the traditional classroom or lecture theatre.

6.2.2.4 …In the Classroom

Pedagogies that support feral learning are already alive and well in formal education. Examples include project and portfolio work; recognition of prior learning (RPL); total immersion programs such as international student exchange; early childhood settings emphasizing self-selected play; and the 'alternative' schools mentioned in the *What is feral learning?* section of this chapter.

6.3   Theories and Concepts

The theoretical roots of feral learning lie in constructivist and transformative learning theory.

6.3.1   Constructivism

According to constructivist theory, the events or information a person comes in contact with are significant not in and of themselves, but for the meaning that person invests them with. In constructivist theory, according to Richardson (2003) "there is an assumption that meaning or knowledge is actively constructed in the human mind" (p. 1625). The author further specifies that in social constructivism the focus is "how the development of that formal knowledge has been created or determined within power, economic, social and political forces" whereas in the psychological approach the focus is "on the ways in which meaning is created within the individual mind and, more recently, how shared meaning is developed within a group process" (p. 1625).

Constructivist theory thus contains many of the elements necessary for genuinely student-centered formal instruction that will nurture the feral learner. However, many of the applications of constructivist theory, such as Reigeluth's (1999) elaboration theory, still have several major limitations for the feral learner, in that they:

- Are supply-push, rather than demand-pull
- Are based on a reductionist framework

- Offer a very limited range of learning pathways and outcomes.

To this extent, constructivist theory has not yet delivered on its potential for the feral learner.

6.3.2   Transformative Learning

Mezirow's (1990, 1991) *transformative learning* theory not only perceives the learner (or client) as being at the centre of the process, it also explicitly frames the learning process as an aspect of personal growth and development. With roots in the work of Rogers and Maslow, transformative learning spans the fields of education and personal development. Mezirow makes a clear distinction between formative (uncritical) learning, which occurs in childhood, and transformative learning, which is the product of critical self-reflection in adulthood. My own view is that both formative and transformative learning may take place throughout life, although the balance between them is likely to change. A learner's capacity to critique their own prior learning, or to be discriminating in their acceptance of new information and value systems is not, in other words, a simple function of childhood or adulthood. Some individuals display this capacity from a very early age. Others may never acquire it. Likewise, some of us are more capable of entertaining entirely new ideas in our maturity and old age than are others.

There are interesting parallels between this idea of transformational change in the individual and the transformative power of change in learning organizations, described by Senge (1990) as "a group of people continually enhancing their capacity to create what they want to create" (p. 42) and learning societies (Faure et al., 1972; J. Visser, 2001). In *The Presence Workbook*, Senge et al. (2004) note that learning and change processes often yield disappointing results because they fail to recognize "the underlying field of potential from which new possibilities emerge" (p. 5). They identify three aspects of transformative and sustainable change, which they call *sensing* (learning to see the familiar from different perspectives), *presencing* (becoming aware and 'present' in a way that allows different visions and interpretations to be acknowledged), and *realizing* (changing our behavior in order to promote the preferred vision for the future).

Compare the above with Mezirow's (1990) definition of transformative learning as "the process of learning through critical self-reflection, which results in …a more inclusive, discriminating, and integrative understanding of one's experience. Learning includes acting on these insights" (p. xvi).

In both views, sustainable change occurs when not only the individual's knowledge base, but their frame(s) of reference for making sense of that knowledge, their 'meaning perspectives' are amended. In this framework, cognitive dissonance becomes a powerful tool. "Anomalies and dilemmas of which the old ways of knowing cannot make sense become catalysts or 'trigger events' that precipitate critical reflection and transformations" (Mezirow, 1990, p. 14).

Transformative learning theory describes the way that experience can change (transform) the way a learner understands their world. These transformations may be incremental, or take the form of discontinuities—gestalt moments in which existing ways of understanding undergo a perceptible shift. The measured pace of traditional curricula makes little allowance for this. Feral learners, whose natural learning patterns do not fall into similar measured incremental steps will therefore spend most of their formal education either behind or ahead of the curriculum.

6.3.3 Flexible Delivery

> Given the convergence of technologies and the development of universal communications and data bases, it is becoming possible for learners of all ages to initiate their own educational pathways and learn what they want, when they want, where they want; the ideal of open learning. (Lundin, 1997, p. 72)

Flexible delivery (Nunan, 1996; Lundin, 1998, 1999) concentrates on creating an effective learning environment focused on meeting learner needs in preference to organizational convenience. Unlike the stereotype of traditional classroom teaching, genuinely flexible delivery does not attempt to dictate when, where or how a student learns but develops a partnership in which the student chooses meaningful learning strategies in pursuit of agreed learning objectives.

Flexible delivery is essential for feral learning in a formal education context. In order to provide a genuinely flexible learning environment for its students, an organization must itself be flexible in its management and culture; in order for it to facilitate learning it must be a learning organization. These requirements are both essential for feral learning. Both become increasingly difficult to maintain in larger institutions, which tend to have large and relatively rigid infrastructure.

To be sustainable, educational institutions need to address the needs not just of the student, but of all their stakeholders including employer groups (for vocational training), parents (for the school sector), government agencies, staff, boards, and other students. All of these mean that it is incredibly difficult in practice, to maintain a clear and unambiguous focus on what each individual may need from their learning experience, and find the resources to provide it. Failing to deal effectively with them, however, leaves educators at risk of focusing on institutional imperatives at the expense of educational ones.

6.3.4 Learning Ecologies

The concept of the *learning ecology* that underlies the *learning landscape* metaphor in this chapter follows Seely Brown (1999), Dimitrov (2000), Visser (2001), and Siemens (2003). Seely Brown defines it as "an environment that is consistent with (not antagonistic to) how learners learn... an open system, dynamic and interdependent, diverse, partially self organizing, adaptive, and fragile" (n.p.). The characteristics each of these authors ascribes to a learning ecology are summarized in Table 6.1 below. This view of the *learning ecology* is substantively broader than the view that underlies some other ecological models such as Ysseldike and Christenson's *TIES-II* (The Instructional Environment System-II), or Frielick's (2004) *ecosystemic process of teaching/learning*, which remain focused on instruction within an institutional setting.

Where other approaches have focused on stripping the environment back to its component parts, the value here is in considering them holistically as a whole ecosystem. The *learning ecology* concept allows us to focus on the interactions between the learner, (*Me*) and their whole environment, (*Not me*), that create changes in both.

6.3.5 *Learning Landscapes*

Counseling and psychology use the metaphor of *internal* and *external landscapes* to describe the differences between the interpretation a person makes of the world around them (internal) and their observable context and behavior (external). This overlaps with the constructivist notion that interpretation is a key aspect of the learning process (Mezirow, 1990).

Each of us operates within an environment (landscape) that has some features in common with others in our peer group(s) and some that are unique to us. The elements that contribute to this landscape will include technologies, teaching & learning strategies, delivery modes (for instruction), physical and social situation, content, social and personal history, ethnicity and culture, social networks, character traits, and a vast array of other influences and interactions. The way the learner interacts with each element is important, and so is the way that various elements interact with each other to create the rich and complex environment in which the learner operates.

In economically developed areas, where learners are exposed to the environment Lundin (1997) describes at the start of the section on 'flexible delivery' above, some of the common features are likely to be:

- Direct, decentralized access to information and opinion.
- Contestable information—multiple sources, contexts, interpretations.
- Immediateness—the internet is always "on", and response times are short compared to physical transfer of materials (e.g. through library interloans, 'snail mail').
- Connectedness—there is always someone out there available to connect with. Social groups can maintain contact on an almost constant basis.
- Availability of a global information base.
- Multi-sensory, multi-media forms of communication.
- Uncertainty—technologies, content & protocols are continually changing. Even the trends and patterns that govern these changes are often unclear.

Table 6.1 Learning ecologies

	Seely Brown (1999)	Dimitrov (2000)	Visser (2001)	Siemens (2003)
Focus	An open, complex adaptive system comprising elements that are dynamic and interdependent. Enables learning to happen everywhere.	Focuses on factors and conditions facilitating the process of learning.	The totality of conditions put in place in which individuals and social entities at different levels of organizational complexity all engage in learning. An environment in which the activity of learning is pervasive and occurs in diverse contexts and at different levels of organizational complexity.	An environment that fosters and supports the creation of communities. Consistent with (not antagonistic to) how learners learn.
Openness	An open system.	Searches for ways to open new possibilities.	Thermodynamically efficient open systems.	
Dynamics	Dynamic and interdependent. A self-catalytic system reinforcing and extending the core competencies.	Dynamic interactions of living creatures, including humans, and their environment - natural and artificial (human-made). (ecology).	Myriad different spaces in which people learn in interaction, and often collaboration, with each other. Capable of accommodating interaction, collaboration, networking and adaptive growth. Evolving.	A dynamic, living, and evolving state. New communities, projects and ideas start with much hype and promotion…and then slowly fade. To create a knowledge sharing ecology, participants need to see a consistently evolving environment.
Robustness			Flexible. Capable of complex, robust, open-ended learning and cognition.	High tolerance for experimentation and failure.
Organization	A collection of overlapping communities of interest. Largely self organizing. Embodies substantial expertise that exists in both written and tacit form.	Facilitates … self-organizing impetus.	Distributed systems.	Informal, not structured. Flexible enough to allow participants to create according to their needs. Decentralized, fostered, connected.

(continued)

Table 6.1 (continued)

	Seely Brown (1999)	Dimitrov (2000)	Visser (2001)	Siemens (2003)
Diversity/complexity	Diverse, overlapping, richly opinionated. Cross pollinating. Combines the small efforts of the many with the large efforts of the few.	Web of interactions exists at multiple levels.	Multiple and complementary perspectives. Allows the whole to acquire a meaning over and above the sum of its parts 'Dialogic efficacy' Incorporates a complex resource infrastructure. Should accommodate all different purposes and modalities of learning in a way that they constitute a whole that is complete in itself.	Tool-rich—many opportunities for users to dialogue and connect. Other characteristics need to be balanced with the need for simplicity. Simple, social approaches work most effectively.
Integrity/consistency	Constantly evolving.	Vital for sustaining the integrity of this web and hence for sustaining the life and its unfolding. (Learning process)	Ability to foster learning that is rooted in the real world. Recognizes the wholeness of knowledge. Integrity is important because of the need for all learning entities to be able to interact with each other.	Requires consistency and time. High social contact (face to face or online) is needed to foster a sense of trust and comfort. Secure and safe environments are critical for trust to develop.

The prevalence of feral learning strategies may be more dependent on culture than on technology. If feral learning is, as this chapter suggests, a natural lifelong process of synthesizing experience as and when we find it and allowing it to modify the way we interact with our environment, then logically it will occur whether the infrastructure is traditional or technological.

6.3.6   Digital Natives and Digital Immigrants

Adams (1999) likened the evolution of the modern communication technology to the evolution of pidgin and creole languages. Like early Internet functions and protocols, pidgin languages are a rough-and-ready collection of bits from here and there, providing a rudimentary functionality but lacking depth, subtlety, or flexibility. According to Adams, the first generation of children born to a particular language community "takes these fractured lumps of language and transforms them into something new, with a rich and organic grammar and vocabulary, which is what we call a Creole....The same thing is happening in communication technology" (n.p.).

Prensky (2001a) speaks of this quantum change in terms of cultural differences between those born and raised in the digital age (digital natives) and previous generations (digital immigrants). He quotes from a variety of sources[1] to say that "children raised with the computer 'think differently from the rest of us. They develop hypertext minds. They leap around.'…'Linear thought processes that dominate educational systems now can actually retard learning for brains developed through game and Web-surfing processes on the computer.'" (2001b, p. 4).

While Prensky's position is by no means universally accepted (see, for example, Merrill in this volume), elements of his view are clearly echoed by other commentators. Prensky's Digital Natives have the non-linear, intuitive characteristics of Silverman's Visual-Spatial learners. More importantly, perhaps, both Adams (1999) and Prensky (2001a, 2001b) draw attention to the fact that there is a huge gap between learners' and teachers' experience of the world. It follows that the touchstones learners and teachers use to make meaning from their experiences may also be very different. So what the educator believes they are observing may not always match what the learner believes they are experiencing. Other authors in this volume (J. Visser; Bransford et al.; LaPointe) similarly refer to the speed and magnitude of change in today's world, and its effect on the transferability of knowledge between generations.

Key differences in the typical learning environments encountered by today's young, and their parents' and grandparents' generations that Prensky (2001a, 2001b) and Adams (1999) identify are summarized in Table 6.2.

---

[1] Prensky references his sources as follows: "William D. Winn, Director of the Learning Center, Human Interface Technology Laboratory, University of Washington, quoted in Moore, *Inferential Focus Briefing*" and "Peter Moore, *Inferential Focus Briefing*, September 30, 1997."

Table 6.2 Changing learning landscapes

Digital immigrants' landscapes tended to be...	Digital natives' landscapes tend to be...
Non-participatory	Interactive
Disconnected (excluding distractions and irrelevancies)	Connected (cell phones, search, IM, social networks)
Slow (limited by physical speed)	Instantaneous (twitch speed)
Constrained	Complex
Disciplined	Creative
Focused (concentration, not multitasking)	Multi-sensory (digital/video games)
One-or two-dimensional (defined by paper representations)	Multidimensional, non-linear (hypertext)
Controlled (by others)	Controllable (by them)

This view, that there is a real difference between the experience and thought processes of those born into the digital age and those who were raised before, is still contested. Intuitively though, it seems likely to me that there is a difference of kind, not simply of degree. If my generation was educated to cope with the rate of change in our world, a first differential, my children's learning must equip them to cope with the changes in that rate of change, a second differential. Marks (2006) voices it as follows:

> My generation draws the Internet as a cloud that connects everyone; the younger generation experiences it as oxygen that supports their digital lives. The old generation sees this as a poisonous gas that has leaked out of their pipes, and they want to seal it up again. (n.p.)

Feral learning is about genuine engagement not simply obedience or discipline. In order to engage learners, educators must first be able to recognize and navigate in the learner's own landscape. This implies a necessity to readjust the traditional power structures inherent in formal education.

If it is necessary to locate the frame of reference for learning experiences in the learner's native landscape (situated learning) and it is one the 'teacher' is unfamiliar with, then what the teacher has to offer is navigation technique (learning skills), rather than geography (curriculum). Clearly in these circumstances the learner, not the teacher, becomes the final arbiter of relevance or validity. We have been familiar with the notion of the teacher as 'guide.' If the above holds, it seems 'teachers' may need to relinquish even that much illusion of control over curriculum and take on the role not of guide, but of tracker.

6.4 Discussion

6.4.1 The Alienation of Learning

Visser (2001) describes learning as "...the disposition of human beings, and of the social entities to which they pertain, to engage in continuous dialogue with the human, social, biological and physical environment, so as to generate intelligent behavior to interact constructively with change" (p. 453).

Learning is not transferable (as anyone knows who has tried to pass on the benefit of their own experience to their children!). It is something that we each experience alone and uniquely, in the difference between who we are in this instant, who we were in the past and who we will be in the future as our experiences—however subtly—change how we interact with the world around us. Typical dictionary definitions refer to learning in one of three ways: (i) the act, process, or experience of gaining knowledge or skill; (ii) knowledge or skill gained through schooling or study; and (iii) behavioral modification especially through experience or conditioning.

From infancy a child learns the first way, gaining experience, knowledge, and skills which it uses to manipulate its environment—or it does not thrive. Once they begin formal education, children become familiar with the second aspect of learning. In the traditional classroom setting they are socialized to regard *being taught* as being equal to *learning*. They must accept that someone other than themselves is the best arbiter of what they need to learn, what they will learn, when to stop learning, and what use their learning will be to them. By the time they finish school this understanding of what it means to learn has been dominant for as much as three quarters of their life.

At the extreme, this process of imposing someone else's values and priorities on the learner becomes indistinguishable from the third meaning given above: Pavlov-style *conditioning* or *behavior modification*. There is a debate within psychology about whether the ends of 'better' behavior justify the means of manipulating another human being without their informed consent. This ethical issue should also concern us as educators.

The traditional classroom thus alienates students from their own learning process. They are trained not so much to *learn*—to enquire for its own sake, because finding out, and achieving greater levels of mastery is fun—but to *be taught*. They must channel their attention and energy into the discrete curricula someone else has determined they *should* learn. Anything they pursue for their own interest or satisfaction, for example by reflecting when they should be writing, or vice versa, is likely to be denigrated as 'off-task.' Ironically, we then expect them to be self-motivated and reflective learners.

The fact that this one term, 'learning' carries such a diversity of meanings is a powerful reason for us to reflect carefully when we use it on which of these meanings we are invoking.

6.4.2 *Survival and Wisdom*

Human learning has two ultimate objectives: survival, and wisdom. Senge (1990), writing about learning organizations, uses the terms *adaptive* for learning that promotes survival and *generative* for learning that creates additional capacity—the organizational counterpart of wisdom. Senge, Scharmer, Jaworski & Flowers (2005) talk of this same distinction in terms of *reactive learning*, which does not challenge existing world views, and *deeper levels of learning*, which move beyond existing preconceptions and ways of interacting with the world to permit genuinely new perceptions or behaviors.

Survival is the objective served by making education compulsory for young children, by teaching '*foundation skills*' and '*core curriculum.*' These strategies are designed to provide all members of society—particularly children—with means and opportunity to gain the skills and knowledge that they will need to survive into a healthy and functional adulthood. The objective of learning beyond what is needed for survival is to become wise.

Ochs (2005) observes that "When you become wise like Eve, you don't let others tell you what is safe for you to learn, try out, explore, or investigate" (p. 9), but rather, "You know what you need to encounter to become wise, and you venture forth. ...You let no one tell you what kind of learning is a waste of your time or what's too serious for you, or not serious enough. You alone are the judge" (p. 9). She also notes the holistic nature of wisdom: "To become wise like Eve, you discover ways to weave together your book learning and your life learning" (p. 10), and, furthermore, "When you become wise like Eve, you regard all ways of learning with respect" (p. 12).

Unfortunately, wisdom is not a fashionable concept in contemporary Western education. Primary schools and universities alike frame their mission statements in terms of wisdom, but present their curriculum as survival learning—to survive well, you must have a career. To have a career, you must be literate and have qualifications.

There is a tacit assumption that wisdom is a natural corollary of getting older, or more qualified. In my experience though, even young children can be interested and competent in the pursuit of wisdom—learning for its own sake, for the joy of knowing, for the ability to enjoy a life rich in understanding. They too may achieve complex and abstract insights into the nature of reality, even if their command of language does not always capture the fullness of the concept. Listen to Anthony (age four) who observed, "Nothing's really alive or dead. Everything's part of everything else. My body could be part of a rock one day. This rock might have been a dinosaur." Perhaps we need to reintroduce the concept of *becoming wise* more explicitly into our discussion of learning and teaching, and into the terms of reference of our educational institutions.

6.4.3   Learning and Being Taught

Learning and *being taught* are not the same. Some of us have observed that students do not always enjoy *being taught*, and have drawn from that the mistaken conclusion that the internal process of *learning* is not intrinsically satisfying. Mulhauser (2006) tells us that we are each our own best authority on our experience and, given the right conditions, we are each capable of fulfilling our own potential. One such condition is the acceptance (*positive regard*) of others whom we respect or depend on.

When we do not have that validation, or even when it is only granted when we behave in ways that are dictated from outside ourselves, then we interfere with the very process of making meaning. Over time, we may lose touch with our ability to make meaning from experience so thoroughly that our intrinsic sense of our own identity may be replaced by pressures from other people. When we depend on the conditionally positive judgments of others, our 'self-concept' may begin to clash with our immediate personal experience and psychological disturbance results.

When we fail to hold our students in *unconditional positive regard*, or fail to reflect critically on our own frames of reference and our professional practice, this error becomes embedded in our practice and our discourse. And, over time, it becomes part of the institutional culture of education. Most of us would concede—in theory—that valid learning happens in all kinds of environments. However, when we put our practitioner hats on, we tend to focus on formal learning environments at the expense of wider contexts. As a result, we end up discussing *formal instruction* and *learning* as if they are the same thing, which they patently are not. Educational institutions provide instruction: an opportunity to learn through formal study. This is valuable. However that process of receiving sequential one-to-many instruction from a series of 'experts' is only one way of learning.

Although we speak of *educating* our children and young people in our schools and universities, in practice we often settle for *training* them, even at degree level. Goal-driven instruction for a specific purpose such as employment is *training*. While training is important and valid, it is only a subset of *formal instruction*. *Training* is characterized by a closed curriculum and a limited set of target outcomes. *Education* implies openness in the curriculum, and a broad range of acceptable goals and outcomes.

We need to be aware of how far and how fast the ground can shift as we talk about learning. To encourage feral learning, we need to prioritize learning over formal instruction and education over training. We cannot afford to let linguistic 'shorthand' mislead us into talking about institutional environments as if they are the only legitimate avenues for learning and teaching.

6.4.4   Changing the System

As a society, we have invested much in traditional ways of thinking about education, and in the physical and human resources that constitute our existing educational institutions. Society is governed by people who have benefited well from traditional education: politicians, professors, policy makers and the like. As caring adults, we naturally want to restrict our children to the relative safety of landscapes familiar to us. These social and political expectations present significant barriers to new ways of thinking about education.

"Education is the propagation of a set of beliefs. We call it 'education' if we already believe in it and 'propaganda' if we don't" (Rhoads, 1997, n.p.). Here's an example. A report of a longitudinal research project into the ongoing effects of early childhood education recently published in New Zealand (Wylie & Hipkins, 2006) concluded that 14-year-olds with no particular interests are likely to be lower achievers in school than those who have active interests such as sports, music, or other hobbies. Researchers identified four student clusters according to their leisure-time pursuits:

1. *Sports players*, likely to regularly play sports, exercise, and less likely to take part in performing arts. 34% of the sample was in this cluster. ...This cluster had the second lowest proportion of young people who enjoyed reading (52%).
2. *Electronic-games/no strong interests*. This group showed a similar level of electronic-game playing as the 'sports players,' but did not engage in other interests regularly. 24% of the sample was in this cluster. There was some relationship with family income: 33% of the low-income group were in this cluster, decreasing to 15% of the high and very high income groups. ...This cluster had the lowest proportion of students who enjoyed reading (34%).
3. *All-rounders*. These students participated in regular sport and exercise, but also liked to read and take part in the performing arts on a regular basis. 28% of the sample was in this cluster. The very high-income group was also more likely to be in this cluster (41%). 67% of this cluster enjoyed reading.
4. *Creative interests*. Students in this cluster also participated in the performing arts, and were regularly involved in making things. They did not take part in sport and exercise on a regular basis. 13% of the students in the study were in this cluster, and 70% of the cluster enjoyed reading.

The lead paragraph in the local newspaper summarized this as 'Research into how children fare at high school has sounded a warning for Generation X-Box kids and their parents.' This message, that competence in new media ('new literacy') is dangerous and destructive to useful learning, is inaccurate and unhelpful but—alas—all too common.

The good news is, many teachers and parents do continually explore new ideas and technologies with their students, and build meaningful links from students' interests to the requirements of the curriculum. Embedding those changes in our social and political infrastructure is not necessarily going to be easy. At some point, the social barriers to meaningful change need to be addressed so our institutions can evolve to the next level, and help our children grow beyond the limitations of their parents.

6.5   Concluding Remarks

Feral learning offers a way of talking about the natural process of learning (adaptation) that we all experience throughout our lives. By providing a label and the beginnings of a framework for thinking about this process, it provides a vehicle for shifting the focus of educational debate away from what teachers do and how students respond to it (teaching-and-learning) to the process of becoming a functional human being or human society, and what is desirable or necessary to enable and nurture it.

The view of feral learning developed in this chapter is an extension of constructivist theory, and draws strongly on the work of Rogers (humanist education) and Mezirow (transformative learning). It is also informed—and constrained—by my own experiences, notably in flexible delivery, eLearning, Early Childhood Education and parenthood.

The concepts of feral learning are not new. The language and impetus for describing it has arisen largely out of the literature on the educational potential of the so-called 'new media.' This does not mean that it is applicable only in that context. What it does mean is that that is the context with which, at the time of writing, I feel competent to comment on.

An understanding of feral learning may help to promote positive outcomes for all kinds of learners, such as able, differently-abled and at-risk students, Internet junkies and gamers, the very young, adult learners, and hobbyists.

Feral learning is a life-long process, incorporating formal and informal, directed and self-selected learning experiences. It may be undertaken alone or in groups, with or without intervention. Feral learning is by nature respectful, transparent, student-led, a-curricular, holistic, complex, and seamless.

Human learning serves two purposes, survival and the pursuit of wisdom. Each carries its own intrinsic rewards. There is—or at least, there can be—a profound difference between the experience of learning and the experience of being taught. While being taught is not always an enjoyable experience, genuine learning is.

There is an urgent need for educators to reinvent the traditional roles of learners and the educational institutions that are supposed to meet their learning needs. Developments in technology (the Internet, mobile phones and video gaming), and educational theory (constructivist and transformative learning theory), and flexible delivery make this possible. The social and personal cost of our evident failure to meet the needs of a significant number of students in the traditional classroom makes it urgent. Some areas that seem to have useful potential in achieving this are: lifelong learning; communities of interest; learning organizations; transformational change; management and spirituality; personal growth and 'self-help;' complexity theory; digital game-based learning; virtual learning environments.

Whatever the pathway we approach it by, one of the keys to promoting effective change in our education systems is to develop more, and more consistent use of strategies that promote feral learning.

6.6 Resources for Further Exploration

Following is a list of resources to start with for those interested in further exploration of the ideas presented in this chapter.

- Society for Organizational Learning (SoL—http://www.solonline.org/): SoL is a widely distributed intentional learning community that is consciously reflective, self-organizing and forward-looking. Its focus is as much corporate and philo-sophical as educational. Articles and references are available along with membership and journal subscriptions.

- elearningpost (http://www.elearningpost.com/): elearningpost is maintained by Maish Naichani and comprises a blog and posted articles. An email digest is also available. Its mission is "to provide quality e-learning and knowledge management content that attracts a diverse and emerging audience."
- Sudbury Valley School (http://www.sudval.org/): The website of the original Sudbury School in Massachusetts. It offers useful and accessible information about the theory and practice of Sudbury's democratic school model as well as links to associated articles, mailing lists, photos and other resources.
- Managing complexity: Some challenges in elearning (http://www.efest.org. nz/2004/2004speakers.html): This is an accessible and interesting introduction to the issue of managing complexity in virtual educational environments. The presentation is in Microsoft PowerPoint format. Download and peruse in Normal view to see the outline and notes.
- Marc Prensky's Web site (http://www.marcprensky.com/): At the time of writing, the blog was not well maintained, but the rest of this site provides readable and engaging articles, information and resources on digital game-based learning. Of particular relevance are Prensky's articles on Digital Natives and Digital Immigrants.
- Pekka Himanen's (2001) *The hacker ethic and the spirit of the information age* is unfortunately not available online at the time of writing. Pekka Himanen describes and explains the culture that has driven the development of the Internet, and is embodied in the way it operates. The prologue by Marcus Torvalds (developer of the Linux operating system) is fascinating in its own right.

6.7 Questions for Comprehension and Application

1. Imagine having the opportunity to create from scratch an educational facility— school, training department or a more limited learning event of your choice—for a particular group of people with given learning needs. Based on what you have read and your own appreciation of the ideas advanced by the author, how would you go about setting this facility up? Discuss implications for curriculum structure and organization; assessment; roles of different actors (students, teachers, etc.); use of media if applicable; organization of activities in space and time and other aspects you deem relevant.
2. Now imagine you are not doing the above from scratch, but rather your starting point is an already existing educational facility that functions in the traditional way. Identify and describe the difficulties you will encounter in making the change. What would you do to help the change process along?
3. Read and critique the 'characteristics' Section (6.2.1) of this chapter. In particular, look for assumptions and implications that underlie the views presented by the author and those cited. How well or poorly do these relate to your own experience and understanding?

References

Adams, D. (1999). *How to stop worrying and learn to love the Internet*. Retrieved July 10, 2006, from http://www.douglasadams.com/dna/19990901–00-a.html.

Bransford, J. D., Slowinski, M., Vye, N., & Mosborg, S. (in this volume). The learning sciences, technology and designs for educational systems: Some thoughts about change. In J. Visser & M. Visser-Valfrey (Eds.), *Learners in a changing learning landscape: Reflections from a dialogue on new roles and expectations* (pp. 37–67). Dordrecht, The Netherlands: Springer.

Britain, S. (2004, October 12). *Managing complexity: Some challenges in elearning*. Keynote Speech presented at eFest 2004, Wellington, New Zealand. Retrieved March 29, 2006, from http://www.efest.org.nz/2004/2004speakers.html.

Britain, S., & Liber, O. (1999, October). *A framework for pedagogical evaluation of virtual learning environments*. Manchester: JISC Technology Applications Program. (Report No. 41). Retrieved February 6, 2007, from http://jisc-1.eduserv.org.uk/ uploaded_documents/jtap-041.doc.

Dimitrov, V. (2000). *Learning ecology for human and machine intelligence*. University of Western Sydney. Retrieved August 17, 2007, from http://www.zulenet.com/VladimirDimitrov/pages/ LearnEcologyHuman.html

Faure, E., Herrera, F., Kaddoura, A. -R., Lopes, H., Petrovsky, A. V., Rahnema, M., & Ward, F. C. (1972) *Learning to be*. Paris: UNESCO. Retrieved August 18, 2007, from http://unesdoc. unesco.org/images/0000/000018/001801e.pdf.

Frielick, S. (2004). Beyond constructivism: An ecological approach to e-learning. In R. Atkinson, C. McBeath, D. Jonas-Dwyer, & R. Phillips (Eds.), *Beyond the comfort zone: Proceedings of the 21st ASCILITE conference*. Perth, 5–8 December, 2004. Retrieved July 12, 2006, from http://www.ascilite.org.au/conferences/perth04/procs/ contents.html.

Gilbertson, D. (2003). '*ADHD*' or '*Latent Entrepreneur Personality Type*'? Retrieved April 4, 2006, from http://www.windeaters.co.nz/publications/innovation_entrepreneurship/ Adhd2_web.pdf.

Harvey, S., & Seeley, K. (1984). An investigation of the relationships among intellectual and creative abilities, extracurricular activities, achievement, and giftedness in a delinquent population. *Gifted Child Quarterly, 28*, 73–79.

Himanen, P. (2001). *The hacker ethic and the spirit of the information age*. London: Secker & Warburg.

LaPointe, D. (in this volume). Will games and emerging technologies influence the learning landscape? In J. Visser & M. Visser-Valfrey (Eds.), *Learners in a changing learning landscape: Reflections from a dialogue on new roles and expectations* (pp. 227–249). Dordrecht, The Netherlands: Springer.

Lundin, R. (1997). Human factors and interactive communications technologies. *The Canadian Journal of Educational Communication, 26*(2), 61–74.

Lundin, R. (1998, September). *Feral learning: Being unreal in a virtual education world*. Paper presented at Learning Technologies'98. Retrieved February 7, 2007, from http://videolinq.tafe. net/attached_docs/pdf/conf1998_RoyLundinFeralLearning.pdf.

Lundin, R. (1999). Flexible teaching and learning: Perspectives and practices. *UniServe Science News, 13*, July 1999, n.p. Retrieved February 7, 2007, from http://science.uniserve.edu.au/ newsletter/vol13/lundin.html.

Marks, J. (1985). *Two kinds of order*. Retrieved April 21, 2006, from http://www.ertnet. demon. co.uk/2kinds.html.

Marks, K. (2006, February 27). Tiered versus Weird. In *Epeus' epigone. Kevin Marks weblog*. Retrieved February 5, 2007, from http://epeus.blogspot.com/2006_02_01_epeus_ archive. html#114086100019819301.

Merrill, M. D. (in this volume). Why basic principles of instruction must be present in the learning landscape, whatever form it takes, for learning to be effective, efficient and engaging. In J. Visser & M. Visser-Valfrey (Eds.), *Learners in a changing learning landscape: Reflections from a dialogue on new roles and expectations* (pp. 267–275). Dordrecht, The Netherlands: Springer.

Mezirow, J. (1990). *Fostering critical reflection in adulthood: A guide to transformative and emancipatory learning*. San Francisco: Jossey-Bass.

Mezirow, J. (1991). *Transformative dimensions of adult learning*. San Francisco: Jossey-Bass.

Mulhauser, G. (2006). *An introduction to person-centred counselling*. Retrieved April 20, 2006, from http://counsellingresource.com/types/person-centred/.

Nunan, T. (1996, July). *Flexible delivery: What is it and why a part of current educational debate?* Paper presented at the Annual Conference of the Higher Education Research and Development Society of Australasia on 'Different Approaches: Theory and Practice in Higher Education,' Perth, 8–12 July, 1996. Retrieved July 16, 2007, from http://www.city.londonmet.ac.uk/deliberations/flex.learning/nunan_fr.html.

Ochs, V. L. (2005). *Sarah laughed: Modern lessons from the wisdom and stories of biblical women*. New York: McGraw-Hill.

Prensky, M. (2001a). Digital natives, digital immigrants. *On the Horizon, 9*(5). Retrieved September 8, 2004, from http://www.marcprensky.com/writing/Prensky%20-%20Digital %20 Natives,%20Digital%20Immigrants%20-%20Part1.pdf.

Prensky, M. (2001b). Digital natives, digital immigrants, Part II: Do they really think differently? *On the Horizon, 9*(6). Retrieved September 8, 2004, from http://www.marcprensky.com/writing/Prensky%20-%20Digital%20Natives,%20Digi tal%20Immigrants%20-%20Part2.pdf.

Reigeluth, C. M. (1999). The elaboration theory: Guidance for scope and sequence decisions. In C. M. Reigeluth (Ed.), *Instructional design theories and models: A new paradigm of instruction theory*. Mahwah, NJ: Lawrence Erlbaum.

Rhoads, K. (1997). Definitions. In *Working psychology*. Retrieved February 6, 2007, from http://www.workingpsychology.com/definit.html.

Richardson, V. (2003). Constructivist pedagogy. *Teachers College Record, 105*(9), 1623–1640. Retrieved March 16, 2006, from http://www.tcrecord.org ID Number: 11559.

Rogers, C. (1967). The interpersonal relationship in the facilitation of learning. In *Humanizing education: The person in the process*. Washington, DC: Association for Supervision and Curriculum Development. Abridged version. Retrieved August 26, 2007, from http://www. mona.uwi.edu/idu/TrashLater/InterpersonalRelationships.rtf.

Seeley, K. (1984). Giftedness and delinquency in perspective. *Journal for the Education of the Gifted, 8*, 59–72.

Seeley, K. (2003). High risk gifted learners. In N. Colangelo & G. A. Davis (Eds.), *Handbook of gifted education* (3rd ed., pp. 444–451). Boston: Allyn & Bacon.

Seely Brown, J. (1999). *Learning, working & playing in the digital age*. Talk presented at the 1999 Conference on Higher Education of the American Association for Higher Education. Retrieved August 18, 2007, from http://serendip.brynmawr.edu/sci_edu/seelybrown/.

Senge, P. (1990). *The fifth discipline: The art & practice of the learning organization*. New York: Currency Doubleday.

Senge, P., Scharmer, O., Jaworski, J., & Flowers, B. S. (2005). *Presence: Exploring profound change in people, organizations and society*. London: Nicholas Brealey.

Siemens, G. (2003, October 17). Learning ecology, communities, and networks: Extending the classroom. In *elearnspace everything elearning*. Retrieved February 6, 2007, from http://www. elearnspace.org/Articles/learning_communities.htm.

Siemens, G. (2007, January 10). Thinning walls. In *elearnspace everything elearning*. Retrieved January 15, 2007, from http://www.elearnspace.org/blog/archives/2007_01. html.

Silverman, L. (2004, May). *At-risk youth and the creative process*. Paper presented at the ARTernatives for At-Rish Youth Conference, Colorado Springs, May 14, 2006. Retrieved August 10, 2006, from http://www.gifteddevelopment.com/Articles/vsl/v04a.pdf.

Silverman, L., & Freed, J. (2006). Strategies for gifted visual-spatial learners. In Visual-Spatial Learners. Retrieved March 20, 2006, from http://www.gifteddevelopment.com/ Articles/vsl/v70.pdf.

United Nations Office of the High Commissioner for Human Rights (1959). *Declaration of the rights of the child*. Proclaimed by General Assembly resolution 1386(XIV) of 20 November 1959. Retrieved March 20, 2006, from http://www.unhchr.ch/html/menu3/ b/25.htm.

Visser, J. (2001). Integrity, completeness and comprehensiveness of the learning environment: Meeting the basic learning needs of all throughout life. In D. N. Aspin, J. D. Chapman, M. J. Hatton, & Y. Sawano (Eds.), *International handbook of lifelong learning* (pp. 447–472). Dordrecht, The Netherlands: Kluwer.

Wylie, C., Hipkins, R. (2006). *Growing independence: Competent learners @14*. Wellington, New Zealand: Ministry of Education. Retrieved August 17, 2007, from http://www.nzcer. org. nz/pdfs/14601.pdf.

Chapter 7
Postsecondary Education in the Changing Learning and Living Landscapes

Yusra Laila Visser

Abstract Today, more than ever before, a person's opportunities within the economic sector of most nations are determined by the extent to which he or she has formally participated in postsecondary education. As a result, postsecondary education is an integral part of the learning and development for many individuals. The overall purpose of this chapter, therefore, is to critically analyze the role of the postsecondary education system in the living and learning landscape, and to explore issues around some of the key ways in which the postsecondary education system is changing. The chapter explores the changing (and at times discordant) views of the purpose of postsecondary education, specifically focusing on three of the most commonly cited expectations of the postsecondary education system: professional training, remedial education, and cultivation of the knowledge worker. The chapter also considers shifting views on the value of a postsecondary education, looking specifically at how such perceptions are changing among both learners and employers. Looking at the effects of the commercialization of postsecondary education, the chapter discusses the adoption of the 'mass education' metaphor, the growing diversity in educational service providers, the prevalence of distance and distributed instructional modalities, and the reduction in funding for postsecondary education. To conclude, the chapter explores the implications of the changing role of the postsecondary education system in the learning landscape, focusing on those implications that most directly impact the learner.

7.1 Introduction

It is in fact nothing short of a miracle that the modern methods of education have not yet entirely strangled the holy curiosity of inquiry; for this delicate little plant, aside from stimulation, stands mainly in need of freedom; without this it goes to wrack and ruin without fail. It is a very grave mistake to think that the enjoyment of seeing and searching can be promoted by means of coercion and a sense of duty. To the contrary, I believe that it

Florida Atlantic University & Learning Development Institute

would be possible to rob even a healthy beast of prey of its voraciousness, if it were possible, with the aid of a whip, to force the beast to devour continuously, even when not hungry, especially if the food, handed out under such coercion, were to be selected accordingly.
                                                                        Albert Einstein, quoted in Gorder (1990, p. 79)

In this chapter I consider the role of formal, postsecondary educational systems in the context of the dynamic and broader learning landscape. While non-formal and informal modes of learning receive considerable attention in today's discussions about lifelong and lifewide learning, formal learning systems remain an important and integral part of the learning landscape, and they retain that status as long as the completion of a postsecondary education continues to positively impact an individual's opportunities in life. There is little reason to believe that the place of postsecondary institutions will soon be threatened. However, they are challenged in their efforts to respond to changing expectations and needs, by virtue of their sheer magnitude, political placement, and their entrenchment in their own historical foundation.

A common thread connecting the diverse components of the learning landscape is the central focus on *learning* as an essential dimension of being. I thus begin this chapter with a brief consideration of those facets of the complex construct of learning that are most central to the discussion of postsecondary education systems in the changing learning landscape. Building on this initial consideration of learning, I give some attention to what we mean when we discuss the learning landscape, and to the place of postsecondary education in the broader learning landscape. Next, I explore in greater detail how the postsecondary education system is changing, both in terms of its internal functioning and in terms of its relation to the broader learning and living landscape. Here, I focus the discussion on three central themes: evolving (and at times discordant) views of the purpose of the postsecondary education system; changing perceptions of the value of a postsecondary education; and changes in the internal and external functioning of the postsecondary education system as a consequence of commercialization. I present for each theme an incomplete and somewhat eclectic series of relevant issues and opportunities and I focus specifically on the implications for the postsecondary learner of these phenomena of change. To conclude the chapter I consider how researchers, practitioners, and policy makers are positioned to impact our understanding and nurturing of postsecondary learners in the changing learning landscape.

This chapter deals with a series of issues and developments that are potentially broad in scope. For this reason, I have chosen to focus my comments on the situation as confronted primarily in the context of US postsecondary education. At various points, I refer to data and sources from Canada, the UK, and continental Europe. This chapter's constraint in the geographic scope is not intended to limit exploration of the relevance of some of the issues presented to societies outside of this rather limited area. Instead, it is intended to aide in the clarity of the discussion by containing the scope of the examples to a situational context that shares a number of fundamental common attributes.

7.2   Learning as Seen from the Learner's Perspective

In exploring the broader theme of 'learners in a changing learning landscape' it is essential to look at the construct of *learning* in adequate depth. In the context of this chapter, where the focus is on adult learning in formal settings, we should best focus on those aspects of the meaning of learning that are connected to our conceptions of *teaching*.

Van Rossum, Deijkers and Hamer (1985) explored conceptions of learning from the learner's perspective, using a phenomenographic methodology. A group of 42 Dutch college students participated in the study. They elucidated their ideas about learning and related concepts in response to open ended questions. The researchers identified five distinct learning conceptions, each affecting the learner's perception of teaching (as cited in Dawson-Tunik, 2004, p. 6):

1. Learning is seen as the augmentation of knowledge through the accumulation of factual information, the teacher's role being one of presenting a variety of facts.
2. Learning is perceived as memorization of knowledge for performing on assessments with teaching being defined from a technological vantage point. Understanding of subject matter is believed to be related to performance on assessments.
3. Learning is viewed as applying knowledge. In this frame of reference good teaching manifests itself in an organized, controlled, and active learning environment.
4. Learning is defined as the process of trying to identify relationships within a discipline and across disciplines. Good teaching consists of giving students the conditions to explore their own learning process and to engage in the process of constructing knowledge.
5. Learning is regarded as personal development. Effective teaching is dialogical in nature and emphasizes opportunities for independent learning.

The categories identified by Van Rossum et al. (1985) are consistent with those identified by Marton, Dall'Alba and Beaty in 1993, although the latter group of researchers supplemented the list with a sixth category, "associated with increased awareness and a sense of learners becoming irreversibly different people as a result of learning" (Cliff, 1996, n.p.). In other words, learning encompasses a process in which the learner changes in the way in which she views phenomena, and consequently the new way of seeing the phenomena changes the learner (Dawson-Tunik, 2004).

It is of interest to note that the categories of perceptions of learning as described above are positioned hierarchically. In other words, the conceptual interpretation of learning ranges from the lowest level in the hierarchy, where learning is viewed as the simple accumulation of factual information, to the highest level in the hierarchy, where learning is viewed as having the capacity to have "a dimension of personal transformative power" (Cliff, 1996, n.p.).

For the purpose of this chapter, we will build on the contributions of the phenomenographic research above in two ways. Firstly, we will keep a focus on *learning* and the *learning landscape* from the vantage point of the learner. Secondly, we will concern ourselves primarily with those perspectives on learning that would, in the context of the research by Van Rossum et al. (1985) and Marton et al. (1993), appear on the higher levels of the hierarchy. In other words, our focus will be on conceptions of learning that emphasize meaning-making; cross- and transdisciplinary understanding and application; independent exploration; dialogical relationships between members of a learning community, and sustained personal growth and development.

7.3   Learning and Living Landscapes

You may not divide the seamless coat of learning. What education has to impart is an intimate sense for the power of ideas, for the beauty of ideas, and for the structure of ideas, together with a particular body of knowledge which has peculiar reference to the life of the being possessing it.

Alfred Whitehead, The Aims of Education (1929, p. 23)

The notion of a *learning landscape* is a broad, complex, and dynamic construct that recognizes at once the commonalities and the idiosyncrasies between discrete points and entities in the broader universe of learning. Recognizing both the aesthetic and ecological dimensions of learning (J. Visser, 2001), it is a landscape that may be seen as made up of numerous other sub-landscapes, such as the media landscape and the instructional landscape (J. Visser, 2003). Much like any 'natural' landscape in the world around us, the metaphor of a learning landscape encompasses conditions and entities that can both foster and hamper growth and development. In this respect, a learning landscape embodies attributes that are similar to what Dewey (1916) describes in *Democracy and Education* as the nature and meaning of environment in education:

In brief, the environment consists of those conditions that promote or hinder, stimulate or inhibit, the characteristic activities of a living being. Water is the environment of a fish because it is necessary to the fish's activities—to its life. The north pole is a significant element in the environment of an arctic explorer, whether he succeeds in reaching it or not, because it defines his activities, makes them what they distinctively are. Just because life signifies not bare passive existence (supposing there is such a thing), but a way of acting, environment or medium signifies what enters into this activity as a sustaining or frustrating condition. (n.p.)

The learning landscape can therefore be likened to the ecological environment in which we, as humans, develop and grow as a result of our interaction with our surroundings. We thus assume the broadest of possible definitions for the *learning landscape*, and might consequently argue with increasing conviction that the *learning landscape* and the *living landscape* are in fact one and the same. Our lives are a perpetual process of interaction with the world around us, and through this process we grow, change, and develop—in short, we learn. Our development as humans, in this context, is mediated through mechanisms that operate largely in ignorance of the boundaries for *levels* and *types* of learning that are neatly established when we study learning in a more detached manner. Informal, non-formal and formal learning will likely all figure prominently in our interactions with the living and learning landscape, and we will learn through both incidental and intentional processes that shape us biologically, mentally, and spiritually.[1] We *are* learning, and learning *is* us.

Later in this chapter we will explore in more depth some of the things that one might categorize under idea of a 'changing learning landscape,' particularly in regard to the place of formalized postsecondary education within it. For the moment, however, let us consider one key way in which the learning landscape is indeed changing, namely, in terms of our very conception of what it is. As rates of change continue to increase, ambiguity becomes ever more prevalent, and we are expected to interact with ever larger amounts of information, we become increasingly resourceful in finding new spaces and opportunities for learning, so that we can meet the challenges that today's world presents us.[2] In so doing, we redefine our conception of the learning landscape, and our awareness of its breadth and depth increases. We become more aware that *learning* is above all else the dominion of the learner, rather than educators or educational establishments. The learning landscape changes as our perception of it changes.

What then, of the formal learning systems that our societies have so carefully cultivated and fostered over the centuries to provide us with planned learning experiences, dedicated learning spaces, defined learning goals and measures, and access to individuals with recognized subject-matter knowledge and pedagogical skills? Such formalized mechanisms seem at times somewhat outdated when we engage ourselves in thinking of the brave new world of learning that lies ahead of us. However, the reality remains that formalized education systems, with all their limitations, are still a formidable entity in the learning landscape. Compulsory primary and/or secondary education is embedded in the rights and responsibilities of citizens of many countries, and under the Education For All (EFA) movement, the United Nations Educational, Scientific, and Cultural Organization (UNESCO) and the international community at large have set as a goal that all children will receive and complete free and compulsory education by 2015 (UNESCO, 2000).While we come closer to achieving the goals of universal access to primary and secondary education, we are also finding that participation in postsecondary education is increasingly becoming a condition for meaningful participation in the economic sector of many countries. For instance, in the United States it is projected that between 2000 and 2015 some 85 percent of new jobs will require postsecondary

---

[1] For further reflection on time spent on formal versus informal learning, see Bransford, Slowinski, Vye, & Mosborg (in this volume).

[2] See J. Visser (in this volume) and Bransford et al. (in this volume) for further exploration of ambiguity in the context of the changing learning landscape.

education (Gunderson, Jones, & Scanland, 2004). In one recent survey of US employers, over one-quarter of respondents projected that they would reduce their hiring of employees with only a high school degree, 60 percent of respondents projected increasing their hiring four-year college degree graduates, and almost 50 percent projected increasing their hiring of two-year degree holding employees (Casner-Lotto & Barrington, 2006). Thus, while the breadth of opportunities for just-in-time, self-directed, and informal learning is considerable, the reality is that formal education systems remain the 'staple' ingredient in the learning journeys for many of us. They deserve, therefore, careful attention and critical analysis when considering learners in the changing learning landscape.

7.4   Changing Perceptions of the Purpose of the Postsecondary Education System

The task of a University is the creation of the future, so far as rational thought, and civilized modes of appreciation, can affect the issue. The future is big with every possibility of achievement and of tragedy.

Alfred Whitehead, Modes of Thought (1938, p. 233)

In the developed world, postsecondary institutions shoulder a considerable amount of the responsibility for providing adults access to instructional opportunities that will enable them to function constructively as independent and interdependent members of society. While attempting to 'make good' on this responsibility, the postsecondary education system appears to face an almost innumerable series of challenges, finding itself in a state of flux both in terms of its internal functioning and in terms of its place in the broader social and living landscapes.

During this turbulent time there is in my view one key systemic challenge that has direct implications for how postsecondary institutions fit into the broader learning landscape, namely that there is little consensus about what a postsecondary education should effectively constitute. Reading through the research and policy documentation for postsecondary institutions, one finds that these institutions are expected to serve any of a myriad of different purposes. Often, the expectations placed on the postsecondary sector are wildly different and, indeed, contradictory. Below we look at three of the most commonly cited expectations for postsecondary education: Professional training, remedial education, and cultivation of the knowledge-worker.

7.4.1   Professional Training and Preparation

Traditionally, the purpose of the postsecondary institution is primarily to take a broadly-prepared secondary school graduate and to expose him or her to the learning experiences needed to develop the pre-defined competencies for effective performance in a specific professional field. A program in Information Technology, for instance, is expected to provide its learners with the sequence and scope of course material that is needed to achieve two goals: to prepare the learner (1) for general effectiveness in the world of work (one way in which this might be achieved is by focusing on the development of analytical and communication skills), and (2) for the specific knowledge and skills associated with working in the field of Information Technology. In many of our postsecondary institutions today, we see systems that have been carefully set up to achieve the goal of this kind of professional training and preparation. At the undergraduate level, the academic program is typically set up so that learners begin with a series of general education courses (designed to shape the learner with the broader set of general skills and knowledge for effective integration into society and the workforce), after which they gradually travel up the academic hierarchy to courses that are increasingly specific to the professional area of concentration that the learner has selected.

Many learners entering the postsecondary system for the first time are likely to be motivated by a desire to receive professional training and preparation in a defined area of specialization. In reality, however, two main factors mitigate the ability of universities and colleges to consider themselves effective in meeting this expectation: (1) the increase in the number of learners in need of remedial education in order to successfully enter an academic program, and (2) the evolving expectations of an economic sector in need of professionals who not only command the skills and knowledge related to the current state of the discipline, but who also command the skills to succeed in what is increasingly referred to as a knowledge-based economy.[3] As a result, universities and colleges have sought to expand their purpose, while new types of postsecondary entities (such as corporate universities) have emerged to fulfill the role of providing a narrow, skills-based professional training.

7.4.2 Remedial Education

Mastery of key entry-level skills is considered a cornerstone for success in any instructional intervention. Postsecondary institutions are therefore increasingly expected to serve as what is perhaps best described as a bridge to *themselves*. In other words, postsecondary institutions are expected to provide inadequately prepared high school graduates with the learning opportunities needed to enter into a postsecondary level academic program of study. According to the National Center for Education Statistics about half of US students admitted to college must complete

---

[3] Skills associated with learner success in a knowledge-based economy are related to the areas that J. Visser (in this volume) posits today's learners should be competent in.

remedial education courses in English and Math before undertaking college-level courses (NCES, 2001).

The growth in the demand for remedial education at the postsecondary level is certainly condemnatory of the condition of the secondary education system and the poorly-conceived policies for standardizing education and assessment in middle and high school. However, the responsibility does not reside on the shoulders of the secondary education system alone—in fact, one might argue that a significant proportion of the responsibility resides with the postsecondary education system, since this is the system that has after all been responsible for the professional preparation of the teachers teaching at the secondary level. Regardless of where the blame resides, however, the consequences are altogether troubling from the vantage point of the learner. A report released by the Commission on the Future of Higher Education (2006), notes that "Among high school graduates who do make it on to post-secondary education, a troubling number of undergraduates waste time—and taxpayer dollars—mastering English and Math skills that they should have learned in high school" (p. x).

The secondary school system's failure to prepare learners for a postsecondary education results in the learner having to dedicate additional time and resources to taking remedial courses in core subjects such as Math and English. What emerges is a situation in which the postsecondary education system functions with a significant conflict of interest: The remedial courses offered at postsecondary institutions do not count as credit toward the learner's intended academic program of study, effectively meaning that whatever time the learner spends on taking remedial courses is added on to the anticipated length of time during which the learner expected to pay tuition to the postsecondary institution. The learner, who would under normal circumstances have paid tuition for four years for an undergraduate degree, may end up paying tuition for five years if she is required to take a full year of remedial coursework. Much like it was once argued that distance education programs had no vested interest in improving completion rates of learners if non-completion meant that tuition could be charged to the same learner over and over again, the impression created in the presence of remedial education programs at postsecondary institutions is that these institutions—increasingly driven by financial motives—have little vested interest reducing the demand for remedial education or the amount of time that the learner spends on taking remedial courses.

The impact of remedial education on the purpose and place of the postsecondary institution in the learning landscape goes beyond only economics. The need for remedial education affects the probability that a learner will earn a postsecondary degree (NCES, 2001). It also affects the major area of study that the learner will concentrate on. Learners who need more than two semesters of remediation are one-sixth as likely to graduate with a baccalaureate degree as learners needing no remedial courses (NCES, 2001). Learners who have been inadequately prepared in secondary-level math will generally be less inclined to pursue postsecondary studies in disciplines where the requirements for math competence are greater (such as the sciences, economics and engineering fields).

7.4.3 Cultivation of the Knowledge Worker

The most socially useful learning in the modern world is the learning of the process of learning; a continuing openness to experience and incorporation into oneself of the process of change.

Carl Rogers, Freedom to Learn (1969, p. 163)

On the one hand the purpose of the postsecondary institution has expanded beyond professional training and preparation to encompass the provision of remedial education opportunities. On the other hand, the postsecondary institution has expanded to encompass a more elusive set of competencies: the preparation of the worker for the knowledge-based economy. The Organization for Economic Cooperation and Development (OECD) defines knowledge-based economies as "economies which are directly based on the production, distribution and use of knowledge and information" (p. 7).[4] Learning and education take on a different role in such a knowledge-based economy:

> Without investments oriented towards both codified and tacit skill development, informational constraints may be a significant factor degrading the allocative efficiency of market economies. Workers will require both formal education and the ability to acquire and apply new theoretical and analytical knowledge; they will increasingly be paid for their codified and tacit knowledge skills rather than for manual work. Education will be the centre of the knowledge-based economy, and learning the tool of individual and organisational advancement. (pp. 13–14)

In a world where knowledge, rather than a more tangible production factor, is the key capital asset in an economy, universities and other postsecondary institutions are increasingly expected to focus on the preparation of learners for a future as knowledge workers (AAUP [American Association of University Professors], 2006). Some, such as the Commission on the Future of Higher Education (2006) argue that postsecondary institutions are inadequately preparing learners for this new environment. In its final report the Commission notes that "unacceptable numbers of college graduates enter the workforce without the skills employers say they need in an economy where, as the truism correctly holds, knowledge matters more than ever" (p. vii). One of the reasons for perceptions of failure of the postsecondary system in this regard may be the lack of clarity in the understanding of what, specifically, constitutes a well-prepared knowledge worker (OECD, 2001). In general, however, it appears that workers in a knowledge-based economy are expected to have higher levels of literacy and/or education, and that they are expected to have more advanced skills in terms of teamwork, leadership, problem solving, and lifelong learning (OECD, 2001). Postsecondary institutions that have traditionally focused on measuring the attainment of product-oriented and observable discipline-

---

[4] One point of reflection is that the term *"knowledge-based economy"* conveys a narrower scope than is perhaps justified for the concept of such an economy. While in the knowledge-based economy an emphasis is placed on the worker's ability to produce, distribute and manipulate knowledge and information, there are critical skills and attitudes that underscore the ability to constructively interact with knowledge in this manner.

specific knowledge and skills are now challenged to develop teaching and assessment methods that are more in line with the process-oriented competencies that are associated with effective practice in the knowledge-based economy.

The impact of the broadened view on the purpose of the postsecondary sector in cultivating the knowledge worker extends well beyond analyzing the competencies of graduates from postsecondary institutions. Higher education institutions are also being expected to contribute to the development and growth of knowledge economies through increased innovation and research partnerships with the private sector. The growing focus on the knowledge economy is further being interpreted by some as meaning that postsecondary institutions must anticipate a world in which learner-as-consumer education models prevail (see also Stirling, in this volume), demand increases for more advanced levels of higher education, institutions have access to a potentially larger and more distributed target audience for their educational goods and services, and competition among postsecondary educational providers increases.[5] Each of these potential changes emerging from a redefined role of the postsecondary education sector in the living and learning landscape has considerable implications for the learner, and we will explore some of those implications in more detail later in the chapter.

7.5 Changing Perceptions of the Value of Postsecondary Education

The previous section of this chapter explores some of the ways in which the purpose of postsecondary education is being challenged and, in some cases, redefined. The discourse around the purpose of postsecondary education yields changes in its perceived value. In the present section I briefly explore the key ways the value of postsecondary education is changing from the vantage point of two major stakeholders in postsecondary education (learners and employers).

7.5.1 From the Vantage Point of the Learner: Higher Demand Coupled with Higher Concerns About Its Worth

We have seen that postsecondary education is becoming an increasingly prevalent 'minimum qualification' for initial and sustained employability in the workforce. Enrollment, consequently, in postsecondary institutions continues to grow. According

---

[5] To explore this issue further, consider accessing "A Test of Leadership: Charting the Future of US Higher Education" (2006), a report of the commission appointed by the US Secretary of Education. This report, and its recommendations, exemplifies the increased emphasis on consumer- and market-driven, results-based paradigms for postsecondary education. The report is available at http://www.ed.gov/about/bdscomm/list/hiedfuture/ reports/final-report.pdf.

to the U.S. Department of Education (NCES, 2006), enrollments in U.S. undergraduate education are expected to continue growing throughout the next decade, reaching a new high each year between 2006 and 2015. Similarly, according to the same source, enrollment in graduate and professional education courses has grown 62 percent between 1976 and 2004, and these enrollment increases are expected to continue between 2006 and 2015. The curious thing about the increase in postsecondary enrollments is that while on the one hand it suggests that learners are increasingly demanding the 'value-added' of the additional academic training and preparation, on the other hand the increased prevalence of postsecondary training in the general population raises questions about how such additional training uniquely benefits each individual learner. Learners wonder whether their learning experiences, educational quality, and subsequent employment options will compare to those of previous generations (Baker, 2001). This question emerges from an increasing concern that, while the quality of education may still be high, the possibility of realizing a postsecondary education degree is shared by a greater percentage of the population than in previous years, and subsequently one might argue that "a university degree is no longer as distinctive as it once was" (p. 2).

For the learner, then, there is the concern that the postsecondary degree is the new high school degree, because postsecondary degrees are increasingly considered a requirement rather than an asset for employment, and because an ever greater percentage of the adult population has completed some postsecondary studies. However, the diminishing 'uniqueness' of a postsecondary degree is only one dimension of the concern that today's students should have about the worth of postsecondary education. With the increased enrollment in postsecondary institutions, and the increased emphasis on postsecondary education as a competitive economic sector, resources are reduced and students are less likely to find within their learning experience the unique dimensions that allow each learner to potentially graduate with a qualitatively different set of insights and experiences to bring into the economic sector. The prevalence of a mass education metaphor in postsecondary education has not only yielded a cattle-herding mentality for the processes and procedures of shuttling a learner through the levels of the education system; it has also infected the very way in which the learner interacts with learning in the formal context. One might argue that it is this mentality, rather than the overbearing emphasis on somewhat outdated notions of learning, that underscores the concerns about the worth of a postsecondary education.

7.5.2 *From the Vantage Point of Employers: Challenges to the Ability of the Postsecondary Education Sector to Prepare Learners for the World of Work*

There is growing concern that aspects of the postsecondary education system are failing to prepare learners for effectiveness in the world of today and tomorrow. Take a recent survey of some 430 human resource professionals on employers' views of the readiness of high school, two-year college, and four-year college graduates entering into the United States workforce. From the '*Are they really ready to work?*' report, a very bleak picture emerges regarding the readiness of high school graduates entering the workforce (over one-half of respondents rate high school graduates as deficient in core skills such as oral/written communication, critical thinking/problem solving, and work ethic/professionalism). However, the report's findings are perhaps most alarming in that additional years of postsecondary education do not yield the magnitude of improvement that one might expect in key skills for successful integration into the workforce (Casner-Lotto & Barrington, 2006). Some highlights from the data relating to employers' assessments of the preparedness of new workforce entrants with degrees from *two-year colleges*:

- Almost half of the survey respondents rated them as deficient in written communication skills.
- One-quarter of respondents rated them as deficient in lifelong learning/self direction and creativity/innovation.
- Over 20 percent of respondents rated them as deficient in critical thinking/ problem solving, oral communications, and ethics/social responsibility.

The report's authors further observe that; "[f]or two-year college-educated entrants, one 'very important' applied skill—Information Technology Application—appears on the Excellence List while seven skills appear on the Deficiency List" (Casner-Lotto & Barrington, 2006, p. 10).

Survey results for employers' assessments of the preparedness of new workforce entrants with degrees from four-year colleges fell short, too (Casner-Lotto & Barrington, 2006):

- Around one-quarter of respondents rated them as deficient in writing skills and leadership skills.
- Approximately 15 percent of respondents rated them as deficient in lifelong learning/self-direction and in creativity/innovation.
- Just less than ten percent of respondents rated them deficient in critical thinking/problem solving and teamwork/collaboration.

While one can argue that postsecondary education is not simply pursued for the purpose of fitting a predetermined professional mold, the reality is also that few individuals pursue a postsecondary education purely for personal enrichment purposes. In the broader learning-living landscape, it appears that postsecondary institutions are losing ground in their efforts to position themselves so that their students develop the competencies needed to be effective in the changing world of work. More troubling, however, is that they may even be losing ground in preparing learners for even the most elemental desired outcomes for adult education, such as writing and problem solving. If employers are expressing profound concerns about the ability of postsecondary programs to adequately prepare prospective employees in basic skills such as writing and essential applied skills such as leadership and lifelong learning, it is society as a whole (not just the learner), which is ultimately is left dealing with the consequences of this systemic failure.

Poor alignment between postsecondary education and workforce education is something that has plagued the education system for some time (Conley, 2005). However, it appears that the distance between the classroom and the 'real-world' work situation is getting more pronounced rather than less pronounced, to the extent that in many of the fastest changing fields, postsecondary education qualifications may be becoming an afterthought, if not a liability. The value of ongoing education in recognized by most entities in the economic sector (in other words, employers do appear to believe that someone with postsecondary education will have developed more competencies needed for success in the workforce than someone who enters into the workforce with only a secondary education). However, the alignment of specialized postsecondary academic curricula with the world of work in that area of specialization is increasingly challenged. Many of the most successful high-tech companies in Silicon Valley, for example, have gone to great lengths to set up recruitment approaches that directly speak to the lack of esteem for a postsecondary education *per se* in terms of enhancing the appreciation for a prospective employee.[6]

Stewart (2006), the founder of a management consulting firm employing some 600 people, recently wrote a revealing piece in the Atlantic Monthly, essentially laying out his case for why he hires graduates from Philosophy programs as opposed to MBA-degree holders in his company. In *The Management Myth*, Stewart argues that cornerstone skills for effective management practices are not effectively taught in classroom MBA curricula, and that MBA curricula instead invoke in their students an unhealthy obsession with faddish approaches and an over reliance on heuristics for management. Having worked in management without holding an MBA himself, Stewart summarizes his impression of the MBA experience as "taking two years out of your life and going deeply into debt, all for the sake of learning how to keep a straight face while using phrases like 'out-of-the-box-thinking,' 'win-win situation,' and 'core competencies' " (p. 1). In his assessment, business school provides little in the way of relevant academic training for business work, while placing an undue emphasis in a cult-like following of the *mouvements du jour*. Likewise, he notes that business school curricula, with their stated emphasis on the development of problem solving skills, in fact fail to tell their students that the problem solving frameworks they are being taught are simply heuristics; "they can lead you to solutions, but they cannot make you think" (p. 8).

---

[6] Google used an innovative strategy for recruitment of engineers, posting a complex mathematical equation on a billboard in Silicon Valley. The billboard read: '{first 10-digit prime found in consecutive digits of e}.com.' Olsen (2006) explains: The answer, 7427466391.com, would lead a puzzle-sleuth to a Web page with yet another equation to solve, with still no sign the game was hosted by Google. (…) Mastering that equation would lead someone to a page on Google Labs, the company's research and development department, which reads: 'One thing we learned while building Google is that it's easier to find what you're looking for if it comes looking for you. What we're looking for are the best engineers in the world. And here you are'." (n.p.)

7.6   Changing Operational Aspects of the Postsecondary Education Sector

It is fair to assume that the changing views of the purpose and value of postsecondary education as discussed above will have a trickle-down effect on a myriad of the more operational aspects of the institutions in the postsecondary education sector. Teaching, instructional delivery, student support and many other facets of day-to-day interaction between the learner and the postsecondary institutions are all undergoing significant change. These changes are explored briefly in this section.

7.6.1   Commercialization and Commoditization

Few people would contest the observation that economic and commercial forces play an increasingly important role in virtually every facet of the postsecondary education system. In a report commissioned by the US Secretary of Education, there is ample evidence the higher education environment being described as a *consumer-driven environment*, a *mature enterprise*, *risk-averse*, and at-risk of losing *market-share* (Commission on the Future of Higher Education, 2006). The commercialization of postsecondary education defines some aspects of the relationship between the postsecondary institution and the learner. Postsecondary institutions tend to characterize the learner in terms of the monetary value of that learner's participation in the system. Learners are inclined to characterize the postsecondary institution's services as commodities that have been purchased, whereby the learner is increasingly placed in the role of being a consumer whose financial investments allow him/her to leverage a certain amount of influence over the manner in which the purchased service is delivered. The relationship between the corporate sector and postsecondary education sector is evolving, too, with a greater number and diversity of vendors involved in defining the *what* and *how* of providing learning opportunities. Instructional and curricular design decisions, such as the delivery of instruction in the distance education mode, are often driven by economic and marketing considerations rather than concerns with social goals, long-term benefit for the learner or instructional effectiveness. Today's learner is impacted by this phenomenon not only in terms of concrete ways in which commercial products enter into the learner's instructional experience (such as the prevalence of one-size-fits-all Learning Management Systems), but also in terms of the things which, as a result of an increased emphasis on commercialization, are rapidly disappearing from the postsecondary learning landscape (such as idiosyncratic instructional tactics and deep-rather-than-broad explorations of instructional topics; things that are not easily justified as falling under the umbrella of efficient, results-driven, consumer-friendly strategies).

Commercialization goes hand-in-hand with commoditization. London (2007), reviewing Neil Postman's *Building a bridge to the 18th Century*, succinctly summarizes the commercialization-commoditization link in education (in this case in the education of children): "Children are no longer viewed as adults in the making, but rather as consumers, as a 'market' to be exploited for commercial gain. And public education has lost an animating sense of purpose, oriented as it is more toward the form than the substance of instruction" (n.p.). Noble (1998), in an impassioned piece about the automation of higher education, argues that decision-making for instructional practices in postsecondary classrooms has transferred from the faculty-student level to the institutional level, driven mostly by a significantly increased emphasis on commoditization and commercialization of teaching. Painting a rather bleak picture, Noble argues that—since the 1970s—higher education has shifted toward a highly commoditized conception of the research function of universities, with detrimental consequences for the teaching function: "Class sizes swelled, teaching staffs and instructional resources were reduced, salaries were frozen, and curricular offering were reduced to the bone" (n.p.). Responding to the crisis that has ensued, instruction was commoditized: "teachers as labor are drawn into a production process designed for the efficient creation of instructional commodities, and hence become subject to all the pressures that have befallen production workers in other industries undergoing rapid technological transformation from above" (n.p.). The movement toward the commoditization of higher education instruction has, according to Noble continued to gain ground with the growth of the digital revolution and the distance learning movement, generating questions for today's postsecondary learners about issues such as "costs, coercion, privacy, equity, and the quality of education" (n.p.).

7.6.2 Adoption of a Mass Education Metaphor

It is interesting to note that many of the countries of the developed world are—in synchronicity—lamenting the loss of their competitive edge relative to other countries in the developed world. Thus the European Union rings the alarm bells regarding the lowered placement of their postsecondary education relative to the United States, while the United States expresses its concerns regarding the way in which it is losing ground relative to European countries.[7] To the extent that some European countries, however, are able to make the case that their higher education sector has fallen short in years gone by, this can in part be attributed to the prevalence of a mass education metaphor in European postsecondary education. Trow (2000) notes in the European context:

---

[7] The European Union's perspective is represented in Lambert and Butler's (2006) *The Future of European Universities: Renaissance or Decay?*, while the US perspective is found in *A Test of Leadership: Charting the Future of US Higher Education* (Commission on the Future of Higher Education, 2006).

> The response of governments was to demand greater productivity. The rationalization of
> university life and management, the pressures for 'efficiency' in operation and outcome, the
> consequent loss of 'slack' resources, the imposition of the criteria and language of business
> and industry, all threaten the autonomy of the university and the capacity of its scholars and
> scientists to pursue long-term studies that do not promise short-term results. (p. 1)

Indeed, postsecondary education systems today are characteristically different
from those of the past in terms of the sheer volume of individuals participating in
them. Baker (2001) aptly describes this difference when stating "the university
experience has gone from a five-star, luxury design to a mass-transit economy
model" (p. 2). The mass education metaphor, because it strikes at the fundamental
aspects of the definition of education, permeates many aspects of the learner's
experience. Earlier in this chapter we explored the implications of increased
enrollment on the perceptions of value of higher education. The mass education
metaphor, however, also affects more mundane but persistent aspects of the learning experiences of today's learners. As enrollments increase, individualized interaction between learners and professors is becoming rarer. Indeed, the amount of
in-depth interaction between professors and learners decreases significantly, with
larger portions of the course-specific communication being mediated through
teaching assistants or pre-packaged instructional communications. An almost
single-minded focus on the formulaic fulfillment of academic requirements fills
the air in educational institutions. Professors are responsible for teaching a
greater number of courses or course sections each semester, resulting in less out-
of-class time being available for things such as instructional planning and generating in-depth feedback to learners' assignments. A view of postsecondary
education as focusing on quantity over quality has also shaped the rationales
behind the infusion of technology into the learning experience. The National
Education Association (n.d.) notes that "Technology is seen by some as the panacea for budgets cuts: some see visions of hundreds of students sitting in front of
monitors, with talking heads providing cheap, mass education" (n.p.).

7.6.3   Growing Diversity in Educational Service Providers

Perhaps one of the most significant factors affecting today's postsecondary learning
landscape is the increase in the sheer number *and* type of educational providers and
businesses seeking to reach—and cultivate—adult audiences for their programs and
services. As a result of growth, learners are offered a potentially larger number of
formal venues for learning. In addition, learners may also expect that the type
of learning experiences they are being offered is changing.

Historically, learners' options for postsecondary education were generally restricted
to colleges/universities and vocational/technical programs. Unless the learner was
willing to undertake their postsecondary education through correspondence instruction, his or her access to educational providers was constrained by time, space, and
geography. These constraints are rapidly falling away for many of today's postsecondary learners, with the growth and proliferation of ever greater numbers of more

diverse postsecondary education providers, such as corporate universities, virtual colleges and universities, educational brokers, and consortia of postsecondary education providers (Middlehurst, 2003).

To contemplate the effect of this phenomenon on the postsecondary learning landscape, consider the phenomenon of the *corporate university*. Christensen, Aaron, and Clark (2003) note that there are some 2,000 corporate universities in the United States (p. 20), and that these institutions target learners who "are interested in achieving some sort of outcome but can't because of lack of money or skills" (p. 21). McDonald's Hamburger University alone trains 700,000 people per year (Marquardt & Kearsley, 1999). These educational providers generally specialize in providing learning opportunities tailored to the industry sector, employee needs, and corporate culture of the company that they serve. Corporate universities have thrived in recent years because they do not seek to complete with traditional academic programs (such as university degree programs), but instead seek to serve the many employees who would not pursue a formal program but who desire access to the types of lessons normally taught in traditional academic programs. Corporate Universities generally do not seek accreditation to award formal terminal qualifications such as university-equivalent degrees (Middlehurst, 2003). There are two obvious ways in which corporate universities have changed the postsecondary learning landscape: (1) they serve an audience that otherwise would have been unlikely to participate in additional postsecondary education, and (2) they have created a niche within the broader learning landscape by offering curricula that seek to forge clear and immediate links between classroom learning and employment-based application.

The proliferation of types of corporate universities is but one small instance of the increase in educational service providers. In a UNESCO-funded report on borderless higher education, Middlehurst (2003) outlines the following commercial sector providers in higher education: private and for-profit providers (such as the University of Phoenix); media and publishing businesses (such as Pearson Education and Thomson Learning); educational services and brokers (such as Learndirect and Western Governors University); and corporate universities (such as McDonald's Hamburger University). The increase in the number and diversity of educational providers involved in postsecondary education affects learners in a multitude of different ways. Those who espouse the merits of a commercial view of education expect that increased competition and commercial involvement in the educational marketplace will encourage all educational providers—including the traditional postsecondary education institutions—to improve the quality and effectiveness of their educational services. However, this argument is often made from the vantage point of the bottom line for the educational provider, rather than from the vantage point of the benefit to the learner and the society to which the learner will contribute. As postsecondary education providers are increasingly under pressure to demonstrate viability and profitability to their financial underwriters (be those corporate investors or governmental entities), they are more inclined to use cost-saving measures whose educational impact is—at best—unclear. The effect of this on public higher education institutions in the U.S. has been particularly disheartening to witness. There is a dramatic increase in the proportion of courses being delivered by adjunct instructors and graduate assistants (neither of whom are typically offered either job security or health insurance and other employment benefits) to deliver courses. Particularly at the undergraduate level, the acquisition of prefabricated, standardized curricula for core courses is becoming increasingly prevalent, leaving faculty members incapacitated with regard to selecting the scope or instructional tactics that would allow them to make the course most dynamic and engaging for the learner.

7.6.4   Increased Prevalence of Distance and Distributed Modalities for Instructional Delivery

The attributes of today's learners actively involved in the postsecondary education formal education component of the learning landscape are arguably quite different from those of years gone by. This is illustrated in the statistics regarding learning attributes in the UK, where almost 20 percent of freshman students are classified as 'mature students,' and over 25 percent of all postsecondary education students are enrolled on a part-time basis (Baker, 2001). In the context of the United States, 40 percent of students in postsecondary institutions today are enrolled on a part-time basis, and the same percentage of students is aged 25 or older. In combination with the increased commercialization of postsecondary education, the changes in the demographics of learners have been a major contributory factor in the movement toward more flexible course and degree programs. Indeed, according to Stokes (2006) some seven percent of higher education learners are currently enrolled in online certificate and degree programs, and it is expected that by 2007 some 1.8 million students in the United States will be enrolled in fully-online programs.

Given the changing attributes and needs of learners in today's postsecondary education landscape, distance and distributed delivery of instruction has become increasingly popular at many institutions. Thus, the large-scale adoption of distance and distributed learning modalities is perhaps one of the most immediately obvious—and most significantly impacting—features of the changing learning landscape in this sector. Motivated by advancements in the enabling technologies, pressures to access and serve a growing student body, and cost and space constraints, postsecondary institutions have undertaken an unprecedented, large-scale adoption of networked technologies in the learning environment. Indeed, the statistics in relation to distance education in postsecondary education speak to a system in flux. According to the National Center of Educational Statistics' *Condition of Education 2006* report, over 60 percent of two- and four-year postsecondary institutions in the United States offered distance education courses during the 2004–05 academic year (NCES, 2006). Interestingly, however, while the majority of these institutions have offered distance learning courses, the distance learning courses are being taught by a significant minority of faculty – some eight percent of full-time faculty and six percent of part-time faculty taught via distance education in 2003 (NCES, 2006). In addition, the NCES (2006) report indicates that "Among full-and part-time staff, those who did not teach distance education carried a lighter course load than their peers who taught distance education" (p. 96). A picture of a turbulent landscape emerges as a result of the simultaneous pervasive integration of distance education into the postsecondary institutions; the surprisingly small proportion of faculty within institutions delivering courses via distance learning; and the inequitable distribution of teaching loads between faculty who are and aren't teaching via distance education.

Distance education and distributed learning have been adopted *en masse* at many institutions explicitly because of the profit gains that were believed to be associated with being able to reduce overhead operation costs, increase the number of students per section, and with indefinitely reassigning and reusing a given course once its content had been develop for efficient Web-based delivery. And, while students in public postsecondary program witness this array of strategies being tested out for financial viability, tuition rates and auxiliary fees have continued to increase well above the rate of inflation.

7.6.5 Reduced Funding

The learning landscape, one might argue, is also changing as a result of changes in the funding of postsecondary education. According to 2005–06 Annual Report of the American Association of University Professors on the Economic Status of the Profession (AAUP, 2006), there are troubling developments on the front of academia as a profession, and one would logically assume that, given the interdependent relationship between teaching and learning, the place of the learner in formal postsecondary education will be affected by this dynamic situation in the university professoriate. The AUUP notes that, while society places increasing pressure on postsecondary education to prepare students for success in the knowledge-based economy, the shift toward larger numbers of part-time teaching faculty and toward fewer tenure-earning faculty lines (among other things) directly threatens the quality of US postsecondary education. Indeed, the AAUP reports that 46 percent of faculty jobs are on a part-time basis, and that over half of new full-time faculty appointments are not tenure-earning positions. In the UK, one way we might look at the funding issue is in terms of public per student spending on postsecondary education. An article in the BBC News World Edition reports that public per student spending at the beginning of the 1990s was over £7,500, but had dropped to around £4,800 a decade later (Baker, 2001), representing a decrease of more than one third. In Canada, funding for public higher education institutions was decreased by 30 percent between 1980 and 2000 (Davenport, 2000).

7.7   Implications for the Learner

A learned man came to me once.
He said, "I know the way, – come."
And I was overjoyed at this.
Together we hastened.
Soon, too soon, were we
Where my eyes were useless,
And I knew not the ways of my feet.
I clung to the hand of my friend;
But at last he cried, "I am lost."

Stephen Crane (1905)

In the previous sections of this chapter I have identified and discussed those aspects of the changing postsecondary education sector that I believe have the most immediate impact on the learner in today's learning landscape. In so doing, I have considered changing perspectives and approaches in relation to the purpose, value, and operations of postsecondary institutions. While each of these changes yields specific implications for the learner, the sum-total of the changes also yields a broader set of recommendations and implications for learners. I have chosen to write this section focusing on the latter set of considerations.

7.7.1   Reconciling Changing Perceptions of Individuals and Employers in Relation to the Value of Postsecondary Education

Learners seeking to enter into today's economy should recognize at once that, while a postsecondary education is becoming increasingly important, mindlessly going through the motions of education at that level will significantly limit the potential economic value of the time and resources invested by the learner. I mention this particularly given the potential inconsistency between public opinion about the economic value of advanced degrees in the knowledge economy, and the data in relation to entry level of skills for jobs in this new economy. For instance, an article in Canada's Financial Post (Francis, 1998, as cited in Davenport, 2000, p. 8) illustrates this discrepancy, observing: "The public is beginning to realize a technical education at a college or vocational school is considerably more valuable than more university degrees." The original source cites an opinion poll among residents of the province of Ontario. Projections of employer needs by the British Columbia Chamber of Commerce (2006), on the other hand, indicate that 66 percent of jobs in British Columbia currently require some form of postsecondary education, a figure that is expected to grow to 70 percent by 2013. The public opinion on this matter may thus not be entirely consistent with employers' needs and views. While technical education is valued in some economic sectors, the phenomenon of the knowledge economy has yielded projections for an ever greater need for a workforce trained in the knowledge, skills, and attitudes that more academic postsecondary education programs have sought to instill in their learners.

7.7.2 Greater Expectations Are Placed on the Learner to Find Intrinsic Motivation for Mindful Engagement in Postsecondary Education

Fulfilling preset academic requirements and demonstrating competence on pre-determined performance measures alone will assure neither the learner nor the broader society that the learner is prepared to seamlessly apply newfound knowledge, skills, and attitudes to some meaningful endeavor. The crux of the issue faced by learners is that they cannot assume that mindlessly wandering through the maze of academic requirements for any postsecondary learning endeavor constitutes a sufficient level of engagement with learning. In this respect, the excessive focus of all levels of education on standards and formulaic fulfillment of academic requirements has done a tremendous disservice to the learner, the education system, and the broader society. Implied in the often complex systems for channeling learners through the myriad of academic procedures and requirements is the idea that satisfactory completion of the administrative requirements is in itself the goal for the learner: '*If class assignments are submitted in this sequence, and with that degree of detail, you have achieved the goals of the class*;' '*If you complete these courses, in this sequence and that timeframe, you will be able to graduate and you will be prepared to apply what you have learned in every situation you face.*' Learners are thus encouraged to focus first and foremost on following a series of academic procedures that more often than not have actually been instituted for the sake of efficiency in the administrative oversight of the academic system rather than because of their inherent logic within the learning and development trajectory of the learner. Such approaches likely instill in learners a sense that they are doing their part in the learning process solely by fulfilling requirements, and therefore logically that the fulfillment of the requirements constitutes adequate and appropriate engagement with learning. In today's dynamic and chaotic world, nothing could of course be further from the truth. Dispelling such misunderstandings is the responsibility of all involved in postsecondary education.

It is becoming evermore important that learners be exposed to a more realistic view that separates the adherence to academic and administrative procedural requirements from more fundamental measures that the learner can use to gauge his or her level of engagement with the learning experience. This involves leveling with learners about how the formal education system works—with all its strengths and weaknesses, and allowing learners to recognize that success in navigating the formal education system does not necessarily constitute success in learning or success in transferring what is learned. In all likelihood, the development of such a realistic view of the parallel roles that the learner plays in fulfilling academic requirements versus capitalizing on the fullness of the learning experience is something that is best achieved well before the learner enters into the postsecondary education context. If learners can develop a more refined view of this distinction from the earliest times of engagement in the formal education process, benefits will be reaped across all sectors of the formal education system. It will instill in learners a sense of appreciation for their potential for autonomy and personal responsibility in all their learning experiences, both formal and informal. It will allow learners to more actively engage in their development as learners and, indeed, as humans. And, it will provide learners with perhaps one of the most critical sets of skills in the world of today and tomorrow: The ability to gauge their personal learning needs and processes.

7.7.3   Learners Have a Greater Range of Options to Choose from When Considering the Kind of Institution They Wish to Attend for Postsecondary Training; However, Making Well-Informed Choices Requires Learners to Develop a Sound Understanding of the Short- and Long-Term Implications of Choosing One within the Myriad of Educational Service Providers Available

In terms of considering the implications of the increased intersection between commercial sectors and postsecondary institutions, learners are likely to experience both benefits and drawbacks. They are likely to generally be positively served by an increase in the number of venues in which the learner may consider pursuing his or her learning needs and goals. While brick-and-mortar universities and colleges may continue to serve the needs of many learners much of the time, the presence of 'additional players' in the postsecondary educational landscape empowers learners to choose alternate educational providers if those providers are likely to be able to meet their needs more efficaciously. However, this changing context for postsecondary education also challenges the learner. For example, in order for learners at the corporate universities to fully take advantage of the learning experiences they are offered, they will have to supplement their corporate university training with additional informal or formal training, if they wish to have their corporate university training not only serve their employer, but also serve their own human development needs. Corporate university curricula obviously do not seek to better prepare the learner to be effective in the workplace for competing corporations, or to develop the 'whole' of the learner, unless the development of the 'whole' translates into quantifiable value-added for the corporation. Instead, corporate universities position their curricula to maximize the likelihood that immediate gains in on-the-job performance are yielded. Interestingly, one of the potentially most enduring effects that the increase in the number and diversity of commercial education providers will have on the learner is perhaps in the destabilization that this may cause in the postsecondary education sector as a whole. The education sector has often been characterized as remarkably stagnant relative to other sectors of society. With the increase in educational providers, the chances increase that a specific educational entity will not be capable of competing in the new postsecondary context. The impact of this is not limited to those commercial entities seeking to serve the postsecondary institutions. When a company like WebCT is acquired by a major competitor, teachers, learners, and staff at all postsecondary institutions using WebCT are immediately affected. And, in a more extreme case, when one of the for-profit postsecondary institutions is not able to remain financially viable, learners who have earned degrees or certificates from that institution suddenly find themselves in the previously unfamiliar situation of having careers and credentials that survive beyond the lifespan of the organization that granted them. In light of these changing dynamics, learners entering the postsecondary sector must become evermore informed consumers—not only considering an institution's reputation, but also factoring in the long term financial viability of the institution and its commercial partners into their decision-making for where to pursue continued studies.

7.7.4 Autonomy, Resourcefulness, and Persistence are Competencies Essential to Success in a Rapidly Changing World; They are also Competencies That Learners Will Be Forced to Develop Expeditiously as They Interact with a Postsecondary Education Sector That Is in Flux

The self-regulatory demands on the learner in the changing learning landscape are considered by many to be considerable. Opportunities for individualized attention and support are diminishing in many postsecondary institutions and instructional modalities are physically distancing the learner from the instructor (NCES, 1999). Moreover, faculty salaries are languishing, and the proportion of adjunct professors in the teaching faculty continue to increase (AAUP, 2006). These factors, far outside of the realm of control of the individual student, change the dynamics in the learning environment and, more broadly, in the educational culture in postsecondary institutions. They also place new demands on the learner in terms of personally investing in the learning process, and in terms of developing an effective self-regulatory and attitudinal disposition when navigating the formalized postsecondary education landscape.

The challenge faced by many learners is that they are confronted with a formal postsecondary education context that likely has little in common with what they were exposed to in their earlier formal training. In other words, there is little alignment between today's postsecondary learning environment and the K-12 learning settings that students graduated from. Learners are therefore unlikely to come equipped with the dispositional attributes most likely to yield success in the postsecondary learning landscape. Nor are they likely to know exactly how to go about developing the desired habits of mind for achievement of personal learning goals using formal postsecondary education as a vehicle. Self-direction relies on the ability of the learner to learn how to learn (Gallagher, 1994), and self-regulatory skills and meta-learning skills development is intertwined with the recognition of the dialogical nature of learning. Morgan (1993) notes that developing a "facility for dialogue" (p. 93) is dependent on a frame of reference in which learner responsibility and autonomy (in the learning process) are recognized. Dialogue and dialogical learning are explored in more detail in the next section.

7.7.5 *Learners Have Less Access to In-Depth, Individualized Interaction with a Professor, but Greater Access to Rich Opportunities for In-Depth Dialogue and Collaboration with Peers and Relevant People Outside the Immediate Instructional Setting*

Combining the impact of increased prevalence of distance and distributed modalities in postsecondary education with the effect of reductions in funding on the frequency and depth of learner-instructor communication, we might also posit that the changing learning landscape makes it more important than ever for learners to develop a constructive disposition toward both asynchronous and synchronous dialogue with peers and individuals outside of the immediate instructional setting. Dialogue—in its many forms—is an integral aspect of learning (Freire, 1976; Morgan, 1993), and effective, meaningful dialogue is essential to the achievement of what Lindemann (1947) referred to as *true* adult education, when he observed that "true adult education is social education" (p. 55). Vygotsky (1978) posits that learning, as a social activity, takes place through communication with others. Yet much of the attention to the dialogical nature of education has traditionally been on its application in real-time, face-to-face dialogue between a learner and an instructor. New demands are placed on the learner in the changing learning landscape, and new methods of dialogical learning have to be assumed; indeed, the medium of communication is considered of central importance to considering the exchange of knowledge and ideas.

According to a survey of distance education at postsecondary institutions conducted by the National Center of Education Statistics (NCES, 1999), "asynchronous Internet instruction, two-way interactive video, and one-way prerecorded video were used by more institutions than any other distance education technologies" (p. 5). Critical to the development of learner competence in social, dialogical learning in today's learning landscape is therefore a renewed focus on the value of written communication as opposed to the auditory verbal exchanges in the traditional classroom.[8]

---

[8] De la Teja and Spannaus (in this volume) explore in more detail the hints provided to learners of non-verbal communication competencies needed for learning.

Ihalainen (1997—cited in Geursen, 2000), observes that there is a potential diffi-culty in "changing existing cultures and long accepted ways of operating" (p. 3). However, I contend that the potential benefits of changing such cultures to fully recognize the unique power of written, asynchronous communication in postsec-ondary education is paramount to helping learners capitalize on this new reality of formal learning. Indeed, Derrida (1967) noted that written communication is not only qualitatively different from verbal communication, but that written communication allows for the expression of thoughts and perceptions in a manner that verbal communication does not.

7.7.6 Empowerment Over, and Responsibility For, the Learning Process Position the Learner in the Postsecondary Education Sector and the Broader Learning Landscape for Sustained Growth and Success

As mentioned earlier, one of the changes in the learning landscape is the greater prevalence of mass models of education as opposed to elite, personalized models of education (Baker, 2001). With the resulting reduction in personalized attention and consideration for individualized educational needs, it appears more important than ever that learners in today's learning landscape develop the skills and habits of mind needed for personal success and for locating support mechanisms outside of only the instructor-student relationship. Succeeding in this is complicated by the increasing number of university courses and programs where instruction is largely or exclusively offered through distance learning modalities that augment the prob-ability that the learner will be physically separated from both the instructor and fellow students during his or her postsecondary education learning experiences. The sum total of conditions and experiences encountered by the learner in the changing postsecondary setting is unfamiliar to most learners entering into the system from a traditional secondary school setting. This lack of familiarity can threaten to make even the best-intentioned person second guess the extent to which they can function as empowered learners.

In truth, however, perhaps one of the most important and overarching compe-tencies that today's learners must develop is a sense of empowerment over—and responsibility for—their learning trajectory. In the postsecondary education setting there are particular conditions and challenges that make this important to the learner's success. However, the postsecondary education sector is far from the only context in which an empowered disposition is essential to success. As with any organic phenomenon, every aspect of the learning and living landscape is in a perpetual state of flux. Learners within such an ecosystem work most harmoni-ously with their environment if they carefully cultivate a disposition of empow-erment and responsibility. And, while the challenges and opportunities facing the learners in today's learning landscape are unique to the specific place in which our societies find themselves, the desire for active, empowered engagement is certainly not something new. Spinoza (1632–1677), in his key work on Ethics, introduces the active affects, believing that it is ethically important that a person be active rather than passive. The active affects (active joy and active passion) emphasize a person's "role as total cause of what they do" (LeBuffe, 2006). Borrowing from Spinoza, perhaps one of the most meaningful effects that the postsecondary education sector can have on learners is in emphasizing the learners' role as the total cause of their learning and growth in the learning and living landscapes.

7.8 Resources for Further Exploration

- Dawson-Tunik, T. L. (2004). "A good education is…" The development of evaluative thought across the life-span. *Genetic, Social, and General Psychology Monographs, 130,* 4–112. This monograph outlines the process and results of research conducted to answer the question, 'How does evaluative reasoning about education change over the course of cognitive development?' In addition, the literature review provides an insightful introduction to the various perspectives on conceptions of education and their evolution over the lifespan.
- Lambert, R., & Butler, N. (2006). *The future of European universities: Renaissance or decay?* London: Center for European Reform. An insightful analysis of the state of European higher education. The report starts with the following lines: "Europe's universities, taken as a group, are failing to provide the intellectual and creative energy that is required to improve the continent's poor economic performance. Too few of them are international centres of research excellence, attracting the best talent from around the world. Their efforts in both teaching and research are limited by a serious, and in many areas desperate, lack of resources" (p. 1). The authors look at country-specific and regional indicators of the troubling condition of higher education in Europe and current reform efforts, and conclude with a series of policy recommendations to address the challenges faced in European postsecondary education.
- Lagemann, E. C. (2000). *An elusive science: The troubling history of education research.* Chicago: University of Chicago Press. This book seeks to elucidate how the field of education (and specifically educational research) has come to have so little credibility. It offers an insightful analysis of the state of the field of education through the lens of the historical development of methods and paradigms in educational research. A review of the book was published in the Harvard Educational Review, and can be accessed at http://www. hepg.org/her/booknote/72.
- U.S. Department of Education (2006). *A test of leadership: Charting the future of U.S. higher education.* Washington, DC: U.S. Department of Education. This is a report of the commission appointed by the US Secretary of Education. It examines the quality of postsecondary education in the United States through the

lens of variables such as accessibility, affordability, accountability and quality. The report concludes with the commission's recommendations for improving U.S. higher education.

7.9 Questions for Comprehension and Application

1. In the *Learning and living landscapes* section of this chapter, reference is made to the impact of the increasing prevalence of ambiguity on learners in today's learning landscape. What are the competencies and habits of mind needed to interact constructively with ever-greater levels of ambiguity? How and where can today's learners best develop the skills for tolerating—or indeed, thriving on—ambiguity?
2. What are some of the key competencies for participation in the knowledge economy? How can these competencies be measured? What, if any, changes are needed in instructional strategies to support the development of competencies for the knowledge economy?
3. The concluding section of this chapter explores the implications of the changing role of postsecondary education for *learners*. However, one can argue that the responsibility for dealing with the postsecondary education's state of flux does not reside only (or even primarily) with the learner. What, then, would be some of the implications for the policy-makers, researchers, and practitioners that shape the postsecondary education reality today?
4. What are some of the ways in which the postsecondary sector and its institutions can adapt to better prepare learners for the rapidly changing world?
5. Imagine that you have been asked to outline the key areas for further research on the postsecondary education sector's changing place in the living and learning landscape. What, from your perspective, are the important questions to be addressed regarding this topic?

References

AAUP (American Association of University Professors) (2006). 2005–06 Report on the economic status of the profession. *Academe, 92*(2), 25–34.

Baker, M. (2001, September 28). University: Is it a Good Education? *BBC News World Edition.* Retrieved October 2, 2006, from http://news.bbc.co.uk/2/hi/uk_news/education/ mike_baker/1569623.stm.

Bernard, R. M., Abrami, P. C., Lou, Y., Borokhovski, E., Wade, A., Wozney, L., Wallet, P. A., Fiset, M., & Huang, B. (2004). How does distance education compare to classroom instruction? A meta-analysis of the empirical literature. *Review of Educational Research, 74*(3), 379–439.

Bransford, J. D., Slowinski, M., Vye, N., & Mosborg, S. (in this volume). The learning sciences, technology and designs for educational systems: Some thoughts about change. In J. Visser & M. Visser-Valfrey (Eds.), *Learners in a changing learning landscape: Reflections from a dialogue on new roles and expectations* (pp. 37–67). Dordrecht, The Netherlands: Springer.

British Columbia Chamber of Commerce (2006). *Expanding opportunities in post-secondary education*. Retrieved December 1, 2006, from http://www.bcchamber.org/files/PDF/BC_ Chamber_Campus_2020_Presentation.pdf.

Casner-Lotto, J., & Barrington, L. (2006). *Are they really ready to work? Employers' perspectives on the basic knowledge and applied skills of new entrants to the 21st century workforce* (Rep. No. BED-06-Workforce). New York: The Conference Board.

Christensen, C. M., Aaron, S., & Clark, W. (2003). Disruption in education. *EDUCAUSE, 38*(1), 45–53.

Cliff, A. F. (1996). Postgraduate students' beliefs about learning and knowledge. *Proceedings HERDSA Conference 1996*. Retrieved October 3, 2006, from http://www.herdsa.org.au/ confs/1996/cliff1.html.

Commission on the Future of Higher Education (2006). *A test of leadership: Charting the future of U.S. higher education*. Washington, DC: U.S. Department of Education.

Conley, D. (2005). *Policy perspectives: What we must do to create a system that prepares students for college success*. Retrieved February 13, 2007, from http://www.wested.org/ online_pubs/ pp-06-01.pdf.

Crane, S. (1905). *The black riders and other lines*. Boston: Small, Maynard & Company.

Davenport, P. (2000, December). *The affordability of lifelong learning in the knowledge economy: A Canadian university perspective*. Paper presented at the OECD/Canada Conference on Lifelong Learning as an Affordable Investment, Ottawa, Canada, December 6–8, 2000. Retrieved December 1, 2006, from http://www.oecd.org/dataoecd/1/ 39/1917484.pdf.

Dawson-Tunik, T. L. (2004). "A good education is..." The development of evaluative thought across the life-span. *Genetic, Social, and General Psychology Monographs, 130*, 4–112.

De la Teja, I., & Spannaus, T. W. (in this volume). New online learning technologies: new online learner competencies. Really? In J. Visser & M. Visser-Valfrey (Eds.), *Learners in a changing learning landscape: Reflections from a dialogue on new roles and expectations* (pp. 187–211). Dordrecht, The Netherlands: Springer.

Derrida, J. (1976). *Of grammatology* (G. C. Spivak, Trans.). Baltimore: Johns Hopkins University Press.

Dewey, J. (1916). *Democracy and Education* (Chap. 2: Education as a Social Function). Retrieved September 4, 2007, from http://www.ilt.columbia.edu/Publications/Projects/ digitexts/dewey/ d_e/chapter02.html.

Freire, P. (1976). *Education: The practice of freedom*. London: Writers & Readers.

Gallagher, J. J. (1994). Teaching and learning: New models. *Annual Review of Psychology, 45*, 171–195.

Geursen, L. (2000). *Dialogue as a means of learning within online distance education*. Retrieved February 2, 2003, from http://flexiblelearning.net.au/nw2000/talkback/p32.htm.

Gorder, C. (1990). *Home schools: An alternative*. Tempe, AZ: Blue Bird.

Gunderson, S., Jones, R., & Scanland, K. (2004). *The jobs revolution: Changing how America works*. Washington, DC: Copywriters Incorporated.

Lagemann, E. C. (2000). *An elusive science: The troubling history of education research*. Chicago: University of Chicago Press.

Lambert, R., & Butler, N. (2006). *The future of European universities: Renaissance or decay?* London: Center for European Reform.

LeBuffe, M. (2006). Spinoza's psychological theory. *Stanford Encyclopedia of Philosophy*. Retrieved December 2, 2006, from http://plato.stanford.edu/entries/spinoza-psychological/.

Lindeman, E. C. (1947). Adult education and the democratic discipline. *Adult Education Journal, 6*, 112–115.

London, S. (2007) *Book review of 'Building a bridge to the 18th Century'* (Neil Postman). Retrieved December 1, 2006, from http://www.scottlondon.com/reviews/postman3.html.

Marquardt, M. J., & Kearsley, G. (1999). *Technology based learning: Maximizing human performance and corporate success*. Boca Raton, FL: St. Lucie Press.

Marton, F., Dall'Alba, G. & Beaty, E. (1993). Conceptions of learning. *International Journal of Educational Research, 19*, 277–300.

Middlehurst R. (2003). The Developing World of Borderless Higher Education: Markets, Providers, Quality Assurance and Qualification' in Conference Proceedings of the First Global Forum on International Quality Assurance, Accreditation and the Recognition of Qualifications. Paris, UNESCO. 25–39.

Morgan, A. (1993). *Improving your students' learning*. London: Kogan Page.

National Education Association (n.d.). *Technology*. Retrieved December 1, 2006, from http://www2.nea.org/he/techno.html.

NCES (National Center for Education Statistics) (1999). *Distance education at postsecondary education institutions: 1997–98* (NCES 2000-013). Washington, DC: NCES. Retrieved September 27, 2007, from http://nces.ed.gov/pubs2000/2000013.pdf.

NCES (National Center for Education Statistics) (2001). *The condition of education 2001* (NCES No. 2001–072). Washington, DC: U.S. Department of Education. Retrieved September 27, 2007, http://nces.ed.gov/pubs2001/2001072.pdf.

NCES (National Center for Education Statistics) (2006). *The condition of education 2006* (NCES No. 2006–071) Washington, DC: U.S. Department of Education. Retrieved September 27, 2007, from http://nces.ed.gov/pubs2006/2006071.pdf.

Noble, D. (1998). Digital diploma mills: The automation of higher education. *First Monday, 3*(1). Retrieved October 5, 2006, from http://www.firstmonday.org/issues/issue3_1/noble/.

Olsen, S. (2006, July 9). *Google recruits eggheads with mystery billboard. CNET news*. Retrieved October 5, 2006, from http://news.com.com/Google + recruits + eggheads + with + mystery + billboard/2100-1023_3-5263941.html.

Organisation for Economic Co-operation and Development (OECD) (1996). *The knowledge-based economy*. Retrieved October 6, 2006, from http://www.oecd.org/dataoecd/51/8/1913021. pdf.

Rogers, C. (1969). *Freedom to learn*. Columbus, OH: Charles E. Merrill Publishing.

Schilpp, P. (1949). *Albert Einstein, philosopher-scientist*. Evanston, IL: The Library of Living Philosophers.

Stewart, M. (2007). The management myth [Electronic Version]. The Atlantic Monthly. Retrieved March 10, 2008, from http://www.theatlantic.com/doc/200606/stewart-business.

Stirling, D. (in this volume). Online learning in context. In J. Visser & M. Visser-Valfrey (Eds.), *Learners in a changing learning landscape: Reflections from a dialogue on new roles and expectations* (pp. 165–186). Dordrecht, The Netherlands: Springer.

Stokes, P. J. (2006). *Hidden in plain sight: Adult learners forge a new tradition in higher education*. Issue Paper. Retrieved December 1, 2006, from http://www.ed.gov/about/ bdscomm/list/ hiedfuture/reports/stokes.pdf.

Trow, M. (2000). *From mass higher education to universal access: The American advantage*. Paper in Research and Occasional Paper Series: CDHE.1.00, Center for Studies in Higher Education, University of California, Berkeley, CA. Retrieved December 1, 2006, from http://cshe.berkeley.edu/publications/docs/PP.Trow.MassHE.1.00.pdf.

UNESCO (2000). *Dakar framework for action. Education for all: Meeting our collective commitments*. Text adopted by the World Education Forum Dakar, Senegal, April 26–28, 2000. Retrieved February 2, 2007, from http://www.unesco.org/education/efa/ed_for_all/ dakfram_eng.shtml.

Van Rossum, E. J., Deijkers, R., & Hamer, R. (1985). Students' learning conceptions and their interpretation of significant educational concepts. *Higher Education, 14*, 617–641.

Visser, J. (2001). *Factors that foster the evolution of a learning society*. LDI Working Paper # 2. Retrieved August 18, 2006, from http://www.learndev.org/dl/FactorsThatFoster.PDF.

Visser, J. (2003). Distance education in the perspective of global issues and concerns. In M. G. Moore & W. G. Anderson (Eds.), *Handbook of distance education* (pp. 793–810). Mahwah, NJ: Lawrence Erlbaum.

Visser, J. (in this volume). Constructive interaction with change: Implications for learners and the environment in which they learn. In J. Visser & M. Visser-Valfrey (Eds.), *Learners in a changing learning landscape: Reflections from a dialogue on new roles and expectations* (pp. 11–35). Dordrecht, The Netherlands: Springer.

Vygotsky, L. (1978). *Mind in society*. Cambridge, MA: Harvard University Press.

Whitehead, A. N. (1929). *The aims of education and other essays*. New York: Macmillan.

Whitehead, A. N. (1938). *Modes of thought*. New York: Macmillan.

Chapter 8
Online Learning in Context

Diana Stirling

Abstract This chapter will explore the implications of courseware design and use in online learning environments for not only individual learner expectations but also expectations of the learning community as a whole. The concept of context density and its importance in formal online learning environments will be stressed. It will be argued that the lack of adumbrations in online communication necessitates explicit communication by participants in the process of co-creating meaning and context density. From this focus on the context embedded in online learning environments the discussion will zoom out to view the larger learning landscape through a wider lens, i.e. the context within which online learning is taking place for individual learners and the global society. While technology offers us the potential to create real change in our approaches to education, such change can only be realized if we proceed with reflective awareness. Before we can see such change, we must be willing to question our assumptions about what we have done so far and envision the truly different, the 'new model that makes the existing model obsolete' in Buckminster Fuller's words. A change in education is not inherent in our new technology; it must be a manifestation of the world in our collective imagination.

8.1 Introduction

> We pass the word around; we ponder how the case is put by different people, we read the poetry; we meditate over the literature; we play the music; we change our minds; we reach an understanding. Society evolves this way, not by shouting each other down, but by the unique capacity of unique, individual human beings to comprehend each other.
>
> Thomas, The Medusa and the Snail (1979, p. 98)

This chapter is going to explore learner expectations in formal online learning environments as they relate to the context embedded in courseware design and its use. E. T. Hall's (1964, 1976) descriptions of context densities and adumbrations serve as a starting point for examining context in these environments. There will also be a

Independent educator and curriculum designer

foray into the political and philosophical underpinnings of courseware design and the expectations that precede and result from their influence on such design.

Many questions will arise in the course of the discussion—questions on the author's mind and, it is hoped, questions inspired by the reader's interaction with the ideas examined and proposed. For my part, I feel as if I'm writing this while in the midst of puzzling over the potential, both positive and negative, of these new online venues for interacting with others. Poised as we are at this juncture, where online enrollments are rapidly increasing and organizations are considering how best to proceed with online instruction, we can choose what is most promising of the many available options or, better still, we can take the time to imagine just what we'd like the future to extend to us and what we'd like to offer in exchange. It can start here, with our efforts toward mutual comprehension.

8.2   The Significance of Context

Jan Visser has posed an intriguing question to inspire our investigation of learner expectations: *Is the online learner a distinct subspecies among the wider species of learners in general?* (Question 1, p. 4 in this volume)

There is evidence from psychology that people behave differently in different situations based on the roles and/or expectations assigned to them. The classic Stanford Prison Experiment (Zimbardo, 1973, 1999–2006), conducted in 1971, is a well known example. Perhaps the online learning environment brings out different aspects of learners (and instructors) than in-person classroom environments do. If so, then considerations of context become paramount. Do the expectations in in-person learning environments differ from those in online learning environments? If so, why do they differ and how? How do expectations in these environments get communicated?

8.2.1   The Stanford Prison Experiment

In the Stanford Prison Experiment, participants were assigned roles arbitrarily (http://www.prisonexp.org/slide-4.htm). Beyond the initial procedures during which 'inmates' were admitted, the experimenters did not explicitly state what behaviors were expected in the given roles (http://www.prisonexp.org/slide-12. htm). Those initial procedures included assigning uniforms to the 'guards' (http://www.prisonexp.org/slide-13.htm) and stripping the 'prisoners,' clothing them in only hospital-type gowns (http://www.prisonexp.org/slide-8.htm and http://www. prisonexp.org/slide-11.htm) and assigning them numbers to be used in place of their names. The physical environment, a portion of the university basement, was altered to simulate a prison environment, with room doors replaced by steel bars (http://www.prisonexp.org/slide-5.htm and http://www.prisonexp.org/slide-6.htm). There were no windows and all clocks were removed.

It is uncanny how quickly the participants in the experiment fell into their roles and how common are the behaviors they exhibited in the 'real world' of prisons. Even the designer of the experiment could not resist the lure of his role as superintendent (http://www.prisonexp.org/slide-27.htm) and lost sight of the fact that the experiment was a simulation. How did the role-players decide what behaviors to express? Sometimes the behaviors were negotiated socially with others in the same context-dependent role (http://www.prisonexp.org/slide-16.htm and http://www.prisonexp.org/slide-17.htm) and sometimes they were determined individually. Once the roles were established, however, decisions were invariably made in accordance with the context. This was so much the case that the experiment had to be concluded early.

8.2.2 Roles, Context and Communication

The Stanford Prison Experiment was an extreme example of simulated role-playing. It could be argued that the roles of guard and prisoner elicit more intense behaviors that other common roles due to the nature of their relationship to one another; i.e. the roles of guard and prisoner are inextricable, inflexible, and based entirely on the disparity of power. Although this book is about education, I am not by any means suggesting that the relationship between teacher and student is equivalent to that between guard and prisoner. While there is typically a power discrepancy between teacher and student in formal learning environments, that discrepancy is not the basis of the relationship. In addition, the role of prisoner is limiting in the sense that it is the dominant, and possibly the only, role played 24/7, and typically is not assumed willingly. In contrast, it is entirely possible (and some say desirable) for teachers to become students and students to be teachers in formal educational environments. As long as a teacher wields the power of the grade, the teacher-student power discrepancy does not disappear, but it is presumably more flexible than that between prisoner and guard. In fact, it is the differences between the guard-prisoner and teacher-student relationships that invite questions crucial to the design and use of online courseware. What I want to focus on here is the significance of context in establishing roles and behaviors, and in particular, how these factors influence communication in formal online learning environments.

In his book *Beyond Culture*, Edward T. Hall (1976) discusses some differences between what he calls "*high-context*" and "*low-context*" communications (pp. 91–93). Here's how Hall explains these differences.

> A high-context (HC) communication or message is one in which most of the information is either in the physical context or internalized in the person, while very little is in the coded, explicit, transmitted part of the message. A low-context (LC) communication is just the opposite; i.e., the mass of the information is vested in the explicit code. (p. 91)

Hall compares communication in the United States with that in Japan as one way of illustrating this concept. The United States is on the low-context end of the spectrum while Japan is on the high-context end. Essentially this means that in the U.S.

communication is typically quite explicit as compared with communication in Japan. In many situations in Japan it is considered offensive to explain a situation directly or to offer suggestions or alternatives when the unexpected happens. Hall gives the example of being moved repeatedly from room to room in a hotel in Japan, and once even being moved from one inn to another without any explanation whatsoever. He was still baffled by this years after it happened. As Hall explains, in the U.S. we don't like to be moved around, particularly without being offered a reason. There are all kinds of implications of status and so forth tied up in issues of space and independence in decision making. He eventually came to understand that, in the context of Japanese culture, he was being treated with the greatest respect. There, being identified with a group is of the utmost importance. Without such identification, one is considered an outsider. By overseeing Hall's stay and making arrangements for him, the Japanese proprietors were conveying the message that he 'belonged' to them, was a part of their group. For them it was the highest form of hospitality.

E. T. Hall's (1976) example highlights the importance of understanding context in intercultural interactions. However, differences of context exist within cultures as well. The following discussion details how and suggests the relevance of such contextual differences in online learning situations.

E. T. Hall's (1976) concept of high- and low-context communications is expressed as a continuum rather than as a dichotomy. He explains his idea in terms of cultures, but for this discussion I should like to apply the concept to situations within cultures as well as to online learning environments.

Imagine that you are with a group of your longtime friends and you are relaxing together, maybe at a party. Further, imagine that you have brought along a new friend who is unknown to the group. Typically there will be lots of phrases and innuendos in the conversation that will be undecipherable to the newcomer. The group of friends together engages in high-context communications, the context having been built up over time by mutual experience and understanding with which the newcomer is unfamiliar. In order for the newcomer to be included, you will have to explicitly explain the details that are encoded in the communications between your longtime friends, thus intentionally creating a context for understanding. If the newcomer is also new to the culture surrounding the group of friends, and if the friendships have existed within that surrounding culture (be it a culture of work, nationality, political ideals, etc.) the context may be even more dense and impenetrable.

In the previous scenario, the newcomer, while welcomed, could not participate in the high-context interactions between longtime friends without an effort being made by group members to explicitly communicate some aspects of their historical context.

What happens when a group of people unknown to one another gathers for the first time in a low-context culture such as the United States? My guess is that if the group has been called together for some purpose, such as to deliberate on a particular problem related to work or study, the contextual framework of the field of endeavor enables higher-context communication than is possible at, say, a large party where friends, friends of friends, and party crashers are in attendance. I suspect that the size of a group may have some bearing on the development of contextual density. I further suspect that time is a factor for groups such as these. A working group may meet or communicate regularly over a period of time, thus further developing the contextual density of their interactions, while those at a large party may expect never to see one another after the party ends. Communication between the partygoers who are strangers to one another may be minimal or nonexistent, the greatest density of context being derived from roles such as 'flirt' or 'host.'

8.2.3 The Power of Roles in Context

The participants in the Stanford Prison Experiment were presumably not known to one another before the experiment began. They did not have a history together that could have established a higher degree of context density than that of a typical group of strangers. The context of their interactions was established by the environment and their roles within it. They became so strongly identified with their roles in such a brief time that they all, including the experimental designer, began to behave in ways that would have been uncharacteristic in contexts such as their ordinary daily lives. There are interesting questions inherent in this situation. For example, what is the relationship between environment and roles? If the basement hadn't been remodeled to simulate a prison environment, if the prisoners had not worn gowns and the guards had not worn uniforms, and if the prisoners had left the simulation and returned to their ordinary lives each evening, would the role-playing have been less convincing to the participants? Finally, does the powerful context generated so quickly in this experiment suggest that some roles, on the level of archetypes perhaps, are inherently dense and therefore serve to enable high-context communication in the absence of other context-dense conditions? If these role-defined communications prevail, what value do they have as compared with other types of communication possibilities?

And what do these questions have to do with online learning environments? These questions will be considered further after we take a look at the non-verbal aspects of communication and just what *presence* means online.

8.2.4 Adumbrations and Presence Online

In his anthropological writings, E. T. Hall (1964) has considered the elements of successful intercultural communication that lie outside of linguistics. He has described his concept of "*adumbration*" (p. 154) as an essential component of the overall context. Hall defines adumbrations as "those indications preceding or surrounding formal communications which enable organisms to engage in the mutual exchange and evaluation of covert information on what each can expect from the other" (p. 154). These are the very factors, typically missing in online interactions, that many educators and learners refer to when they discuss the differences between communication online and in-person communication. A variety of efforts has been made to incorporate adumbrative elements into online communication, things like emoticons (such as ☺) and textual descriptions (e.g., <sigh>) of emotional behaviors (also see Raybourn, 2001, p. 250).

How important are these adumbrations in online communication and particularly in formal online learning environments? This writing of E. T. Hall's (1964) predates online learning environments, but he says of in-person communications that without the adumbrative features, the results can be "catastrophic" (p. 154) and further hypothesizes that "the specific technical communication on the overt level is seldom seriously misinterpreted, even in cross-cultural contexts, if the adumbrative part is read correctly. What is most often misinterpreted is the adumbration" (p. 161). Are there adumbrative features in online communications (beyond the simple ones mentioned above) and, if so, what are they? If not, how are online interactions affected by the lack of such features?

It can be argued that the lack of physical presence online has both positive and negative value. Such lack might mitigate reactions to characteristics that could otherwise result in stereotyping or inhibitions. To a certain extent, it is up to each participant whether or not to reveal personal information, such as ethnic background or disability status, online. In person, many of these characteristics are obvious from the outset. It could be argued that these physical characteristics comprise a portion of the communications (intentional or otherwise) that exist in in-person communications. The lack of such information might be seen as of positive value for affording greater parity to participants who may be marginalized in other contexts.

Another potentially positive value is the lag time in communications that often exists online. If a participant desires, s/he may edit any comment before posting. This is obviously an option in person as well, i.e. one can stop and think before speaking, but the extra time required to type and post may afford the online 'speaker' a window of opportunity in which to reconsider the point about to be made. Were the same speaker engaged in an in-person discussion, the emotional aspects of the response might be more obvious, regardless of what words were actually spoken. This lag time in communications can also be seen to be of negative value, however. The flow of a discussion is often different in text-based online environments than in person. Due to differences in connection and typing speeds, for example, a response to a particular comment may appear after the conversation has taken a turn in a different direction, making the discussion disjointed and confusing. Although this can happen in person as well, it is easier to keep track of who said what when there are visual and kinesthetic cues that physical presence affords.

With regard to Beaudoin's (in this volume) topic of the 'invisible learner,' it seems possible that, even though these silent learners populate in-person classrooms as well as those online, it is actually the absence of adumbrative features that underlies Beaudoin's concerns. McGrath and Prinz (2001) talk about presence in person as being expressed on a continuum from silence to "full on" (p. 101). If Beaudoin and his silent student share the same physical space, the adumbrative features (eye contact or lack of it, body posture, non-linguistic verbal expressions, etc.) result in some communication. However, in a typical text-based online learning environment it is difficult, if not impossible, to communicate across the continuum—it's all or nothing. A student can log in and be silent, and the instructor has no idea whether or not that student is actually 'present' or has gone off to eat dinner or talk on the phone. So, whether or not a lack of physical presence online is seen as an advantage or a disadvantage, it could be argued that, at least in some online environments, establishing some sense of presence is relevant and important.

But just how is a sense of presence established online?

A number of researchers are examining the concept of presence in collaborative virtual environments (CVEs) (Büscher, O'Brien, Rodden, & Trevor, 2001; Hindmarsh, Fraser, Heath, & Benford, 2001; Huxor, 2001; McGrath & Prinz, 2001; Raybourn, 2001). The researchers mentioned here are particularly concerned with varieties of CVEs and how presence is mediated in them. Before exploring this, though, the question arises as to the relevance of CVEs to this discussion with its focus on formal online learning environments. The potential relevance lies in the possibility of designing online learning environments to support collaboration. If such environments are deemed desirable, then a look at what seems to work and where the challenges lie might be instructive. Whether or not such environments are desirable will be addressed later in this chapter, when the motives and forces underlying courseware design are examined more closely.

By observing participants interacting in and with large-scale CVEs at a media museum, Büscher's group (2001) came to the conclusion that "presence is not an individually owned, private quality, but one that is embedded in the sociality of our existence in the world" (p. 79). This reminds me of the tree falling in the forest question: *If a tree falls in a forest and there is nobody there to hear it, does it make a sound?* Our analogous question for Beaudoin's (in this volume) class might be: *If a student is logged in for class but never makes a 'sound,' can s/he said to be present?* In other words, does presence require a witness? If so, what constitutes witnessing?

In her discussion of CVEs used for gaming, Raybourn (2001) points to the degree of control one has with regard to the image presented of oneself in an online environment. Citing Cushman and Cahn (1985), she argues that "self-concepts are not determined by *who* others think we are, but rather by *how* the presentation of the self is co-constructed and maintained by both parties in interaction (p. 249). I might amend that to say *all* parties in interaction. At the same time, as mentioned above, in the absence of physical characteristics for others to view (in online environments that don't support video conferencing, for example), each partici-pant has an opportunity to consciously construct the persona(s) that s/he chooses to present. These personas, and thus the online presence, are constructed solely of communication events (Raybourn, 2001, p. 249) and it is the history of these events that establishes presence in the online environment. If that is the case, it could be said that as presence is being co-created in an online environment, so is the density of the context being enhanced. Thus, it could be argued that facilitation of interactions between participants contributes significantly to the quality and depth of online experiences.

This idea of the social construction of presence seems apropos in collaborative virtual environments. Collaboration necessarily requires participation and communication. There must be a mutual sense of presence in order for the necessary communication to take place. Later in this chapter, however, these questions of presence will be revisited in the context of human-machine interactions. In that context, expectations of and by learners may be quite different from those engendered by human collaboration.

There is some discussion about whether 3-D environments are more conducive to a sense of presence than those which are entirely text-based (McGrath & Prinz, 2001; Raybourn, 2001; Huxor, 2001), and one answer seems to be *it depends*. On what does it depend? Some of the factors being explored in 3-D environments are: ease of navigation of the environment (McGrath & Prinz, 2001; Büscher et. al., 2001), ease of communication in the environment (McGrath & Prinz, 2001) and the ability to shift perspectives within the environment (Büscher et al., 2001; Zhang & Furnas, 2005). These concerns are not specific to 3-D environments; designers of all kinds of online environments must take them into account. But where it might once have been assumed that a 3-D environment would necessarily be an improvement over an entirely text-based one (Huxor, 2001) the adoption of 3-D environments outside the gaming community has been slow. Why might this be the case? It might be due to the lack of technical ability of the courseware designers, it could be prohibitive cost in money, time and bandwidth, or it could be that designers and users don't see the added investment as worthwhile in terms of the potential or real benefits of these environments for educational purposes.

Still, there are some intriguing possibilities available in 3-D environments that are not possible otherwise. One of these possibilities is the choice of an avatar, a figural representation of oneself, to stand in and represent one's presence online. Although the use of an avatar cannot approach the subtlety of in-person interactions, some interesting work has been done involving what McGrath and Prinz (2001) call *symbolic acting* in an online work environment. In their system, an avatar representing an individual performs some non-verbal actions based on the individual's activity on their desktop.

> For example, in the Forum Meeting Space, when you have a window obscuring the visualization of the space your avatar is seen to be looking at a document because the Envoy [a software agent] interprets that desktop situation into a symbolic action displaying that your attention is elsewhere. (p. 103)

Some of the drawbacks to these features in McGrath and Prinz's study were that the female avatar was characterized as everything from "amusing to offensive" (p. 109) and that the animation for indicating that someone was "engaged" (p. 110), as in the previous example, was often misunderstood. Apparently it was no better at conveying whether the individual was engaged in listening, had gone off to lunch, or was simply bored than would be evident in a purely text-based environment.

One of the potential advantages of the 3-D working space is the facilitation of chance encounters (Huxor, 2001). Huxor's work has been with virtual office spaces, however, where the lack of opportunity for chance encounters that one might experience in a brick-and-mortar environment can be viewed as a disadvantage of the virtual space. In Huxor's virtual office chance encounters are facilitated, not simply by the fact of colleagues being online at the same time, but by two of them being in the vicinity of the same content simultaneously. In his scenario, the communication of the encounter is conducted via chat software. However, due to the limitations of the text chat as compared with a voice conversation, he admits that the chance encounter typically leads to a telephone conversation.

8.3 Formal Online Learning Environments and Context Density

Back to Visser's question about the online learner as a subspecies (Question 1, p. 4 in this volume). If these considerations of context are valid, then it may be that the interactions in online environments are complicated by the lack of both context density and adumbrative features. Even though the learners themselves may study in a variety of environments in person and online, their interactions in online learning situations might be quite different from those in their in-person classrooms.

I should like to suggest that typical online learning environments are necessarily low-context, particularly those that are entirely text-based, and that some of the difficulties encountered in these environments have to do with a lack of adumbrative features in purely text-based communications. The participants in online classes may live in different parts of the world and be from different cultural backgrounds. They may never have an opportunity to meet in person. If the class meets synchronously, some participants may be sipping their morning coffee while others have just tucked their children into bed. There may be differences in skill levels in terms of interacting with the mediating technology or differences in infrastructures, causing communication delays (or even failures) for some participants. Further complications can arise when participants come from cultures with inherently different context densities.

When these widely diverse participants meet online for the first time, they do not simply appear out of nowhere. They log in in the context of their individual lives, coffee in hand, the warmth of a child's touch on the cheek, tense from a long commute home, or any of a myriad of other possibilities. In asynchronous learning environments, the discrepancies of context may be even more pronounced as not only the time of day, but the time with regard to events in the global community will differ. Again, this is not so different from correspondence by letter in the days of snail mail. The real difference here lies in the speed with which these asynchronous messages are delivered and the fact that, except in the case of pen pals, letters are/were typically exchanged between people who knew one another or had a business relationship of some kind.

This lack of shared context density in online environments means that, in order to foster high-quality interactions and facilitate collaboration, communication, including intentions and expectations, needs to be made explicit. Due to the lack of shared context density that is inherent in many, if not most, formal online learning environments, I suggest that they must all be approached as if they were the sites of intercultural communications. Whether the participants self-identify as being culturally homogeneous or not, unless they have relationships with one another outside the online classroom or have a history of online communications with one another, the fact that they will be interacting without the benefit of adumbrative features that help to create context density necessitates a greater awareness of the role those implicit qualities play in in-person communication.

In the absence of explicit communication, individuals in online environments naturally attempt to interpret communications in terms of their own personal experiences, making inferences based on assumptions formed in other contexts. This situation is not unlike that which faces anyone who interacts with others from unfamiliar cultures, and it is fraught with the same dangers (as well as the same expansive possibilities). Naturally, these potential barriers to understanding occur in all kinds of environments, including in-person classes, but in computer mediated learning situations, the lack of adumbrative features further complicates the ability to infer intentions and meanings. The lack of visual, kinesthetic and auditory cues online means that clarity in communication must depend on the explicit expression of assumptions and intentions. In order to achieve this kind of communication, a message sender must possess the meta-cognitive ability to unpack and address the assumptions behind and intention of the message to be sent. Likewise, the message receiver needs to be able to identify the personal context within which the message is being interpreted and to question the assumptions there that may confuse the interpretation of the sender's intention. Raybourn (2001) declares that "effective intercultural communication cannot successfully occur without awareness, negotiation, collaboration, and the co-creation of meaning" (p. 251). This comment applies equally to effective online communication.

In the absence of opportunities to co-create meaning and context density, I suspect that participants rely on their perceived roles in the online environment for contextual clues. The Stanford Prison Experiment as well as the hypothetical party situation mentioned earlier, invite speculation in this area. If such is the case, how is the quality of the online interactions affected by reliance on roles as a substitute for explicit communication or a history of meaning co-creation? My own experience has been that this situation does occur, and that there is great danger of misinterpretation, particularly of an instructor's intentions (*instructor* being a more powerful role than *student*), when roles rather than explicit communication are relied upon.

So far, this discussion has focused mainly on formal online learning environments that are designed after the classroom setting, i.e. with a group of learners who meet with an instructor, either synchronously or asynchronously, to navigate curricular material. But there is another type of formal online environment that deserves mention here. That is the programmed environment in which a student completes a prescribed number of steps, often culminating in a multiple-choice assessment. Many online tutorials are of this variety. This type of environment may be entirely or mostly computer-mediated. In the next section, some of the motivating factors behind courseware design will be explored, including the differences between those that inspire online collaboration in learning and those that support entirely computer mediated design.

8.4 Does Educational Philosophy Drive Educational Design?

Having considered the importance of context in formal online environments, I'd like to turn now to the factors that seem to be driving design in education in general and in online courseware specifically.

Do choices in educational design emerge from educational philosophy? Or do other factors play a greater role—things like expediency, cost effectiveness, and so on? While the buzz words in education today include terms like *constructivism* and *student-centered learning*, are these ideals being achieved in the online learning environments of organizations that claim them to be desirable? If so, how do their online environments and course design support student-centered and constructivist approaches? If not, how could these environments be characterized?

First, however, a clarification of the terms *constructivism* and *student-centered* as they are used here will help ensure that the author and the reader share a sense of their meanings.

8.4.1 Constructivism

In the last century, the work of progressive thinkers such as Dewey and Piaget invited educators to re-examine a model of education in which students were seen as passive recipients of knowledge assembled by others (teachers and parents, for example) in favor of a view of students who constructed their own understanding (Dewey, 1916; Papert, 2003). Although there may be as many varieties of constructivism as there are theorists, this concept of the individual construction of understanding is a vital connecting principle. The constructivist approach values the process of individual construction of knowledge through personal experience. Duckworth (1996), an educator whose work is strongly grounded in that of Piaget, encourages learners to become aware of their own ways of thinking and transforming conscious experience (see also M. Hall, in this volume). This approach requires that the teacher stay attentive and actively engaged in the learners' own reasoning processes. One important way the teacher stays engaged is by asking open-ended questions that offer opportunities for the learners to examine and test their own ideas. Here Duckworth describes the process.

> Instead of explaining to the students, then, I ask them to explain what they think and why.
> I find the following results. First, in trying to make their thoughts clear for other people,
> students achieve greater clarity for themselves....Second, the students themselves

determine what it is they want to understand….Third, people come to depend on themselves: They are the judges of what they know and believe. They know why they believe it, what questions they still have about it, their degree of uncertainty about it, what they want to know about it next, how it relates to what other people think. Any other 'explanation' they encounter must establish its place within what they know. Fourth, students recognize the powerful experience of having their ideas taken seriously, rather than simply screened for correspondence to what the teacher wanted [sic]. Fifth, students learn an enormous amount from each other….Finally, learners come to recognize knowledge as a human construction, since they have constructed their own knowledge and they know that they have. (pp. 158–159)

This focus on learners' processes has often been referred to as *student-centered*. However, the constructivist approach is more than just student-centered, it is *learner-directed* as well. The difference between what has come to be known as student-centered and that which is learner-directed is subtle but significant.

8.4.2 Learner-Directed/Student-Centered: What's the Difference?

Learner-directed education takes time. It allows, in fact encourages, learners to follow their own unique trains of thought. The instructor's role is to follow the learner, asking open-ended questions to facilitate the learner's process of discovery and integration of the new. While there are often pre-determined concepts that the instructor expects learners to encounter in situations arranged to support student explorations, the constructivist process, like the questions that are a vital part of it, is often open-ended. Espousing the belief that learners incorporate best what they have personally experienced, constructivist educators who recognize the importance of learner-directed learning may allow for the re-invention of the wheel, so to speak, by each individual learner. On the positive side, such an approach may help learners develop metacognitive skills that are vital to higher-order thinking. Additionally, learner-directed methods may lead to innovative problem-solving and be especially appropriate for real world problem-based curricula. Still, the bottom line is: learner-directed education can be inefficient and thus, expensive.

Is learner-directed education student-centered? Yes. Is student-centered education learner-directed (and therefore constructivist in approach)? Not necessarily.

For example, the TDeLS e-learning system (Fujii, Yukita, Koike, & Kunii, 2004) allows learners a great deal of choice in how they will approach the learning materials. They can choose to have materials serialized on demand, or they can allow TDeLS to automatically choose the order of the materials (p. 7).[1] The algorithm for serialization offers materials based on previous choices of the learner (p. 8). For example, if the learner has previously shown a preference to approach a topic breadth-first, the algorithm offers those options first. Likewise, for the one who prefers to explore

---

[1] Pagination used is from electronic version.

one sub-topic in depth before moving on, TDeLS serializes based on that preference. The student has the option to switch from one to the other in the combined method. TDeLS might be considered student-centered in the sense that the order of presentation of materials is based on the student's history and preferences. However, the course materials are all chosen in advance and the purpose of the courseware is to "lead [the students] to the final goal efficiently" (p. 11). Thus, TDeLS could not be said to be learner-directed, nor does it claim to be.

The distinction between that which is student-centered and that which is learner-directed is significant in this discussion because expectations in student-centered environments that are not learner-directed differ from those in truly constructivist, learner-directed environments. The expectations differ no matter what the educational setting. Consequently, this distinction has implications for choices in courseware design that the designer would do well to consider in advance.

How do those expectations differ? The most fundamental difference is that in learner-directed environments, the learner or learners are expected *to co-create the learning experience via exploration of a learning landscape without discrete boundaries.* In contrast, in the student-centered environment, the learners are expected *to make choices within a clearly delineated learning domain.*

8.4.3 Constructivism in the Virtual Classroom?

So, what form does a constructivist approach take in formal online learning environments? Well, any form that works for the participants. The key to designing environments that successfully support co-creation of learning is to make the environments as open as possible. Do these environments need a lot of bells and whistles? Not necessarily. Rather than focusing on the specifics of designed learning environments, the most effective approach might be to do away with thinking about formal environments as containers and begin thinking of them as portals. Portals to where? To the entire world! This is the function that the most effective constructivist classrooms play in physical reality, and so it can be in virtual spaces as well. In fact, when the virtual learning environment is seen this way, the assumed barriers between our lives online and offline begin to blur. The limitations of software become moot as we use everything and anything that is available, online or offline, to support our collaborative and individual efforts. This is what we do anyway in our lives, but the artificial distinction between when we are *learning* and when we are *living* persists.

What is the point of having formal learning environments at all in this scenario? One role these environments can play is that of connecting mentors with learners. Does this have to be done formally? No, but learning institutions can cultivate their ability to serve in this way if they so choose. Many universities, for example, recruit accomplished researchers who might offer unique insights to learners interested in their fields. Another function of formal learning institutions is to provide witness to or verification of learning experiences. This is a role that may or may not change in the future. For example, in many societies, credentials count for a large part in one's being selected for employment, and the status attributed to the credentials depends on the status of the formal institution that issued them. In the future, selection may rely more on one's initiative in seeking out one's own learning experiences or on demonstrations of ability (portfolios, for example).

8.4.4   The Learner as Consumer and the Marketing Mindset

Mass Customization will be as important in the 21st century as Mass Production was in the 20th.

B. Joseph Pine II

The factory model of education was influenced by the Industrial Revolution and a mindset that valued efficiency above all. These days, the business model seems to prevail, and business terminology has been adopted by all kinds of institutions that were once seen to have very different objectives from those of business. For example, I work in a library. For many years, the users of library services were referred to as *patrons*. This seems an appropriate term as library services are provided as a public service, paid for by all property owners whether or not they are library users and available to all persons, whether or not they are property owners. The person who comes through the door to get directions, use a computer, conduct research, or check out materials, is not required to pay for these services; no commercial transaction takes place. Even so, these days we who work in the library are encouraged to refer to library users as *customers*. Every library staff member is required to attend a series of customer service trainings. This change in terminology reflects a change in perspective, a shift to a business mindset in a public service organization. This shift to the usage of business terminology has become quite pervasive in the United States. It can be seen in health care and education, as well as in library services.

A recent opinion piece in the New York Times (Salgo, 2006, p. A27) addresses this issue in the context of health care in the United States. The author argues that the change in terminology from *patients* to *customers* has been part of an overall attempt to commodify health care at the expense of the doctor-patient relationship. He maintains that the power to change the system resides with the patients themselves, who must demand to be treated with respect. They should 'shop around' until they find a doctor who will do just that. While elements of this argument are debatable (e.g., do patients really have as much power in the health care system as consumers do in the world of commerce?) the assertion that terminology is important in defining relationships is worth considering.

While we in education still refer to students as *students*, or *learners* (that's a shift in terminology for another discussion), rather than *customers*, there is ample evidence of the business paradigm at work in educational settings as well. In my work as a high school teacher, for example, I was required to attend *customer service* in-service trainings just as I am at the library. The interesting thing about the application of business principles to education is that, in fact, many educational institutions are businesses. This is particularly true in the realm of online education as the proliferation and financial success of schools like Capella University and the University of Phoenix demonstrate. Is there any evidence of a distinction between education as business and education as something else entirely (*what?*) in discussions, at conferences, or in the minds of students, administrators and instructors? Ought there to be a distinction? If so, what should the distinction be?

One of the dangers of applying the business mindset to services that were once considered other than business is that the bottom line becomes the major motivator of practice and the principal measure of success. In education, this means that learners are equated with products and test scores become the bottom line.

I recently encountered an article in the New York Times (Dillon, 2006, p. A14) with the headline "Panel Considers Revamping College Aid and Accrediting" and the subtitle "Business and Academic Leaders at Odds." According to the article, the U.S. Education Secretary has set up a commission comprised of business leaders and academics "to examine college costs and accountability."[2] One investment banker on the panel has compared state colleges and universities to "Soviet-style factories"—criticizing, not what he perceives of as the factory mentality, but rather the Soviet version, which he derides as inefficient. Another commission member is quoted as saying, "We want these people in academia to get real about the problems and issues." What qualifies business executives to sit on a national commission assigned to advise about educational policy? There seems to be an assumption, based on the composition of the commission, that business executives are somehow more attuned to the 'problems and issues' in education than are the educators themselves. In fact, the commission is chaired by Charles Miller (http://www.ed.gov/about/bdscomm/list/hiedfuture/bios/miller.pdf), a private investor who is credited with spearheading the statewide public school 'accountability' system in Texas that became the model for the controversial No Child Left Behind Act. One issue that the panel is considering is standardized testing for higher education. It may not come as a surprise that another member of the commission is Jonathan Grayer (http://www.ed.gov/about/bdscomm/list/hiedfuture/bios/grayer.pdf), Chairman and CEO of Kaplan, Inc. According to his bio on the site, Mr. Grayer has a background in marketing and business. "Grayer's vision" as it is described in the bio, "is helping transform the for-profit education industry" (n.p.). It is interesting, then, that he has been selected to advise about national policy affecting non-profit higher education. It could be argued that this commission merely reflects the current direction of the political wind in the U.S., but government commissions are not the only place where one finds evidence of the business paradigm being applied to what is widely publicized as the failure of education.

The same week that The New York Times ran the article mentioned above, the magazine Edutopia, a publication of the George Lucas Educational Foundation,

---

[2] For more information about the Commission and its activities, see http: //www.ed. gov/about/ bdscomm/list/hiedfuture/.

published an article called *Risky Business* (Daly, 2006). The caption that runs along the bottom of the title pages reads: "With the economic future of the U.S. tied to our public education system, business leaders are scrambling to push for change" (pp. 42–43). The article leads with highlighted text that ends by explaining that business leaders believe "if the U.S. economy had the same success rate with its products as our public educational system has with its students, ...our days as an economic powerhouse would be numbered" (p. 43). Idealistic educators sometimes think that the factory model is far behind us, but here, in this quote which overtly compares products and students, is an example of how deeply rooted its paradigm remains. Since our economy depends far less on manufacturing today than in the past, the business paradigm has eclipsed the manufacturing one, but the language for evaluating education still reflects a view of education that must justify itself in terms of products delivered against money invested.

The business model uses terminology like *quality assurance* and *mass customization*. What are the implications of the application of these terms in educational settings?

> Throughout higher education's ongoing methodological evolution the issue of quality is a constant. There was consensus among the speakers in a conference session on quality assurance that quality is developed not by one faculty member acting independently, but by standardizing the course outline and general approach by the institution; that is, by the faculty as a whole, with expertise in course content, learning theory, and the range of elements that are involved in creating a course. This approach is hardly traditional, but perhaps the home institutions of these panelists provide examples: they represented Capella University, the University of Phoenix, and the University of Maryland University College. (Witherspoon, 2005)

So, at least if the previous comment is any indication, *standardization* for *quality assurance* is one aspect of the application of a business mindset to education. Apparently, some of the business leaders on the commission mentioned above seem to agree.

Standardization, by its very nature, is antithetical to a learner-directed approach, as each individual learner is bound to choose a unique path toward understanding. However, standardization does not preclude a student-centered approach, which can be provided through *mass customization*. Mass customization is a term from the business world (cited in Pine, 2003, p. 4). The distinction between mass customization and what Piller (2005) calls "conventional (craft) customization" (p. 2) lies in the fact that "the space within which a mass customization offering is able to satisfy a customer's need is finite" (pp. 1–2) whereas "a traditional (craft) customizer re-invents not only its products but also its processes for each individual customer" (p. 2). Piller also makes a distinction between *customization* and *personalization*. By his definition, personalization "involves intense communication and interaction between two parties" (p. 3) while customization is a more general modification of product or service components (p. 3).

Mass customization seems to be an effective marketing tool. What is the appeal of mass customization to the consumer? Mass customization allows the consumer to feel like s/he is getting individual attention and provides the opportunity to purchase a product that is a better fit or better suited to a particular need than the off-the-shelf product might be. Piller (2005) uses Land's End (http://www.landsend.com) as an example of a company that has had personalization via their customizable virtual model since 1999, but the personalization is followed simply by an offering of ready-made products in their inventory. Land's End also offers mass customization through a service that allows customers to order trousers and shirts on a made-to-order basis. Piller comments that one weakness of their customization process is that it is not paired with personalization (i.e. no guidance is offered regarding style, fabric, cut, etc.); however, when I logged on to the site on April 6, 2006, live chat with a customer service representative was available while shopping. This may be the link that Piller suggests was missing from Land's End's services.

Piller's (2005) examples of the difference between personalization and customization raise a couple of questions. One question is *Can one or both of the parties involved in the interaction of personalization be a machine?* Piller's answer would have to be, 'Yes,' since he uses the virtual model as an example of a service that offers personalization. Thus, according to Piller's view of personalization and mass customization, both of these processes can be mediated by machines; neither of them requires interaction between two humans. One human interacting with a computer program will suffice to meet his criteria.

What would the adoption of these concepts to formal online educational courseware design look like? What would mass customization look like in an educational setting? Can e-learning personalization be accomplished by courseware rather than involving a human instructor? In the future, will courseware and instructional designers replace instructors entirely in the online educational scenario? Can the objectives of educational institutions as well as those of online learners be achieved without direct instructor involvement in some circumstances? If so, in what context would such an approach be appropriate?

TDeLs, mentioned previously, might be considered a mass customization product. Although the choices offered are limited to breadth-first, depth-first, or a combination of the two, still, there is some choice involved. I call this application of the business model to education, which in my mind is simply a shift from a manufacturing to a marketing mindset, the *flexible factory* approach.

What is the value of the flexible factory approach? When is it appropriate? What is the value of the constructivist approach? When is it appropriate? Is it possible to have a combination of these two in a single courseware design? If so, how, and when would such a design be appropriate?

Even though I lean clearly toward the constructivist philosophy and believe utterly in the importance of learners understanding, experientially, the concept that multiplication is streamlined addition, there is no doubt in my mind that memorizing the multiplication tables will lighten the learner's burden in future mathematical explorations. Thus, I would argue that there is no one right answer to the best approach to courseware design, but that it depends on the circumstances and objectives (by which I don't necessarily mean the measurable outcomes drilled into teachers-in-training as vital to an effective lesson plan) of the learning experience. Whatever one's personal philosophy, it would seem that the flexible factory model is here, at least for the time being. Our obligation is to use it judiciously. We make a grave error when we try to limit our possibilities to one approach. By the same token, it is vital to remember that we have a responsibility to consider the possibilities, take chances, and try alternatives. If educators and designers don't continue to explore and create, what will the consequences be for formal education?

8.5 Summing Up

The Stanford Prison Experiment (Zimbardo, 1973, 1999–2006) opened the eyes of the researchers and participants involved to the relevance of context in determining roles and behaviors. E. T. Hall (1976) approached the idea of context in terms of cultural interactions, outlining a framework within which to understand communications in terms of context density. Using these ideas as a starting point, I have explored their possible application to understanding how participants in online learning environments interact.

A discussion of what it means to 'be' online necessarily requires an examination of presence. E. T. Hall's (1964) discussion of adumbrations was brought to bear on the current considerations of how presence is expressed online. Further, questions about the construction of presence individually and socially were raised. The relevance of context density to the construction of online identity was explored, and I argued that, in the absence of a history of interactions (either online or in person), online environments are necessarily low-context. Keeping that in mind, I have suggested that more effective online learning situations call for proactive, explicit communication. Without such explicit communication, I suspect that participants in online learning environments make communication assumptions based on perceived roles and personal history. It seems likely that the opportunities for miscommunication are compounded by reliance on these kinds of assumptions in the absence of explicit, context-relevant communication.

Next, the discussion moved to an exploration of what factors influence the design of formal online learning environments. I have made a distinction here between student-centered and learner-directed educational philosophies, arguing that learner-directed approaches can truly be considered constructivist, while those claiming to be student-centered may or may not be. I believe this distinction is significant, but it is often overlooked in discussions in which these terms are used interchangeably. I have explained the significance in terms of a crucial difference in the design of educational environments, i.e. that student-centered environments may be designed for mass customization with a marketing mindset, while in learner-directed environments learners actively co-create the design. Thus, instead of simply 'personalizing' a predetermined product for mass consumption, learner-directed environments emerge from the communities they serve. Another possible consequence of the mass marketing mindset in educational design is the ever greater reliance on business professionals in the making of decisions about education. I have offered some examples of how this trend is currently manifesting itself in the United States for the reader's consideration.

In closing, I should like to take a look at some of the future possibilities for the evolving learning landscape.

8.6   Future Possibilities

There is no doubt that the context of our daily lives is changing and thus, we, as learners, are changing. I recently overheard a librarian complaining that people in his workshops were not paying attention as they used to; these days, he said, they are carrying on chat conversations simultaneously. He said he had read an article decrying the same behavior in university classrooms. He was arguing that we needed to change the young people so that they would pay attention as their predecessors did. In my view, there are two erroneous assumptions behind his argument: (1) that the predecessors of today's young people paid more attention in class than do today's youth, and (2) that it is possible or desirable to require learners to pretend that classroom learning is somehow separate from everyday living. I argued that our ways of approaching learning situations have got to change instead.

It is one thing to *talk* about changing, however, and an entirely different thing to actually change. I have attended countless presentations over the years (and even as recently as a few weeks ago) where the presenters have talked at some point about including all learners through the use of multiple ways of learning. Typically, these presenters refer to Howard Gardner's theory of multiple intelligences (see http://www.howardgardner.com/). Invariably, the presenters have lectured, sometimes for several hours, and after mentioning the multiple intelligences, involve the 'audience' in a single activity designed to illustrate Gardner's ideas. Seldom have I experienced a presentation that actually incorporated Gardner's ideas throughout. Gardner introduced his theory of multiple intelligences more than 20 years ago.

The disconnect between the way we live our lives and the way we approach formal learning environments has become even greater as we have more and more technical options for communicating. It seems to me that this issue has to be addressed if we are going to make real progress. Take the ubiquity of cell phones and in general of handheld devices used for communicating as well as organizing, playing games, etc. Will the desktop online learning environment become obsolete as learners rely more and more on communicating while traveling, sitting in coffee shops or even while on vacation? What are the design implications for a change such as this? How can formal learning environmental design take positive advantage of these more flexible ways of engaging with learners in various contexts?

Another significant trend today is that of communicating with 'strangers' without regard to status or distance. The burgeoning popularity of online sites such as My Space (http://www.myspace.com) attests to the attractiveness of such options. What this means for learners is that mentors are often just an email message away. This could change our entire way of approaching what and how we want to learn.

The control and ownership of information is another area in which there are big changes underway. In academia, the control of information has long been in the hands of major academic publishers. With the advent of open access journal projects, such control may be shifting. Before the advent of personal computers and search engines, librarians were considered primarily responsible for the organization and retrieval of information. Now the role of the librarian is changing and the organization and retrieval of information has taken on many new forms.

All these changes have implications for the future contexts of learning, both formal and informal. A discussion of the online learner cannot be well served by ignoring the consequences of these changes. In the overall learning landscape, the topography is no more constant than that of the earth's surface, despite their apparent differences of scale. So, the most effective approach to addressing learner expectations is to begin by addressing the expectations of the learning environments themselves and our places within them. From there, it's a matter of imagination.

8.7   Resources for Further Exploration

- Active Worlds (http://www.activeworlds.com/) has support for educators who want to use 3-D CVEs in their classrooms. Possibilities abound!
- CABWEB (http://www.cabweb.net/portal/index.php) is a project of Collaboration Across Borders and acts as a portal for collaboration and discussions about higher education. Join a discussion or project, or start one of your own.
- The Center for Open and Sustainable Learning (http://cosl.usu.edu/projects/) is working to equalize educational opportunities globally via open source projects and materials.
- To find out more about the work, ideas and research of Professor Emeritus Philip G. Zimbardo (originator of the Stanford Prison Experiment), visit http://www.zimbardo.com/zimbardo.html.

8.8   Questions for Comprehension and Application

1. Consider the online gaming environments referred to in LaPointe's chapter (in this volume) and virtual spaces such as those one can create in Second Life (referred to in the chapter by Bransford, Slowinski, Vye & Mosborg, in this volume). How would you apply E. T. Hall's ideas about context density to interactions in such online environments?
2. The free availability of online learning materials from educational institutions, organizations of many kinds, and individuals puts self-directed, lifelong learning well within the grasp of anyone with an Internet connection and an understanding of how to interact with digital materials. (One must take into account that many

of these materials are provided only in English, however.) Those who enjoy working independently have ample opportunity to do so, while those who prefer learning with others can assemble study or discussion groups around these free materials. The overall learning context potentially becomes more actively the domain of the learner. Discuss the implications of this possible context change for the design of formal learning courseware; the design of curricula; the objectives of formal education; the certification/evaluation requirements which are now the norm in the educational and occupational arenas; and for educational equity or the lack thereof.

References

Beaudoin, M. F. (in this volume). Reflections on seeking the 'invisible' learner. In J. Visser & M. Visser-Valfrey (Eds.), *Learners in a changing learning landscape: Reflections from a dialogue on new roles and expectations* (pp. 213–226). Dordrecht, The Netherlands: Springer.

Bransford, J. D., Slowinski, M., Vye, N., & Mosborg, S. (in this volume). The learning sciences, technology and designs for educational systems: Some thoughts about change. In J. Visser & M. Visser-Valfrey (Eds.), *Learners in a changing learning landscape: Reflections from a dialogue on new roles and expectations* (pp. 37–67). Dordrecht, The Netherlands: Springer.

Büscher, M., O'Brien, J., Rodden, T., & Trevor, J. (2001). "He's behind you": The experience of presence in shared virtual environments. In E. F. Churchill, D. N. Snowdon, & A. J. Munro (Eds.), *Collaborative virtual environments* (pp. 77–98). London: Springer.

Cushman, D. P., & Cahn, Jr., D. D. (1985). *Communication in interpersonal relationships*. Albany, NY: State University of New York Press.

Daly, J. (2006). Risky business. *Edutopia, 2*(3), 42–47.

Dewey, J. (1916). *Democracy and education*. Retrieved April 2, 2006, from http://www.ilt.columbia.edu/Publications/dewey.html.

Dillon, S. (2006, April 12). Panel considers revamping college aid and accrediting: Business and academic leaders at odds. *The New York Times*, A14.

Duckworth, E. (1996). *"The having of wonderful ideas" and other essays on teaching and learning* (2nd ed.). New York: Teachers College Press.

Fujii, N., Yukita, S., Koike, N., & Kuni, T. (2004, October–December). An e-learning system based on the top-down method and cellular models. *International Journal of Distance Education, 2*(4), 77–93. Electronic version (with different pagination) retrieved via Proquest Jan. 27, 2006.

Hall, E. T. (1964). Adumbration as a feature of intercultural communication. *American Anthropologist*, New Series, Vol. 66, No. 6, Part 2: The Ethnography of Communication, 154–163. Retrieved via JSTOR, January 22, 2006.

Hall, E. T. (1976). *Beyond culture*. New York: Anchor.

Hall, M. (in this volume). Getting to know the feral learner. In J. Visser & M. Visser-Valfrey (Eds.), *Learners in a changing learning landscape: Reflections from a dialogue on new roles and expectations* (pp. 109–133). Dordrecht, The Netherlands: Springer.

Hindmarsh, J., Fraser, M., Heath, C., & Benford, S. (2001). Virtually missing the point: Configuring CVEs for object-focused interaction. In E. F. Churchill, D. N. Snowdon, & A. J. Munro (Eds.), *Collaborative virtual environments* (pp. 115–142). London: Springer.

Huxor, A. (2001). The role of the personal in social workspaces: Reflections on working in AlphaWorld. In E. F. Churchill, D. N. Snowdon, & A. J. Munro (Eds.), *Collaborative virtual environments* (pp. 282–296). London: Springer.

LaPointe, D. (in this volume). Will games and emerging technologies influence the learning landscape? In J. Visser & M. Visser-Valfrey (Eds.), *Learners in a changing learning landscape: Reflections from a dialogue on new roles and expectations* (pp. 227–249). Dordrecht, The Netherlands: Springer.

McGrath, A., & Prinz, W. (2001). All that is solid melts into software. In E. F. Churchill, D. N. Snowdon, & A. J. Munro (Eds.), *Collaborative virtual environments* (pp. 99–114). London: Springer.

Papert, S. (2003). *Jean Piaget. [Electronic Version] The Time 100: The most important people of the century.* Retrieved April 2, 2006, from http://www.time.com/time/time100/scientist/profile/piaget.html.

Piller, F. (2005). *Glossary: Mass customization, open innovation, personalization and customer integration. Frank Piller's web site on mass customization & open integration.* Retrieved April 6, 2006, from http://www.mass-customization.de/glossary.htm.

Pine, B. J. (2003). Introduction. In F. T. Piller, R. Reichwald, & M. Tseng (Eds.), *Proceedings of the 2003 world congress on mass customization and personalization* (p. 4). Germany: Technische Universitat Munchen.

Raybourn, E. M. (2001). Designing an emergent culture of negotiation in collaborative virtual communities: The DomeCityMOO simulation. In E. F. Churchill, D. N. Snowdon, & A. J. Munro (Eds.), *Collaborative virtual environments* (pp. 247–264). London: Springer.

Salgo, P. (2006, March 22). [Editorial] The doctor will see you for exactly seven minutes. *The New York Times*, A27.

Thomas, L. (1979). *The Medusa and the snail.* New York: Bantam.

Witherspoon, J. (2005). *Building the academic ecosystem: Implications of e-learning.* Retrieved April 6, 2006, from http://www.wcet.info/resources/publications/documents/WCETandAcademicEcosystem_000.pdf.

Zhang, X., & Furnas, G. (2005). mCVEs: Using cross-scale collaboration to support user interaction with multiscale structures. *Presence: Teleoperators and Virtual Environments 14*(1), 31–46.

Zimbardo, P. G. (September, 1973). A study of prisoners and guards in a simulated prison. *Naval Research Reviews.* Washington, DC: Office of Naval Research. Retrieved July 30, 2006, from http://www.zimbardo.com/downloads/1973%20A%20Study%20of%20Prisoners%20 and%20Guards,%20Naval%20Research%20Reviews.pdf.

Zimbardo, P. G. (1999–2006). *The Stanford prison experiment.* Retrieved July 30, 2006, from http://www.prisonexp.org.

Chapter 9
New Online Learning Technologies: New Online Learner Competencies. Really?

Ileana de la Teja[1] and Timothy W. Spannaus[2]

Abstract Numerous organizations contend that online learning is different from learning in a classroom and that to be successful online it is essential to possess specific skills and characteristics. On the other hand, several studies comparing online and face-to-face learning argue that there is no significant difference in the effectiveness of both learning modes, thus suggesting that there may not be a significant difference either in the competencies required to get the same results whether learning online or face-to-face. The usual question is, are the online learner competencies different from those of the face-to-face learner? Our belief is that this is the wrong question. Rather, we argue, the specific set of competencies required in any setting for a particular learning event is driven by the strategy of the event, not whether it is online or face-to-face. Our analysis is based on the characteristics and skills of the online learner as described by the hints and tips some higher education organizations offer to their target public to become successful online learners. Given that most online learning now imitates classroom instruction, it is likely that the new competencies required specifically for online learning, if any, have not yet emerged. We suggest that three factors, the use of technology, the degree of collaboration, and the extent to which students or the instructor manage the use of time are far more important determinants of the competencies required than whether a class is online or face-to-face. We invite the reader to consider other factors to further explore the topic, believing that a clearer understanding of the online learner competencies will produce more informed choices and, consequently, more effective interventions in online learning.

9.1 Introduction

This chapter was inspired by an ongoing project of the International Board of Standards for Training, Performance and Instruction (ibstpi), in relation to the online learner competencies, and by discussions generated at Téluq, the distance

---

[1] Télé-université, Québec

[2] Wayne State University, Detroit

education university of the Université du Québec à Montréal, where a competency approach to learning is used in the design and development of online learning resources and activities. From those discussions, involving a variety of individuals with different backgrounds and perspectives, it became clear that online learner competencies are more challenging and difficult to 'capture' than other sets of competencies previously developed by ibstpi, such as those for instructional designers, instructors, training managers and evaluators. Why is this so?

A first look into this query was presented in the context of the Presidential Workshop and Panel Session at the International Convention of the Association for Educational Communications and Technology (AECT) in 2005 (De la Teja, 2005). Debates on related subjects stimulated our interest in further investigating what the particulars of online learner competencies are in relation to face-to-face learner competencies, and how the learner is different from other actors that make their competency profiling special.

Exploring the challenge to building an online learner competencies profile took a more precise orientation when realizing that studies comparing online and face-to-face learning report mixed results. Whereas some of them consider there is no significant difference (e.g., Allen & Seaman, 2003; Russell, 2001), others insist on the advantages of online learning over face-to-face learning (e.g., Sahin, 2006; Kassop, 2003). Moreover, in the context of higher education, numerous organizations advocate that online learning is different from face-to-face learning and invite their students to assess their aptness to online learning before enrolling in a program. Based on results from quizzes and self-assessment tests offered on their Web sites, some organizations even conclude that online learning is not for everyone (e.g., Wayne County Community College District, 2005). Those who do not possess the characteristics and competencies required should not consider online learning.

These selective criteria for online learning are surprising in more than one way given the slight empirical foundations supporting the competencies purported by most of those organizations. If, according to ibstpi, one of the characteristics of competencies is that they can be developed through training (Richey, Fields, & Foxon, 2000), we think that no individual should ignore her possibilities for learning online because of lack of competencies. It is critical thus to identify in a systematic way what are the competencies of a successful online learner in order to empower the learner and help other actors of the learning process to make more valuable interventions, for example, allowing the instructor to provide appropriate assistance, helping the instructional designer to design effective online activities and learning resources, and facilitating the manager's task.

A quick search on the Web shows the absence of robust lists of competencies or competencies profiles for the online learner; however, there are multiple sites with hints on how to become a successful online learner in educational or corporate settings (see, among others sites, ComputerSchools.com, 2001; Illinois Online Network, 2007; University of Guelph, 2006; Watkins, 2005; WorldWideLearn, 1999). The present study examines around 500 hints offered by 30 organizations including 20 from higher education in order to explore some avenues to better understanding the particulars of the competencies of the online learner vis-à-vis those required by the face-to-face learner, as well as to have a better grip on the challenges related to the development of online learner competencies. Inspired by ibstpi's competencies development model it focuses on the foundational research step aiming to identify information essential to the development of a competencies profile, such as the characteristics of the online learner, values, expected standards, and knowledge, skills and attitudes.

During our exploration study, different conceptual and methodological issues emerged regarding the development of online learner competencies. It would be impossible to cover all of them or to address them in depth in this chapter. It is our intention to put some of them forward and inspire the reader to further reflect on the online learner competencies.

This chapter has been structured as follows: First, the nature of competencies and competency modeling is discussed, followed by an analysis of the hints we found that are intended to help the online learner. Many examples of the hints from college and university Web sites are included for clarification. The subsequent discussion considers whether the hints for online learning are in fact distinctive from those that would apply to a learner in a face-to-face setting. We conclude that the distinction of online and face-to-face learning is not as useful as looking at the use of technology, degree of collaboration, and the extent to which students or instructors manage time.

9.2   Grounding the Competencies on Foundational Research

9.2.1   The Online Learner Examined in This Study

The vast array of literature on competencies seems to converge in one point: there is a myriad of definitions of competencies (Cheetham & Chivers, 2005; Hoge, Tondora, & Marrelli, 2005; Kierstead, 1998). Despite the lack of consensus on one definition, it is however agreed that a competency includes three components: knowledge, skills and attitudes (KSA) (Lucia & Lepsinger, 1999; Marrelli, 2001; McLagan, 1997; Mirabile, 1997; Nolan, 1998).

To identify these components, and according to the generic ibstpi Competency Development Model, it is essential to start with foundational research, which is based on the characterization of the actor, namely in terms of behaviours, values, and vision of the future. These "provide the major input into the identification and validation of the knowledge, skills, and attitudes critical to a particular job role". (Richey et al., 2000, p. 33). This study takes on the foundational research process as a starting point to identifying main characteristics of the online learner with a view to developing a competencies profile of the online learner.

To set the background of the analysis it is important to identify the online learner to whom the competencies profile will be relevant. It is worth noticing that a clear definition of online learner is rarely presented on the Web sites examined in this study. Sometimes, the online learner is characterized as a person using computers to acquire knowledge and skills. In most cases, the role of the online learner is set through the description of the type of activities that can be undertaken in the online learning context, for example, learning that can be engaged in by electronic means such as videoconferencing, CD-ROMs and computer-based learning tools. In some cases the technology factor is integrated in a very general way by mentioning that the online learner is an individual who accesses information, sends in assignments and talks with classmates and tutors online.

Although on most Web sites analyzed in this study online learning refers to the technological context within which learning takes place or the means of course delivery, it is difficult to say who qualifies as an online learner. Given that the hints are provided by higher education organizations, we can infer that the online learner refers to a learner enrolled in a formal learning setting. In our opinion, the definition of an online learner is not limited to an individual who takes all her courses of a program online; it suffices rather to use online technology for learning purposes, including within the framework of a face-to-face classroom or in non-academic settings. The Sloan Consortium provides for a range of terms, including web-facilitated, blended/hybrid and online, to cover a range of uses of technology from 1% to 100%, measuring how extensively technology is being used within a course. (Zero percent is defined as traditional delivery.) (Allen & Seaman, 2006). Moreover, the pervasive use of technologies in the learning context seems to increasingly blur the frontiers between the online learner and the conventional learner.

9.2.2   Competencies Versus Hints

The first logical step for someone looking for a list of online learner competencies would be to do a search on the Web. However, a Boolean search using different entries related to online learner competencies shows very few sites directly related to online learner competencies. Interestingly, most of the sites on competencies for online learning point to the online instructor. The competencies of the key actor of the online learning process, the learner, seem to have been overlooked, and the support for online learners is relegated to lists of characteristics and skills of the successful online learner, as well as hints and recommendations to become one.

This type of support, referred in this chapter as 'hints,' is worth analyzing because it reveals what an organization parses out of the online learner, such as values, expectations and priorities, as well as the knowledge, skills and attitudes that she requires to fulfill the learning goals.

Hints are practical recommendations, presented in a roundabout way. They are not comprehensive and do not distinctly categorize the challenges nor the learning activities engaged in by an online learner.

In this study we use 'hints' and 'tips' synonymously. They are, at best, guidelines to help a student achieve the (usually unstated) goal of learning. That is a very generic, broad goal, and consequently the hints and tips are stated broadly and generically. None claim to be standards or best practices, but guidelines or attitudes that students may find helpful. Typically the hints refer to being assertive; applying flexibility and humor; using relaxation techniques to focus better; valuing the journey, caring for good online written communication. Some are provided almost as clues, as if online learning were a game or puzzle (e.g., online learning is NOT easier than learning in the traditional classroom; some tasks are best done alone; get in the 'student frame of mind'). A few are stated as warnings, particularly those about staying up to date with the class assignments (e.g., don't fall behind in your work!; don't procrastinate; you will not SEE an instructor who reminds you to turn your homework in on time).

9.2.3   Interest in Hints

Although there are few studies on the use of hints in learning and problem solving (Do Nacimento, 2005; Hseih, Smith, & Stephanou, 2004), several authors have recognized the importance of offering some hints to help individuals using online learning and have published lists of hints, to be used mainly in corporate settings (Tang, 2000; Slaidinis, 2004; Masie, 2004; Warnakulasooriya & Prichard, 2005; eLearning Guild, 2005). In most of these publications the hints target the instructor.

The hints analyzed in this chapter focus on the learner, and more precisely on the learner enrolled in higher education online courses. They are available online through the Web sites of organizations such as colleges or universities. The listings of hints don't seem to follow a particular order and some organizations appear to share listings or parts of them. Unfortunately, the source of the hints is rarely documented, making it difficult to know how the hints were gathered and if they have been validated, although a few organizations mention that they are based on experience but don't provide further detail.

In spite of the lack of clear methodology surrounding the hints, they are interesting sources of information about existing perceptions of the online learner and online learning in general. For example, the provision of hints implies an assumption that there is a perceived need for assistance and the belief that the learner may benefit from a certain sort of guidance to help her go through the online learning experience.

Other than acknowledging the existence of complex situations or obstacles that may hinder the way to the goal of the targeted audience, the lists of hints also presupposes that there is a goal or end that the learner is expected to attain. Furthermore, hints suggest that the nature of assistance required by the online learner can be informal and not necessarily explicit.

9.3   Analyzing the Hints

9.3.1   Online Learners' Roles, Activities and Tools

Online technology is the manifest characteristic that distinguishes learning as we knew it from online learning. Hence, the analysis of the online learning tools and their recommended use is important to understanding the particular nature of the online learner. Patterns of expected performance and conduct set forth the roles that actors are called to play in the learning process. Generally, two roles are recognized: learner and tutor (Anderson, 2004). They portray the relationship with the content, receiver-giver, passive-active. However, in online learning, the learner plays different roles and these roles are played with other actors such as instructor, evaluator, instructional designer, training manager, etc. (Paquette, Ricciardi-Rigault, De la Teja, & Paquin, 1997).

The analysis of the hints indicates some roles that the learner plays, such as technician, learner, instructor, evaluator, manager, and designer. The scene becomes more intricate when one considers that each actor can play various roles during the online learning process. Playing different roles means using the tools in different ways because in a learning context, different actors can use the same tools for different purposes. All of the actors may use a learning object repository, but in different ways. Online learners for example, may use the repository to search for information. For the instructional designer the intent could be to reference his/her work in order to reuse it later; the instructor may analyze materials for further use, and the manager could use the repository to track the updating of materials.

In general, the main online tools that the hints refer to are search engines and some asynchronous communication tools such as email, forums, conferences and discussion boards. Other computer related tools, although not necessarily online, are calendars, printers and word processors, more specifically the use of spell checking and cut and paste functions. It is interesting though that the online learner could use online technology to complete her tasks more effectively, but only a few hints point to appropriate tools to increase the value of the use of technology.

It would be difficult to determine which tools are instrumental to the online learner's success because each course may have its own pedagogical requirements. According to the course design some roles may be more prevalent than others, thus necessitating a specific set of tools and particular functions.

Helping the learner differentiate which tools to use to achieve a particular end is not apparent in most hints. The pedagogical value of different communication tools is not included. Orientation on the use of certain tools could be appreciated; for example, when should the learner use one-to-one (email) or one-to many (discussion boards or email lists)? When should she use asynchronous or synchronous tools? Which strategies may benefit from communication tools? What tools does the learner use for group critiques in fine or performing arts vs. managing individual feedback from an instructor on a paper? How to moderate a discussion or organize a thread?

The tools included in hints focus on asynchronous tools, mainly the 'traditional' electronic mail and discussion forums. Little is said about distribution lists, news groups, blogs, or Wikis. Very little is said about synchronous tools such as chat, video streaming, or videoconferences.

Good manners are stressed in hints, but few tips are given on how to make the most out of the tools. For example, contrary to an online conference, in the chat accidental grammatical slips and typos can be tolerated; the dialogue is improvised and similar to oral conversation, but can be fragmented and more dispersed. Furthermore, chat has possibilities that are different from face-to-face conversations, such as being scrolled, saved, or tracked, which can promote more reflective communication.

The proactive approach is not exclusive to online learning—sharing responsibility is also important in a classroom. The tactics of initiating, guiding a discussion and moderating are absent among the hints analyzed and should be included.

Taking on additional roles such as leader or observer are not explored. Most activities are seen as part of ready-made models provided in the course.

9.3.2 Expectations Regarding the Online Learner

The analysis of the hints resulted in a rich source of information on behaviors and values expected from the online learner, including characteristics of the successful online learner, study habits, similarities and differences with face-to-face learners, course conduct, use of the online learning environment, as well as various problems that can be met in online learning.

9.3.2.1 Readiness for Online Learning

The characteristics of the successful online learner provided by some Web sites are usually suggested as a benchmark against which it is possible to assess one's readiness for online learning. Among the characteristics of successful online learners are self-motivation, self-discipline, being self-directed, having good organization and time management skills, commitment, ability to adapt to new learning environments, and pro-activeness. It is equally recommended to possess or develop some attitudes and qualities such as being an active participant, flexible and patient, calm, inquisitive, having a positive attitude and acceptance of critical thinking, being assertive, constant and prepared to share work and ideas, and to collaborate.

Some characteristics are thought to be advantageous to online learning, like 'be constant, get to chat sessions on time, post things on the discussion board when you are meant to' or 'willingness to learn to use the technology (the hardware and software) to complete course work.' However, most characteristics are generic and can equally be applied to learning settings not requiring online technology. Although the need for strong autonomy has received increased attention in recent years in the online learning literature (e.g., Arnold, 2006; Bouchard, 2003), it is important to recall that online technology itself does not require autonomy from the learner but that the way technology is used in an online course may require a certain level of autonomy. It is possible to use online technology to deliver courses that take the learner by the hand or that leave most of the responsibility to the instructor, thus requiring little autonomy from the learner. Conversely, face-to-face courses can also be designed for autonomous, self-disciplined and self-motivated learners.

Characteristics presented in very short phrases such as 'visual learner,' 'goal directed' or 'be academic' are left to limitless interpretation and are of little value to the online learner. In addition, given the potential of online learning to stretching geopolitical boundaries and reaching learners from different parts of the world, some characteristics of successful online learners may be of limited validity if they are not examined under a multicultural perspective. In the case of 'autonomy' or 'self-discipline,' for example, as Usuki (2003) suggests, the concepts are based on Western values and may not be easily transposed to and appreciated in the Asian context.

9.3.2.2   Study Habits and Pedagogical Considerations

The characteristics of the successful online learner are often blended with recommended study habits and pedagogical considerations. For the study habits, special attention is paid to the importance of scheduling and setting goals, time and stress management, preventing procrastination, and preparing for tests. The following are sample hints:

- Be very organized
- Create a binder and calendar for each online course
- Schedule your study sessions and make a specific goal for each study session
- Prepare for assignments and tests

It is often emphasized that these study habits are more crucial for online or distance learners; however, studies and numerous education Web sites (see for example Kizlik, 2007; Brown & Miller, 2007; Western Nevada Community College, 2007) indicate that successful learners in face-to-face settings do possess the same study habits.

As is the case with other learners, the online learner needs to get prepared for a course. Basic preparation habits are fundamentally the same but, in the case of online learning, they translate into setting up the online learning environment, including software, hardware, service providers and appropriate lighting conditions for screen reading. The analyzed Web sites also stress the importance of avoiding distractions, getting familiar with the online materials and the Web site of the course.

Recommendations also include pedagogical considerations such as encouragement to the online learners to participate regularly in the class and to ask for assistance when problems or questions arise. Being solicited to get involved and contribute to the course may be well known to a majority of learners outside online learning (Brophy & Evertson, 1976; Gardner, Heward, & Grossi, 1994; Marmolejo, Wilder, & Bradley, 2004). One must not lose sight, though, of the fact that participation may be essential for some online courses, for example those requiring collaboration or inspired by a classroom teacher-learner interaction, whereas participation or communicating with others is not necessarily required or desired in self-paced online courses.

The lack of visual and auditory cues in online learning is frequently brought forward as one of the reasons to insist on the importance of the learner to be assertive in online learning settings (Vrasidas & McIsaac, 2000). Nonetheless, the media that are systematically recommended for establishing an online presence focus on written communication through forums and email messages, which do not convey the missing body language or gestures. This orientation can be influenced by current limitations of technology and may change with time. In fact, one recommendation alludes to a variety of forms of communication: 'It often helps to develop a brief outline before responding to questions whether they are submitted in writing, via e-mail, orally or on video/audio tape.' However, in general, the multimedia characteristics of online learning are overlooked and no particular recommendations are provided for studying with multiple multimedia sources, taking notes from multimedia sources or making multimedia presentations.

9.3.2.3   Comparison with Face to Face Learners

Most viewpoints stress the similarity between online and face-to-face learning, whereas others point at distinctive characteristics. Example of opinions expressing resemblance are: 'e-Learning requires the same flexibility as if you are reading a book;' 'Taking ink-created notes is just as important with e-learning as in any other type of learning environment;' 'Distance education courses have the same requirements as on-campus courses, and attendance may play a role in your final grade;' 'Online learning is NOT easier than learning in the traditional classroom;' and 'The most important key to any type of learning is to find your own rhythm and stride and have fun with the whole process.' Some opinions contrast online and face-to-face learning, e.g., 'Studying on a computer screen requires different uses of the mind and eyes;' 'Most students find that online courses take more time than traditional courses. Just think, all that time you save by not driving to campus and sitting in class, should be devoted to studying.' In general, the opinions offered in the lists of hints and recommendations rarely refer the learner to authoritative sources which would lend greater validity to these statements.

9.3.2.4   Course Conduct

Hints including advice on study habits and behavior comprise taking care of the eyes 'when reading from the computer screen.' Other type of advice regards how to respond to others when interacting with them through online technology. Namely, it is advised to use 'proper netiquette,' avoiding emotive reactions to postings, and being open to receive criticism, as indicated in the following hint: 'If you become upset or angry with something someone has posted, take a deep breath (or three or four!), wait twenty-four hours, and then respond.'

9.3.2.5   Maximizing the Online Setting

Some hints provided to online learners regard the learning process, which, other than starting by setting up the equipment and the right services and having a test to diagnose readiness to online learning, can be useful as well to face-to-face learners. Among the generic indications one can find getting familiar with the learning environment, logging on regularly, checking email on a regular basis, staying in touch with the instructor, monitoring oneself, and avoiding interruptions and distractions, such as by 'making sure you have a private space where you can study.' The importance of creating an appropriate workspace is also stressed on several college and university Web sites for learners in face-to-face settings. Stressing the need for a private space puts into question the 'learning anywhere, anytime' truism developed around online learning.

9.3.2.6   Breakdown Prevention and Notices

It is worth noticing that few hints provide signposts confirming advancement on the 'right path,' leaving the online learner without indications on how to measure their progress on learning to learn.

In general, all hints are 'canned,' non-provoking statements provided by an unknown authority. They leave little room for creativity and rarely encourage the online learner to find his/her own way. This is particularly important given that online learning is a relatively recent experience in the education and training fields and knowledge on how to 'get there' is still an unknown path.

9.3.3   Online Learner Skills

By examining hints, we identified the perceived problems, and values and behavior put forward by the organizations providing the hints. In this part of the chapter, we analyze the main skills required, according to those organizations, from the online learner, i.e. computer literacy, management skills and communication skills, and try to distinguish these from skills required in the face-to-face setting.

9.3.3.1   Computer Literacy Skills

A number of the hints offered for the online learner deal directly or indirectly with technology, though most of them do not. The hints fall naturally into two groups, those which specifically address a technology competency and those which do so indirectly or by means of an assumption. For example, in the first group are those hints that advise the learner that they need 'basic computer skills,' or that they need to be able to conduct searches on the Internet. In this group of hints that directly specify a competency are those that discuss typing, Internet access, and searching. None of these hints specify in more detail what skills are included in basic computer skills.

Many more hints assume some already existing competencies with the use of technology. Some, for example, suggest that, in responding to a post on a discussion board, the student first write the response using a word processor, then copy and paste the text onto the discussion board. The hint clearly assumes that the student already has a particular computer competency. Typical hints in this group discuss best ways to respond to a discussion board or email, suggestions to download and print course documents, use of chat environments, or instant messaging and email.

Few, if any, of these competencies (or the hints from which they are derived) are peculiar to the online learner. As McDonald (2004) points out, today's learner must be computer literate. While not every face-to-face class uses a discussion board, many do. Certainly, basic computer skills are required in any learning context, as is Internet searching or use of a word processor. In high-technology classrooms, instructors are more likely to complain about overuse of Google or Wikipedia for research for assignments in any instructional context than about the student who doesn't know how to conduct a basic Internet search and relies instead on the library.

9.3.3.2 Management Skills

This category refers to management of information or resources, rather than time or self-management, which is discussed below in self-monitoring. Resources here are broadly defined, to include the software tools available to the learner, other students, instructor or teaching assistants, and advisors.

Many of the hints offer recommendations for managing the learning process, information resources, or the tools available, including the course management system and software. Typical are the following ones:

- Find out help available for technical and software problems or guidance
- Participate in online discussions, asking questions using email, and sharing your expertise during online forums to learn and share from online interaction with other learners and colleagues
- Rely on and be responsible to your colleagues in a course
- Print out the syllabus and calendar, but modifying its appearance and layout to visually suit you
- Spend time before the class begins scoping out the 'lay of the land,' knowing where each instructor puts assignments, lectures, readings, etc. as each course may be slightly different

Some of these hints apply to both blended and online learning, if not to all of face-to-face learning. The hint suggesting that the learners 'formulate their response off-line' applies only to electronic media and not a face-to-face classroom discussion. Similarly hints referring specifically to online tools, such as online discussions, e-learning activities, or making sure the learner knows where assignments, lectures and readings are located, have specific reference to online learning. Rephrased to avoid references to specific technological tools, all could apply as well to face-to-face. For example, participating in classroom discussions, asking questions and sharing expertise is important in any learning context, whether the communication is computer mediated or not.

What may vary among blended, online and face-to-face learning is the relative importance of these hints. Clearly, finding out what help is available for technical and software problems is of much greater importance to blended or online learning than to learning in a face-to-face context. Curiously, we found only one hint that discusses organizing course materials. Moreover, that hint uses traditional terminology of 'binder' and 'calendar' rather than referring to 'folders' or 'directories' on the learner's computer or the organizer software found on PDAs or in personal information management software such as Outlook, Notes or Evolution. In online classes, the majority of course materials are offered in digital form, as documents or Web sites. It is relatively easy for the learner to download the materials but organizing the storage is critical if the student is to be able to retrieve and access it in a purposeful manner. The learner will also be adding content of his or her own creation, in the form of notes and assignments.

Although less in number, self-monitoring and metacognitive strategies are also present in the hints. As with the other skills, they are not exclusive to the online learner, and are a regular component in various national programs (Brockband & McGill, 1998; Brown & Miller, 2007; Weinstein & Rogers, 1985). It is however worth noticing that reminders about deadlines or prompts and activities to motivate the learner can be designed in an online course. Moreover, online technologies offer more possibilities for self-monitoring, and for creating self-discipline than ever. Use of such possibilities needs to be integrated appropriately in the design of online courses and highlighted in the hints.

9.3.3.3 Communication Skills

The central role of communication in online learning is highlighted on most Web sites and some of them include 'enjoying online communication' and 'being a good communicator' as essential characteristics of the successful online learner. Given that the concept of communication is broad and the hints do not provide a clear definition of the term, for operational purposes, Lasswell's aphorism "Who says what to whom to what effect" (Lasswell, Lerner, & Pool, 1952, p. 12), can be used as a guide to examine the hints regarding communication skills. In order to put communication in the context of online learning, the online technology needs to be put forward in the maxim: 'Who says what to whom to what effect with what tools.'

With that in mind, it is possible to say that, clearly, hints suggest that the main interlocutor of the successful online learner is the instructor. The content of the communication is opened but, as indicated below, in general it aims at getting help and clarifications, as well as reporting on progress. Peers and 'study buddies' are also part of the persons with whom the online learner is recommended to establish contact, usually trough email and conferences. Among others, communicating with peers should help establishing collaboration and forming study groups with classmates. Also, making contact with experienced students and 'finding out easy spots and hard spots' of a course is one of the suggestions offered. On the other hand, the socializing value of communicating with colleagues is not considered in the hints.

Other than the instructor and classmates, few hints consider the importance of communicating with other faculty members. An exception is the hint suggesting that learners exchange ideas and discuss learning needs with a learning specialist. Communicating with instructional designers, technicians, managers and subject matter experts, does not seem to be a priority in the hints.

According to the analyzed hints, the communication skills can be demonstrated, in a variety of ways:

- Application of principles of netiquette (not specified in the hints) and the risky use of humor.
- Behaving properly. This characteristic is not particular to online learning and in fact, some hints acknowledge the similarities with conduct in face-to-face learning settings, as suggested by this hint: 'Remember that the Internet is a public place. Speak and behave as you would in a classroom.'
- Reflecting on responses, choosing comments.
- Being open to criticism. Some hints alert the online learner about the risk of feeling criticized and put forward the value of constructive critique.
- Being comfortable in expressing oneself in writing. Except for a hint regarding communicating through visual and oral language, the other ones focus on written communication, maintaining that it is fundamental to success.
- Being present. Some hints interested in promoting participation encourage informal communication, e.g., 'Don't worry too much about typing mistakes.'
- Initiating interactions.
- Taking advantage of anonymity, as an opportunity for learners concerned about image or cultural prejudices.
- Giving time to the instructor for notification.

Among the main tools proposed by hints about communicating are online conferences (discussion boards) and email. All of them presuppose written communication. One site recommends the learner to express ideas effectively regardless of the media, including video and audio tapes. In one case, a hint brings up the phone, fax machine and on-campus visits to communicate with the instructor. Some hints urge the learner to participate but do not specify the type of recommended tool, and when indicated, little is said on how to make the most out of the learning experience.

As learners in face-to-face learning settings, the online learners have an interest in mastering communication skills to ensure effective interaction with the instructor and with other learners. Particular to online learning is the possibility of synchronous communication at a distance, comprising students of other countries. However, the hints don't pay attention to the impact of this type of communication that may need to consider the 'use of language appropriate to the context and culture.' This communication skill is part of the fundamental competencies of communication in various standards developed by the International Board of Standards for Training, Performance and Instruction.

It is interesting to notice that hints related to communication skills focus on the ability to express ideas clearly in a person-to-person interaction, and do not consider communicating with a machine. This may be a key skill for an online learner needing to communicate, for example, with an agent integrated in the site of the course.

Some studies suggest that chats and informal synchronous conversations have a strong resemblance to speech (Creswell, Schwartzmyer, & Srihari, 2007; Kačmárová, 2005; Volckaert-Legrier & Bernicot, 2005) and thus have less strict grammatical rules than certain conferences and forums. Unfortunately, the hints do not specify when to use formal or informal language, leaving it up to the learner to find out when to apply one or the other as well as to discover what tools are most appropriate for the different purposes of communication.

9.4   No Significant Difference?

The analysis of the hints shows that the majority of them could easily apply to learners in general, and very few—most of which are directly related to the use of certain functions of the technology—are specifically relevant to the online learner. What may be important in this comparison is the relative importance of different competencies between online and face-to-face settings. Technology is essential to the online learner; for the face-to-face learner, it will depend on specific circumstances, such as those noted above. For the learner in a traditional environment, self-management may be less important than for the learner in the online world, but as discussed below, the differences may depend more on the instructional strategy than on the environment.

As in the case of the instructor (Klein, Spector, Grabowski, & De la Teja, 2004; Spector & De la Teja, 2001), the competencies for online and face-to-face learners will be manifested in different ways. Asking and responding to questions, receiving and giving feedback, staying connected with classmates, and speaking up, for example, are all important to all learners, but the specific way in which a learner does those things will depend on the context.

9.5   Defining the Successful Online Learner

The hints analyzed in this study have a specific audience in mind: the adult learner enrolled in a higher education formal (accredited) online course. Consequently, it is understandable that the online learner's success is defined by the accomplishment of the requirements of such a course. The hints for becoming a successful online learner, therefore, point to the accreditation criteria established by an organization. These conditions for success do not correspond necessarily to interests in corporate or non-academic settings. Moreover, learners having their own learning goals and using online technology to attain them may have personal standards for success.

Given the diversity of criteria that the concept of successful learner encompasses, would it be more appropriate to talk about becoming a *competent* online learner instead of a *successful* online learner? As the question moves to the competencies arena, one is confronted, as mentioned in the first section of this chapter, with the fact that little is known about competencies for online learners.

9.5.1   Why There are No Online Learner Competencies

Conceptual and methodological challenges can help to explain the lack of online learner competencies. The definition of competency, for example, is usually related to the competency-based approach initiated by McClelland (1973) to introduce the use of competencies instead of academic aptitude or intelligence, as a non-biased way of measuring and predicting job performance, professional career development and employee selection. The methodology used to identify a competencies profile was mainly based on a job analysis and the performance standards were set by comparing average and outstanding performers (Boyatzis, 1982).

The competency approach was initially applied in a job context, for human management purposes. In academia and training settings this approach emerged with the incorporation of the competencies in the design of their programs as an answer to preparing future employees to fulfill job needs demands (Jennings, 1991; Kerka, 1998). With this orientation in mind, a successful learner (i.e., competent learner), refers to an individual engaged in a program or set of activities, who is able to demonstrate performance of the 'content' competencies included in the program. The latter concept of success focuses on specific content and goals but falls short of describing the learner's knowledge, skills and attitudes that are transferable from one content to other, and are useful to attain different goals, including personal, organizational and societal ones. Furthermore, as long as the content or performance criteria planned in the learning activities are demonstrated, the technology used by the learner to develop the competencies seems accessory. In this sense, a successful online learner would be a learner who 'happens' to use online technology to effectively demonstrate performance of the competencies required in a program. Competencies have been considered only in achieving cognitive objectives, which are inadequate to meet the needs of the whole person, the contributor to her organization, and to society.

The successful online learner demonstrates management skills, including self-management, computer skills, and communication skills. These skills are demonstrated through the use of different tools, taken generally, not limited to computer or online tools. Online tools are one category of these tools, others of which might be calendars, telephones, the written word beyond the screen, or reminders posted on a real, non-electronic bulletin board. Use of each these tools requires certain competencies. In the case of computer tools, the learner may need to develop specific skills, which are those needed specifically for online learning. The point here is to separate online learning skills from the skills needed for learning generally.

Tools of whatever nature extend the capabilities of the actor. A hammer is a more effective tool to drive a wooden peg than a person's fist or a rock. Television extends the view of the person beyond the line of sight. The Internet allows a person to communicate almost instantaneously with people anywhere the Net reaches, extending the communication capabilities far beyond those of words written in a physical medium such as stone, or later, paper. Such capabilities, it should be noted, may be extended in time and in space. (But there is an interesting issue with the extension in time. Words expressed digitally may allow communication over great distances in a brief time. Words carved in stone, while a reader will have to travel to where the stone is or the stone will have to be brought to the reader for the words to be read, may be visible after millennia have passed. The digital words, if they survive at all, will likely be unreadable.)

After all of this, learning is still the key task. The use of tools facilitates performing the task. With each new tool, there is a need to master the tool (new competencies) but also the use of the tool, and mastery of it, will likely change the nature of the process and through this the tool itself.

The learner is now faced with different types of learning experiences, using a variety of learning strategies and integrating online tools in many ways. Each experience will be different because her abilities will be different, requiring the competency to adapt and be able to identify and develop the required learner competencies, such as being able to identify the learning needs at individual, organizational and social levels; choosing the appropriate learning solution; adapting the existing resources to her needs; managing the learning environment; and monitoring and evaluating the learning process.

9.5.2 *Considerations Regarding the Building an Online Learner Competencies Profile*

The hints analyzed for this chapter focus on improving learning, but look at it from a viewpoint of transition from a traditional classroom environment. We as learners have not yet used the tools for a long enough period that the tools change the process of learning, or that a new, improved process can necessitate the development of new tools.

The hints aim at a novice or someone at the entry level of computer knowledge or skill. They do not purport to advance the moderately experienced learner to a more advanced level at this point. They do not propose, for the most part, any new ways of managing time, information, or the self.

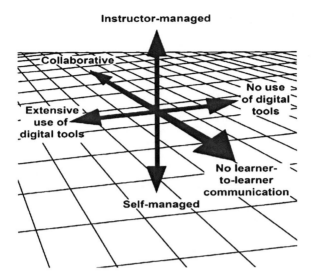

Fig. 9.1 Three parameters used to define the competencies

We may think of the three categories of competencies—management, communication, and computer tools—as defining a three-dimensional space, since the three categories are to some extent independent of each other (see Fig. 9.1). What complicates the problem is that different tools foster different strategies. Norman (1993) discussed the affordances, strengths or weaknesses of particular technologies, as a way of differentiating the support each provides for certain tasks.

Any particular learning experience may be placed in this space to identify its use of the three categories, from entirely instructor-managed to totally self-managed learning, from studying alone to collaborative learning, and from no use of computer technology to extensive use of such technology. Depending on where a learning event is placed in this three-dimensional space, the competencies demanded of a learner will vary. The hints analyzed emphasize only one of the eight possible segments in which the three-dimensional space is seen to be divided by the above dimensions, namely the portion of space characterized by no use of digital tools, instructor-managed processes, and collaboration.

At this point, we do not yet know, for instance, what competencies may be required for another area in our three-dimensional space, such as the one indicated in Fig. 9.2, which is characterized by high levels of self-management by the student, high use of technology, and high levels of collaboration. The problem comes from the nature of competency definition. We want to know what differentiates the high performer from the average performer, but we have too few examples of high performers in this region of the space.

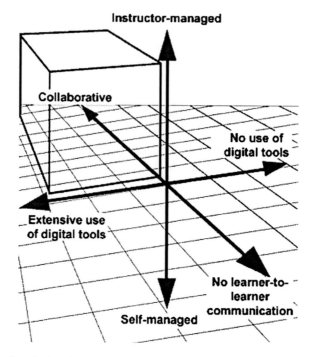

Fig. 9.2 Location of a learning event in a particular portion of the space

In the absence of a competency model, it is however possible to support the learner with hints. The hints can be thoughtful, based on hypothesized models of performance, and perceptions of the needs of the learner. While such hints may be useful, they will not be empirically validated, just as those studied for this chapter lack validation.

Useful hints need to consider different learning strategies, tools, and management demands in order to allow the learner to establish links among the three categories of competencies, take on different roles, communicate with other actors, and pass from one level of technology use to another, as many gamers do while engaging over time in digital games.

The elaboration of hints requires some degree of educated guesswork on the nature of the support a learner will need, the possible difficulties she will face, and tactics for improving performance. Increased success of learners in these advanced environments requires development of these hints, drawing on the experiences of successful learners, designers, instructors and managers.

9.5.3 Value of Hints

In this chapter we have analyzed the hints with a view to identifying principles in the construction of an online learning competencies profile. The analysis of these hints has provided us with rich information on the differences—or lack thereof—between the online learner and the face-to-face learner, but the hints have also

revealed themselves as potentially valuable pedagogical tools for raising the awareness of certain knowledge, skills, and attitudes for successful learning, and leaving
to the learner the responsibility to develop such competencies. This section of the
chapter finishes with a brief description of the qualities of the hints that require
further exploration in future research, as well as some considerations to be taken
into account in the development of hints.

To be most useful, hints for learners are deliberate, thoughtful statements, not
spontaneous or improvised, intended to help the learner reach the goal of successfully completing a course or program of study. Most are brief, one or two sentences,
and therefore not explicit, but indicators of a direction to go or a tactic to attempt.

The best hints would be based on trustworthy sources. Many hints appear verbatim on several unrelated sites, suggesting that they are reliable and that they have
been used by many online learning providers.

Finally, for the hints to be most effective, the provider should know the context,
the problem and goal, the audience, and when the hint might be most helpful.
The provider should have identified potential problems or traps, such as procrastination, and determined ways to either avoid or ameliorate the problem. Successful
learners themselves might be sources of useful hints from their own first-hand experience. Research or systematic observation can also produce reliable, effective hints.

9.6   Conclusions

The purpose of this exploratory study was to identify elements to build an online
learner competencies profile as a tool to support the learner using online technology. A first analysis of literature put in evidence a lack of competency models for
this actor, and, on the other hand, showed that different higher education organizations offer lists of hints to their clientele to become successful online learners.

From the analysis of the hints, we conclude that the knowledge, skills and attitudes recommended by these organizations to the online learner may be very similar
to those of the face-to-face learner. In this sense, there is no significant difference.

Insisting on the distinction of face-to-face and online learner may not be a proper
way to further understanding of the competencies that learners require to use online
technology effectively. Setting up lists of competencies that are particular to the
online learner by arguing that they are different from the traditional learner's competencies brings us back to the technology vs. method debate between Clark and Kozma
in the early nineties (Clark, 1994; Kozma, 1994). Focusing on this divide may result
in either 'glorifying' or 'dismissing' the technology, but losing sight of the learner's role.

The answer to the question suggested in the title of this chapter inquiring
whether or not the new technology requires the development of new competencies
for the learner can be: yes *or* no, but also yes *and* no. The importance is not to lose
sight of the goal: learning and the key actor, i.e. the learner. The suggestion in this
chapter is that online learning is not the important dimension, but the use of
technology, collaboration, and locus of management (instructor or learner) are far
more important in any learning context.

At the start of the dialogue on which this book is based, Visser asked the question: "Is the online learner a distinct subspecies among the wider species of learners in general?" (Visser, Question 1, p. 4 in this volume). Part of the answer could be: No, because the instructional strategies, use of technology, and locus of management are critical factors, not merely the fact that something happens online or not.

Furthermore, as the processes and tools evolve, we anticipate further differentiation in the competencies required of the online and face-to-face learner. Some of those changes will be in the competencies concerned with use of the tools. But others will be driven by changes in instructional strategies, as the collaboration across time and space made possible by the World Wide Web, the growth of repositories of learning objects, the overlapping roles of designer, manager, learner and instructor, and other changes, including those that we cannot as yet see, *will* make new demands on learners' skills and characteristics.

The model proposed in this study suggests three dimensions to help locating where a learner may require support in a particular learning situation regardless of the technology involved. Hopefully this will be useful for program and course designers in providing the right hints or in developing the appropriate lists of competencies, instead of randomly throwing a lifeline wherever there is a problem.

9.7 Resources for Further Exploration

For further exploration of some of the issues touched upon in this chapter, we encourage readers to check out the additional resources listed below under the headings of 'no significant and significant differences' and 'competencies.'

9.7.1 No Significant and Significant Differences

- Ramage, T. (2002). *The 'No Significant Difference' phenomenon: A literature review*. Retrieved January 25, 2007, from http://www.usq. edu.au/electpub/e-jist/docs/html2002/ramage.html.
- The Web site of the *No significant difference phenomenon* available at http://nosignificantdifference.org.
- McDonald, J. (2002). Is 'As Good As Face-To-Face' as good as it gets? *Journal of Asynchronous Learning Networks, 6*(2), 10–23.

9.7.2 Competencies

- The Web site of the *International board of standards for training, performance and instruction*, available at http://www.ibstpi.org.

- Foxon, M., Richey, R. C., Roberts, R., & Spannaus, T. (2003). *Training manager competencies: The standards* (3rd ed.). Syracuse, NY: ERIC Clearinghouse on Information and Technology.
- Richey, R., Fields, D., & Foxon, M. (with Roberts, R.C.; Spannaus, T., & Spector, J.M.) (2001). *Instructional design competencies: The standards* (3rd ed.). Syracuse, NY: Eric Clearinghouse on Information and Technology.
- Klein, J. D., Spector, J. M., Grabowski, B., & De la Teja, I. (2004). *Instructor competencies: Standards for face-to-face, online and blended settings* (Revised 3rd ed.). Greenwich, CT: Information Age Publishing.

9.8 Questions for Comprehension and Application

1. Throughout this chapter, the authors have been trying to come to grips with the question: 'What does it mean to be a successful learner?' They have provided, hopefully, some useful insights, but they are aware that further exploration is needed. Such further exploration is among the goals of this book. Readers are therefore encouraged to reflect on this same question from their own experiential background and based on their independent study of examples and the literature at large, considering any or all of the following questions: What are the criteria to measure the success of an online learner? Who establishes the parameters, and based on what? Is there such a thing as a 'success scale' for online learners? Is course completion, which is widely used as a measure of success, a satisfactory measure of success? Argue for and against it. Are grades a useful measure? How? In some settings, return on investment might be useful. What settings? How might it be useful?

2. Reference is made in this chapter to the practice engaged in by different institutions to advise their prospective students regarding their readiness for online learning. Going by your own experience, your reading of this chapter, and your autonomous exploration of the literature, do you think it is possible for a learner to assess her readiness for online learning? If so, how would she go about it? Is it possible to predict if a learner will be successful in an online environment according to the absence/presence of certain skills? What are your arguments? If it is true that online learning might not work for everyone, how could a learner know? How would you justify excluding learners who are not ready for online learning? Or can you? Finally, discuss the validity—or lack thereof—of your choice of tests of readiness that can be found on the Web.

3. Discuss the plausibility of establishing a competencies profile for online learners. What would such a profile look like? How would the developers of such a profile accommodate the wide range of learners?

4. Does learning in informal online settings require different skills than those required of online learners in formal online settings? Would this be different for academic and non-academic learning? What are some examples of informal online learning of both kinds? Does informal learning pose the same requirements

as formal learning for such things as careful scheduling of time, or providing a quiet space? Why or why not?

5. How do the dimensions of the learning environment discussed in this chapter (technology, management, collaboration) interact with each other? What is your experience with these dimensions? Can you think of other dimensions that might be helpful in describing learning environments and the skills learners require to be successful?

References

Allen, I. E., & Seaman, J. (2003). *Seizing the opportunity: The quality and extent of online education in the United States, 2002–2003*. Needham, MA: Sloan Center for Online Education. Retrieved September 12, 2007 from http://www.sloan-c.org/publications/ survey/pdf/sizing_the_opportunity.pdf.

Allen, I.E. & Seaman, J. (2006). *Making the grade: Online education in the United States*. Needham, MA: Sloan Consortium.

Anderson, T. (2004). Toward a theory of online learning. In T. Anderson & F. Elloumi (Eds.), *Theory and practice of online learning* (Chap. 2). Retrieved September 12, 2007, from http:// cde.athabascau.ca/online_book/index.html.

Arnold, L. (2006). Understanding and promoting autonomy in UK online higher education. *International Journal of Instructional Technology & Distance Learning, 3*(7), n.p. Retrieved September 30, 2007, from http://itdl.org/Journal/Jul_06/article03.htm.

Bouchard, P. (2003). *Four dimensions of learner autonomy*. Retrieved September 30, 2007, from http://www.oise.utoronto.ca/CASAE/cnf2003/2003_papers/paulbouchard-2CAS03en g.pdf.

Boyatzis, R. E. (1982). *The competent manager: A model for effective performance*. New York: Wiley.

Brockband, A., & McGill, I. (1998). *Facilitating reflective learning in higher education*. London: Society for Research into Higher Education and Open University Press.

Brophy, J., & Evertson, C. (1976). *Learning from teaching: A developmental approach*. Boston: Allyn & Bacon.

Brown, S. A, & Miller, D. E. (2007). *The active learner: Successful study strategies* (3rd ed.). New York: Oxford University Press.

Cheetham, G., & Chivers, G. (2005). *Professions, competence and informal learning*. Northampton, MA: Edward Elgar.

Clark, R. E. (1994). Media will never influence learning. *Educational Technology Research and Development, 42*(2), 21–29.

Cole, J. (2005). *Using Moodle: Teaching with the popular open source course management system*. Sebastopol, CA: O'Reilly Community Press.

ComputerSchools.com (2001). *Tips and strategies for the successful online student*. Retrieved September 12, 2007, from http://www.computerschools.com/interviews/elearning/.

Creswell, C., Schwartzmyer, N., & Srihari, R. (2007). Information extraction for multi-participant, task-oriented, synchronous, computer-mediated communication: a corpus study of chat data. In *Proceedings of the IJCAI-2007 workshop on analytics for noisy unstructured text data* (pp. 131–138). Retrieved September 12, 2007 from http://research.ihost.com/and2007/cd/ Proceedings_files/p131.pdf.

De la Teja, I. (2005, October). Reflections on the online learner competencies. In J. Visser (Chair), *Presidential Workshop and Panel Session on Learners in a changing learning landscape: New roles and expectations—A dialogue motivated by an ibstpi research project*. International Convention of the Association for Educational Communications and Technology (AECT), Orlando, FL, October 15–18, 2005. Retrieved September 12, 2007, from www.learndev.org/dl/ ibstpi-AECT2005-DeLaTeja.pdf.

Do Nacimento, H. D. (2005). User hints: A guide to interactive optimization. *Future Generation Computer Systems, 21*(7), 1177–1191.

eLearning Guild (2005). *834 Tips for successful online instruction*. eLearning Guild. Retrieved on September 12, 2007 from http://www.elearningguild.com/content.cfm?selec tion = doc.541

Gardner, R. III., Heward, W., & Grossi, T. (1994). Effects of response cards on student participation and academic achievement: A systematic replication with inner-city students during whole-class science instruction. *Journal of Applied Behavior Analysis, 27*(1), 63–71.

Hoge, M. A, Tondora, J., & Marrelli, A. F. (2005), The fundamentals of workforce competency: Implications for behavioral health. *Administration and Policy in Mental Health, 32*(5), 509–531.

Hseih, W. -L., Smith, B. K., & Stephanou, S. E. (2004). *It is more about telling interesting stories: Use explicit hints in storytelling to help college students solve ill-defined problems*. ERIC Reproduction Service No. ED485034. Retrieved September 30, 2007, from http://www.eric.ed.gov/ERICDocs/data/ericdocs2sql/content_storage_01/0000019b/80/1b/a7/21.pdf.

Illinois Online Network (2007). *Illinois online network: Supporting online education throughout the world*. Retrieved September 12, 2007, from http://www.ion.illinois.edu/ resources/tutorials/pedagogy/tips.asp.

International Board of Standards for Training, Performance and Instruction (n.d.). *Web site of the international board of standards for training, performance and instruction (ibstpi)*. Retrieved September 30, 2007, from www.ibstpi.org.

Jennings, L. (1991, November). *A critical analysis of the competency-based approach in education and training*. Paper presented at The National Conference of Australian Association for Research in Education, Gold Coast, Queensland, Australia.

Kačmárová, A. (2005). Internet chatting inside out. *SKASE Journal of Theoretical Linguistics, 2*(1), 55–84. Retrieved September 12, 2007, from http://www.skase.sk/Volumes/JTL02/05.pdf.

Kassop, M. (2003). *Ten ways online education matches, or surpasses, face-to-face learning. The Technology Source, May/June*. Retrieved September 12, 2007, from http://technologysource.org/article/ten_ways_online_education_matches_or_surpasses_facetoface_learning.

Kerka, S. (1998). *Competency-based education and training: Myths and realities*. Retrieved September 12, 2007, from http://www.calpro-online.org/eric/docgen.asp?tbl = mr&ID = 65.

Kierstead, J. (1998). *Competencies and KSAOs*. Retrieved March 12, 2008 from http://www.psagency-agencefp.ca/research/personnel/comp_ksao_e.pdf

Kizlik, R.J. (2007). *Monster learning skills*. Retrieved Sept. 12, 2007 from http://www.adprima.com/MLS/mlsinfopage.htm

Klein, J. D., Spector, M. J., Grabowski, B., & De la Teja, I. (2004). *Instructor competencies: Standards for face-to-face, online, and blended settings*. Greenwich, CT: Information Age Publishing.

Kozma, R. B. (1994) Will media influence learning? Reframing the debate. *Educational Technology Research and Development, 42*(2), 7–19.

Lasswell, H. D., Lerner, D., & Pool, I. de S. (1952). *The comparative study of symbols: An introduction*. Stanford, CA: Stanford University Press.

Lucia, A., & Lepsinger, R. (1999). *The art and science of competency models: Pinpointing critical success factors in organizations*. San Francisco: Jossey-Bass/Pfeiffer.

Marmolejo, E., Wilder, D., & Bradley, L. (2004). A preliminary analysis of the effects of response cards on student performance and participation in an upper division university course. *Journal of Applied Behavior Analysis, 37*(3), 405–410.

Marrelli, A. (2001). *Introduction to competency modeling*. New York: American Express.

Masie, E. (2004). *701 eLearning tips. The Masie center*. Retrieved September 12, 2007, from http://www.masie.com/701tips/book/701_e-Learning_Tips.pdf.

McClelland, D. C. (1973). Testing for competence rather than for 'intelligence.' *American Psychologist, 28*(1), 1–14.

McDonald, D. (2004). Computer literacy skills for computer information systems majors: A case study. *Journal of Information Systems Education, 15*, 19–34.

McLagan, P. (1997). Competencies: The next generation. *Training and Development Journal, 51*(5), 40–47.

Meyer, K. (2002). *Quality in distance education: Focus on on-line learning.* ASHE-ERIC Higher education report, Volume 29, Number 4. San Francisco: Jossey-Bass.

Mirabile, R. (1997). Everything you wanted to know about competency modeling. *Training and Development Journal, 51*(8), 73–78.

Morrison, G. R. (1994). The media effects question: Unresolveable or asking the right question. *Educational Technology Research & Development, 42*(2), 41–44.

Ngwenya, J., Annand, D., & Wang, E. (2004). Supporting asynchronous discussions among online learners. In T. Anderson & F. Elloumi (Eds.), *Theory and practice of online learning* (Chap. 13, pp. 319–348). Alberta, Canada. Athabasca University. Retrieved September 12, 2007, from http://cde.athabascau.ca/online_book/ch13.html.

Nolan, P. (1998). Competencies drive decision making. *Nursing Management, 29*(3), 27–29.

Norman, D. A. (1993). *Things that make us smart: Defending human attributes in the age of the machine.* Cambridge, MA: Perseus Publishing.

Paquette, G., Ricciardi-Rigault, C., De la Teja, I., & Paquin, C. (1997). Le Campus Virtuel: Un réseau d'acteurs et de resources (The virtual campus: A network of actors and resources). *Revue de l'Association canadienne d'éducation à distance/Canadian Association for Distance Education, 12*(1–2), 85–101.

Richey, R. C., Fields, D. C., & Foxon, M. (2000). *Instructional design competencies: The standards.* Syracuse, NY: ERIC Clearinghouse on Information & Technology.

Russell, T. (2001). *The no significant difference phenomenon: A comparative research annotated bibliography on technology for distance education.* Montgomery, Alabama: IDECC.

Sahin, M. S. (2006). *Overcoming the "No Significant Difference" phenomenon in distance education by internet.* 2nd International Open and Distance Learning Symposium. Anadolu University, Turkey. Retrieved September 12, 2007, from http://www.aof.edu.tr/iodl2006/ Proceedings/ book/papers/paper_16.pdf.

Slaidinis, I. (2004). *Guide des bonnes pratiques à l'usage des acteurs du e-Learning (Best practices guide for actors in e-Learning). European Center of Excellence for e-Learning.* Retrieved September 12, 2007, from http://conseil-recherche-innovation.net/download/ EEE/Guide%20 de%20bonnes%20pratiques%20%C3%A0%20l'usage%20des%20acteurs%20du%20e-learning.pdf.

Spector, J. M., & De la Teja, I. (2001). *Competencies for online teaching. Eric clearing house on information and technology. Syracuse, ED456841.* Retrieved September 12, 2007, from http:// www.ericdigests.org/2002-2/teaching.htm.

Tang, B. A. (2000). *10 Tips to optimize your e-Learning. Learning Circuits, ASTD.* Retrieved September 12, 2007, from http://www.learningcircuits.org/2000/nov2000/ nov2000_elearn.html.

University of Guelph (2006). *Open online: Online distance education at the University of Guelph.* Retrieved September 12, 2007, from http://www.open.uoguelph.ca/online/online _learning/ for_you.cfm.

Usuki, M. (2003) Learner beliefs about language learning and learner autonomy: A reconsideration. In A. Barfield & M. Nix (Eds.), *Learner and teacher autonomy in Japan 1: Autonomy you ask!* Tokyo: Learner Development Special Interest Group of the Japan Association of Language Teachers.

Visser, J. (in this volume). Let the dialogue begin: An introduction. In J. Visser & M. Visser-Valfrey (Eds.), *Learners in a changing learning landscape: Reflections from a dialogue on new roles and expectations* (pp. 1–10). Dordrecht, The Netherlands: Springer.

Volckaert-Legrier, O., & Bernicot, J. (2005). *Le courrier électronique au collège: comparaison avec l'oral par téléphone et l'écrit traditionnel envoyé par fax (Email in college: Comparison with oral communication by telephone and traditional written communication by fax).* Retrieved September 12, 2007, from http://www.unice.fr/ LPEQ/Jetcsic/DOCUMENTS/ JETCSIC%20Volckaert-legrier.pdf.

Vrasidas, C., & McIsaac, M. S. (2000). Principles of pedagogy and evaluation for web-based learning. *Educational Media International, 37*(2), 105–111.

Warnakulasooriya, R., & Prichard, D. (2005). *Hints really help!* Retrieved September 12, 2007, from http://relate.mit.edu/hints.pdf.

Watkins, R. (2005). *Preparing learners for online success. Learning Circuits: ASTD.* Retrieved September 12, 2007, from http://www.learningcircuits.org/2005/sep2005/ watkins.htm.

Wayne County Community College District (2005). *Is distance learning for you?* Retrieved October 1, 2007, from http://www.wcccd.edu/distance_learning/distance_learning.asp.

Weinstein, C. E., & Rogers, B. T. (1985). Comprehension monitoring: The neglected learning strategy. *Journal of Developmental Education, 9*(1), 6–29.

Western Nevada Community College (2007). *Counseling services: Developing college study skills.* Retrieved on September 12, 2007, from http://www.wnc.edu/studentservices/ counseling/ studyskills.php.

White, K. W., & Baker, J. D. (Eds.) (2004). *The student guide to successful online learning: A handbook of tips, strategies, and techniques.* Needham Heights, MA: Allyn & Bacon.

WorldWideLearn (1999). *Traits of successful online students: Is online learning for you?* Retrieved September 12, 2007, from http://www.worldwidelearn.com/elearning-essentials/ learning-online.htm.

Chapter 10
Reflections on Seeking the 'Invisible' Online Learner

Michael F. Beaudoin

Abstract While much has been written regarding the learning behaviors of students participating in online courses, little research has been conducted to ascertain whether or not students are still engaged and actually learning even when not visibly involved in online discourse with other students and faculty. This work summarizes a preliminary study of inactive students enrolled in an online graduate course, augmented by further reflections of the author, based on experience and observation of online student behaviors over a five-year period following the initial study. These findings identify how much time is spent in course related activity, what the reasons are for 'invisibility,' and if preferred learning styles influence their online behavior. The data shows that these students do, in fact, spend a significant amount of time in learning related tasks, even when not visibly participating, and they feel they are still learning and benefiting from this low-profile approach to their online studies. Preliminary analyses of course grades indicate that the mean grade is better for high-visibility learners than for no-visibility learners. Subsequent reflections reinforce these findings, and suggest that further research on so-called invisible learners is a critical area of investigation to better understand the dynamics of asynchronous learning and teaching at a distance.

10.1 Introduction

In 1999, I was asked to evaluate a new course offered as a pilot in an online Master's of Distance Education program delivered jointly by University of Maryland University College and Oldenburg University (Germany). The following year, I had the opportunity to observe the course online, and subsequently, I revised and mentored this same course (Foundations of Distance Education), which I occasionally taught over the next three years. In these various roles, I acquired a keen interest in the phenomenon that has been referred to by Helmut Fritsch (1997) as

University of New England

J. Visser and M. Visser-Valfrey (eds.), *Learners in a Changing Learning Landscape*,   213
© Springer Science+Business Media B.V. 2008

'witness' learners, and which I have subsequently referred to as 'invisible' learners. This inquiry resulted in a study of learners defined as such, and to several publications and presentations on various aspects of that research (Beaudoin, 2002a, 2002b, 2002c, 2003).

Now, with the added benefit of five more years experience designing and teaching a variety of online courses in three graduate programs for three institutions, it seems an appropriate time to reflect further as a practitioner, and to augment my prior investigation with more observation, anecdotal reporting, and analysis regarding the so-called 'invisible' student. It is my hope that the earlier work, coupled with more recent practice, will generate further interest in this phenomenon, and also will foster an on-going exchange of ideas and opinions among colleagues who are also intrigued by e-pedagogy, especially as it applies to the teaching-learning dynamic with students who appear less actively engaged in online discourse.

As interactive modalities increasingly facilitate the connectivity across time and space between students and teacher, and students with other students, attention to the phenomenon of online interaction has gained heightened interest among those seeking to understand and enhance the teaching-learning process at a distance. In considering learning activity in this particular environment, we might assume that it correlates closely to what is visible (i.e., students' written words that appear on the monitor), and conclude that if there is no visible online activity, then little or no learning is likely to occur. Assuming that some learning might indeed occur even when students in online courses are not posting comments, what could be contributing to this tendency to 'lurk' on the periphery of course activity? Are they auto-didactic learners who prefer to remain as anonymous and autonomous as possible? Do they forsake opportunities to participate because thinking about what to write online is more formal and less spontaneous than oral, face-to-face dialogue typically is? Do they frequently have a thought that they are mentally composing, but others often seem to express the same idea before they can do so? Are they having technical difficulties mastering the intricacies of the particular online platform being used? Or are they simply too busy to actively and regularly participate?

What we may not see in asynchronous environments, literally and figuratively, is what else is going on that contributes to participants' learning. It is easy to assume that unless learners in online formats are actively participating by posting frequent and relevant contributions, they may be benefiting relatively little from this more passive experience. And, we might assume that unless students are posting comments that are directly related to the designated topic in, for example, a threaded discussion forum, their learning is likely to be further compromised. Thus, for those students who, even if they do regularly log on, but who do not engage at all in a particular discussion, or who seem to be offering irrelevant or, at best, tangential remarks, we might conclude that they neither contribute to, nor benefit from, the experience. Some distance education theorists argue that the dialogue between student and teacher is the essential defining element of distance education. Holmberg (1981) stated that it should consist of guided didactic conversation. It is curious that, although an historical tenet of distance education is the notion of learners autonomously constructing their own knowledge, instructors facilitating the learning process for distant students often become alarmed when dialogue wanes in their courses.

Fritsch (1999), director of the Center for Research in Distance Education at the FernUniversität in Hagen (Germany), offers an insightful appraisal of the level of student participation as measured by the frequency of online entries at specific points in time as a course progresses. He developed the notion of 'witness learners' (i.e., students who are not actively participating via written contributions at a particular point, but who nevertheless are still engaged in the process as observers (witnesses) of the written exchanges taking place online between other students. He argues that learning, even in this more passive and less visible mode, is still occurring. His assumptions were supported by his findings as a result of his evaluation of a virtual seminar offered jointly by the University of Maryland and Oldenburg University. This was the working assumption that this study sought to investigate.

10.2 Methodology

An online master's degree program offered by the University of Maryland and Oldenburg University enrolled two sections of the Foundation of Distance Education course in the Fall of 2000. Mid-way through the semester, it was noticed that 24 out of a total of 55 students in the two sections had not actively participated (i.e., they posted no online messages during one or both of the modules wherein two prominent guest faculty, who had authored the required textbooks, were both conducting a week-long online conference with each cohort).

Since the course format requires online participation to successfully complete academic requirements, and because the articulation of ideas (whether presented on paper or transmitted electronically) is viewed as an inherently critical element of the learning process, this behavior is seen as an activity that ultimately serves as a key criterion for ascertaining academic success.

A questionnaire was designed and administered to these 24 seemingly 'inactive' students, with the intention of identifying the primary factors influencing their non-participation in this particular component of the course. This author designed the 29-question instrument, and then transmitted it electronically to the target population, midway through the academic term. It should be noted that this study did not take into account gender, native language, and whether or not this was the respondents' first online course.

10.3 Findings

All twenty-four students responded within the prescribed deadline. The first set of nine questions asked for data regarding the total number of hours spent during the two-week conference period on various course related activities. The activity that commanded the greatest amount of time was reading assignments—an average of 12 hours over the two-week conference period. An average of 7.6 hours was spent logging on to the course site, and reading others students' comments.

The second set of questions posed to these low-visibility students asked them to identify factors (checking all that apply from a list of ten provided) that deterred them from posting comments. Three-fourths of them responded that they simply preferred to read what others wrote, or that they had thoughts but others made similar comments before they could post anything themselves. Only four students indicated that time constraints limited the amount of time they could spend writing comments.

The last set of questions was intended to obtain data related to students' learning styles in an online environment, and asked them to respond with a Yes or No to ten items. All but one of the 24 respondents indicated that they were often processing ideas gained from the course even when not visibly participating. Nineteen (19) said they felt they were learning just as much or more from reading other students' comments than from writing their own. About half identified themselves as 'autonomous' learners less inclined to be active in group learning, regardless of the instructional medium. Many emphasized that they spend long hours on the course, and that they have gained much from the course, however little it may appear that they participated; only two confided that online courses did not seem to be their preferred way to learn.

Summing up respondents' comments regarding the primary reasons given for non-participation, the factor cited most often is that online learning is a new experience, and students need time to become acclimated to using it. Three admitted that their limited interaction online is similar to how they would behave in a traditional classroom setting. Several expressed intentionality to write comments more frequently, but didn't because by the time they were ready to do so, several others had already posted similar ideas. It was also clear that many were reluctant to offer online comments just for the sake of being 'present.' Four students admitted to being self-conscious about writing in this forum, one due to being a non-native English speaker/writer, another to being shy, and the other two were just not sure how best to express themselves. Interestingly, two stated that they frequently compose messages, but didn't post them; it may well be that this behavior is a more common phenomenon than we might have initially conjectured.

A preliminary analysis of final course grades offers intriguing evidence that performance cannot be easily correlated to participation or that frequent participation necessarily leads to better performance on graded assignments. The statistics show that the mean grades are better for the high-visibility students than the no-visibility students, yet low-visibility students seem to do somewhat better than the visible (average) students. This suggests that fully engaged, highly participatory learners tend to perform strongly in graded assignments, but that minimal online participation does not compromise grades and, in fact, may reveal that these low-visibility students are dedicating more time to reflection and processing of course material that translates to stronger performance on assignments than those submitted by students participating at an average level.

10.4 Discussion

What might we discover, at least preliminarily, from this data? Regarding how much time is spent on course-related activity, even though little of it is visible to the faculty or to other students, we can state that our intuitive assumption is correct that some activity, though mostly invisible, is taking place. Indeed, if over a two week period in the lives of busy adult students, each spends an average total of 44.6 hours engaged in these various course-related tasks, it must be assumed that some learning is taking place in an ongoing fashion. While it may be tempting to question if students really do, in fact, spend as much time as is claimed on these activities, we must nonetheless accept their self-perceptions, as we are not in a position to perceive what actually occurs outside the online environment. It is quite remarkable, given that this respondent group was identified on the basis of low participation, that such a significant amount of time (i.e., 22+ hours per week) is presumably devoted to academic activity in this one course.

It is evident from the responses regarding reasons for low participation that a significant factor affecting online activity for some students is a certain level of discomfort with the electronic environment, causing some hesitancy to contribute, and then the moment is lost. Most students want to 'get it right' before they commit themselves to online dialogue because the written format seems so 'public.' It may be that online discourse feels more formal and premeditated, while classroom discussion lends itself to a more spontaneous, informal exchange that is not recorded and therefore is less likely to be retained. That three-fourths of the respondents in our study indicated they prefer to read rather than write may suggest a learning style preference, but it could also relate to a lack of familiarity and facility with the medium. And, although it might be suspected that time constraints would be used frequently as an explanation for low participation, the data revealed that lack of time was a relatively negligible factor.

It is important to recognize that students' inclination to interact can depend on a variety of factors, including age, personality, learning style, professional experience, etc. As Kearsley (1995) and others have noted, it may be that the more autonomous, self-directed learner is also more reflective, and so requires less stimulation and reinforcement from interacting with more 'other-directed' peers. And it may be that the perception that there are avenues for interaction is just as important as actually utilizing them. Fulford and Zhang (1993) found that a key factor in student satisfaction in an ITV course was not the extent to which students actively participated, but rather their perception that interaction was possible and was occurring, as needed. This suggests that if courses are designed to provide interactive features, and there is evidence that interaction is taking place or even that the potential for it exists, than knowing it is available may be as important as actually utilizing it.

It should be emphasized here that we are not endorsing low-visibility behavior in online courses as a desirable trait; the purpose of the study was to begin to better understand those factors contributing to low-visibility participation at certain points as a course progresses, and to determine if learning-related activities might be occurring 'behind the scenes.' It is noted here as well that respondents were not queried as to whether or not the presence of two esteemed distance education scholars as guest faculty in the course during this period might have perhaps intimidated them to some degree, and thus have reduced their level of participation.

10.5   Reflections

With the benefit of mentoring a variety of online courses in the five years since the 2000 study, I attempt here to further examine, through experience and observation, these same dynamics regarding the invisible online student, in hopes of better understanding and more effectively supporting these learners. I have modified and/ or expanded on the questions originally posed in the 2000 study of students who are typically less active in an online course, in the sense that they do not participate as frequently as others in online dialogue via postings. The rationale/motivation for reformulating these particular questions is that virtually (sorry for the pun here) every online course I have mentored over the past five years includes one or more such learners, and they present a special challenge to the distance educator who wishes to honor differing learning styles, while not compromising the course effectiveness. If we can better understand what is going on with this learner behavior, then we might better adopt instructional approaches that appropriately accommodate the situation for all learners.

10.5.1   Questions Derived From the 2000 Study

The five questions that follow first are all derived from the original study carried out in 2000. They will be followed in the subsequent section by eight questions that were not raised previously.

10.5.1.1   Should the Online Instructor Be Lenient in Assessing the Invisible Learner's Minimal Participation in Online Dialogue if Other Course Requirements are Satisfactorily Met?

The value and importance of online participation in threaded discussions must be emphasized from the outset of any online course, especially if the instructor intends to factor that activity into student assessment. To not do so early only exacerbates the situation when the instructor eventually notes minimal participation by some, and so must then become the enforcer, possibly creating an atmosphere of 'forced' interaction. To allow minimal participation by some students, with the thought that they will simply have to suffer the consequences later when graded, is likely to incur the ire of more engaged students, some whom will go so far as to admonish the instructor for not explicitly clarifying expectations in this regard. In the end, strong performance in other course components cannot fully compensate for mediocre performance in online dialogue.

10.5.1.2 Given That Online Course Environments are Generally Enhanced by a Community of Scholars Actively Contributing to the Course, Especially via Online Discussions, Can It Be Argued That the Invisible Learner's Behavior Is Parasitic, in That S/He Frequently Takes from, but Seldom Contributes to, the Course?

The online instructor should make his/her position quite clear at the outset as to the parameters of participation and performance, and also what the rationale is for such expected behaviors. Explaining the nature and purpose of learning communities or other desired collaborative activities may not ensure adequate participation by all, but at least it provides a cue from the instructor that one type of involvement is highly valued. Of course, if the instructor does not him/herself exhibit the type of online behavior expected of students, the demand for interaction becomes problematic to encourage or enforce.

10.5.1.3 Is the Evidence Consistent That Invisible Learners, Despite Their Minimal Engagement in Online Interaction with Instructor and Peers, Actually Do Learn and Perform on Graded Assignments as Well as, or Even Better Than, the More Visibly Active Students?

In five years of observing and assessing the work of online students, the pattern described in the 2000 study seems to be consistent—that the invisible student generally does as well as the moderately visible student, but not as well as the highly visible peers. This does suggest, as was noted in the earlier work, that the so-called 'lurkers' may often represent the more reticent students who feel they are quite engaged, learning and satisfying course requirements, even if only posting minimally. Still, it must be said that there are typically one or two of these students who are not only not visible, but who are also largely disengaged from the entire course, hoping to satisfy minimum course requirements and salvage at least a passing grade.

10.5.1.4 Does the More 'Public' Aspect of the Online Environment Hinder Certain Types of Learners from Actively Participating, or Might the Absence of Face-to-Face Interaction Actually Encourage More Expression of Ideas and Opinions?

I am convinced that, in many courses I have mentored in the past several years, the richness of online discourse has been significantly greater than it would have been with the same student populations in classroom-based courses. This is especially the case, I believe, with diverse classes containing, for example, students of varying ages and experience. Consider the following: In an issues-oriented course (American Education) I have taught both face-to-face (f-2-f) and online, I have always emphasized the importance of full participation in discussions. Despite my efforts to establish a supportive and comfortable environment, in either milieu, for the frank expression of opinions and ideas, the younger college-age students in my f-2-f classes have generally been reluctant to express themselves as much as the older adult students. Yet, when this same course was offered for the first time online, with the same demographic mix, the degree of candor and boldness of expression among the younger students was noticeably equal to that of their older counterparts from the very first week's threaded discussion. It does seem to me that the online setting allows for a certain sense of anonymity, and tends to equalize the legitimacy of anyone's thoughts, regardless of age and experience.

10.5.1.5 Might the Low Visibility of Some Students Be a Function of Little or No Prior Experience with Online Studies?

Students new to the online course environment are generally able to adapt rather quickly, and there is little evidence that their lack of familiarity with a particular platform inhibits their participation. A recent example of this is a course I mentored which I developed just prior to it being offered and, consequently, enrolled students were informed relatively late that it would be delivered online. Four students, in particular, expressed annoyance or apprehension upon becoming aware of this, explaining that they had no prior experience with online courses and wondered if this would compromise their ability to successfully complete their studies and ultimately affect their final grade. Yet, barely three weeks into the course, these same four students had all contacted me to express their pleasure with the course, and all were at least as visible as their peers, most of whom had taken online courses before. In fact, it is interesting to speculate if perhaps it is the very newness of the experience that makes them especially active, as they are eager to master the medium as effectively as others do.

10.5.2 Questions Not Raised in the Earlier Study

Augmenting the initial set of questions posed above, my subsequent experience as an online instructor has prompted a new round of questions; these are presented below, with preliminary responses. This expanded line of inquiry might constitute the basis for a more comprehensive follow-up study.

10.5.2.1 Does an 'Invisible' Instructor Influence Student Interaction?

Online teachers serve as powerful role models, for better or worse, for what is expected of students. Minimal visible presence from faculty especially in threaded discussions; slow response time to queries; or tardy feedback regarding assigned work—all these faculty behaviors can give unintended cues to students that online interaction does not seem to be especially valued by the instructor, and so need not be a student's high priority either.

10.5.2.2 Does a Dominant Interaction Pattern Among Course Peers Influence That of Others? Do Inactive Students Tend to Reduce the Participation Level of Their More Active Peers, and Do the More Active Students Prompt Some Inactive Ones to Participate More?

It seems that more active students are likely to gradually increase the participation level of some less active peers, but leas active students generally do not prompt a lower level of participation among active students. However, those few who could be characterized as 'hyper-active' students (needing to post incessantly about everything) are likely to intimidate inactive students to remain so, and to sometimes annoy the more average participants, many of whom are astute enough to recognize that quantity does not obfuscate the absence of quality.

10.5.2.3 Do Regular and Ongoing Postings Enhance Threaded Discussions, or Is It Sufficient for Students to Post Occasionally, Such as on Weekends When They May Have More Time to Devote to Their Studies?

While not as problematic as the totally invisible student, the 'weekly visitor' can certainly represent a vexing behavior for the online instructor. This is the student who can almost always be counted on to make a single 11th hour (literally) appearance, as s/he typically posts late in the evening on the final day of a particular unit of study. This 'batching' approach results in the student never actually participating in any ongoing threaded discussion with peers, but rather simply trying to summarize his/her comments and reactions relating to an entire week's topic(s) in one convenient, catch-all posting. At that point, even though these students generally tend to be quite reflective and articulate, their contribution is somewhat anti-climactic, as most other students have by then completed their postings, and may already be turning their attention to the next unit's readings and thinking about what they want to post on the new topic.

10.5.2.4 Does a Cohort Group in An Online Course Affect Participation Levels of New Students?

Fairly consistently, groups of students who track through a series of courses together adopt a 'cliquish' style of interactive behavior (e.g., addressing one another directly by name in postings, frequently engaging in personal chat), so much so that this can make new students (and even the instructor) feel like interlopers. In these situations, instructors should attempt to neutralize this by creating a separate venue for off-topic conversation. Also, by avoiding addressing students directly by name at the beginning of a posting, instructors may influence students to do likewise.

10.5.2.5   Does the Type of Questions Posed by the Instructor as Discussion Prompts Influence the Style and Frequency of Response Postings?

If the instructor tends to pose questions requiring 'just the facts' replies, rather than those that elicit more expansive answers, reflective learners will be less enthusiastic in responding to that kind of questioning. In this situation, the instructor can inadvertently discourage engagement from those students who may have the most to offer. Questions based on assigned readings ought not to be designed to merely confirm that students can provide accurate information from those sources, but that they can synthesize ideas, arrive at new meanings, and convincingly articulate their understanding and insight.

10.5.2.6   What Is the Effect of High-Expertise Older Learners on Younger Learners with Little Work Experience and Little Familiarity with the Subject Matter? Does This Disparity in Age and Experience Influence Participation of Younger Students?

My experience suggests that the anonymity provided by the online setting tends to diminish, or at least make less obvious, such differences, and so these have a negligible influence on participation levels. To be sure, the low-expertise student's postings may not be quite as sophisticated as those of a high-expertise peer, but this does not seem to discourage activity. It is obviously important that the online instructor avoid too frequently posing questions and soliciting comments that are primarily based on experience or expertise.

10.5.2.7   Does Use of Instructor-Authored Readings Influence the Nature/ Tone of Learners' Comments?

It might be presumed that students would be more reluctant to challenge material they are asked to comment on if written by their course instructor. In my experience, students with less expertise in the area of study are generally reluctant to challenge any published author, regardless of whether s/he happens to be their teacher or not. Graduate students at an advanced stage of study and who may already be quite accomplished practitioners in the field of study, are more inclined to comment candidly and critically, even if it relates to the work of an instructor/author.

10.5.2.8   Does Use of More Elaborate Platform Features (e.g., Graphic Displays, Video Clips, and Other Visuals) Elicit More Engagement Than a Text-Focused Online Course Environment?

While it might be assumed that younger students, who are products of the interactive digital age, are likely to be more responsive to entertaining technological accoutrements, it seems that most mature students could care less about such online enhancements, provided that the instructor establishes and the platform provides a supportive and responsive learning environment in which students can progress satisfactorily toward their learning goals. Students' positive or negative responses to online courses are much more likely influenced by instructor behavior, than by elaborate technical features that can, in fact, become a distraction.

10.6 Conclusions

These ruminations and responses could be perceived as another attempt to formulate yet another set of 'best practices.' But it is perhaps more accurate to define these reflections as a series of inquiries aimed at discovering if the process by which students ultimately learn approximates what faculty initially intended in designing course content and in facilitating the course's progress. In the end, it should be acknowledged that online instructors really do not teach; rather, they create conditions for learning. The more traditional view of pedagogy might be described as largely a matter of structuring content so that students may move logically in a linear direction via a managed process. But, as we have gained experience and insight into the realm of online pedagogy, we have discovered that learning is not so much a managed and linear process, as it is a fostered process, one by which the learner forages; that is, looking for tools to assist in identifying and solving problems.

There is an inherently evolutionary process underway for both teacher and learner in the online environment. Both, to a lesser or greater degree, are experiencing a transition in their respective functions, both undergoing a quite profound redefinition of the teaching-learning relationship. One is trying, in effect, to disengage from his/her historical role, while the other is expected to move to higher levels of engagement. For both, it truly requires an 'unfreezing' process of unlearning old habits. In a 2001 study this author conducted of fifty faculty members in five institutions transitioning from classroom to distance teaching, subjects were asked what they considered to be their most important role. Among them, 38% selected the option of 'mentor' and 32% identified themselves primarily as 'facilitators.' Only 22% referred to themselves as 'teachers' and 8% chose a variety of other terms. As instructors and learners make the transition from face-to-face interaction to a relationship that transcends time and space, each undergoes a fundamental role change, as both seek new ways of knowing and new levels of meaning. This present work hopefully provides a modest contribution to that understanding.

The anecdotal reflections on the 'invisible' learner that are summarized in the preceding section generally reinforce findings of the earlier study. What is now proposed to be done is to pose these questions—from 2000 and 2006—in a more comprehensive follow-up study that could serve as a 'book-end' project, complementing findings from the initial study with these more preliminary assumptions based on experience and observation. This would provide a series of three investigations, to determine if the invisible online behavior chronicled here would remain largely consistent throughout each investigation and analysis. It is hoped that this would provide a sufficient amount of data and discussion to prompt others to conduct their own research regarding the 'invisible' learner. And in considering further this invisibility factor, it would be useful to remind ourselves that, from students' perspective, there is also the not uncommon situation of the invisible instructor in many online courses. There is perhaps no more frequent criticism from online course consumers than 'Where is the instructor?' Indeed, it would be worthwhile to examine correlations between a relatively invisible instructor and a high incidence of student invisibility in that course.

Ultimately, can we arrive at any preliminary insights about what transpires 'below the surface' in an online context that either helps or hinders learning? We can probably conclude that essentially the same 'witness learning' phenomenon occurs in both formats—classroom and online. Certainly, most students are actively engaged in learning activities, often in an auto-didactic fashion, even though there may be relatively little obvious manifestation of that activity. It could be suggested that the image of an iceberg serves as a useful analogy here, in that most of its mass is hidden beneath the surface, just as is the case with our invisible students' learning.

It is premature to declare that a certain level of interaction in online discourse is an essential ingredient to student success or course effectiveness. In fact, all online learners are invisible to the teacher; that some are less visible than others is not necessarily an indicator that the benefits of the learning experience are being compromised. Those who are involved in the instruction and assessment of online learning are reminded that although the medium is technology-based, the actual learning remains largely an invisible process, just as it is in courses at fixed times and places. We are reminded here of Dewey's observation regarding a critical element of the teaching process: to create conditions for 'productive inquiry' that takes place independent from the teacher. In the online learning environment, teachers must be attentive to process as well as content to ensure that this inquiry is indeed occurring, however invisible it may be to them.

10.7   Resources for Further Exploration

Because there has been relatively little attention given to date in distance education research and literature to the 'invisible' learner, it is somewhat difficult to identify and recommend any body of work beyond the resources noted in the accompanying list of references that has made a substantive contribution to this topic. However, the author has noted a growing number of articles in recent issues (2002 onward) of the *American Journal of Distance Education* that present worthwhile research in a number of related areas, and so could be useful to others' particular interest in the invisible learner. Topics include: student learning styles; cognitive engagement; interaction strategies; persistence of distant learners;

student self-efficacy and self-concept; relationship of social presence and interaction; analysis of group interaction; developing self-direction; learners' experiences of starting an online course; and finally, bridging the transactional distance gap. Many of these areas of study would seem to offer promising material for further research applied to the invisible learner.

10.8 Questions for Comprehension and Application

1. Those wishing to further consider the phenomenon discussed in this work may find it useful to consider the more specific questions posed here in relation to the invisible learner within the broader context of an important, and still remarkably relevant, set of more general questions relating to online interaction posed by Kearsley (1995).

    - Is frequency of interaction a useful measure of student success and course effectiveness?
    - Is interaction of greater value for some learners than others?
    - Does interaction affect achievement of learning outcomes?
    - Does increased interaction enhance student satisfaction?
    - Are forms of visible interaction more important than invisible course-related activities?
    - Does the pattern of interaction change over a course? If so, why, and should it change?
    - Consider these questions and formulate answers to them, preferably in a context in which they can be discussed with others, taking into account the issues raised in this chapter as well as your own experience in teaching or learning online.

2. One of the reflections in this chapter concerns the question: 'Does the type of questions posed by the instructor as discussion prompts influence the style and frequency of response postings?' The kind of questioning both students and instructors engage in probably goes to the heart of what it means to maintain a meaningful didactic conversation (Holmberg, 1981). Imagine yourself being an actor—student or instructor—in an online dialogue about issues of your choice that you feel comfortable with. You wish your fellow participants in the dialogue to explore the issues in depth. Within that area, invent three questions that elicit ongoing dialogue beyond 'mere facts' and that are conducive to reflective exploration of the issues at stake.

3. Assuming that you have access to archived online teaching-learning dialogues, preferably ones in which you yourself participated, explore some of those you have access to and identify the parts of them where you feel that new insights were established among those who participated. Analyze the kind of questioning that took place and interpret it against the backdrop of the requirement that such questioning should aim for more than 'just the facts.'

References

Beaudoin, M. (2002a). Learning or lurking? Tracking the 'invisible' online student. *The Internet and Higher Education, 5*(2), 147–155.

Beaudoin, M. (2002b). Finding the elusive online student. *Online Classroom,* 4–5.

Beaudoin, M. (2002c). From campus to cyberspace: The transition of classroom faculty to distance teaching roles. *Educational Pathways, 1*(6), 6.

Beaudoin, M. (2003). Is the 'invisible' online student learning or lurking? In E. Rubin & U. Bernath (Eds.), *Reflections on teaching and learning in an online master program. A case study* (pp. 121–129). Oldenburg, Germany: Bibliotheks- und Informationssystems der Universität Oldenburg. ASF Series # 6.

Dewey, J. (1971). *Experience and education.* New York: Macmillan.

Fritsch, H. (1999). Host contacted, waiting for reply. In U. Bernath, & E. Rubin (Eds.), *Final report and documentation of the virtual seminar for professional development in distance education* (pp. 355–378). Oldenburg, Germany: Bibliotheks- und Informationssystems der Universität Oldenburg.

Fulford, C. P. & Zhang, S. (1993). Perceptions of interaction: The critical predictor in distance education. *The American Journal of Distance Education, 7*(3), 8–21.

Holmberg, B. (1981). *Status and trends of distance education.* London: Kogan Page.

Kearsley, G. (1995). The nature and value of interaction in distance education. In M. Beaudoin (Ed.), *Distance Education Symposium 3: Instruction* (pp. 83–92). University Park, PA: American Center for the Study of Distance Education.

Chapter 11
Will Games and Emerging Technologies Influence the Learning Landscape?

Deborah LaPointe

Abstract Read newspapers and professional educational journals, attend a national or state conference, or review the offerings of a university catalog, and you soon encounter statistics like 92 percent of children ages 2–17 play video and computer games (Beck & Wade, 2004); 60 percent of Americans play interactive games on a regular basis (Kirriemuir, 2002); 78 percent of American families have video game equipment in their homes (Simpson, 2005). You will also read that 78 percent of 18–29 year olds use the Internet in their daily lives (Ramaley & Zia, 2005), yet only 38 percent of college students report using the Internet in their classes (Ramaley & Zia, 2005). Outside the classroom, students are creating a new shared culture, showing us new ways to learn and communicate and make sense of physical and virtual identities and worlds. They are showing us that what happens in virtual worlds is often just as meaningful as what happens offline (Taylor, 2006). They work autonomously or with others—playing with others online who may protect and advise them or playing next to others who play the same game. They know where to obtain helpful resources. However, these mainly young gamers do not just play games and consult resources; they create game guides, answers to FAQs, maps, overviews, strategies, fanfic (fanfiction—stories about the gaming characters or settings written by game fans rather than by game creators), and character-planning guides. All of this adds up to a different kind of play and developmental environment, which influences a different developmental process and way of seeing the world and thinking than experienced by generations before.

11.1 Introduction

The statistics mentioned in the abstract above suggest a substantial disconnect between the use of technology in students' personal daily lives and in their academic coursework under a teacher's direction (Ramaley & Zia, 2005; Hartman,

University of New Mexico

J. Visser and M. Visser-Valfrey (eds.), *Learners in a Changing Learning Landscape*,   227
© Springer Science+Business Media B.V. 2008

Moskal, & Dziuban, 2005). Some of the disconnect may be related to the fact that many instructors and instructional designers did not grow up playing computer and video games and have as of yet not started playing games; we may misunderstand, overlook, and undervalue games.

Games are not the only technology we have not experienced. Neither are games the only technology supporting virtual communication, physical and virtual identities, convenient access to resources and information, and social networking. Other new technologies are also changing the way we communicate, receive and process information, and learn. These emerging technologies are interactive, interpersonal, and group communication tools with graphical user interfaces that are potentially usable by anyone. They are already influential in our students' lives outside the classroom and set expectations for what technologies can do, as reflected in statements such as, "Whenever I go to school, I have to power down" (Prensky, 2006, p. 10) or "The cookies on my daughter's computer know more about her interests than her teachers do" (Prensky, 2006, p. 11).

For clarity's sake, I shall now first describe key concepts used in this chapter—video games, online games, computer games, and simulations. Simulations engage learners in situations or events that would be too costly, difficult, problematic, or hazardous in the real world (Gredler, 1996). The learner becomes engaged in complex, evolving situations and relationships (Bonk & Dennen, 2005), and the focus is on the player's serious, authentic responsibilities (Gredler, 1996). Games are competitive, goal-oriented, rule-based, and tend to foster skill development by focusing on fun, rules, and a goal that entices the players to exert effort to win or achieve (Gredler, 1996; Koster, 2005). Video games require a console and a TV set like Nintendo, Sega, and Xbox; computer games require a PC; and online games require an Internet connection. Video games are generally focused on action and adventure; players choose a character. A surprisingly long list of video games can be found at http://en.wikipedia.org/wiki/List_of_computer_ and_video_games. Typical computer games are solitaire, poker, and board games that do not require a character but also include WarCraft, The Sims, and Civilization. One more type of game must be mentioned—MMORPGs—which is an acronym for massively multiplayer online role playing games—or MMOGs—massively multiplayer online games. MMORPGs or MMOGs host thousands of players who participate in games in real-time using the Internet (Taylor, 2006).

This chapter also reviews mobile technology, wikis, blogs, video blogs, MySpace, Friendster, and Flickr—emerging technologies that our students are using and with which we instructors and instructional designers should become familiar. They already use these technologies to connect people and their information (Warlick, 2005). We now need to determine whether we should include them in our portfolio of instructional technologies.

11.2   Games and Emerging Technologies are Challenging Our Assumptions

Games and the emerging technologies are challenging our assumptions about user behavior, information needs, and learning (Hartman et al., 2005). Games and the emerging technologies provide rich multimedia capabilities that offer greater levels of interactivity through modeling, animations, simulations, voice and video applications, changing the way in which and with whom users can interact. People create identities for themselves, establish social networks, and take on roles and responsibilities. These capabilities make it convenient for students to express themselves and contribute information and commentary at an unprecedented scale (Ramaley & Zia, 2005). Games allow players to assume different roles, see the world from diverse perspectives, and share newly informed insights. In contrast, students identify the interaction facilitated by technology in the classroom as lacking the immediacy they experience in their daily lives and as unmindful that they view classmates as a source of knowledge and help rather than as competition (Zurita & Nussbaum, 2004).

Some predict that games will be another medium of expression for almost any idea. Games and the new emerging technologies may be revealing to us what it means to be educated in the 21st century. Our students, like those before them, have to be able to read, evaluate the credibility of, use, and cite a wide range of resources. However, today ideas are expressed through spoken, written, and visual resources for a variety of purposes to communicate with a variety of audiences (Richardson, 2006). Video and computer games are another medium of expression of ideas and information, for example, the games *Food Force, September 12, Darfur is Dying, Peacemaker*, and *A Force More Powerful* (Thompson, 2006). We will need to use these technologies in the classroom to enrich education and prepare learners to learn and communicate through this medium, so they will be able to join their chosen professional community of practice. These technologies may more fully engage students less likely to complete a degree and help learners experience the competence and control they normally do not experience.

We currently lack research to help us determine the impact of games (and the emerging technologies) on learning. Some researchers assert that games promote experiencing the world from different perspectives, help developing problem solving skills, lead to understanding complex systems, and allow transfer in a safe environment. Conversely, games have been maligned and charged with the "corruption of youth, blamed for shortened attention spans, and heralded as a precursor to a society of alienated, socially incompetent automatons" (Chaplin & Ruby, 2005, p. 1). Some of the emerging technologies have been criticized for their very advantages—the ease and immediacy of interacting online; the open nature of publishing content and commentary; and presenting a virtual self different from the physical self. The very nature of the emerging technologies can sometimes result in exposure to inaccurate, false, and inappropriate content.

11.3 Show Me the Games of Your Children

Our students have grown up in a time and culture different from ours. Such an obvious yet simple statement is important. For the culture and its practices play a large role in shaping the development of individual minds and embed a particular language of thought and an internalized representational process that stem from the individual's participation at the particular time (Vygotsky, 2000). In any society, people get their ideas about life, what is important, and who they want to be from the messages of their culture (Chaplin & Ruby, 2005). Their development is also impacted by the tools, technologies, and artifacts used by each culture to store knowledge and to achieve the goals to which tools' activities are directed. The technologies available as a generation matures influence their behaviors, attitudes, and expectations (Hartman et al., 2005).

Some of the tools and technologies our students have been using since the age of two involve computer and video gaming and Internet-based communication software. The computer and the game console became standard home entertainment equipment in the 1990s, and the typical child since that time has grown up playing video games at home (Rushkoff, 1996). Such distinctive early experiences become instrumental in the development of individuals (Bownds, 1999; John-Steiner, 1997). Years of computer use develop hypertext minds and parallel cognitive structures in young gamers in contrast to the sequential cognitive structures (Prensky, 2001) of their instructors. "The wiring connections in our brains...depend on features of the sensory and motor environment in which we grow up after birth" (Bownds, 1999, p. 11). Or, as anthropologists say, "Show me the games of your children, and I'll show you the next 100 years" (Chaplin & Ruby, 2005, p. 201). Castronova (2005) believes we are already seeing evidence to support the anthropologists' statement when he writes that (a) the commerce flow generated by people's buying and selling virtual items like magic wands, spaceships, and armor amounts to $30 million annually in the United States and (b) the average age of gamers increases with each passing year, including the fact that 60 percent of parents are playing games with their children at least once a month.

Reviewing those games, tools, and technologies and determining the advantages offered will help us understand our students' language of thought and the internalized representational processes they acquired during their developmental years. Understanding the advantages will help us think through the design of stimulating, significant learning environments that promote the social exchange students currently experience with each other and the complex learning (Jochems, van Merriënboer, & Koper, 2004) that our students will need for their professional lives tomorrow. These authors describe complex learning as the coordination of the myriad skills needed to solve new problems with a focus not just on content but on problem solving, critical thinking, learning to learn, self-regulation, and self-assessment. Meaningful learning environments designed around authentic tasks where learners can practice the coordination of these skills are needed. Many of us teaching today did not learn and develop in such rich, complex times. Deciding whether gaming and other technologies are something we should bring into the classroom requires some serious accommodation of our existing schema.

11.4   Our Early Years

Many of us now teaching were born in the 1940s, 1950s, and 1960s. The majority of us are women (79 percent) with an average age over 40 (Simpson, 2005). Writing from an American perspective, I should add that many of us were taught in a culture and school system that were preparing students to be scientists and mathematicians at a time America strove to land someone on the Moon before other nations would do so. We sat in long rows of desks and memorized state capitals, times tables, the operation of simple machines, the systems of the body, numerous verses from Shakespeare, and many rules. We solved many pages of textbook math problems each night; we completed fill-in-the-blank, multiple choice, and matching tests. We worked alone and were trained to store a collection of arbitrary facts.

For education then was the transmission of specific bodies of knowledge and skills. Our cultural and educational model was to leave out a myriad of details to formulate a basic pattern (Gee, 2003) and focus on the attributes of an object or idea with little or no focus on forces outside the object (Nisbett, 2003). Our culture focused on individualistic representation, inductive logic, giving rise to a physics of mechanical units, psychology of associated ideas, social theory of individual rights, an economics of utilitarian calculus, a legal system based on common law, a religious system based on sects, and a state based on guarantees of individual freedom (Hess, 1995) regardless of circumstances. We came to expect to live by abstract principles, applicable to everyone.

Those were the days of the behaviorists. Learning was defined as a more or less permanent change in behavior that could be "detected by observing the organism over a period of time" (Driscoll, 1994, p. 29). Learning had to be defined in this manner as cognitive processes could not be otherwise validated, and education was not concerned at the time with how knowledge was constructed. Learning occurred through reinforcement of behaviors, and teachers facilitated learning through extrinsic motivation. Our learning was assessed through practices that measured reproduction of prescribed content (Garrison & Archer, 2000).

It is important for us to recognize these patterns for they initiate a learner into a set of practices, literacies, and customs central to that culture and age. The time and the way a child grows up and plays subsequently come to define and impact his or her preferred mode of thought and ways of attaching meaning to experiences (John-Steiner, 1997), traits, behaviors, values, and beliefs (Beck & Wade, 2004) and embodies an accumulated set of cultural values and beliefs (Wells & Claxton, 2002).

Great learners and great accomplishments did come from these earlier educational practices. However, some learners were left out when the teacher was required to deliver the same material to 30 learners in one room within a given period of time. Harm to the quality of learning of many of the learners in the classroom and the loss of a great deal of potential learning were inevitable (Meighan, 1996). In contrast, we now know that learning styles differ; we know that change is a constant in the many complex systems we find ourselves living and working in; and we should, therefore, vary the learning situation accordingly. Possibly more learners can contribute worthy accomplishments when learning environments are designed around assumptions that are different from the ones held by the behaviorists and include additional instructional methodologies and technologies.

11.5   Our Students—The Young Gamers

The students in our university and college classes today share the same biology as we Baby Boomers; however, they are processing information differently from us based on their disparate developmental experiences. The students in our classes today include young gamers from the Net Generation (born 1981–1994) plus learners who predate the Internet (Matures born before 1947, Baby Boomers born 1946–1964, and Generation X born 1965–1980). These groups of students grew up in different cultures, and all experienced diverse childhoods. They grew up playing differently, grew up in dissimilar times, picked up habits and attitudes from friends, relatives, teachers, and colleagues, and inculcated different worldviews.

Many factors impact how we work, play, and socialize. More of these factors have been changed by technology, probably more so in the last 70 years than in the preceding 2000 years. Baby Boomers grew up with transistor radios, $33\frac{1}{3}$ and 45 rpm records, CB radios, eight-track tapes, portable typewriters, and dial tone telephones; Generation X grew up with CDs, personal computers, and e-mail; the Net Generation has grown up with GameBoys, MP3 players, cell phones, PDAs, and digital video recorders (Hartman et al., 2005) and text messaging. Matures and Baby Boomers accordingly grew up expecting that someone else had already selected what they would listen to, in what order; they expected to be out of range of listening to music and to be out of touch with their friends as they traveled; they grew accustomed to buying an LP and liking only one track. They thought of music as a recorded physical commodity—LP, cassette tape, or CD (Williams, 2006)—and came to learn that someone else provided the content they read in newspapers and books. By contrast, their young students sample new music on the Internet, pay for and download the tracks they like, creating playlists for their MP3 players and cell phones. They share their playlists over peer-to-peer networks, using CDs basically to burn their songs on. They are rarely separated from their friends as their cell phones afford sharing photos and text messaging even when talking is prohibited or while they are on a family vacation. They create, modify, and publish content on blogs and wikis.

11.6 Sociocultural Perspective

Today we recognize that society and culture have a profound effect upon cognitive processes. People learn through experiencing and making sense of the world. They learn content and learn in ways that are shared with groups of people who carry distinctive social practices. Vygotsky (2000) stressed that higher order mental functions are socially and culturally formed, and an individual's conceptual development evolves from experiences and interaction with others. Interaction with others is mediated by language and other semiotic devices. Analysis of those experiences occurs through interaction with others and through internal reflection, leading to reconstruction at a higher order. Vygotsky thus theorized that one's potential can be achieved through collaboration with more capable others. This suggests that learning comes from intellectual action and involves others who help us understand the field structure and relations among objects in the environment.

In contrast, many of us Baby Boomers grew up practicing drill and skill, which Vygotsky (2000) suggested shows no sign of conscious comprehension and does not include understanding the field structure and the interrelationships among objects in the field—the whole. Through interaction with others, learners come to see an idea, subject matter, or content as socially valued. The value commitments of members of a community provide the basis for the satisfactory conduct of a way of life (Bruner, 1990). Through discourse, shared meaning is made and experience is structured and organized as knowledge (Halliday, 1993). As well, it is through discourse with others that a way or a preferred mode of thought becomes important.

While many Baby Boomers in the United States learned to focus on objects, rules, and attributes, their Eastern friends learned "to see objects and events not in isolation but embedded in a meaningful whole in which the elements are constantly changing and rearranging themselves" (Nisbett, 2003, p. 27). Baby Boomers played with "Chatty Cathy" and "Barbie" dolls and Tonka trucks and rode Schwinn bicycles. However, their three-year-old sons, daughters, nieces, and nephews now play video games on the V.Smile video gaming system, learning problem solving, logic, vocabulary, colors, and telling time. Our six-year-old and nine-year-old neighbors are using *The Sims* as their dolls, giving them their own characters and personalities, personal effects, taking care of their comfort, fun, hygiene, finances, and social life. Maintaining the dolls' happiness is the goal of the game. However, *The Sims* dolls do not always listen, and keeping them happy is difficult as they have their idiosyncratic and varied desires (Schiesel, 2006), and their happiness is influenced by a complex world inhabited by other characters and situations, resulting in the continually emerging evolution of the dolls.

We did not see life's complexity modeled for us; we read texts using words to describe worlds, or we watched a stream of sounds and images in a film (Chaplin & Ruby, 2005). Games offer an advantage for preparing players to be agents in open systems. Our students are learning how motion informs and refines vision; they are gaining knowledge of how to act in response to what is seen and testing the visual guidance of action that cannot be obtained by passively extracting visual features from the environment (Bownds, 1999, p. 180); they are interacting in immersive three-dimensional environments. They can influence what happens. The differences are important for the elements that we are taught to perceive and pay attention to influence our cultural processes and thinking habits, cognitive tools, and ways of interacting with others.

As mentioned earlier in this chapter, we Baby Boomers were taught to 'do our own work,' and when we needed help, we sought help from the authority figure in the classroom. Our students know they can learn from and with each other. They share tips and preparation-to-play selections before starting a game. Some post written tips, walk-throughs, detailed accounts of how to handle the monster or zone, specifying the pacing of the encounter, posting pictures and documentation (Taylor, 2006). So, whereas we entered the workplace, expecting a central authority to assign us tasks, our students expect to work as members of self-directed teams, who share and create new knowledge and technologies (Hess, 1995). The skills needed are decidedly different.

11.7 Technological Perspective

What is in the technology that so influences behaviors, attitudes, and communication? Specifically for those of us looking ahead to new learning landscapes, we, like Salomon (1977), ask, 'What makes a difference in cognition and learning when we add technology to the learning environment?'

Tapscott (1998) makes an interesting point when he suggests that *technology* is a term used only for and by people who were born before it was invented. While we Baby Boomers may wonder if wikis, texting, gaming, mobblogging are appropriate technologies, the young gamers do not see technology at all; they see people, information, games, applications, services, friends, and resources (Tapscott, 1998). They do not talk about technology; they photoshare, swarm, and blog; they talk about finding the key, building a Web site, writing a friend, researching a rain forest; they text message, use IM, and learn how to copyright their lyrics by researching the Web.

Tapscott (1998) believes the difference is between assimilating technology, which is what young gamers do, and accommodating it, which is what Baby Boomers do. He describes accommodation as a much more difficult learning process. According to Driscoll (1994), assimilation occurs when a child, for example, perceives new objects or events in terms of existing schemes and operations. The child with largely broad and undifferentiated schemas uses an object without first wondering if he or she is using the object appropriately. The infant puts things in his or her mouth, grasps, throws, and shakes them—uses them in as many situations as is possible. Our young gamers do not enroll in formal training to learn a new technology; they tinker and explore, following Levi-Strauss's (1968) concept of bricolage. In contrast, accommodation occurs when existing schemes or operations must be modified to account for a new experience. Accommodation requires a shift in thinking about all the aspects of the task.

From an educational technology and communication perspective, we have long researched and debated whether media are delivery vehicles for instruction with little or no direct influence on learning. Through the years, we have determined that at least three factors can make a difference in learning: (a) the technology involved; (b) the content transmitted; and (c) the symbolic codes into which the messages are coded (Salomon, 1977). Salomon suggested that it is the symbolic code into which an idea is coded that makes the largest and most important difference in learning. For what generates and governs learning are the mental processes activated by the instructional stimulus. A verbal description of an object and a picture of it differ not only in appearance; they also require different mental skills to process the conveyed information, according to Salomon. Each medium has a wide range of symbolic codes; each combination of codes may have different effects on mental skills or processes. Repeated exposure to games enhances (a) representational competence, defined as the ability to read visual images as representations of three-dimensional space; (b) multidimensional visual-spatial skills (the ability to create mental maps; (c) inductive discovery; and (d) attentional deployment (the ability to focus on several things simultaneously and respond faster to unexpected stimuli (Prensky, 2006). These cognitive effects, in turn, determine the way the material is processed and learned (Salomon, 1977), interacting with individual learner differences.

11.8   Young Gamers and Games

Games play a daily part in the lives of almost every child. As far as the US is concerned, the gaming industry attracts more than 60 percent of the American population (Kirriemuir, 2002), and its estimated revenue of $7 billion (Herz & Macedonia, 2002) to $9 billion (Vaknin, 2002) is projected to soon pass both the record industry and the home video sales market (Snider, 2002). Bonk and Dennen (2005) write that it is generally and widely said that wherever you are, there is a good chance that you are near a game. The young gamers (over the age of ten) now number 90 million in the US and are so numerous that by sheer volume, Beck and Wade (2004) predict they will automatically change popular culture and other social landscapes.

According to the Pew Internet & American Life Project (Jones, 2003), for college students, gaming is commonplace and woven into the fabric of everyday life. Seventy percent reported playing video, computer, and online games at least once in a while, and students reported that gaming affords a way to spend more time with friends, make more friends, as well as improve existing friendships. Playing games is a social activity and part of many other tasks—taking a break from studying or walking to the next class. Nearly two-thirds agreed that gaming helped them pass time when friends were unavailable.

Beck and Wade (2004) suggest the gamers have spent endless amounts of time building their skills in a world that was created solely for them. They have grown up together, speaking a unique vocabulary only they understand—cheat codes, fragging, strafing, mule, water ski, and brick. The players have been influenced by games' common elements. What are those common elements? First, games have a recognized goal (Herz & Macedonia, 2002). The components of every game include fun, play, competition, goals, rules, and winning. As to winning, *The Sims* is an exception as no points can be scored (Schiesel, 2006). Second, games are designed to absorb all of the player's attention, causing them to ignore interruptions. Third, games respond to the gamer, who has an enormous range of controls and choices. The learner selects and makes his or her initial preparations; achieves milestones; teaches him or herself by trying things out and taking risks; gains access to new weapons, tactics, resources, and levels; takes on increasingly challenging opponents and obstacles; and assumes different roles or character identities. Feedback from the game mediates the goal and the learner's behavior. Fourth, games reward technical skills and foster skill development by providing entertaining challenges for the player.

These shared gaming experiences, however, go deeper than sharing a leisure-time experience. Their values and skills have shaped their performance (Beck & Wade, 2004) in several ways. While the Pew study (Jones, 2003) suggests that an important trend is the integration of gaming into other activities, Gee (2003) categorizes video games as a semiotic domain, which he defines as any set of practices that recruits one or more modalities to communicate distinctive types of meanings. When a learner enters a domain, he or she learns to experience, see, feel, and operate on the world in new ways; gains the capacity to join a social group of people who share the domain as distinctive social practices; gains the resources needed for future learning; begins to think about the domain at a meta-level as a complex system of interrelated parts; and begins to think about how to innovate in the domain. To do so, the learner has to learn how to situate meanings for that domain in the sorts of situations the domain involves.

Steinkuehler's (2003) ethnographic research on Lineage supports Gee's (2003) principle of participants becoming members of a semiotic domain. Steinkuehler found that through participation in valued practices or activities, one's character or online identity acquires essential knowledge of the game content, point system, goods available, social status, social connections or networks that move the player from the sidelines or fringes of the game to a more important or knowledgeable player within it. Those who master the social and material practices assist new gamers (Castronova, 2005) and grant newcomers increasing control of the learning situation over time. This sounds very similar to a description of a community of practice.

Games provide a story and a context for the goals the players are to achieve. The embodied nature of game gives meaning to players' actions and consequences. Every movement, word, deed, artifact, or action is an invitation to the player's next action. Actually, words, deeds, artifacts, and actions take on different meanings at different times. Players do not memorize meanings but learn to be prepared for what may come. Green and Bavelier's (2003) research suggests that the dynamic nature of interacting in games increases players' visual attention resources, providing learners with more resources to attend to problems over time and helping them filter out unimportant details and identify the most important aspects.

According to Gee (2003), there are 42 learning principles implicitly built into the more effective games. Gee's list of 42 principles is summarized in this chapter into 5 categories. First, all aspects of the learning environment are set up to encourage active and critical learning, where learning means doing something. There are multiple routes to doing something and making progress, so learners can rely on their own strengths and styles of learning. Second, learning involves mastering semiotic domains and participating in the groups connected to them through embodied experiences. Skills are not learned in isolation or out of context but by engaging in the domain. Real-world consequences are lowered, and learning situations are ordered, so early cases lead to generalizations that are useful for later situations. Third, learners participate in extended engagement as taking on and playing with identities as learners relate and reflect on their multiple identities, leading to the learners' discovery of themselves and their potential and current capacities. Fourth, meaning and knowledge are built through various modalities, not just words; knowledge is stored in material objects and in the environment. Learners receive explicit information on demand and just in time. Finally, the learner is an insider, teacher, and producer, able to customize the learning experience and domain/game. Gee adds that the power of good games resides in ways in which they meld learning and identity while Thompson (2006) believes the essence of games is their ability to teach how complex systems work.

Learning designed following these principles creates engaged learning experiences where learners are "captured heart and mind," cognitively and affectively (Quinn, 2005, p. 12) and metacognitively. When Quinn describes an engaged learning experience as one where there is a challenging goal set in a believable theme, where the learners have to struggle to achieve the goal, the context is meaningful, and decisions have consequences, he may as well be describing games.

The message of this chapter is not that games are the sole source for active learning. Rather, the purpose is to suggest that designers and instructors think not just in terms of content representation but consider seriously Quinn's (2005) call to design learning *experiences* for today's learners who need active learning environments to acquire the skills for tomorrow's complex learning. The world they are living and working in requires a different set of skills and ways of thinking than the world the older generation entered when it left college in the 1970s and 1980s. Today's learners need to experience the entire learning cycle as proposed by Kolb (1984) of experience, reflection and integration with prior knowledge, forming a new hypothesis, testing it through experience, trial and error, and again reflect, integrate, and continue the cycle (Zull, 2002) with others.

We know that no one technology or instructional idea is a panacea, and we currently use a mix of teaching methodologies and technologies. The following section describes other emerging technologies that we can examine and discover ways to use in our classrooms.

11.9   Emerging Technologies

Motivation is a key factor in the success or failure of education (National Research Council, 2004). The National Research Council's report asserts that the primary ingredients for fostering involvement and motivation to learn are (a) forming a connection between a learner and the social context in which learning will take place and (b) making the curriculum and instructions relevant to learners' experiences, cultures, and long-term goals. Can some of the emerging technologies be used to create the engaging features of games or form a connection between learners and the social context, making the instruction relevant to experiences and goals? If that is our hope, then as we look at emerging technologies, we need to be asking ourselves the following questions: How will this emerging technology help facilitate Kolb's (1984) active learning cycle?

How will this technology create a rich learning experience with a challenging goal, control and choice, a believable theme, meaningful context, and consequential decisions? How will this technology help learners learn about themselves? How will this technology help learners find meaning distributed across people, objects, tools, symbols, technology, and the environment? How will this technology support and improve teaching and learning outcomes? Does this technology provide students with the digital literacies required to live and work in contemporary society?

The following paragraphs describe emerging technologies that our students already use in their daily lives.

11.9.1   Friendster

Friendster is a Web site founded by Jonathan Abrams, a former Netscape engineer, designed to promote social networking. Friendster allows members to post stories, photos, and information about themselves and to network through online chats and blogs. It has seven million registered members. Users present a sense of their identity by publishing their profiles and linking with their friends and friends of friends to date, find jobs or apartments, and participate in other networking activities. Users show their relationships with each other as friends by referencing each other's profiles. Friends write testimonials to each other, which, after approval, appear on a user's profile. In a sense, users not only represent themselves online, they also help form the representations of their friends and their friends' friends. Users send e-mail invitations to each other to be friends, and users can accept or deny an invitation to be someone's friend. In this way, users can control who can see their profile.

Many other social networking sites exist and are popular with our young students—MySpace, Xanga, Facebook, and Bebo (Rawe, 2006). At the time of writing, nearly 250,000 new accounts are created on MySpace each day. However, none of the information has to be true. The news media report frequently about privacy concerns and the inability of the social networking sites to monitor daily exchanges to protect young users from online predators.

11.9.2   SMS

SMS is the acronym for *Short Message Service* that is available on cell phones. SMS has been used in the Australian school system to notify parents of student absences from classes. SMS could also be used to notify students of changes in due dates for assignments, changes to rooms for classes, delayed start times, and emergencies (ACT Department of Education and Training, 2005), test scores, and grades. Instructors could send learners data and clues for analysis, diagnosis, and response (Prensky, 2006) throughout the week in problem-based learning environments.

11.9.3   Mobile Devices—Digital Backpack

mLearning is the ability to engage in learning anywhere, anytime and on any mobile device—PDA, cell phone, tablet PC, laptop, smart phone, and GPS device. mLearning takes students out of the classroom and into relevant settings—the environment, community, and workplace—where they can learn directly in the course of real-world engagement in real-world timeframes. Students' cell phones are already equipped with digital cameras and Web browsers that download and play music and feature-length movies plus send and receive e-mails. Instructors can send GPS coordinates and maps for important locations in the community (known as geocaching) relevant to a unit of study, learning sequences, resources, photos, and individual feedback related to the students' needs.

mLearning programs usually use on-going Internet or mobile phone connectivity; however, the students could download information and resources while connected and still use the information without a live connection out in the community. Students can share documents with each other sending them from close range using the beaming features of their PDAs. mLearning could be used to simulate games like the mobile phone game discussed in the next section. Students learn by performing authentic activities through interacting with the environment or community, and those authentic activities stimulate learning (Georgiev, Georgieva, & Smrikarov, 2004).

11.9.4   I Like Frank

In March 2004, Blast Theory (n.d.) unveiled the world's first 3G mixed reality game, *I Like Frank* in Adelaid. *I Like Frank* took place online at www.ilikefrank.com and on the streets using 3G phones. Players in the real city interacted with players in the virtual city as they searched for Frank through the streets of Adelaide. The players built relationships, exchanged information, and tested the possibilities of a hybrid game space.

Online Players moved through a virtual model of the city, opening location-specific photos of the city. Online Players had to find a Street Player to go to that location and retrieve an object shown in the photo. Street Players found postcards in different locations, each postcard contained questions to answer. Street Players received phone messages inviting them to answer the questions posed on the postcards and address the postcards to their online players. Street Players were also invited to follow the footsteps of Frank to a 'Future Land.' The Online Players were able to enter a virtual Adelaide where Frank was waiting in a photographic 'Future Land.'

Windows Live Local could be used with the mobile devices and games like 'I Like Frank.' Learners can locate friends and information and get easy-to-read maps, directions, and satellite photos on Windows Live Local. They can get bird's eye views of most major cities, see multiple destinations on one map, and customize their map views.

11.9.5 Blogs

Weblogs or blogs are easily created and updateable Web sites that permit authors to publish instantly to the Internet (Richardson, 2006). Blogs can convey personal, individual records, group collaborations, or institutional voices. A crucial feature of blogs is the ability to add links and photos and to frame postings in the context of the links that they cite (Downes, 2004). Readers can add information and comment on the blog's contents. Blogs can serve as reflective journals; a class portal for posting the syllabus, class schedule, assignments, and handouts; e-portfolios; and source materials.

Downes (2004) summarizes the educational value of blogging as reading what is of interest—culture, community, ideas—and then engaging with the content and with the blog authors through reflecting, criticizing, questioning, and reacting. A blog can also be a method for eliciting feedback and review of learning materials and professional papers. Blogs can incorporate podcasting and vodcasting to create rich media learning environments. Examples of interesting blogs can be found at Stephen Downes blog http://www.downes.ca/; Edublog http://www.edublogs.org/; and Blogger http://www.blogger.com/start.

After learning about blogs and discovering the hundreds of blogs with interesting, relevant content, learning about RSS or *Real Simple Syndication* is crucial. RSS allows blog readers to subscribe to the blogs they enjoy without having to visit the blogs to read new content. RSS uses an aggregator to collect new content from the blogs a reader enjoys. When the blog reader is ready, he or she opens the aggregator to read the new content. Bloglines.com is a popular RSS aggregator.

11.9.6 Moblogs and Photoblogs

A moblog is a combination of blog and mobile technology such as a mobile phone. Essentially a moblog refers to posting items to a blog using a mobile phone or other mobile device, using a moblog client loaded into the phone. The user then collects images, text and videos onto the phone and posts the collection to his or her blog.

A photoblog is a form of blog, which has its emphasis on the use of photographs rather than on text; however, a photoblog may include a limited amount of text. Differences between moblogs and photoblogs are largely semantic. Both are conceptually like blogs, but with a moblog, the emphasis is on updating from a mobile device. In an educational context, either could be used as part of the learning activities in the visual arts, photography, a digital storytelling exercise, or as stimulus for creating writing. They could also be used to provide sequenced and annotated photographs of particular processes involved in developing a particular skill.

11.9.7   Flickr

Flickr.com is social software, which refers to the practice of connecting people and information (Warlick, 2005). Flickr.com emphasizes photo hosting and sharing to capture daily events, vacations, community highlights, and even the features of Jane Goodall's African camp (Richardson, 2006). It is thus similar to a photoblog. Users can add notes to photographs that pop up whenever readers roll their mouse over the photographs. Users can hold discussions about the photographs and the ideas or customs they represent. To see examples of Flickr, visit http://www.flickr.com/.

11.9.8   Wikis

A wiki is Web-based social software and publishing system that enables anyone to view, contribute to, update, comment on, or edit the content of a Web page. *Wiki* comes from the Hawaiian word for 'quick,' which is a fitting descriptor as a wiki provides quick and easy Web publishing. It is a collaborative publishing system that can be used for a variety of purposes. Its users do not have to learn HTML or any Web authoring program.

Corporations use wikis to manage documents and share information with customers. In an education context, wikis can support collaborative learning activities and enable students to develop content in group situations. Instructors and students can create an online text for the course curriculum. Sternstein (2005) views the Wikipedia, probably the best known of many existing wiki applications, as a self-correcting and self-evolving encyclopedia created and updated by its community of users.

The Center for Scholarly Technology at the University of Southern California developed a wiki pedagogy (Higdon, 2006) relating wiki users and purposes. Higdon identifies users as (a) students who contribute to, comment on, revise and study wiki content; (b) instructors who assess, edit, and delete student contributions to the wiki content; (c) departments who review and syndicate content; and (d) external accreditors who review posted content. Wikis provide spaces and opportunities for such things as student journaling; the establishment of portfolios; the collaborative development of knowledge bases; collaborative writing; research coordination and collaboration; curricular and cross-disciplinary coordination; conducting conferences and colloquia; syndication/aggregation of Web resources; and inter-term project management. Interesting wikis can be found at http://www.marveldatabase. com/ (the Marvel Database Project); http://tviv.org/ (a compendium of television knowledge anyone can edit); http://www.wikihow.com/ (the wikiHow collaborative writing project to build the world's largest, highest quality how-to manual); and http:// flatclassroomproject.wikispaces.com/ (the Flat Classroom Project).

The greatest advantage of a wiki is probably also its greatest disadvantage, namely the ability for anyone to easily create, revise, and modify content. Thus, incorrect information, spam, and malicious postings pose potential problems for users and hosting institutions. Keen (2007) goes further, suggesting that wikis and other Web 2.0 technologies will bring about the end of culture as we know it.

11.9.9 Swarming (Mobbing or Meetups)

The term 'swarming' is normally used to describe animal or insect behavior, as in a swarm of bees. Today swarming is also used to conceptualize human behavior. Arquilla and Ronfeldt (2003) use the term 'swarm intelligence' to describe the idea that individually, social insects (and humans) are only minimally intelligent, and their work together is largely self-organized and unsupervised. However, collectively they are both capable of finding highly efficient solutions to difficult problems and can adapt automatically to changing environments. Arquilla and Ronfeldt refer to the development by social researchers of mathematical models to describe and study the swarming behavior. Such models are now being applied in business settings.

Bryan Alexander (2004) suggests the application of 'learning swarms' to learning environments by having students with a common interest come together quickly to experience or participate in a learning event. Mobile devices of various kinds have been used to generate swarms for political, learning, or social purposes. Rheingold (2002) has used the term 'smart mobs' to refer to the same concept.

11.9.10 Sharewood Picnic

Interesting emerging technologies appear weekly. To learn more about emerging technologies that may be used in the classroom, instructors and designers can regularly check Robin Good's *Sharewood Picnic*, a weekly basket of hand-picked technologies discovered during the previous week. Sharewood Picnic offers new Web sites, software tools, and online resources that may find their way into our students' lives and into our classrooms. Sharewood Picnic can be found at http://www.masternewmedia.org/news/ 2006/01/22/new_media_picks_of_the.htm.

As will be obvious, the emerging technologies briefly reviewed in this section are social and collaborative in nature. Students frequently use these emerging technologies outside the classroom well before they are known to their teachers. They already perceive the social affordances of these technologies, contacting peers and experts online and browsing the resources of the Web. They bring additional contacts into the classroom with the teacher no longer serving as the sole authority. Classes can thus have a network of people with a range of opinions and experiences. Whether the instructors and designers of instruction perceive any educational affordances of these emerging technologies depends upon whether they can perceive a relationship among the properties of the technologies, the characteristics of the learners, and the goals of the instruction.

Research through the years has taught us to focus beyond the technologies and onto the human and social construction as well as the broader political, social, and economic context. Instructors and designers must thus focus on how technologies and the humans support the courses and programs to ensure pedagogical quality. Bringing emerging technologies into the classroom leads to accompanying challenges. Emerging technologies are rarely part of the university's core infrastructure and many universities are often not adequately prepared to handle the network traffic resulting from the use of a new technology, as evidenced when students began Instant Messaging, downloading movies, and sharing music and videos. Emerging technologies bring increased potential for incompatibilities among all the technologies used, support issues, security threats, privacy worries, intellectual property concerns, and consumption of bandwidth. It is thus not realistic to suggest that we must necessarily adopt and use every new technology. However, we do have to observe and learn what our students are using now as that may be a forecast for the future and it influences our students' perceptions of current use of technology in the classroom.

11.10   Issues for Further Consideration

Future research is needed to test Gee's (2003), Beck and Wade's (2004), and Prensky's (2006) ideas about gaming, engaged learning experiences, and the emerging technologies (Bonk & Dennen, 2005). We need to look at games critically and determine if games fully engage Kolb's learning cycle and provide learning opportunities for all, especially for those not served by lecture and multiple-choice tests. We also need to determine if games and other technologies are helping students identify assumptions, points of view, and inferences.

Early research suggests that games and simulations are good ways to foster critical thinking skills, increase communication among participants, and increase learners' available resources for problem solving. Research has also brought problems and issues to light. First, recent research has suggested that contrary to popular belief, games are tightly rule and goal based. Players do not actually have the freedom to do whatever they want but are required to take on particular ways of thinking and acting. If that is so, we need to bring this to the learners' attention during debriefing. Second, the feedback provided to gamers is *unsupervised feedback* as opposed to *supervised feedback*. Supervised feedback is evaluative input provided by an instructor, supervisor, or another person providing external feedback to the learner. Games provide unsupervised feedback, meaning the learner provides feedback to himself or herself by intuiting or detecting information from the game with the results of his or her actions to predict how to self-assess and handle subsequent events. Third, the age-old problem of transfer from the classroom to the real world may be a dilemma for gaming. Real-worldliness generally has many more dimensions than simulations, games, and case studies, which creates a scaling up problem. The scaling up problem concerns whether the learner can scale up from playing games (or participating in any instructional strategy) to incorporate all relevant (and unprepackaged) dimensions in the real world and still perform the task (Churchland & Sejnowski, 1999). This, too, needs to be mentioned in debriefings.

Finally, Bateman and Boon (2006) write that current games are designed for hardcore gamers, those who are willing to play for long periods of time on their own, are predominantly logical and methodical, are strongly goal oriented, enjoy conflict, and tend to overachieve. Bateman and Boon (2006) categorize hardcore gamers as a Myers-Briggs Introvert, strong in Thinking, and Judging. As games are becoming increasingly more prevalent throughout our culture, Bateman and Boon (2006) hope that the attributes of the other 16 types within the Myers-Briggs typology will be incorporated into future game designs as well.

11.11   Conclusion

We do not know how games and emerging technologies influence thinking and behavior. Every new learning technology brings with it new conceptual issues that must be disentangled in order to discover its technological and pedagogical potential (Roschelle, 2004). We do not even know if games work as we are currently just at the prototype level (Thompson, 2006). We may not understand why our students like and use games and the emerging interactive technologies. We also do not have many educational examples of how games work to meet complex, significant learning challenges.

We do know shifts have been brought about by games and the emerging Internet technologies. We have not as yet developed pedagogies to accompany these new technologies. Upon what learning theory would such games be built? Who ensures the connection is made between the active learning, social connectedness, and the learner control that learners crave? Who ensures players make good use of information and experiences gained through games and reflect upon those experiences? Who ensures learners evaluate the credibility of the information they find?

Castronova (2005) concludes his book, with "we should take a serious look at the games we have begun to play" (p. 283). We, too, should take a serious, open-minded, informed look at games and the emerging technologies that surround them. For those who never played the games, they should go one step further: take the risk and play the games that have begun.

11.12   Resources for Further Exploration

The following short annotated list of five references is presented for your further exploration of the ideas presented in this chapter.

Koster, R. (2005). *A theory of fun for game design*. Scottsdale, AZ: Paraglyph Press. Koster is the former lead designer for *Star War Galaxies* and is chief creative officer at Sony Online Entertainment. First of all, let me say that Koster's book is fun to read. However, the information presented is serious. Koster discusses why some games are boring while some games are initially fun but become boring. That takes a discussion of cognitive science, what fun is, what games teach, and the nature of human interaction.

Chaplin, H. & Ruby, A. (2005). *SMARTBOMB*. New York: Workman Publishing. Chaplin and Ruby tell the story of the humans and the forces behind the videogame industry from the 1950s, including the creators of *Sim City, the Xbox, Doom, Nintendo, Star War Galaxies, Quake*, and *Grant Theft Auto*.

TechTrends Games and Learning issue (September/October, 2005), Vol. 49, No. 5. This issue provides six articles and a Guest Editor's Note by Kurt Squire related to topics such as *Evolution in the Classroom: What Teachers Need to Know about the Video Game Generation* by Elizabeth Simpson; *Women, Video Gaming & Learning: Beyond Stereotypes* by Elisabeth Hayes; *Increasing Student Engagement by Using Morrowmind to Analyze Choices and Consequences* by Maya Kadakia; *From Users to Designers: Building a Self-Organizing Game-Based Learning Environment* by Kurt Squire; *Children's Narratives Development through Computer Game Authoring* by Judy Robertson and Judith Good; and *IDT Portfolio: "Life of a Star" Museum Exhibit* by Jill Hughes.

Marc Prensky's Web site, available at www.marcprensky.com/writing.

The *Serious Games* Web site (www.seriousgamessource.com/) and *Social Impact Games* Web site (www.socialimpactgames.com) are devoted to using games as a teaching tool. Both sites hope to illustrate that games are a medium of expression of almost any idea. Check out *Peacemaker*, a video game in which players assume roles of the Israeli prime minister or the Palestinian president; *A Force More Powerful*, a game that teaches the principles of nonviolence; *Food Force*, released by the United Nations to help people understand the difficulties of dispensing aid to war zones; and *Darfur is Dying*, where players try to support their village).

11.13   Questions for Comprehension and Application

1. Despite the multiple active learning principles at work in games, will it be possible for instructional designers and instructors to offer games in their traditional, online learning, or blended classrooms any time soon? Why or why not? Will schools, colleges, and universities be the last players to bring games into the classroom? Will corporations use games for professional and staff development? Why or why not?

2. How will we begin to meet Bonk and Dennen's (2005) call for research to determine the effectiveness of games in promoting complex learning? How will we determine what kinds of knowledge learners take away from a game? How will we determine when knowledge gained is transformed into appropriate action? How would you design a rigorous research study to answer these questions?

3. Elizabeth Hayes (2005) writes that despite the growing number of games and gamers around the world, "gaming continues to be a very gendered practice" (p. 23). Most of the gamers are under 30 while our classrooms are filled by learners from 18 to 88. Will we be able to design games to enhance complex learning that will appeal to a wide variety of learners with diverse developmental and adult backgrounds? What attributes of women, older learners, and diverse Myers-Briggs personality types are currently being left unmet in games? Do game designers have an obligation to include these attributes?

4. We currently have not found unified agreement that learning should be fun and entertaining. What assumptions are we making if we believe that blending entertainment and learning will lead to complex learning? What assumptions are we making if we believe that we should not blend learning and entertainment?

5. Do games support declarative, procedural, or contextual knowledge? How so?

6. This chapter as well as the chapter by Hall (in this volume) repeat Prensky's (2001, October) claim that years of computer use develop hypertext minds and parallel cognitive structures in young gamers. Merrill (in this volume) expresses serious doubts about the same claim. Compare the chapters and cases made, draw on additional literature, consider validity of arguments or lack thereof, and make up your own mind.

References

ACT Department of Education and Training (2005). *Emerging Technologies: A Framework for Thinking*. (Final Report). Dulwich, South Australia. Retrieved March 22, 2006, from http://www.decs.act.gov.au/publicat/pdf/emergingtechnologies.pdf

Alexander, B. (2004, September/October). Going nomadic: Mobile learning in higher education. [Electronic version]. *EDUCAUSE Review, 39*(5).

Arquilla, J., & Ronfeldt, D. (2003, September 29). *Swarming - The next new major warfighting doctrine? Aviation Week & Space Technology*. Retrieved June 2, 2006, from http://www.sci.fi/~fta/swarming.htm.

Bateman, C., & Boon, R. (2006). *21st Century Game Design*. Hingham, MA: Charles River Media.

Beck, J. C., & Wade, M. (2004). *Got game: How the gamer generation is reshaping business forever*. Boston: Harvard Business School Press.

Blast Theory (n.d.). *I like Frank*. Retrieved March 22, 2006, from http://www.blasttheory. co.uk/bt/work_ilikefrank.html.

Bonk, C. J., & Dennen, V. P. (2005). *Massive multiplayer online gaming: A research framework for military training and education*. (Technical Report 2005–1). Advanced Distributed Learning Initiative Readiness and Training, Office of the Under Secretary of Defense for Personnel and Readiness. Retrieved May 5, 2006, from http://www.adlnet. gov/downloads/downloadpage.aspx?ID = 100.

Bownds, M. D. (1999). *The biology of the mind: Origins and structures of mind, brain, and consciousness.* Bethesda, MD: Fitzgerald Science Press.

Bruner, J. (1990). *Acts of meaning.* Cambridge, MA: Harvard University Press.

Castronova, E. (2005). *Synthetic worlds: The business and culture of online games.* Chicago: The University of Chicago Press.

Chaplin, H., & Ruby, A. (2005). *SMARTBOMB.* New York: Workman Publishing.

Churchland, P. S., & Sejnowski, T. J. (1999). *The computational brain.* Cambridge, MA: MIT Press.

Downes, S. (2004, September/October). Educational blogging. *EDUCAUSE Review, 39*(5), 14–26.

Driscoll, M. P. (1994). *The psychology of learning for instruction.* Boston: Allyn & Bacon.

Garrison, D. R., & Archer, W. (2000). *A transactional perspective on teaching and learning: A framework for adult and higher education.* New York: Pergamon.

Gee, J. P. (2003). *What video games have to teach us about learning and literacy.* New York: Palgrave Macmillan.

Georgiev, T., Georgieva, E., & Smrikarov, A. (2004). *M-learning: A new stage of e-learning.* Paper presented at the 2006 *International Conference on Computer Systems and Technologies.* Retrieved August 1, 2006, from http://ecet.ecs.ru.acad.bg/cst05/Docs/cp/ sIV/IV.14.pdf.

Gredler, M. E. (1996). Educational games and simulations: A technology in search of a (research) paradigm. In D. H. Jonassen (Ed.), *Handbook of research for educational communications and technology* (pp. 521–540). New York: Simon & Schuster Macmillan.

Green, S. C., & Bavelier, D. (2003). Action video game modifies visual selective attention. *Nature, 423,* 534–537.

Hall, M. (in this volume). Getting to know the feral learner. In J. Visser & M. Visser-Valfrey (Eds.), *Learners in a changing learning landscape: Reflections from a dialogue on new roles and expectations* (pp. 109–133). Dordrecht, The Netherlands: Springer.

Halliday, M. A. K. (1993). Towards a language-based theory of learning. *Linguistics and Education, 5,* 93–116.

Hartman, J., Moskal, P., & Dziuban, C. (2005). Preparing the academy of today for the learner of tomorrow. In D. G. Oblinger & J. L. Oblinger (Eds.), *Educating the net generation.* Retrieved March 3, 2006, from http://www.educause.edu/educatingthenetgen.

Hayes, E. (2005). Women, video gaming and learning: Beyond stereotypes. *TechTrends: Linking Research & Practice to Improve Learning, 49*(5), 23–28.

Herz, J. C., & Macedonia, M. R. (2002, April). Computer games and the military: Two views. *Defense Horizons, 11.* Retrieved May 3, 2004, from http://www.ndu.edu/inss/DefHor/ DH11/ DH11.htm/.

Hess, D. J. (1995). *Science & Technology in a Multicultural World.* New York: Columbia University Press.

Higdon, J. (2006). *Pedagogies of wikis.* The Center for Scholarly Technology University of Southern California. Retrieved May 1, 2006, from http://www.educause.edu/ir/library/pdf/ ELI0626.pdf.

Jochems, W., van Merriënboer, J., & Koper, R. (2004). An introduction to integrated e-learning. In W. Jochems, J. van merrienboer, & R. Koper (Eds.) *Integrated e-learning: Implications for pedagogy, technology & organization* (pp. 1–12). New York: RoutledgeFalmer.

John-Steiner, V. (1997). *Notebooks of the mind: Explorations of thinking, revised edition.* New York: Oxford University Press.

Jones, S. (2003). *Let the games begin: Gaming technology and entertainment among college students.* Washington, DC: Pew Internet & American Life Project.

Keen, A. (2007). *The cult of the amateur.* New York: Doubleday.

Kirriemuir, J. (2002, February). Video gaming, education and digital learning technologies. *D-Lib, 8*(2). Retrieved April 10, 2006, from http://www.dlib.org/dlib/february02/ kirriemuir/ 02kirriemuir.html.

Kolb, D. A. (1984). *Experiential learning: Experience as the source of learning and development.* Englewood Cliffs, NJ: Prentice-Hall.

Koster, R. (2005). *A theory of fun for game design.* Scottsdale, AZ: Paraglyph Press.

Levi-Strauss, C. (1968). *The savage mind (nature of human society)*. Chicago: University of Chicago Press.

Meighan, R. (1996). The implications of home-based education effectiveness research for open schooling. In T. Evans & D. Nation, (Eds.) *Opening education: Policies and practices from open and distance education* (pp. 48–62). New York: Routledge.

Merrill, M. D. (in this volume). Why basic principles of instruction must be present in the learning landscape, whatever form it takes, for learning to be effective, efficient and engaging. In J. Visser & M. Visser-Valfrey (Eds.), *Learners in a changing learning landscape: Reflections from a dialogue on new roles and expectations* (pp. 267–275). Dordrecht, The Netherlands: Springer.

National Research Council (2004). *Engaging schools: Fostering high school students' motivation to learn*. Washington, DC: National Academy Press. Retrieved April 10, 2006, from http://www.nap.edu/catalog/10421.html.

Nisbett, R. E. (2003). *The geography of thought: How Asians and Westerners think differently ... and why*. New York: Simon & Schuster.

Prensky, M. (2001, October). Digital natives, digital immigrants, Part I. *On the Horizon, 9*(5). Retrieved July 4, 2006, from http://www.marcprensky.com/writing/.

Prensky, M. (2006). *Don't bother me, mom—I'm learning*. St. Paul, MN: Paragon House.

Quinn, C. N. (2005). *Engaging learning*. San Francisco: Pfeiffer.

Ramaley, J., & Zia, L. (2005). The real versus the possible: Closing the gaps in engagement and learning. In D. G. Oblinger & J. L. Oblinger (Eds.), *Educating the net generation*. Retrieved March 3, 2006, from http://www.educause.edu/educatingthenetgen/.

Rawe, J. (2006, July 3). How safe is MySpace? *Time, 168*, 35–36.

Rheingold, H. (2002). *Smart mobs: The next social revolution*. Cambridge, MA: Perseus Books Group.

Richardson, W. (2006). *Blogs, wikis, podcasts, and other powerful web tools for classrooms*. Thousand Oaks, CA: Corwin Press.

Roschelle, J. (2004). Keynote paper: Unlocking the learning value of wireless mobile devices. *Journal of Computer Assisted Learning, 19*, 26–272.

Rushkoff, D. (1996). *Playing the future: How kids' culture can teach us to thrive in an age of chaos*. New York: HarperCollins.

Salomon, G. (1977). A cognitive approach to media. In J. Ackerman & L. Lipsitz (Eds.), *Instructional television: Status & directions* (pp. 99–120). Englewood Cliffs, NJ: Educational Technology Publications.

Schiesel, S. (2006, May 7). Welcome to the new dollhouse. *The New York Times, Arts & Leisure, 1*, 10.

Simpson, E. S. (2005). What teachers need to know about the video game generation. *Tech Trends, 49*(5), 17–22.

Snider, M. (2002, May 23). Where movies end, games begin. *USA Today*. Retrieved May 14, 2002, from http://www.usatoday.com/tech/techreviews/2002/5/23/e3.htm.

Steinkuehler, C. A. (2003). *Massively multiplayer online videogames as a constellation of literacy practices*. Paper presented at the International Conference on Literacy, Ghent, Belgium. Retrieved May 13, 2006, from http://website.education.wisc.edu/steinkuehler/.

Sternstein, A. (2005, April 4). Wiki means fast: Online collaborative sites open to everyone enable the sharing of ideas. *Federal computer week*. Retrieved May 1, 2006, from http://www.fcw.com/article88467-04-04-05-Print.

Tapscott, D. (1998). *Growing up digital: The rise of the net generation*. San Francisco: McGraw-Hill.

Taylor, T. L. (2006). *Play between the worlds: Exploring online game culture*. Cambridge, MA: MIT Press.

Thompson, C. (2006, July 23). Saving the world, one video game at a time. *The New York Times, 1*, 28.

Vaknin, S. (2002, February 2). TrendSiters: Games people play. *Electronic Book Web*. Retrieved May 13, 2004, from http://12.108.175.91/ebookweb/discuss/msgReader$1405.

Vygotsky, L. (2000). The problem and the approach. In A. Kozulin (Ed.). *Thought and language* (pp. 1–11). Cambridge, MA: MIT Press.

Warlick, D. F. (2005). *Raw materials for the mind: Information, technology, and teaching & learning in the twenty-first century* (4th ed.). Raleigh, NC: The Landmark Project.

Wells, G., & Claxton, G. (2002). Introduction: Sociocultural perspectives on the future of education. In G. Wells & G. Claxton (Eds.), *Learning for life in the 21st century* (pp. 1–18). Malden, MA: Blackwell.

Williams, A. (2006, July 16). The graying of the record store. *The New York Times*, Section 9, 1, 8.

Zull, J. E. (2002). *The art of changing the brain: Exploring the practice of teaching by exploring the biology of learning*. Sterling, VA: Stylus Publishing, LLC.

Zurita, G., & Nussbaum, M. (2004). A constructivist mobile learning environment supported by a wireless handheld environment. *Journal of Computer Assisted Learning, 20*, 235–243.

Chapter 12
What Makes Good Online Instruction Good?:
New Opportunities and Old Barriers

J. Michael Spector

Abstract This book is about changes in learning and instruction and implications for learners, teachers, designers and policy makers. Many of the relevant changes are related to new technologies and developing views of how, when, where and why people manage to learn different kinds of things more or less effectively. This chapter focuses on distance learning technologies and questions pertaining to the evaluation of a particular kind of distance learning—online instruction. Criteria that appear relevant to assessing effectiveness are presented and discussed. Arguments for and against online instruction being held to different quality standards are presented. The chapter concludes with remarks about the personalities of online learning groups and how these might affect learning outcomes.

12.1 Introduction and Initial Questions

I recall my father characterizing a teacher as the ear that listens, the eye that reflects, the voice that encourages, the hand that guides, the face that does not turn away.[1] While others may characterize teachers differently, many educators with whom I have shared this characterization agree that they find themselves engaged in these activities (listening, reflecting, encouraging, guiding, supporting) in spite of differences in content and context. Educators want to help others, and these activities often seem relevant to helping. The others to be helped are their students, who are variously engaged in activities aimed at understanding events and phenomena. One might then characterize students as generally trying to change themselves in one way or another. For example, a student may be trying to understand how fossils of apparently non-existent creatures came to be embedded in rocks in the Burgess Shale (Gould, 1989), while another student may be trying to understand how large

---

Learning Systems Institute, Florida State University

[1] My father was a Rabbi and he made this comment with regard to Rabbis, whom he regarded as teachers first and foremost. Instead of 'encourages' he used the word 'comforts'.

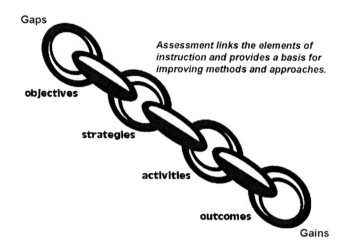

Fig. 12.1 Assessment and the instructional chain

and far away a star barely visible in the night sky would have to be in order to appear as a small spot of light from earth (Sagan, 1980). Students are trying to change themselves—to improve their understanding or performance in some way or other. Teachers try to help them achieve their goals. In this sense, educators want to help students change. Educators are agents of change, as are students.

Just as students engaged in various programs of study generally want to succeed in making the desired changes in their understanding (knowledge, skills and attitudes), so do their teachers, tutors, trainers and other educators who become involved with such efforts. People generally like to succeed—this is not a surprise. In order to establish that one has succeeded or to know to what extent various decisions and efforts have been worthwhile, it helps to have measures and indicators of success. Moreover, if an educator wishes to systematically improve a course or instructional sequence, it helps to have measures and indicators that provide conceptual and causal linkages from current states of understanding (with gaps and deficiencies identified), to goals and objectives, to instructional plans and designed activities, to actual activities and student performances, and finally to individual and aggregated outcomes (Fig. 12.1). In this important sense, the assessment of individual learning and performance informs the evaluation of a course or program of study. Measuring individual changes (hopefully these will be gains) in knowledge, skills and attitudes is an essential aspect of determining the effectiveness of a program of study.

12.1.1 What Makes a Course Good?

What makes a good or successful course good or successful? Given an answer to that question, what role do the knowledge, skills and attitudes of learners play in success? Which knowledge, skills, and attitudes are particularly critical to the success of individual learners and the effectiveness of the course? In other words, how do individual learners know they are improving, and how do instructors know a course has been successful? These are obvious questions that students, instructors and administrators often ask. The answers are less than obvious, however.

In *Choruses from the Rock*, T. S. Eliot (1934) says that "the good man is the builder if he builds what is good" (see http://en.wikiquote.org/wiki/ T._S._Eliot #Choruses_from_The_Rock_.281934.29). One could likewise say that a course is good if the outcomes are good. Good outcomes appear to be a critical measure of success, at the individual level of learner assessment and aggregated at the course level for purposes of program or course evaluation. Good outcomes would seem to involve making desired gains against identified gaps in knowledge, attitudes and levels of performance. However, it is probably the rare course that begins with a pre-test to identify those gaps. Moreover, it is probably the rare course that ends with a post-test aimed again at those initial gaps. In short, whereas change is an essential aspect of learning, it seems that few courses are designed to measure relevant changes. Typically, measures of knowledge and performance on particular items comprise end-of-course assessments that are not related to gaps or gains. The first challenge, then, is to determine what gains in knowledge and performance made by students can be attributed to a course. Without knowing the gaps that existed initially, this is difficult to determine. Still, students, teachers and administrators appear to be more or less satisfied with end-of-course assessments—'this is where this student is now' and 'most students who complete this course know these things and can perform these tasks.' While such end-of-course assessments might satisfy some of those involved, there is insufficient basis to determine which aspects (if any) of the course or the teacher or the student contributed to the measured levels of knowledge and performance.

Students may additionally be asked about their experiences via simple one-dimensional scales, which all too often contain items that have not been tested for reliability or validity and rarely contain information about students (Abrami, Apollonia, & Cohen, 1990). The hope is that these simple course/teacher satisfaction ratings will give some indication with regard to things about the course or the teacher that may have facilitated or inhibited gains in knowledge and performance. For a variety of reasons, however, teacher and course evaluations by students provide very little substantial evidence upon which one can base conclusions with regard to aspects of a course or a teacher or a student that contributed to or inhibited improvements in learning and performance (Marsh, 1987; Wilson, 1998). There may be value in these student evaluations, in that responses to open-ended questions often give teachers meaningful feedback about things that might be improved (Scriven, 1995). However, due to problems of validity and reliability, and the lack of pre-course measures, student evaluations have serious deficiencies as instruments upon which to decide if a course was successful in achieving intended objectives.

It would seem likely that course experiences that teachers and students would deem to be good often result when there is a critical mass of learners with some relevant knowledge, skills and attitudes, with positive attitudes being especially important (Boone & Butler Kahle, 1998; Chen & Hoshower, 2003; Filak & Sheldon, 2003). If so, it would be critical to gather attitudinal and motivational data at the beginning of a course and take these measures into account when evaluating the course. This is rarely done. However, some researchers take career preference as an indication of a relevant attitude, and changes in these preferences can and have been measured and used as indicators of a successful course (Yager & Yager, 1985).

An interesting case along these lines occurred at the United States Air Force Academy in the 1980s and 1990s [this summary is based on personal knowledge of the situation]. Most entering cadets would indicate a preference for aeronautical engineering as a major. After the first course in aeronautical engineering, which was taught in a very traditional manner, many cadets would change their major to something else. The course was re-designed to be highly experiential with the support of sophisticated interactive simulations. Data on a standard final exam for the course for nearly 30 years was examined to see whether knowledge and performance changes (as measured on the final exam) existed. While the course redesign was radical and extensive, there were virtually no changes in final exam scores. What did change significantly was the number of cadets who changed their major to something other than aeronautical engineering—fewer cadets changed their majors to something else after taking the re-designed course. This course redesign effort was a success, especially in terms of the objective to have cadets major in aeronautical engineering, in spite of lack of evidence with regard to improved knowledge and performance.

One conclusion to be drawn from this case is that a course need not be better than one it is replacing in terms of knowledge and performance outcomes in order to be regarded as successful. A second conclusion that is worth noting is that sustaining interest in an area is perhaps a worthwhile goal and this can be easily measured—much more easily measured than knowledge and performance in areas of substantial complexity, such as aeronautical engineering.

What makes a good course good? As difficult as this question is to answer, it deserves a response of some kind. A good course is one that sustains interest and promotes understanding. This conclusion is not surprising when one considers that one of the most reliable predictors of performance is time spent mastering a task (Ericsson, 2004; Slavin, 1998). Admitting to not knowing something that one wants to know (*humility*) and believing that one can learn if some effort is expended (*optimism*) appear critical to success. In other words, determining relevant levels of humility and optimism (readiness and willingness to invest time and effort to learn) on the part of learners before and after a course appear highly relevant to the determination of how good the course has been. Of course one also wants to see gains in knowledge and performance. A good course is one that promotes understanding, as indicated by measures of knowledge and performance, and that sustains interest, as indicated by preferences and subsequent actions on the part of students.

12.1.2 Do Online Courses Differ from Face-to-Face Courses?

What might be different in answering what makes a good course good with regard to face-to-face and online courses? Nothing mentioned thus far has been specific to the setting in which learning and instruction take place, although the successful re-design of the aeronautical engineering course discussed in the previous section moved much of the instruction from a lecture-based, classroom setting to an interactive computer laboratory-based, small group setting. This point is worth emphasizing—good courses are those that promote understanding and sustain interest, regardless of setting. This may seem obvious, but the consequences of accepting this conclusion are perhaps radical.

Let us reconsider the aeronautical engineering case described earlier. The learning outcomes as measured on the final exam were no better for the re-designed course than for the traditional lecture course, yet there were measurable differences in attitudes and preferences. Suppose the re-designed course had been offered entirely online. For the purposes of this discussion, an online course is one that is offered through the World Wide Web with no face-to-face meetings of any kind. While what will be argued here can be applied to blended courses, the discussion will proceed more easily if the focus remains on online courses as compared with face-to-face courses. Many online courses exist. An online version of the traditional aeronautical engineering course might have been just as successful as the simulation-based laboratory version of the course, using the same set of metrics (final exam scores, attrition data, changes in course major). In principle, at least, one can imagine this outcome. Yet there would perhaps be more resistance to accepting an online version of aeronautical engineering than the lecture or laboratory versions of that course. Is this true, and, if so, why?

Online courses are often held to different standards than face-to-face courses (Spector, Doughty, & Yonai, 2003). Courses taught in different settings and formats might well have different standards appropriate to certain aspects of the course. For example, accessibility in face-to-face courses might involve things like parking and ramps for wheelchairs, whereas in online courses accessibility might involve things like Internet connections and screen readers for the vision impaired. However, when one considers learning outcomes or improvements in performance and understanding, differences in standards are difficult to defend, although many expect more in terms of improved learning from an online course than a face-to-face course (Spector et al., 2003). Having said this, is there evidence to support a bias for or against online courses? A recent meta-analysis (Bernard et al., 2004) suggests that there is a great deal of variability in terms of both achievement and attitudes with regard to online courses, just as there is with regard to face-to-face courses.

Evidence of a negative bias towards online courses can be found in beliefs with regard to attrition. Many believe that online courses have much higher drop-out rates than do their face-to-face counterparts (Storrings, 2005). However, when one looks at the attrition data for online courses (attrition includes those who withdrew after the add-drop deadline for courses and was not consistent across universities, although it was the same deadline for online and face-to-face courses), one again finds no significant differences and the same kinds of variability that one finds in face-to-face courses (Spector et al., 2003; Storrings, 2005).

The somewhat radical conclusion that can be drawn is that academic standards for online courses need not be set excessively high. Many face-to-face courses, especially large lecture courses, do not show evidence of improved understanding and often fail to sustain student interest. It does not take all that much to outperform large lecture courses on many of the standard metrics, and the time flexibility offered by online courses is attractive for many students (Spector et al., 2003). Of course online teachers would like to do better (as would classroom teachers), but doing as well as classroom teachers in terms of academic achievement ought to be good enough, since other benefits of online instruction may exist.

Caveat discipulus—let the student beware. The applicable advice with regard to student expectations about a course is that the student should expect to spend more time reading and be willing to be responsible for keeping up with assignments and activities (Spector, 2005; Spector et al., 2003). When students have realistic expectations, they are less likely to become discouraged (Boekarts, Pintrich, & Zeidner, 2000; Storrings, 2005).

Students who have choices with regard to courses and instructors often ask other students about their experiences in those courses or with those instructors. Indeed, online databases of professor ratings are widely used by college undergraduates (see http://www.ratingsonline.com/index.phtml and http://www.ratemyprofessors. com/index.jsp for example). What may not be easily extracted from such sources is how familiar and fluent online teachers are with the details of an online learning environment or with various techniques for conducting engaging online activities (e.g., facilitating online discussions). Online environments require teachers to develop specific competencies (Klein, Spector, Grabowski, & De la Teja, 2004; Spector & De la Teja, 2001). The good news in this regard is that many universities recognize that specific competencies are required for effective online instruction and are developing courses, workshops and seminars to help teachers develop those competencies. The bad news is that, by comparison, not much is being done to improve face-to-face teaching (Spector, 2000).

Are online courses different from face-to-face courses? Yes, many differences exist, particularly with regard to the specific knowledge, skills and expectations that teachers and students ought to have in order to succeed. Given that standards for judging the success of online courses ought to be comparable to those used to judge the success of face-to-face courses, along with the fact that more emphasis is being placed on preparing and supporting online teachers, one might expect online teaching and learning to reap huge benefits.

It is worth noting that preparation of online teachers is very uneven across higher education institutions (these remarks are based on personal experience rather than published research). For example, universities that primarily deliver courses online generally take teacher preparation very seriously. Télé-université, the distance learning part of the University of Québec, requires online teachers to complete several rigorous training courses involving the design of online instruction as well as online facilitation and course management. Similar online teacher preparation is required by Capella University, Jones International University, Nova Southeastern University, the University of Phoenix, Open Universities in Europe, and other prominent online universities. In contrast with extensive teacher preparation at prominent online institutions, the training and preparation for online instructors provided by universities which engage primarily in residential education is generally less rigorous and in many cases non-existent. Other obstacles to systemic improvement in online teaching remain and will be addressed after a few remarks exploring the notion of course personalities.

12.1.3 Do Online Courses Develop Personalities?

Many people have claimed that face-to-face classroom groups develop identifiable behavioral patterns (*personalities*) and, further, that these might affect which instructional strategies and activities are likely to be successful (see Fredricks, Blumenfeld, & Paris, 2004, for a general discussion of school engagement). Is this also true with regard to online courses?

Facilitation skills are difficult to master for many instructors (Klein et al., 2004; Lowman, 1995). There is much variability in facilitating discussions due to class size, subject area, expected learner outcomes, learner prerequisites, and so on (Hadfield, 1992; Johnson & Johnson, 1991). Many teachers say that they also have to make adjustments in face-to-face settings due to the overall classroom dynamics and the behavior of certain individuals (e.g., those who tend to speak out on every topic as well as those who avoid speaking at all costs). These challenges and situations also exist in online settings with different groups exhibiting quite different dynamics (Ganesan, 2004). For example, facilitating synchronous chat sessions is quite different from facilitating asynchronous discussion threads. Differences include the grouping of students and the rules of engagement, among other things.

As claimed earlier, it seems to be the case that having a critical mass of students with relevant knowledge and positive attitudes contributes much to the success of a course. Teachers cannot typically control who signs up for a course, so it is difficult to guarantee that a core group of students with requisite knowledge and with both humility and optimism (readiness and willingness to learn) will exist to create the dynamics of a successful course—online or otherwise. What is a teacher to do, then?

One possible strategy is to treat a class—a group of students—as if they represented a single, intelligent organism with the desired characteristics and personality that seem to contribute to effective learning. That is to say that it may well make good sense to talk about classroom personalities and attitudes just as we talk about individual attitudes and personalities. Moreover, just as we can imagine doing things to an individual to encourage an attitude of optimistic humility and develop inquisitive and open personalities, we might imagine doing things to groups to encourage a classroom to become a community of inquiry. While this sounds idealistic and lofty, it may be practiced in the form of enlightened behavioral reinforcement, even in online settings. For example, an online class, considered collectively, may appear overly reticent in discussion threads or reluctant to explore alternative explanations or unwilling to invest time and effort in offline activities. One *trick* that has worked for one teacher is to introduce cartoons each week that appear relevant to the topic being discussed. The cartoons may appear less threatening than scholarly articles but provide a point of entry into a key idea in the assigned reading. Another trick that has worked for a teacher in a similar situation is to create an imaginary student, add that student to the course, and then log-in as that student and participate in discussions as another student. The teacher would then later log-in as the teacher and engage the imaginary student in discussion and perhaps raise specific questions about the imaginary student's remarks to encourage others to respond. This particular tactic may raise some ethical concerns with regard to intentional misrepresentation, but that teacher did eventually reveal to the students the purpose of this unusual form of online facilitation.

Do online courses develop personalities? It seems that online teachers talk and behave as if they do (Ganesan, 2004). Moreover, talking and behaving as if online courses have personalities is one way that online teachers can reflect on specific strategies and consider alternative approaches. A teacher might well adopt the point of view that each class represents an experiment in a sustained effort to discover an effective method to facilitate learning. On a small scale, this is likely the case with regard, for example, to setting up chat sessions. The first time around, an instructor may discover that a chat session with 20 students is not feasible and gets out of control very quickly. Such an experience might be considered an experiment. The results of the experiment suggest that chat sessions should not be designed to engage so many people simultaneously. A subsequent experiment might cut the size in half to see how that affects the quality of the session. Training online teachers might be designed to allow such experiments to be carried out prior to having the teacher meet the first online course. Of course one can simply tell teachers that chat groups should be small, but experiencing the consequences of unwieldy chat groups is likely to provide a longer lasting and more meaningful learning experience for teachers.

12.2   Barriers to Success

My three questions aimed at answering what makes a good online course good (Learning Development Institute, 2005) arose as a result of my involvement with the International Board of Standards for Training, Performance, and Instruction (*ibstpi*; see http://www.ibstpi.org). My efforts with the Board in the last nine years have been concerned with competencies for instructional designers, especially those designing technology intensive learning environments, and more recently with competencies for online instructors and learners. These three questions also arose in conjunction with online graduate courses and programs in instructional design and technology at Syracuse University and at Florida State University.

The opportunity to work with *ibstpi* colleagues in identifying relevant knowledge, skills, attitudes and values that pertain to online learning and instruction has been enriching (Klein et al., 2004; Richey et al., 2001). We examined research, talked with many experienced practitioners, conducted interviews and surveys, and shared our knowledge and experiences. I worked with a doctoral student who conducted a qualitative investigation of the practices, perceptions, and approaches of highly experienced online teachers (Ganesan, 2004). I worked with another doctoral student on issues pertaining to attrition in online courses (Storrings, 2005). We investigated; we discussed; we published papers and books—the stuff on which academics thrive.

My experience with regard to university programs, however, has been quite different. The faculty involved with developing and implementing online courses and programs have generally been enthusiastic and very knowledgeable. However, there was noticeable resistance from faculty and administrators not involved with online learning and instruction—especially in departments that did not make use of online learning in any of its many forms. Skepticism is fine; entrenched and dogmatic resistance is downright discouraging, especially from highly educated colleagues and administrators.

In addition to the skepticism from those not involved with online learning and instruction, there are several institutional barriers to success that are worth mentioning (Spector et al., 2003). One barrier involves the treatment of junior faculty at colleges and universities. Because online instruction involves relatively recent technologies, it is not surprising to find younger, untenured faculty more inclined to explore online teaching than more senior faculty who have grown quite accustomed to classroom lectures and their arsenal of overhead transparencies and PowerPoint® slides. However, it is now reasonably well documented that online teaching requires more time than teaching in the classroom—as much as twice the time commitment is commonly required to lead an online class, and this extra time does not include the course development time and is reported by those who have taught the online course several times previously (Ganesan, 2004; Spector, 2005). Having established that the extra time is not a consequence of a new course design, one might wonder why more time is required. Just as students report spending more time reading all of the comments posted by various class members, so do online instructors (Spector et al., 2003). Moreover, online teachers generally take time to respond to the various comments, sometimes individually and sometimes to the entire class. In terms of time, this is far less efficient than responding in person in a classroom setting. Teaching online will take time away from scholarly writing, which is typically the most significant factor in deciding upon tenure for junior faculty at many universities. In short, those most interested and qualified to teach online, may suffer with regard to chances for promotion and tenure.

In spite of the fact that online teaching places significant time burdens on teachers, many institutions do not offer additional compensation and few provide recognition for the extra time required to teach online. Worse yet, some institutions, only allow faculty to teach online as an overload course reimbursed at an adjunct rate of pay rather than in place of a face-to-face lecture course or at their normal rate of pay.

Such policies strongly suggest that universities do not regard online teaching to require much time or special expertise, in spite of overwhelming evidence to the contrary.

Still, many faculty members interested in using technology to improve their teaching and reach students whom they would not otherwise reach agree to teach online. For those faculty not at major research universities, one might then argue that teaching rather than publishing is the primary determinant in promotion and tenure. Even when this is true there are barriers. Typically committees are established to observe and evaluate teaching. Often those simple-minded student evaluations discussed earlier play a role in evaluating online teachers, just as they are often used to evaluate classroom teachers. At least that much is comparably bad for both face-to-face and online teachers. When it comes to observing the teaching, however, many committees simply do not know how to go about observing a teacher in an online course. Many professors have never taken an online course, so they have no idea about what the experience ought to be like. They are not even sure what kinds of questions they might ask students.

Few institutions have guidelines for evaluating online teaching, although these are slowly being developed. An interesting ethical issue concerns the physical observation by an evaluation committee of a course. In a classroom setting, the presence of outsiders is immediately obvious and often the purpose of the outsiders is made known to the class. The analogous situation is difficult to implement online. It may violate university policy to allow outsiders into an online classroom without prior notification to students. Moreover, it would seem fair to create relatively analogous situations to classroom evaluations, since faculty who teach in both environments are typically reviewed for tenure and promotion. If the presence and purpose of observers were known in one case and not in another, it would not seem that an equitable basis for comparison had been established.

Additionally, few online teachers know how to help an evaluation committee evaluate their online instruction. It is not only threaded discussions that might deserve examination. There are typically numerous email exchanges and often other forms of teacher-student communication to be considered.

The barriers that exist with regard to fairly compensating and evaluating online teachers are compounded by unusually restrictive hurdles created for implementing online courses. Again this is the notion that online courses are being held to completely different standards than face-to-face courses. One version of this institutional barrier comes in the form of a requirement for a unit wishing to offer an online version of a course to submit a completely new course description and justification to be approved by the entire faculty senate and perhaps other units on campus. Such a procedure assumes that the approving bodies have the relevant expertise to assess descriptions of online courses and introduces a significant delay in the process. Perhaps these extra hurdles and delays are not so bad, since it is generally not especially effective to create page-turning versions of lecture-based courses. Well, such online courses may not be any better than their lecture-based counterparts, but they are rarely worse in terms of learning outcomes (i.e., when the so-called *ceiling effect* falls through the floor with all groups achieving very little, if anything, in terms of persistent knowledge or performance gains). Still, one might like to see procedures and policies that encouraged the development of good online courses, but that requires taking the assessment and evaluation issues quite seriously, which few institutions do.

What would it be like to remove some or all of these barriers to progress at traditional universities attempting to introduce more technology, more online instruction and more blended learning into their course offerings? I am not certain. I doubt that it is possible or feasible to change university practice overnight. Establishing additional procedures and bureaucracy to manage change processes is not likely to have the desired outcome of fostering innovation and improving quality. What, then, can be realistically done? A university could hire progressive university leaders. Another thing a university could do is to encourage faculty to experiment with various technologies, including online teaching. After all, one often learns by experimenting and especially by failing (Schank & Fano, 1995).

12.3 Assessing Effectiveness

In order to decide what makes a good online course good, one must take assessment and evaluation seriously. What does that mean? Recalling the instructional chain in Fig. 12.1, it means that one makes an effort to identify gaps in knowledge, performance and attitudes. Presumably this requires the development and validation of various instruments, perhaps including interviews with those who have mastered the knowledge and skills covered in the course as well as tests that reliably indicate relative levels of expertise. When the knowledge domain is complex and involves many interrelated components with nonlinear and delayed effects (e.g., aeronautical engineering), multiple approaches to solving problems are likely as are multiple acceptable solutions. This of course makes assessing what has been learned more difficult, although not impossible (Spector & Koszalka, 2004).

Regardless of the difficulties involved in assessing progress and improvements in learning, there seems to be value in making a serious attempt to do so. I have called this attempt the WYMIWYG (*What You Measure Is What You Get*) principle previously (Spector, 2001). The logic is both traditional and simple. As a student or as a teacher, you do not know really what you have achieved until you make and take relevant measurements. Of particular relevance are measures taken before and after an instructional sequence so as to examine the possible effects of that sequence. Given the earlier emphasis on both promoting understanding and sustaining interest, measures should include not only knowledge and performance items but also attitudinal items. Moreover, what students actually decide to do once they complete their course is worth considering. Perhaps they will take another online course; perhaps not. Perhaps they will change their majors; perhaps not. Perhaps they will themselves become online tutors; perhaps not. It is, after all, what people do that genuinely makes a difference, and it is also that which tells us that a difference has been made. What someone might say in response to a course evaluation survey given on the last day of class may not be as indicative of what that person truly believes as what that person does once the course has ended. What online teachers do should make a measurable difference.

12.4 Concluding Remarks

The thread running through my comments is that online courses have many significant things in common with face-to-face courses. As researchers, we have tended to focus more on the differences. The thread of similarity discussed herein has perhaps developed as a practical way to respond to those who regard online teaching as an alien ritual performed by people wearing masks whispering in the dark. There is a complementary thread that pertains to quality. Like many others, I would like to do what I do well—at least every now and again. Satisfying that occasional desire for quality requires understanding what is likely to contribute to quality—not only from my perspective but from the perspective of students and those who may employ or work with my students afterwards.

The latter question is really a question of conscience. Stated simply, it comes to this: What good will come from what I am now doing and will likely do tomorrow? After tripping over this question while wondering about in academic darkness, I have come to this conclusion: I do not know. Not only do I not know what good will come from what I am doing, I do not know in general what will result from what I am doing.

In Plato's *Protagoras*, Socrates and Protagoras discuss the nature of virtue. Socrates proposes and apparently convinces Protagoras that if one knows what the right thing to do is in a particular situation, then one is compelled to do it; failure to do what is right implies ignorance. This claim is interesting and somewhat paradoxical in its own right, but my concern here is somewhat different. For Socrates, the indication of understanding virtue (goodness) was based entirely on action or performance. Socrates perhaps introduced the first performance-based criterion for understanding. There is also the implication that there may be a difference between what one says and what one does. Saying the right thing, at least in the cases Socrates considered (most of which involved values and virtue), is not a sufficient indication of understanding; one must also do what is right. In the words of O. K. Bouwsma (1975), "surely your life will show what you think of yourself."

Issues pertaining to the nature of values and virtue are involved in deciding what makes a good online course good. I have suggested the general principle that performance is a reliable indication of knowledge in many complex domains. In order to determine how good any intentional learning situation is, online or otherwise, one might examine performance on representative problems in that domain. Performance is not the only indicator of learning. Learning is a process that occurs over time. Evidence suggests that sustained periods of focused and reflective practice result in improved performance. This would imply that another indication that learning is occurring might be commitment or motivation to continue. While the first measure might be characterized as the hitting-the-target measure, the latter measure might be characterized as the stickiness (*stick-to-it*) measure. Learning is a sticky business—a stick-to-it enterprise, that is.

12.5 Resources for Further Exploration

I recommend the following books and online resources for further exploration regarding the issues discussed in this chapter.

12.5.1 Books

Bransford, J. D., Brown, A. L., & Cocking, R. R. (Eds.) (1999). How people learn: Brain, mind experience and school. Washington, DC: National Academy Press.

Dewey (1938). Experience and education. New York: Touchstone Books.

Dörner, D. (1996). The logic of failure: Why things go wrong and what we can do to make them right. (R. & R. Kimber, Trans.). New York: Metropolitan Books.

Robbins, J. (Ed.) (1999). The pleasure of finding things out: The best short works of Richard P. Feynman. Cambridge, MA: Perseus Books.

Moore, J. (Ed.) (2005). Elements of quality online education: Engaging communities – Wisdom from the Sloan Consortium. Needham, MA: The Sloan-C.

Norman, D. A. (1993). Things that make us smart: Defending human attributes in the age of the machine. Cambridge, MA: Perseus Books.

Spector, J. M., Ohrazda, C., Van Schaack, A., & Wiley, D. A. (Eds.) (2005). Innovations in instructional technology: Essays in honor of M. David Merrill. Mahwah, NJ: Lawrence Erlbaum.

12.5.2 Online Resources

The International Board of Standards for Training, Performance and Instruction—standards and competencies for evaluators, designers, instructors, and training managers: http://www.ibstpi.org.

MERLOT—Multimedia Educational Resources for Learning and Online Teaching: http://www.merlot.org/Home.po.

NEA (the National Education Association in the USA) Online Teaching and Learning Resources: http://www2.nea.org/he/abouthe/techip.html.

The Sloan Consortium—Faculty Satisfaction—institutional rewards: http://www. sloan-c.org/effective/details4.asp?FS_ID = 41.

University of Texas at Austin, Division of Instructional Innovation and Assessment—Instructional Technologies—evaluating online learning: http://www.utexas.edu/ academic/cit/services/courseware/resources/evallearning.html.

12.6 Questions for Comprehension and Application

1. Should faculty who lead online courses receive special recognition or compensation for doing so? While it may appear that the argument in this chapter appears to support an affirmative response, there are many aspects to consider in exploring this question. Treating any group of faculty differently from another has likely consequences. Feelings of superiority or inferiority can interfere with the quality of an educational organization. Moreover, the issue of blended learning environments was not addressed in this chapter. Blended environments that integrate aspects of both face-to-face and online teaching are becoming more and more common. Finally, technology and learning systems are evolving. Traditional distinctions—such as working vs. learning, face-to-face vs. online learning, gathering lessons learned vs. conducting educational research—are likely to become further blurred.

2. How should an online teacher be evaluated? Perhaps special recognition or compensation for online teachers is a complicated issue. Nonetheless, it is reasonable to ask whether an online teacher is performing to expectations. What criteria and measures seem appropriate specifically for online teachers? Do these criteria and measures have identifiable counterparts in evaluation procedures for face-to-face teachers? Are there criteria and measures used in evaluating face-to-face teachers that do not have conceivable counterparts in the evaluation of online teachers?

3. Should leading an online course require more time than leading a face-to-face course? While there is substantial evidence to suggest that leading an online course may require more time on the part of an instructor than leading a face-to-face course, could this be a result of those leading the course not making effective use of technology? Could it be a result of learning to use the technology rather than a result of leading a course in a different format? Should instructors and administrators expect economies of scale with regard to online teaching that are only now beginning to appear due to the novelty of the technologies involved?

4. What kinds of special training are appropriate to prepare teachers for online environments? Given the notion that online environments present different opportunities and challenges for learning and instruction, what steps might an institution take to ensure responsible and responsive online teaching? Would special teacher training be part of such an institutional policy or approach to online teaching? If so, what might such training be like? Would it include a blend of pedagogical and technological issues? Why might a college or university require special training in pedagogy for online teachers while requiring none for their face-to-face counterparts?

5. What kinds of special training are appropriate to prepare students for online environments? Should students be offered special training or support to help them succeed in online courses? Is such support available for students in face-to-face courses? If not, should it be? What kind of specialized training might

students require in order to be successful in an online course? How might institutions change to make it possible to provide more effective online teaching and learning?

References

Abrami, R. C., Apollonia, S., & Cohen, P. A. (1990). Validity of student ratings of instruction: What we know and what we do not. *Journal of Educational Psychology, 82*(2), 219–231.

Bernard, R. M., Abrami, P. C., Lou, Y., Borokhovski, E., Wade, A., Wozney, L., Wallet, P. A., Fiset, M., & Huang, B. (2004). How does distance education compare with classroom instruction? A meta-analysis of empirical literature. *Review of Educational Research, 74*(3), 379–439.

Boekarts, M., Pintrich, P. R., & Zeidner, M. (Eds.) (2000). *Handbook of self-regulation: Theory, research and applications.* San Diego, CA: Academic.

Boone, W., & Butler Kahle, J. (1998). Student perceptions of instruction, peer interest, and adult support for middle school science: Differences by race and gender. *Journal of Women and Minorities in Science and Engineering, 4*, 333–340.

Bouwsma, O. K. (1975). *Unpublished seminar notes.* Austin, TX: University of Texas.

Chen, Y., & Hoshower, L. B. (2003). Student evaluation of teaching effectiveness: An assessment of student perception and motivation. *Assessment & Evaluation in Higher Education, 28*(1), 71–88.

Eliot, T. S. (1934). *The rock.* London: Faber & Faber.

Ericsson, K. A. (2004). Deliberate practice and the acquisition and maintenance of expert performance in medicine and related domains. *Academic Medicine, 10*, S1–S12.

Filak, V. F., & Sheldon, K. N. (2003). Student psychological need satisfaction and college teacher–course evaluations. *Educational Psychology, 23*(3), 235–247.

Fredricks, J. A., Blumenfeld, P. C., & Paris, A. H. (2004). School engagement: Potential of the concept, state of the evidence. *Review of Educational Research, 74*(1), 59–109.

Ganesan, R. (2004, July). *Perceptions and practices of expert teachers in Technology-based distance and distributed learning environments.* Unpublished dissertation. Syracuse, NY: School of Education, Syracuse University.

Gould, S. J. (1989). *Wonderful life: The Burgess Shale and the nature of history.* New York: W. W. Norton.

Hadfield, J. (1992). *Classroom dynamics.* Oxford: Oxford University Press.

Johnson, D. W., & Johnson, R. T. (1991). *Learning together and alone: Cooperative, competitive, and individualistic learning* (3rd ed.). Englewood Cliffs, NJ: Prentice-Hall.

Klein, J. D., Spector, J. M., Grabowski, B., & de la Teja, I. (2004). *Instructor competencies: Standards for face-to-face, online and blended settings.* Greenwich, CT: Information Age Publishing.

Learning Development Institute (2005). *Presidential workshop and panel session on learners in a changing learning landscape: Questions formulated by participating members.* Retrieved September 7, 2007, from http://www.learndev.org/ibstpi-AECT2005. html#anchor1672398.

Lowman, J. (1995). *Mastering the techniques of teaching* (2nd ed.). San Francisco: Jossey-Bass.

Marsh, H. W. (1987). Student evaluations of university teaching: Research findings, methodological issues, and directions for future research. *International Journal of Educational Research, 11*, 253–388.

Richey, R. C., Fields, D. C., & Foxon, M. with Roberts, R. C., Spannaus, T., & Spector, J. M. (2001). *Instructional design competencies: The standards* (3rd ed.). Syracuse, NY: ERIC Clearinghouse on Information and Technology.

Sagan, C. (1980). *Cosmos.* New York: Random House.

Schank, R. C., & Fano, A. E. (1995). Memory and expectations in learning, language and visual understanding. *Artificial Intelligence Review, 9*(4–5), 261–271.

Scriven, M. (1995). Student ratings offer useful input to teacher evaluations. *Practical Assessment, Research & Evaluation, 4*(7). Retrieved March 6, 2006, from http://PAREonline.net/getvn.asp?v = 4&n = 7.

Slavin, R. E. (1998). Effects of student teams and peer tutoring on academic achievement and time on task. *Journal of experimental education, 48*, 253–257.

Spector, J. M. (2000). Trends and issues in educational technology: How far we have not come. *Update Semiannual Bulletin, 21*(2). Published by the ERIC Clearinghouse on Information &Technology, Syracuse University, Syracuse, NY. Retrieved on April 4, 2006, from http://suedweb.syr.edu/faculty/spector/publications/trends-tech-educ-eric.pdf.

Spector, J. M. (2001). An overview of progress and problems in educational technology. *Interactive Educational Multimedia, 3*, 27–37.

Spector, J. M. (2005). Time demands in online instruction. *Distance Education, 26*(1), 3–25.

Spector, J. M., & De la Teja, I. (2001, December). *Competencies for online teaching. ERIC Digest EDO-IR-2001–09*. Syracuse, NY: ERIC Information Technology Clearinghouse. Retrieved March 5, 2006, from *http://www.eric.ed.gov/*.

Spector, J. M., & Koszalka, T. A. (2004). *The DEEP methodology for assessing learning in complex domains* (Final report to the National Science Foundation Evaluative Research and Evaluation Capacity Building). Syracuse, NY: Syracuse University.

Spector, J. M., Doughty, P. L., & Yonai, B. A. (2003). *Cost and learning effects of alternative e-collaboration methods in online settings* (Final report for the Andrew W. Mellon Foundation Cost Effective Use of Technology in Teaching Initiative). Syracuse, NY: Syracuse University.

Storrings, D. A. (2005). *Attrition in distance education: A meta-analysis.* Unpublished dissertation. Syracuse, NY: School of Education, Syracuse University.

Wilson, R. (1998, January). New research casts doubt on value of student evaluations of professors. *Chronicle of Higher Education,* Jan. 16, 1998, A12.

Yager, R., & Yager, S. (1985). Changes in perceptions of science for third, seventh, and eleventh grade students. *Journal of Research in Science Teaching, 22*(4), 347–358.

Chapter 13
Why Basic Principles of Instruction Must Be Present in the Learning Landscape, Whatever Form It Takes, for Learning to Be Effective, Efficient and Engaging

M. David Merrill

Abstract While today's opportunities and contexts for learning are far more varied than they were only a decade or two ago the underlying learning mechanisms of individual learners have not changed. It is important as we explore these different learning landscapes that we don't naively assume that because the landscape has changed dramatically the learners have also changed. There are fundamental instructional strategies, determined primarily by the type of content to be taught rather than by learning styles or by the form of instructional affordance, that are necessary for effective, efficient and engaging learning of specified knowledge and skill to occur. Those learning activities that best promoted learning in the past are those learning activities that will best promote learning in the future. Yet, we have all observed that many instructional environments fail. However, on close examination it is also evident that these learning environments also fail to implement these known instructional strategies resulting in ineffective and inefficient learning outcomes. As we explore the shifting learning landscape it is critical that we don't assume that because existing instructional environments often fail that the fundamental strategies of instruction have also failed. Most often these strategies have never been adequately implemented in the first place.

13.1   Introduction

The thing that hath been, it is that which shall be and that which is done is that which shall be done and there is no new thing under the sun....
There is no remembrance of former things....

Ecclesiastes 1:9, 11

I take this opportunity to restate some of my underlying assumptions about instruction (Merrill, Drake, Lacy, Pratt, & ID2_Research_Group, 1996):

- There are known instructional strategies. If an instructional experience or environment does not include the instructional strategies required for the acquisition of the desired knowledge or skill, then effective, efficient, and engaging learning of the desired outcome will not occur.

Utah State University; Florida State University; & Brigham Young University, Hawaii

- Appropriate instructional strategies can be discovered. They are natural principles which do exist, and which nature will reveal as a result of careful scientific inquiry. These instructional strategies can be verified by empirical test.
- *Students* are persons who submit themselves to the acquisition of specific knowledge and skill from instruction, *learners* are persons who derive meaning and change their behavior based on their experiences. All of us are learners, but only those who submit themselves to deliberate instructional situations for the purpose of acquiring specified knowledge and skill are students.
- Learners today are not significantly different from those of a decade ago, a generation ago, or a century ago. The basic learning mechanisms by which learners acquire knowledge and skill have remained constant amid societal change. While far less understood, the science of instruction is just as stable as the science of biology, physics, or chemistry. The principles of biology do not change with changes in society; neither do the principles of learning and instruction.

I am not naïve about the dramatic changes that have occurred in the *learning landscape* as identified by the papers in this collection. But it is important that we asked ourselves what has changed and what has remained the same? The opportunities for learning and instruction are certainly much more varied than a generation ago. The amount of information available is many times greater than was true for previous generations. Thanks to the Internet the easy access to this information would have been inconceivable to our grandparents. But does this mean that the basic mechanisms of learning have changed? Does this mean that learners today learn differently than their parents or grandparents?

13.2   Learners Are Not Significantly Different

I disagree with Prensky (2001, cited by Hall in this volume). In the quotation that follows I have thus modified his assertion by adding the words *do not* in square brackets. "Children raised with the computer [do not] think differently from the rest of us. They [do not] develop hypertext minds." They certainly have much MTV experience with its jumps from image to image but such a technique has neither been demonstrated to be effective instruction nor to promote goal directed learning. In 1991 IBM spent millions of dollars to produce a multimedia *CD-ROM, Columbus: Encounter, Discovery and Beyond.* They hired a former Hollywood filmmaker, Robert Abel, who was familiar with MTV type entertainment. It was a very high quality hypermedia presentation. Most informal reports[1] indicate that it didn't

---

[1] I searched diligently for any research that was done demonstrating the effectiveness of this product. When the product was released there were a number of articles praising this work as the ultimate in multimedia education. But after this initial flurry of hype there is a significant silence about this product in the literature. The only research report that mentions this product was a dissertation done at the University of Georgia under the direction of Tom Reeves. In personal communication Dr. Reeves indicated that lack of cooperation in the use of the product caused them to drop their investigation. I contacted IBM Education who indicated that the product has been dropped and they were unable to identify any reports investigating its effectiveness.

work. MTV is great for entertainment but it is not good instruction. The label *'digital natives'* makes good press, sells books and promotes lectures but the scientific data used to back-up Prensky's claims is questionable at best. It is very unlikely that these young people have significantly different learning mechanisms than their parents. Adaptation by evolution takes thousands of years not a single generation.

13.3 There are Known Instructional Strategies

I have previously articulated empirically supported instructional principles (see Table 13.1) that have been found to facilitate effective, efficient and engaging goal-directed learning of complex tasks (Merrill, 2002a, 2007, in press). Similar principles are also

Table 13.1 First principles of instruction[2]

Task-centered principle
- Learning is promoted when instruction is in the context of **whole real-world tasks**.
- Learning is promoted when learners are engaged in a **task-centered** instructional strategy involving a **progression** of whole real-world tasks.

Activation principle
- Learning is promoted when learners **activate** relevant cognitive structures by being directed to recall, describe or demonstrate relevant **prior knowledge** or experience.
- Activation is enhanced when learners recall or acquire a **structure** for organizing the new knowledge, when this structure is the basis for guidance during demonstration, is the basis for coaching during application, and is a basis for reflection during integration.

Demonstration principle
- Learning is promoted when learners observe a **demonstration** of the skills to be learned that is **consistent** with the type of content being taught.
- Demonstrations are enhanced when learners are **guided** to relate general information or an organizing structure to specific instances.
- Demonstrations are enhanced when learners observe **media** that is relevant to the content and appropriately used.

Application principle
- Learning is promoted when learners engage in **application** of their newly acquired knowledge or skill that is **consistent** with the type of content being taught.
- Application is effective only when learners receive intrinsic or corrective **feedback**.
- Application is enhanced when learners are coached and when this **coaching** is gradually withdrawn for each subsequent task.
- Application is enhanced when learners observe **media** that is appropriately used.

Integration principle
- Learning is promoted when learners **integrate** their new knowledge into their everyday life by being directed to reflect-on, discuss, or defend their new knowledge or skill.
- Integration is enhanced when learners create, invent, or explore **personal ways** to use their new knowledge or skill.
- Integration is enhanced when learners **publicly demonstrate** their new knowledge or skill.

---

[2] Copyright M. David Merrill 2007

identified in the present volume (Bransford, Slowinski, Vye, & Mosborg, in this volume; Van Merriënboer & Stoyanov, in this volume). Building on the work of Gagne (1985) Component Display Theory (Merrill, 1983, 1994, 1997) identified necessary conditions (strategies) for effective, efficient and engaging instruction for information-about, parts-of, kinds-of, how-to and what-happens instructional outcomes. This content by strategy interaction takes precedence over learning styles and delivery system (Merrill, 2002b). After trying to determine if there are new online competencies required, De la Teja & Spannaus (in this volume) state that "...the specific set of competencies required in any setting for a particular learning event is driven by the strategy of the event, not whether it is online or face-to-face" (p. 187). Instruction that implements these principles has been found to be more effective, efficient and engaging when compared to instruction that does not (Frick, Chadha, Wang, Watson, & Green, 2007; Mendenhall et al., 2006; Thomson, 2002).

How do these principles of instruction impact the changing learning landscape? The thesis of this paper is that these basic principles of instruction must be present in the learning landscape whatever form it takes for goal-directed learning to be effective, efficient, and engaging.

13.4 Instruction is a Goal-Driven Activity

Do the categories *effective*, *efficient*, and *engaging* constitute appropriate criteria for instruction? Learning always occurs. Learning may be incidental. Learning is not necessarily goal directed. On the other hand instruction is a goal-directed activity. Instruction is a deliberate attempt to structure a learning environment so that students will acquire specified knowledge or skill. The purpose of instruction is to facilitate learning. Facilitate means that the learning is more efficient, effective and engaging than learning that might occur without this intervention. Obviously we are all *feral* learners, but such learners are unlikely to have either the previous knowledge of the content or sufficient skill in applying principles of instruction to efficiently direct their own learning. All of us are feral learners in many things but when it is necessary to acquire specific knowledge and skill directing our own learning is likely to lead to chaos and anarchy.

Does this definition mean that instruction is always an instructor directed activity? Certainly not! Learners can select the goals to be accomplished either from a menu of options or in more open ended learning situations (*student-centered* versus *learner-directed* (Stirling, in this volume). But selecting goals is significantly different from selecting the learning strategies to accomplish these goals. Research on learner control has demonstrated that only learners with high previous knowledge or highly developed metacognitive skills are effective in directing their own learning and that guided learner control is better than open-ended control (Clark & Mayer, 2003; Merrill, 1980, 1984). Does this mean that only tutorial instruction is effective instruction? Again, certainly not! However, it does mean that when there are more open learning environments there is even a greater need to be sure that the learners are guided by established principles of instruction.

13.5   Guided Instruction Works Best

There have been a variety of demonstrations of open-ended, learner-led learning environments. Unfortunately when these experiments are carefully scrutinized the data show that they don't work (Kirschner, Sweller, & Clark, 2006; Mayer, 2004).

> Although unguided or minimally guided instructional approaches are very popular and intuitively appealing, ... these approaches ignore both the structures that constitute human cognitive architecture and evidence from empirical studies over the past half-century that consistently indicate that minimally guided instruction is less effective and less efficient than instructional approaches that place a strong emphasis on guidance of the student learning process (Kirschner et al., 2006, p. 75).
>
> The author's thesis is that there is sufficient research evidence to make any reasonable person skeptical about the benefits of discovery learning—practiced under the guise of cognitive constructivism or social constructivism—as a preferred instructional method. ... Overall, the constructivist view of learning may be best supported by methods of instruction that involve cognitive activity rather than behavioral activity, instructional guidance rather than pure discovery, and curricular focus rather than unstructured exploration (Mayor, 2004, p. 14).

I have often chided my colleagues who are studying communities of learners that they are studying "pooled ignorance." Why would I make such a pejorative comment? Let me explain. If the community consists of solely naïve learners, who have neither previous knowledge of the content under consideration nor any previous knowledge of effective instructional strategies then it is unlikely that specified learning will occur unless they add to their environment someone or some source who has the necessary content knowledge and who provides strategies that are required for effective learning. At their best such communities are extremely inefficient while they struggle to find the necessary knowledge and skill to promote learning.

My colleagues counter by citing many successful such learning communities. But who make up these communities? Usually they consist of knowledgeable folks who are drawn together by some common interest for which members of the community already have considerable expertise. This is not the appropriate comparison group for the initial acquisition of knowledge and skill. There is no question that such communities of knowledgeable individuals are valuable to share information and to help one another solve problems. But is this instruction?

Can open ended learning environments be instructional? According to my definition they are instructional only if learners in such an environment seek to acquire specific knowledge and skill, that is, they establish for themselves a learning goal. As soon as learners seek to acquire a specific learning goal then such environments can only be effective and efficient if they are structured in such a way that the desired content is readily available and that this content is available in ways that implement effective strategies for efficient, effective and engaging learning. Setting up such an open environment that supports goal driven learning takes even more sophisticated instructional design than the design of more direct instruction. Do participants in such environments have sufficient knowledge and skill to structure effective instructional experiences for themselves? Is it necessary that open learning environments that support the acquisition of specific learning goals require design by a source outside the participants? Too often such open ended environments are unstructured and result in a "sink or swim" learner-directed problem solving which, as previously noted, when submitted to careful scrutiny fail to produce sufficient learning outcomes. Of course some learning does occur but do the learners acquire the knowledge and skill they desire in an expedient way? Too often not!

13.6 Education Versus Training

Direct instruction is often equated with training and training is contrasted with education. Training is seen as the less desirable option appropriate only for vocational education in the work place. But is this a meaningful contrast? The best education always involves some training. The best training always involves some education. Training is involved with the acquisition of specific knowledge and skill. Some would say that the world changes so fast that the skill needed is how to acquire skills rather than the skills themselves. But isn't learning how to acquire skill itself a skill? Don't we learn how to acquire skill by acquiring specific skill? Is it possible to acquire the ability to acquire skill in the abstract without learning some specific skill? If education is the development of the "whole person" or the development of character don't these goals also require the acquisition of knowledge and skill?

Schools are often seen as ineffective, inefficient and even debilitating. It is difficult to argue with this assessment. However, failure to implement effective instructional strategies should not be equated with an inappropriate philosophy but rather with an ineffective implementation of any philosophy. The claim that so called "instructivism" believes in passive learners waiting for information to be poured into their open minds is at best a straw man. Those of us who have spent our careers trying to find ways to develop effective direct instruction never believed in the *tabula rasa* view of human learning, i.e. that direct instruction is an attempt to pour information into the head of the student without active involvement on their part, nor that those involved in instructional design have ignored the learner and concentrated solely on the instructor or the instructional system. Most of my instructional design colleagues would acknowledge that knowledge is constructed by active participation on the part of the learner. But it does not follow that learners should direct their own learning, can only learn in open ended environments, and that all learning is a result of social interaction. In our view instructional design is not just about teaching but rather it is all about facilitating learning in structured as well as less structured environments.

13.7 Resources for Further Exploration

Online presentations concerning first principles are available at two Web sites.

The first was delivered in Utrecht, The Netherlands, February 17, 2006. The presentation is available in three parts at the following URLs: (1) http://cito.byuh.

edu/merrill/Merrill_1/Merrill-1.html; (2) http://cito.byuh. edu/merrill/Merrill_2/ Merrill-2.html; and (3) http://cito.byuh.edu/merrill/ Merrill_3/Merrill-3.html.

The second presentation was to a group of faculty and students at Florida State University on April 6, 2007. It can be accessed at the following URL: http://mediasite.oddl.fsu.edu/mediasite/Viewer/?peid = 5625589e-436b-4fd8-9282-53131a64fc71.

For additional papers on First Principles of Instruction see the author's web sites at http://cito.byuh.edu/merrill and http://www.mdavidmerrill.com.

There are also several recent books that I would recommend that argue for principles for effective instruction. The following sources present principles for effective, efficient and engaging instruction.

Allen, M. W. (2003). *Michael Allen's guide to e-learning*. New York: Wiley.

Clark, R. C., & Mayer, R. E. (2003). *E-Learning and the science of instruction*. San Francisco: Jossey-Bass/Pfeiffer.

Foshay, W. R. R., Silber, K. H., & Stelnicki, M. B. (2003). *Writing training materials that work: How to train anyone to do anything*. San Francisco: Jossey-Bass/Pfeiffer.

Mayer, R. E. (2001). *Multimedia learning*. Cambridge: Cambridge University Press.

Van Merriënboer, J. J. G. (1997). *Training complex cognitive skills: A four-component instructional design model for technical training*. Englewood Cliffs, NJ: Educational Technology Publications.

Van Merriënboer, J. J. G., & Kirschner, P. A. (2007). *Ten steps to complex learning*. Hillsdale, NJ: Lawrence Erlbaum.

13.8 Questions for Comprehension and Application

1. The author argues for the importance of implementing principles of instruction whether in direct instruction or more open ended learning environments. Do you feel that the principles stated agree with the literature and your experience? What principles do you feel might have been omitted?

2. The author argues for implementing principles of instruction in open-ended learning environments. This poses a challenge for a new type of instructional design. As a designer of an open-ended learning environment how would you implement such principles? How would you evaluate learning outcomes in such learning environments?

3. The title of this book expresses an overall concern with and interest in the implications for learning and learners of changes in the learning landscape. Using a quote from Ecclesiastes at the beginning of the present chapter, the author posits—by way of a counterpoint to the central concern of the book—a different concern, arguing that we should be cautious with getting overly excited about the changes we are witnessing. Reflect on, and, if possible, discuss with co-readers of this book the merit of the author's argument, relating it to your own learning experience and the existing knowledge base about learning and instruction. What, when contemplating change in the learning landscape, is mere hype and what is not? Argue your point, consulting also earlier chapters in this book.

References

Bransford, J. D., Slowinski, M., Vye, N., & Mosborg, S. (in this volume). The learning sciences, technology and designs for educational systems: Some thoughts about change. In J. Visser & M. Visser-Valfrey (Eds.), *Learners in a changing learning landscape: Reflections from a dialogue on new roles and expectations* (pp. 37–67). Dordrecht, The Netherlands: Springer.

Clark, R. C., & Mayer, R. E. (2003). *E-Learning and the science of instruction.* San Francisco: Jossey-Bass/Pfeiffer.

De la Teja, I., & Spannaus, T. W. (in this volume). New online learning technologies: new online learner competencies. Really? In J. Visser & M. Visser-Valfrey (Eds.), *Learners in a changing learning landscape: Reflections from a dialogue on new roles and expectations* (pp. 187–211). Dordrecht, The Netherlands: Springer.

Frick, T., Chadha, R., Wang, Y., Watson, C., & Green, P. (2007). *Theory-based course evaluation: Nine scales for measuring teaching and learning quality.* Unpublished manuscript, Bloomington, IN.

Gagne, R. M. (1985). *The conditions of learning and theory of instruction* (4th ed.). New York: Holt, Rinehart & Winston.

Hall, M. (in this volume). Getting to know the feral learner. In J. Visser & M. Visser-Valfrey (Eds.), *Learners in a changing learning landscape: Reflections from a dialogue on new roles and expectations* (pp. 109–133). Dordrecht, The Netherlands: Springer.

Kirschner, P. A., Sweller, J., & Clark, R. E. (2006). Why minimal guidance during instruction does not work: an analysis of the failure of constructivist, discovery, problem-based, experiential, and inquiry-based teaching. *Educational Psychologist, 41*(2), 75–86.

Mayer, R. E. (2004). Should there be a three-strikes rule against pure discovery learning? *American Psychologist, 59*(1), 14–19.

Mendenhall, A., Buhanan, C. W., Suhaka, M., Mills, G., Gibson, G. V., & Merrill, M. D. (2006). A task-centered approach to entrepreneurship. *TechTrends, 50*(4), 84–89.

Merrill, M. D. (1980). Learner control in computer-based learning. *Computers and Education, 4,* 77–95.

Merrill, M. D. (1983). Chapter 9 – Component display theory. In C. M. Reigeluth (Ed.), *Instructional design theories and models: An overview of their current status.* Hillsdale, NJ: Lawrence Erlbaum.

Merrill, M. D. (1984). Chapter 17 – What is learner control? In R. Bass & C. R. Dills (Eds.), *Instructional development: The state of the art II.* Dubuque: Kendall/Hunt Publishing.

Merrill, M. D. (1994). *Instructional design theory.* Englewood Cliffs, NJ: Educational Technology Publications.

Merrill, M. D. (1997). Instructional strategies that teach. *CBT Solutions* (November/December), 1–11.

Merrill, M. D. (2002a). First principles of instruction. *Educational Technology Research and Development, 50*(3), 43–59.

Merrill, M. D. (2002b). Instructional Strategies and Learning Styles: Which takes precedence? In R. A. Reiser & J. V. Dempsey (Eds.), *Trends and issues in instructional design and technology* (pp. 99–106). Upper Saddle River, NJ: Merrill/Prentice-Hall.

Merrill, M. D. (2007). First principles of instruction: A synthesis. In R. A. Reiser & J. V. Dempsey (Eds.), *Trends and Issues in Instructional Design and Technology* (Vol. 2, pp. 62–71, 2nd ed.). Upper Saddle River, NJ: Merrill/Prentice-Hall.

Merrill, M. D. (in press). First principles of instruction. In C. M. Reigeluth & A. Carr (Eds.), *Instructional design theories and models III* (Vol. III). Hillsdale, NJ: Lawrence Erlbaum.

Merrill, M. D., Drake, L., Lacy, M. J., Pratt, J., & ID2_Research_Group (1996). Reclaiming instructional design. *Educational Technology, 36*(5), 5–7.

Prensky, M. (2001). Digital natives, digital immigrants, part II: Do they really think differently? *On the horizon, NCB University Press, 9*(6), 1–9.

Stirling, D. (in this volume). Online learning in context. In J. Visser & M. Visser-Valfrey (Eds.), *Learners in a changing learning landscape: Reflections from a dialogue on new roles and expectations* (pp. 165–186). Dordrecht, The Netherlands: Springer.

Thomson. (2002). *Thomson job impact study: The next generation of learning.* (*www.netg.com*). Naperville, IL: NETg.

Van Merriënboer, J. J. G., & Stoyanov, S. (in this volume). Learners in a changing learning landscape: Reflections from an instructional design perspective. In J. Visser & M. Visser-Valfrey (Eds.), *Learners in a changing learning landscape: Reflections from a dialogue on new roles and expectations* (pp. 69–90). Dordrecht, The Netherlands: Springer.

Chapter 14
We Question, We Reflect, and We Question Again, Therefore We Are ...: An Analysis of the Evolving Dialogue Around the Central Themes in This Book

Muriel Visser-Valfrey

Abstract This chapter analyzes the evolution of a dialogue around the central theme of this book—learners in a changing learning landscape—from its inception prior to the Workshop and Presidential Session held at the 2005 annual conference of the Association for Educational Communications and Technology (AECT), through the lively discussions at the AECT meeting itself, and followed by the drafting, collaborative review and revision of the chapters that form part of this book. A coding frame generated from the initial description of the purpose of the book is used to conduct a content analysis of the 32 questions which were formulated in preparation for the initial workshop in 2005. The same coding frame is then applied to the chapters in this book and used as a basis for a critical reflection on the nature and evolution of the dialogue. The resulting analysis highlights how the dialogue evolved, singles out some areas of agreement and discord and provides indications of where reflection, discussion and research around the critical themes identified could be strengthened.

14.1 Introduction

This book reflects a two and a half year discussion among scholars, students and practitioners concerning learners—online and otherwise—and the overall setting, the 'landscape,' in which they learn. In their journey of reflection on "what learners ought to be equipped with in order to flourish in today's changing learning landscape" (Jan Visser,[1] pp. 12), the contributors to the discussion and to this book addressed many different dimensions of learning; the learning landscape; and the extent to and the way in which the needs of learners are being met.

Learning Development Institute

[1] This chapter makes reference to all other chapters in this book. These chapters are not listed in the 'references' section. Verbatim quotes associated with the names of contributing authors to this book are referenced by page number only.

J. Visser and M. Visser-Valfrey (eds.), *Learners in a Changing Learning Landscape*,
© Springer Science+Business Media B.V. 2008

Producing this book is thus a step in a process and will hopefully mark the beginning of an even richer process of reflection and dialogue among a much wider community. Having reached this crossroads the overarching question becomes 'So what?' In other words: What did we learn from this dialogue so far? What questions have been at least partially answered? What new questions arose during the process of discussion? And where could and should we go from here? A cursory look at these questions is the subject of this chapter. And because the process by which this dialogue was conducted has some unique features, the reader is invited throughout the reading of this chapter, and while exploring the book in general, to also consider the 'How' question, namely: How did the discussion evolve? How did the process through which the dialogue was conducted contribute to its outcomes? What were its unique features? And how could one capitalize on this experience in moving the discussion forward beyond the contributions in this book?

14.2 Methodology

This chapter reflects on the first set of questions above—the 'What' questions—by using qualitative content analysis to pull together the main themes of the discussion. In doing so, the records of the dialogue that took place between the participants in this process—from its inception prior to the workshop in October 2005, through the Presidential Session at the AECT which directly followed it, to the drafting, review and revising of the chapters which form part of this book—were reviewed and subjected to content analysis techniques. Content analysis is defined by Holsti (1969) as a "technique for making inferences by objectively and systematically identifying specified characteristics of messages" (p. 14).

In order to carry out the content analysis, the rationale for the dialogue as originally formulated in the description of the AECT Workshop and Presidential Session (Learning Development Institute, 2005) was used to identify the key themes for the analysis. Three overall themes were identified from that description, namely:

1. The *learning landscape*—with dimensions related to:
   a. The modalities through which people learn
   b. The context (including spatial and temporal frames) for learning
   c. The purpose for which they learn
2. The *learner*—defined as an actor in the learning landscape engaged in the act of learning both in formal and informal contexts.
3. And *learning* as a concept and a process that refers to what we understand by learning and how this influences the manner in which learning and instruction take place.

The 32 questions generated at the start of the process by the initial group of 10 participants in the dialogue (Learning Development Institute, 2005) were then subjected to content analysis from two perspectives. Firstly, the analysis focused on the relative frequency with which the above three themes were brought up in the questions to get a sense of the focus of the dialogue. Secondly, the questions were then further analyzed to identify the sub-themes that underlie each of the main thematic areas. Sapsford and Jupp's (1996) iterative method for the analysis of unstructured data was used in this process to generate the sub-themes for this analysis.

The themes and sub-themes identified through the review of the 32 questions were then used for the analysis of the abstracts and the chapters in this book. In addition, in reviewing the chapters a comparison was made between the 32 questions originally raised by the authors and those that were actually addressed in the book to identify what issues were discussed more prominently and consequently which areas were covered less comprehensively in the final discussion. Finally, the chapters were reviewed with the intent of identifying additional themes and questions, not previously identified, that emerged during the process. The main purpose of this process of analysis was thus to capture and document the dynamics of the dialogue and to highlight the key themes that have emerged.

There is by necessity a risk of bias in this content analysis. It was done by one person and was not independently verified by others. The reader is thus invited to make her or his independent judgment. By systematically reviewing and documenting the process and highlighting its outcomes in this chapter, it is hoped that this analysis will constitute an opportunity to the reader—even if only to bounce off ideas—for further reflection and discussion around the key themes of this book.

14.3   Questions, Answers, and More Questions ...

The next section examines the results of the analysis in some detail. The chapter contains three sections, focusing respectively on the analysis of the questions, the fine-tuning of the coding framework, and a discussion of the analysis of the book as a whole.

14.3.1   Paving the Road to Understanding with Questions

At the outset, 32 questions were generated for the dialogue, with most collaborators contributing three or four questions. For each of the questions the proponent wrote a short rationale of 'underlying thoughts' (for detail see Learning Development Institute, 2005). This description was essential to the content analysis since it explained the ideas behind the questions and was thus critical to understanding and classifying the topics covered.

The table below provides an overview of the results of the content analysis of the questions against the three categories identified. A brief definition of each of the main themes is provided. The purpose at this stage was to identify the dominant theme of each question. Although every attempt was made to identify only one

Table 14.1 Overview of major thematic dimensions of the analysis

Theme	The learning landscape	The learner	Learning as concept and process
Definition of theme	The modalities by, purposes for and contexts within which learning occurs.	The actors in the learning landscape engaged in the act of learning, both in formal and informal contexts.	What is understood by learning and how this influences the manner in which learning and instruction take place.
Questions related to the theme	Q2 Q4 Q8 Q11 Q20	Q1 Q6 Q7 Q12 Q13 Q14 Q15 Q16 Q17 Q18 Q21 Q23 Q24 Q25 Q26 Q28 Q32	Q3 Q5 Q9 Q10 Q12 Q19 Q20 Q22 Q26 Q27 Q29 Q30 Q31
Number of questions per theme	5	17	13

dominant theme, three among the 32 questions (Questions 10, 12 and 19) clearly covered multiple themes and were therefore classified twice in Table 14.1 above.

The sheer volume of documentation (audio and written) on the website for this project (Learning Development Institute, 2005) testifies to the interest that the overall theme generated and to the complexity of the issue at hand. This quantitative analysis of the dominant themes in the questions highlights that at the onset of this dialogue the bulk of the reflection centered around issues related to the learner. What we understand by learning and how this influences the learning process occupied a second, less important, place. By contrast, the learning landscape itself—although covering three sub-themes—was the dominant theme in only five of the 32 questions. In other words in the process of reflecting on what learners ought to be equipped with in order to flourish in a changing learning landscape it was clearly the learner who was seen as central. This bias may in part be a consequence of the particular audience—instructors, instructional designers, researchers of learning and instruction, and students— that was involved in the dialogue. Had the same questions been asked of technologists, the focus of questioning might have been very different! It may also be a consequence of the fact that almost everyone has at one time been either a student or a teacher or both. From both perspectives one is traditionally conditioned to think that learning is what a learner does thanks to the teaching of a teacher. Our ideas about learning are thus tainted and frequently biased by our upbringing.

Of course, the discussion had to start somewhere. In this case it was the learners who captured the initial imagination and thus provided a valid starting point for the dialogue. It will be interesting, though, to consider further on in this chapter to what extent the thematic focus on learners in the pattern of questioning was maintained. However, before we move on, we first explore what the main thrust of questioning was within the three broad thematic areas.

14.3.1.1 The Learner at the Center of Inquiry

With the learner being the center of inquiry, a wide variety of issues was raised. At a fundamental level, Jan Visser raised the question whether it is relevant and useful to talk about 'online learners' as a distinct category, given the changing and blurring boundaries between the settings in which people learn. A number of the questions also reflected on distinct categories of learners and whether and how their existence and characteristics have implications for the learning strategies and modalities. In this context, Michael Beaudoin's questioning focuses on the invisible learner and explores whether that individual's behavior in the online context is merely parasitic and how instructors should deal with such learners. With respect to online learners as a specific category Christina Rogoza questions the extent to which learning environments—and in particular online environments—accommodate cultural and epistemological diversity among learners and encourage them to open up their personal learning space.

A further shared area of questioning among contributors to the discussion concerned the dispositions of learners and in particular those of online learners. Diana Stirling proposes to examine in particular what role learner expectations play in the overall learning experience, while Michael Spector focuses on knowledge, attitudes and skills of online learners in an attempt to understand what contributes to successful (online) learning and thus what makes a good course good. Under this general heading, one of John Bransford's questions draws attention to the fact that learning is a lifelong process and that a good understanding of expectations of the learning process held by the learner and embodied in the environment may therefore be even more pertinent and urgent.

A related set of questions raised concerns the extent to which educators and instructional designers really understand what makes a successful online learner and how the learning environment—in particular the software component of it—communicates expectations. Building on this is the question of whether and how understanding learner success can have implications for learning modalities and strategies (Ileana de la Teja). And also how the changing world and learning landscape has implications for what learners may need to know (John Bransford). In this context Yusra Visser questions the opportunity costs of different instructional modalities for learners and whether we are able to measure these costs and what the "ramifications of these considerations [are] for public universities' adherence to their missions" (Learning Development Institute, 2005, Question 28, n.p.). We clearly see in these questions that although the learner may be central, the other key themes of the dialogue are also being brought into the discussion. In addition related themes of instructors and institutional settings—not initially explicitly part of the coding frame—are raised here.

Finally, under the overall theme of learners it is interesting to note that, although the mission statement of the Orlando Workshop and Presidential Session (Learning Development Institute, 2005) refers to learners in general, many of the questions around learners generated by the participants in the dialogue concern specifically the online environment, even as some of the contributors are questioning the usefulness of this very concept. The reader of this book may want to reflect on extent to which we may need to rethink such concepts and to consider what alternative foci for inquiry might be appropriate.

14.3.1.2 Learning as Concept and Process

Learning as a concept or process occupied a solid second place in terms of the number of questions that focused on this issue. Questions posed included critically exploring what learning actually means in an ever-faster changing learning landscape (Jan Visser and Jeroen van Merriënboer); how the understanding and definition of learning influences the nature of the learning process (Christina Rogoza); and how our conception of learning necessarily influences the definition of competencies of the learner (Ileana de la Teja). As was the case with the questions that were formulated under the first theme, there was a concern with whether online learning is in itself a useful concept in our quest for understanding or whether we should be abandoning it altogether (Jeroen van Merriënboer).

Still under the heading of learning, some of the contributors seek to explore through their questions what it is that we need to be learning, raising the issue about learning of complex skills (Jeroen van Merriënboer and Michael Spector) and levels/hierarchies of learning (Jan Visser and Yusra Visser), considered to be especially important in today's world. John Bransford questions whether true learning may need to involve unlearning as a first step.

14.3.1.3 Querying the Learning Landscape

A smaller but not unimportant number of the questions addressed the learning landscape as such. However, within this overall broad category, almost all questions centered around the modalities for learning (online, face-to-face, or blended), and the software and hardware involved—as opposed to the broader context within which we learn and the purpose for which learning takes place. Within the sub-theme of modalities in particular the influence of technology and technological developments on the nature of learning (which has become more complex, rapid, and ever-changing) and on the means by which we learn are raised by Deb LaPointe. Christina Rogoza asks at a fundamental level whether computer based collaborative learning rests on different epistemological assumptions while Diana Stirling in two related questions wishes to explore the design of software and the use of online tools by instructors, particularly as concerns communication around expectations. John Bransford proposes to explore whether online environments (can) produce opportunities that are more interesting than traditional ones and in a related question Yusra Visser raises the issue of the extent to which we have evidence that allows us to make statements about the effectiveness and even superiority of different modalities of learning.

With respect to the other two dimensions of the learning landscape—context and purpose—fewer but nevertheless very important questions were put forward. Thus

Jan Visser proposed reflecting on what the key changes are in the learning landscape and suggests putting those into a hierarchical order of challenges to the learner. With respect to the purpose for which we learn Mike Spector suggests looking at what makes a course successful and what skills and attitudes of learners determine success.

Analyzing the 32 questions in this manner provides interesting food for thought and gives a sense of the wide range of issues that brought together the participants in the dialogue. Doing the analysis also makes it possible to develop the coding frame with a number of sub-themes that emerged from the analysis. The result is shown in Table 14.2 below. It is important to note, though, that these themes do not stand alone and that there is in the questions (and also in the chapters in this book as we will see below) a rich interaction between the main themes and sub-themes.

14.3.2 Questions as Building Blocks to Further Reflection—How Did the Nature of the Dialogue Evolve?

The 32 questions were discussed at length among the various proponents during the Orlando workshop in 2005 and this was followed by a lively debate with an extended audience of scholars, students and practitioners who participated in the Presidential Session that followed the workshop at the 2005 AECT meeting. The chapters in this book are the result of this initial dialogue and of further reflection, reading, and online discussions among the participants. During this process authors conversed with others (in some cases resulting in additional contributors being brought in as authors and co-authors) and accessed and reflected on drafts of each other's chapters. Having analyzed and presented above the focus of the questions that arose at the initial discussion, the remainder of this chapter will examine how the dialogue around these issues evolved

Table 14.2 Overview of sub-themes under each of the major dimensions of analysis

Learning landscape	The learner	Learning as a concept and process
• Context (dynamic, ambiguous, complex) • Modalities (particularly regarding technology) • Purpose (lifelong and lifewide)	• Characteristics • Categories/types • Expectations • Culture • Environment • Skills and competencies (necessary and desirable)	• Definition of learning • Stages of learning • Hierarchies or levels of learning • Types of learning (online, face to face, etc.) • Methodologies • Interveners (instructors, institutions, etc.)

and an attempt will be made to tease out some issues for further exploration. The same three broad coding categories, as well as the sub-themes identified in the more detailed coding frame of Table 14.2 above, are thus used in the next section to review the abstracts and the chapters in the book. In presenting the findings a deliberate choice was made to provide a small selection of relevant examples rather than to comprehensively list all the instances in which a certain theme or issue came up. Readers will be able to add to these on the basis of their explorations of each chapter.

The next section provides an overview of the main findings of this second level of analysis, which is followed in the final section of the chapter by conclusions and the identification of areas for further reflection.

14.3.2.1   Some Questions Continue to Be a Central Part of the Discussion as the Dialogue Continues

The analysis of the chapters testifies to the fact that the dialogue matured and became both broader and more complex after the initial formulation of the questions. At a general level we see some contributors quite closely following the original questions that they posed. This is the case of Michael Spector's chapter on *'What makes good online instruction good'* and of Jan Visser who explores in great detail his original questions on the meaning of learning and the nature of the changes to the learning landscape, as well as whether the term 'online learners' is really relevant and useful in the current context.

Authors also use the dialogue to start building on each other's reflections and, by doing so, to explore in much more detail the ramifications of their original inquiry. Thus we see for instance Jeroen van Merriënboer and Slavi Stoyanov building on Jan Visser's analysis of societal and technological problems and opportunities in a fast changing learning landscape to discuss the particular challenge of ill-structured problems, of authentic reference situations in problem solving, and of the increasing importance of domain-general competencies as well as other emerging topics. Yusra Visser builds further on Jan Visser's analysis by discussing critically how increasing rates of change in society are affecting both the depth and the breadth of the learning landscape, how it contributes to increasing levels of ambiguity and to the necessity of ensuring that we become aware of the fact that "learning is above all else the dominion of the learner, rather than of educators or educational establishments" (p. 139). John Bransford, Mary Slowinski, Nancy Vye and Susan Mosborg use this discussion of the evolving nature of the learning landscape to reflect, through a practical example, on the relative importance and the benefit and drawbacks of learning in both formal and informal environments and particularly on the negative consequences of recognizing the relevance of only one of these settings. This ongoing dialogue between authors enriches the discussion and generates new questions, as can be gauged particularly from the 'questions for further reflection' at the end of each chapter, which occasionally build links between different chapters in the book.

14.3.2.2   Some Questions Are 'Better Left Alone'—At Least for Now

We also see questions being 'left alone' or left by the wayside by their proponents in favor of a different and new line of inquiry. Yusra Visser's chapter is a case in point. It examines the changing nature of learning, the role of formal postsecondary education systems in the broader learning landscape and considers implications for the learner—a line of reflection and inquiry which was not originally part of her listed concerns and which adds a new and relevant area of reflection to the dialogue. As such she does not directly address her initial questions concerning the nature and impact of embodied learning on learning environments; the opportunity costs from the learners vantage point of different instructional modalities; whether there is evidence of the possible superiority of distance education and what the implications of this would be; and finally what the effect of anonymity is on the learner, learning and performance in an online environment.

Similarly, John Bransford and his colleagues of the LIFE Center provide a dynamic discussion of the changing context inherent in the learning landscape and reflect in depth on whether and how modern day technologies change the educational landscape. However, the authors do not explicitly discuss two of Bransford's original questions as to whether online learning environments provide learning opportunities that are more interesting and productive than traditional ones and whether online environments are primarily suited for knowledge seekers as opposed to problem solvers.

Some questions remain only partially answered. The importance of getting to know the expectations of online learners, inherent in the question posed by Ileana de la Teja at the start of the dialogue: "Are online learners getting what they want/need?" (Question 25, p. 7) remains only partially addressed.

14.3.2.3   But 'Better Left Alone' Questions Still Resurface in the Discussion

Interestingly, some of the discarded questions are subsequently at least partly addressed in the contributions by other authors. Thus Jeroen van Merriënboer and Slavi Stoyanov reflect in their chapter quite extensively on the question initially posed by John Bransford as to whether online environments cater primarily to problem solvers or knowledge seekers in their discussion on learning, on different kinds of learners, and on online learning environments. The process of letting go of questions, of re-integrating them in the dialogue, and of adding additional ones is a fundamental part of the evolving nature of the dialogue around the learner and learning landscapes. There are various examples of this interesting phenomenon throughout this book.

14.3.2.4   Besides, Areas of Divergence Emerge

What areas of divergence exist? Where is there disagreement? One theme that runs through the book regards technology. There is clearly a consensus that technology drives change and that it poses challenges as well as provides opportunities. But there is a marked discord on the extent to which technology is really changing things fundamentally and lives up to the expectations it generates. A group of authors converge on the point that there seems to be too much 'hype' around technology and that the evidence that it has lived up to its promise and has fundamentally changed the nature of learning is simply not there. Others speculate and put forward arguments (see for example Mary Hall's discussion on feral learning) that technology has not only fundamentally changed the learning landscape by offering opportunities for learning that did not exist before, but that the advent of technology has also changed how individuals learn. Deb LaPointe's chapter argues that "all of this adds up to a different kind of play and developmental environment, which influences a different developmental process and a way of seeing the world and thinking than experienced by generations before" (p. 286).

14.3.2.5 New Areas of Inquiry are Added and Explored

The deviation from original questions, the way in which authors build on each other's analysis and the areas in which authors disagree are all a testimony to the evolving nature of the dialogue around the overall theme over the more than two years that this project developed and matured. In this context it becomes interesting to reflect on whether the fact that certain questions were changed means that these are less relevant to the dialogue, or whether simply in the course of the discussion and reflection other thematic areas and questions became more pressing. Thus we also find through the analysis that new themes emerged, in part because the group expanded to include new members who were not at the discussion in Orlando. Mary Hall—a new member to the group—explores an area that was not originally part of the dialogue by looking at the characteristics of feral learning environments and the capacity of the formal education system to nurture the feral learner. Dave Merrill—also a new addition—adds to the reflection by examining and arguing for the importance of basic principles of instruction, regardless of the context in which learning takes place. Another example is, as we saw above, Yusra Visser's reflection on the role of formal post secondary institutions in the context of the dynamic and broader learning landscape. These 'unanswered' and only partially answered questions, together with the new avenues of discussion that emerged, will hopefully lead the reader of this book to critically reflect on the dialogue and on the extent to which these questions and avenues constitute possible areas for further reflection and research.

14.3.3 How Were the Three Initial Themes—Learning Landscape; Learner; and Learning as a Concept and Process—Addressed?

Finally, and given the three broad coding categories defined at the outset of this analysis, what are some of the key issues that emerged from the analysis of the contributions to this book regarding the landscape, the learner and learning as a concept and process?

We see reflections on the nature of the changing context of the learning landscape start becoming a much more central part of the discussion in a number of chapters. Jan Visser; Jeroen van Merriënboer & Slavi Stoyanov; John Bransford, Mary Slowinski, Nancy Vye, & Susan Mosborg; and Yusra Visser all discuss at length the changes that characterize today's learning environment and which pose a particular challenge to learners as well as to those who design instructional interventions and facilitate learning. This detailed analysis stands in contrast to the approach by some other authors in the volume who acknowledge at the outset of their discussion that the landscape has changed but who choose not to reflect on the changes themselves in detail. These differences of approach may be a matter of practical choice; they may also reflect different views regarding the importance of an explicit examination of the changes that occurred.

A preoccupation with technology as the main driving force of change in the learning landscape also continues to be somewhat dominant. Only very few authors examine other changes such as those brought on by conflicts, by environmental change, by migration, by epidemics, by the shifting balance of political and economic power, and by cultural change.

We see that the learner—around which the majority of the 32 questions were formulated—continues to be central also in the dialogue as it is documented in this book. Thus, as already mentioned, Michael Beaudoin reflects at length on the phenomenon of 'invisible learners' in online environments. Deb LaPointe discusses in detail the extent to which we are ready to facilitate learning for young gamers, for individuals from a rich mix of cultures, as well as for learners who predate the Internet. Other authors add further categorizations of learners such as the feral learners in Mary Hall's chapter and the expert learner in the chapter by Jeroen van Merriënboer and Slavi Stoyanov.

Overall, in these discussions we see the learner being more firmly discussed as part of the learning landscape as a whole. The discussion looks at the learners as individuals but also at learning as a collective exercise and at groups of learners as developing a personality of their own with implications for instructional strategies and settings. We also see other authors joining Jan Visser in calling into question the usefulness of the terms 'online learning' and 'online learners' in a fast changing learning landscape.

Various definitions of learning are discussed as well as how to measure whether learning took place. Yusra Visser makes reference to six conceptions of learning of which the higher order involves learners becoming irreversibly changed as a consequence of learning. In this context it is interesting to see Michael Spector proposing to measure learning not in the form of classical outcomes (such as acquired knowledge and skills) but rather in terms of the evidence of 'sustained interest' in a given area. And John Bransford et al., Jan Visser and Yusra Visser all focus on the need to examine whether the learning process may need to focus much more strongly on fostering the capacity to tolerate (increasing) ambiguity in a changing world.

In discussing learning there is a clear focus on its lifelong nature and the implications of this for how we deal with formal learning environments (see for example the chapter by John Bransford et al.). The importance of the role played by beliefs about learning and how these may differ according to the perspective of various actors in the process—the institution, the instructor, and the learner—emerges prominently from Christina Rogoza's epistemological considerations.

Finally, contributors continue to ferry between focusing on online learning and looking at learning from a more holistic perspective. Thus some chapters focus specifically on online learners while others feel that the discussion on learning can only usefully take place if we remove this 'unhelpful' and somewhat outdated designation of certain learners as being of the online variety.

14.4 Concluding Remarks

Content analysis is about fitting content into categories. Teasing out commonalities and classifying arguments in such a rich and varied dialogue inevitably does not do justice to the depth and breadth of thinking presented in this book. Nevertheless, the perspectives, concerns, interests and points of contention that brought together this small community clearly resulted in a rich dialogue. From a process perspective, the manner in which the dialogue around this book was managed encourages us to think about how the way in which the dialogue was conducted may have contributed to the outcome that the reader has in hand.

Shakespeare alluded to the fundamental importance of our existence as human beings with his challenging 'To be or not to be, that is the question.' The central thread through this book is that learning is fundamental to our present being and to our continuing 'being' as humans. This book does not provide the answer but should propel us to explore in increasing depth and breadth the real meaning of learning.

14.5 Resources for Further Exploration

Hsieh, H. & Shannon, S. (2005). Three approaches to qualitative content analysis. *Qualitative health research* (Vol. 15, No. 9, pp. 1277–1288). London: Sage.

Visser, M., Hsu, C., & Kalinskaya, S. (2003). *The story behind the headlines—HIV/AIDS in a leading South African newspaper*. Paper presented at the National Communication Association (NCA) Conference (sponsored by NCA's International and Intercultural Division), Miami, November 19–23, 2003.

14.6 Questions for Comprehension and Application

- The first part of this chapter reports on a content analysis of the 32 questions that were formulated by participants at the onset of the dialogue. Table 14.1 lists the question numbers under each of the three main coding categories. Critically review this categorization either by yourself or collaboratively with others. Do you agree with how each of the questions was coded? Do you think the coding categories are sufficiently well defined? How difficult was it to decide on the correct category? What does this tell you about the advantages and limitations of using content analysis? And finally, how relevant do you think it is to use content analysis for the purpose of this kind of exercise? Argue your position.

- One of the unique features of this book is the process by which it was created. This process is explained in the introductory chapter (Chapter 1, pp. 1–10) and is also referred to in the present chapter as well as by a number of the authors in their chapters as having been very stimulating and vital to the learning process that went alongside writing the book. If you were to design a strategy for moving forward the dialogue now that this book has been published, what key steps and activities would you suggest and how would you ensure that the further dialogue is 'captured' so that others can also reflect on it?

References

Holsti, O. R. (1969). *Content analysis for the social sciences and humanities*. Reading, MA: Addison-Wesley.

Learning Development Institute (2005). Web site of the Presidential Workshop and Panel Session at the International Convention of the Association for Educational Communications and Technology on *Learners in a changing learning landscape: New roles and expectations*, October 18–22, 2005, Orlando, FL. Retrieved October 5, 2007, from http://www.learndev.org/ibstpi-AECT2005.html.

Sapsford, R., & Jupp, V. (1996). *Data collection and analysis*. London: Sage.

Name Index

Subject Index

Page numbers coming in bold represent the footnotes

Printed in the United States
123832LV00003B/178/P